English for Academic Purposes

Also published in
Oxford Handbooks for Language Teachers

Teaching American English Pronunciation
Peter Avery and Susan Ehrlich

Designing and Analyzing Language Tests
Nathan T. Carr

ESOL: A Critical Guide
Melanie Cooke and James Simpson

Success in English Teaching
Paul Davies and Eric Pearse

Doing Second Language Research
James Dean Brown and Theodore S. Rodgers

From Experience to Knowledge
Julian Edge and Sue Garton

Teaching Business English
Mark Ellis and Christine Johnson

Intercultural Business Communication
Robert Gibson

Teaching and Learning in the Language Classroom
Tricia Hedge

Teaching Second Language Reading
Thom Hudson

Teaching English Overseas: An Introduction
Sandra Lee McKay

Teaching English as an International Language
Sandra Lee McKay

How Languages are Learned 4th Edition
Patsy M. Lightbown and Nina Spada

Communication in the Language Classroom
Tony Lynch

Teaching Second Language Listening
Tony Lynch

Teaching Young Language Learners
Annamaria Pinter

The Oxford ESOL Handbook
Philida Schellekens

Exploring Learner Language
Elaine Tarone and Bonnie Swierzbin

Doing Task-based Teaching
Jane Willis and Dave Willis

Explaining English Grammar
George Yule

Technology Enhanced Language Learning
Aisha Walker and Goodith White

English for Academic Purposes

Edward de Chazal

OXFORD
UNIVERSITY PRESS

OXFORD
UNIVERSITY PRESS

Great Clarendon Street, Oxford, OX2 6DP, United Kingdom

Oxford University Press is a department of the University of Oxford.
It furthers the University's objective of excellence in research, scholarship,
and education by publishing worldwide. Oxford is a registered trade
mark of Oxford University Press in the UK and in certain other countries

ISBN: 978 0 19 442371 7

Printed in China

This book is printed on paper from certified and well-managed sources

PUBLISHER'S ACKNOWLEDGEMENTS

*The author and publisher are grateful to those who have given permission to
reproduce the following extracts and adaptations of copyright material*: p24
Extract from 'Theorizing and practicing critical English for academic
purposes' by Sarah Benesch, Journal of English for Academic Purposes,
Vol 8, Issue 2, pp.81–85. Copyright 2009. Reproduced by permission
of Elsevier; p24 Extract from 'Different not Deficit: Towards a More
Critical EAP Pedagogy' by F. Cotton, *EAP in a Globalizing World: English as
an Academic Lingua Franca* (Proceedings of the 2007 BALEAP conference)
edited by Melinda Whong. © Garnet Publishing Ltd 2007. Reproduced
by permission; p36 Extract from *English for Academic Purposes: An
Advanced Resource Book* by Ken Hyland. Published by Routledge, 2006.
Reproduced by permission of Ken Hyland; p36 Extract from *Theory and
Concepts of English for Academic Purposes* by Ian Bruce, Palgrave Macmillan,
May 2011. Reproduced by permission of Palgrave Macmillan; p37
Extract from 'Culture shock? Genre shock?' by Christine B. Feak,
English for Specific Academic Purposes (Proceedings of the 2009 BALEAP
Conference) edited by Sian Etherington. © Garnet Publishing Ltd
2009. Reproduced by permission; p37 Extract from 'Discipline and
divergence: evidence of specificity in EAP' by Ken Hyland, English
for Specific Academic Purposes (Proceedings of the 2009 BALEAP
Conference) edited by Sian Etherington. © Garnet Publishing Ltd

2009. Reproduced by permission; p44 Extract from the Bangor
University Guide to MA Courses in Linguistics 1990–1 by P. Scholfield.
Reproduced by permission of Bangor University; p59 Extract from
Genre Analysis: English in Academic and Research Settings by John Swales,
Cambridge University Press, 1990. © Cambridge University Press
1990. Reproduced by permission; p68 Extract from *Evolution: A Very
Short Introduction* by Brian Charlesworth and Deborah Charlesworth,
Oxford University Press, Jun 2003. Reproduced by permission of
Oxford University Press; p85 Extract from 'Confronting the Coffee
Crisis: Can Fair Trade, Organic, and Specialty Coffees Reduce Small-
Scale Farmer Vulnerability in Northern Nicaragua?' by Christopher
Bacon, World Development, Vol 33, Issue 3, March 2005, Elsevier.
Reproduced by permission of Elsevier; p89 Table 1.11 from *Longman
Grammar of Spoken and Written English* by Douglas Biber, Susan Conrad
and Geoffrey Leech, Pearson Education Limited, 1999. © Pearson
Education Limited 1999. Reproduced by permission; p95 Extract
from Table 3: Academic Discourse from 'Competency Framework
for Teachers of English for Academic Purposes' by BALEAP, August
2008. Reproduced by permission of BALEAP; p97 Extract from *Child
Public Health, 2nd Edition* by Mitch Blair, Sarah Stewart-Brown, Tony
Waterston and Rachel Crowther, Oxford University Press, Nov 2003.
Reproduced by permission of Oxford University Press; p135 Extract
from *Critical Thinking Skills for Education Students* by Brenda Judge,
Elaine McCreery and Patrick Jones, Learning Matters, July 2009.
Reproduced by permission of Sage Publications Ltd; p153 Extract from
First Ecology: Ecological Principles and Environmental Issues by Alan Beeby
and Anne-Maria Brennan, Oxford University Press, November 2007.
Reproduced by permission of Oxford University Press; p183 Extract
from *Business Research Methods, 3rd Edition* by Alan Bryman and Emma
Bell, Oxford University Press, March 2011. Reproduced by permission
of Oxford University Press; p186 Extract reproduced with permission
from John Clanchy & Brigid Ballard, *Essay Writing for Students: A
Practical Guide* © 1992, Pearson Australia, p.244. Reproduced by
permission; p187 Extract from
'Disciplinary discourses: writer stance in research articles' by Ken
Hyland from *Writing: Texts, Processes, and Practices* edited by Ken Hyland
and Chris Candlin. Routledge, 1999. Reproduced by permission of
Taylor & Francis Books UK; p189 Data from *Genres across the Disciplines:
Student Writing in Higher Education* by Hilary Nesi and Sheena Gardner,
Cambridge University Press, 2012. © Cambridge University Press,
2012. Reproduced by permission; p194 Figure 10 from *Genre Analysis:
English in Academic and Research Settings* by John Swales, Cambridge
University Press, 1990. © Cambridge University Press 1990. Reproduced
by permission; p201 Extract from *Sociology, 4th Edition* by James Fulcher
and John Scott, Oxford University Press, March 2011. Reproduced by
permission of Oxford University Press; p226–7 Extract from *Oxford
EAP: Advanced/C1 Student's Book* by Edward de Chazal and Julie Moore,
Oxford University Press, September 2013. Reproduced by permission
of Oxford University Press; p249 Adapted table from 'Can Do
Framework for EAP syllabus design and assessment' by BALEAP, 2013.
Reproduced by permission of BALEAP; p314 The IELTS 9-band scale,
www.ielts.org. Reproduced with permission of Cambridge English
Language Assessment © UCLES 2013; p316 Extract from 'Interpreting
the PTE Academic Score Report' by Pearson Language testing, 2012.
Reproduced by permission of Pearson Education Ltd; p317 Table 11.9
for Band Score by IELTS, www.ielts.org. Reproduced with permission
of Cambridge English Language Assessment © UCLES 2013; p335
Abridged comment by Pete Etchells, 09:54 22 March 2013, http://
deevybee.blogspot.co.uk. Reproduced by permission of Pete Etchells;
pp343–4 Extract from 'The pipeline' by Frank Gannon, EMBO reports,
Vol 9, Issue 1, January 2008, Nature Publishing Group. Reprinted by
permission from Macmillan Publishers Ltd, copyright 2008; pp344–5
Extract from *Sociology, 4th Edition* by James Fulcher and John Scott,
Oxford University Press, March 2011. Reproduced by permission of
Oxford University Press.

Sources: www.wikipedia.org

To my students and teaching colleagues, since 1987

How much greater than knowledge is understanding

CONTENTS

ACKNOWLEDGEMENTS

First of all, I would like to thank Aisha Walker of the University of Leeds for writing the final chapter, 'Technologies', and Liz Austin of the University of Essex for contributing greatly to Chapter 11, Assessment.

I would also like to thank the two readers: John Swales, Professor Emeritus of Linguistics at the University of Michigan, and Lindy Woodrow, Senior Lecturer in TESOL at the University of Sydney, for their extremely helpful and insightful responses to the manuscript.

At Oxford University Press (OUP), I acknowledge a debt of gratitude to Catherine Kncafscy for originally commissioning this book, Keith Layfield for running with it, and Julia Bell for taking it to its final stages of completion. As part of the wider OUP team I would like to thank Shaun Wilden for providing early material on technologies and resources, plus publishers, sales and marketing staff, administration staff, and editors, notably the editor of the book, Andrew Dilger and copy editor Anna Cowper. All have contributed to and supported me and this book in important ways.

At University College London (UCL), where I taught from 2002 to 2011, I would like to thank my former colleagues in the Language Centre (now the Centre for Languages and International Education); also Professor Donald Gillies, who studied under Karl Popper when at the London School of Economics and Political Science, and has kindly given permission for his lecture material on Bacon and Popper to be used in the first section of Chapter 5. In addition, I would like to acknowledge the influence and support of staff and students at other London University colleges at which I have studied, including those at Westfield College (now incorporated into Queen Mary College), the Central School of Speech and Drama, and the Institute of Education – special thanks there to Amos Paran and Catherine Walter (now at the University of Oxford Department of Continuing Education) for guiding me in my early investigations of noun phrases.

Various courses have offered me relevant content and stimulation, notably my MA in Teaching English as a Second or Foreign Language at Bangor, University College of North Wales, particularly my dissertation supervisor Phil Scholfield, now at the University of Essex; and the Certificate in the Advanced Study of Education in English for Specific Purposes led by Mike Scott and an inspiring team including Geoff and Susan Thompson at the University of Liverpool.

I have also learned greatly from my EAP teaching colleagues earlier in my career in the 1990s, notably at Bilkent University in Ankara, under the direction first of Desmond Thomas (now at the University of Essex) and subsequently John

O'Dwyer. The Bilkent teaching staff at that time have gone on to pioneer EAP teaching throughout Turkey and beyond. I gained further invaluable experience leading the team which set up the academic military English programme for officers at the Joint Command and Staff College in Kuwait.

I would additionally like to acknowledge the ongoing support and friendship of other independent authors, particularly Fiona Aish, Jo Tomlinson, Sheila Thorn, Sam McCarter, Louis Rogers, and Julie Moore, who kindly gave permission for a small number of glossary items she wrote for *Oxford EAP Advanced/C1* to be incorporated into the Glossary in this book.

There are two professional organizations I would like to acknowledge: IATEFL (the International Association of Teachers of English as a Foreign Language) and BALEAP (the global forum for EAP professionals). These two teachers' associations offer outstanding networking opportunities and inspiration for teachers of English and EAP, particularly through their publications, conferences, and events. A considerable amount of material in this book found its first outing in presentations I have given at IATEFL and BALEAP, which represent excellent opportunities to disseminate new ideas and raise questions.

Many further ideas were encountered in innumerable presentations and training events, and the classroom. For this reason I would like to thank past students, colleagues, presenters, trainers, and audiences in presentations for raising interesting questions and ideas.

Lastly, I thank my family for their enormous patience and understanding, as ever.

ABBREVIATIONS AND ACRONYMS

ALTE	Association of Language Testers in Europe
AWL	Academic Word List
APA	American Psychological Association
BALEAP	the global forum for EAP professionals (formerly the British Association of Lecturers in English for Academic Purposes)
CAE	Certificate in Advanced English (Cambridge)
CaRS/CARS	create a research space
CBI	content-based instruction
CDA	critical discourse analysis
CEAP	critical English for academic purposes
CEFR	Council of Europe Framework of Reference for Languages
CLIL	content and language integrated learning
CLT	communicative language teaching
CPD	continuing professional development
CPE	Certificate of Proficiency in English (Cambridge)
DELTA	Diploma in English Language Teaching to Adults (Cambridge)
EAP	English for academic purposes
EFL	English as a foreign language
EGAP	English for general academic purposes
EIL	English as an international language
ELF	English as a lingua franca
ELT	English language teaching
EMI	English (as the) medium of instruction
EOP	English for occupational purposes
ERPP	English for research publication purposes
ESAP	English for specific academic purposes
ESL	English as a second language
ESOL	English for speakers of other languages
ESP	English for specific purposes

EST	English for science and technology
FCE	First Certificate in English (Cambridge)
GCSE	General Certificate of Secondary Education
IATEFL	International Association of Teachers of English as a Foreign Language
IB	International Baccalaureate
IELTS	International English Language Testing System
ISI	Institute for Scientific Information
KET	Key English Test (Cambridge)
LMS	learning management system
MBA	Master of Business Administration
MLA	Modern Language Association of America
MOOC	massive open online course
PET	Preliminary English Test (Cambridge)
PLS	private language school
PTE	Pearson Test of English
SFL	systemic functional linguistics
STEM	science, technology, engineering, mathematics
TBL	task-based learning
TEFL	teaching English as a foreign language
TESL	teaching English as a second language
TESOL	teachers of English/teaching English to speakers of other languages
TOEFL	Test of English as a Foreign Language
TOEIC	Test of English for International Communication
UNESCO	United Nations Educational, Scientific and Cultural Organization
VLE	virtual learning environment
WAC	writing across the curriculum
WiD	writing in the disciplines

INTRODUCTION

Background and context

When I started teaching English as a Foreign Language (EFL) in 1987, the teaching certificate I did in London had a short session on English for specific purposes (ESP), but no mention was made of English for academic purposes (EAP). It probably took a year or two before I ever heard about EAP. In the context of my teaching certificate at International House London, ESP meant business English. Business students, we were told, are motivated, and have interesting lives involving travel. Our trainers also said that in order to teach business English, we would need technical language, and also to be interested in business. My trainee notes, well saved, also reveal that, in ESP, fluency is more important than accuracy, and finally that 'if you're not interested in ESP, don't touch it with a barge pole'.

How far these observations hold true today, if they did indeed hold true then, can remain a matter for discussion. For teachers starting to teach EAP, some of whom will have taught business English, and nearly all of whom will have their own experiences of studying in higher or further education, there are likely to be different concerns: How do I go about teaching EAP? Should I use different techniques and methodologies to those in business and general English contexts? Where can I find good materials? What do my students expect of me? How will I cope with the demands of an intensive **pre-sessional** programme? Which aspects of language should I prioritize? What can I do to improve my students' writing and speaking? What exactly is EAP anyway?

This book is written for these teachers, and indeed all teachers of EAP worldwide, and aims to address questions such as these. It introduces and defines the field of EAP and offers many practical applications of the theories and ideas which are currently in circulation. EAP teachers at all levels of experience can benefit from the ideas and approaches presented. As with academic textbooks in general, the material in this book is presented to be interpreted, applied, and critiqued. Above all, this book is written to be purposeful and relevant to the needs of EAP teachers working in a wide variety of contexts around the world.

Purpose and organization

This book aims to give EAP teachers at all levels of experience a comprehensive, up to date, and coherent account of the field of English for academic purposes, offering an accessible description of EAP practice, which is thoroughly grounded in current theories and developments in the field.

Chapter 1 opens the discussion by setting out 'The field of EAP', which is seen as a research-informed practice influenced by many theoretical and practical approaches over a period of more than half a century. Chapter 2, 'Teaching and learning', presents a context in which EAP students can be seen as resources of knowledge and experience rather than deficient students in need of remedial training. This chapter discusses teacher competences and current issues in EAP teaching and methodology. In Chapter 3, 'Texts', academic texts are presented as sources of knowledge and **argument**, and are described and analysed to emphasize their meaning and use for EAP teaching and learning. Chapter 4, 'Language', casts academic language as agent of meaning: it is through reusable language forms and patterns that original, complex, and abstract meanings can be expressed. This chapter argues for an inclusive approach to language analysis and teaching which recognizes the fundamental inseparability of vocabulary and grammar. Chapter 5, 'Critical thinking', sees the critical thinker as reflector and challenger. **Critical thinking** is **essential** in academic contexts, and starts with the practice of reflecting on the meanings expressed in texts, and the wider context of the texts themselves.

Opening a sequence of chapters covering the four skills, Chapter 6, 'Reading', explores the role of the academic reader as processor and evaluator. Academic reading is purposeful and productive, and by emphasizing these processing and evaluating roles, EAP teachers can develop their students' efficiency in reading and processing the information for their own use. This material leads to Chapter 7, 'Writing', in which the academic writer is cast as architect of meaning. Based on their reading and thinking, academic writers carry out multiple roles, including assembling and constructing a meaningful new text and managing the writing project. Chapter 8, 'Listening', highlights the role of the academic listener as interpreter and recorder through their work in decoding spoken texts and noting down meanings. Chapter 9, 'Speaking', consolidates the sequence of chapters on skills by illustrating the academic speaker as reporter and persuader, particularly using material they have read, listened to, and critiqued.

Following this sequence of skills-focused chapters, Chapter 10, 'Materials', looks at principled ways of using, evaluating, and writing materials which reflect the position of EAP teachers in relation to the influences presented in Chapter 1, the issues discussed in Chapter 2, and the series of approaches described in this chapter. EAP materials are seen as objective-driven tasks leading to independence, since student independence is an ultimate aim of EAP. Chapter 11, 'Assessment', considers the roles and types of assessments in EAP, showing assessments as tools to determine students' academic progression through the EAP programme and into their chosen **discipline**. Finally, Chapter 12, 'Technologies', positions technologies as resources for communication and learning. By maximizing the use of the available technologies, EAP teachers and students can enhance the effectiveness of their teaching and learning.

The final part of the book offers a conclusion to briefly sum up the main arguments in the book as a whole, a glossary of terms used, a bibliography of works cited in the text, and an index.

1

THE FIELD OF EAP

EAP as a research-informed practice

English for Academic Purposes (EAP) has evolved from its modest roots in the 1960s to become an emerging global phenomenon. University education is globalizing, English is becoming established as the medium of instruction in a diverse range of contexts, and international students are becoming increasingly mobile. Whilst EAP has developed to meet these students' needs, it is not only students, but also their teaching staff who are becoming increasingly mobile. A small but growing area of EAP involves teaching these academics, which is discussed briefly in Chapter 2.

To understand what EAP is and how it reached this stage of development, it is useful to look briefly at its current context, before going back half a century to its beginnings. During this time, EAP has been influenced by linguistics and educational research, and a number of trends, theories, and practices from different parts of the world, which go some way to explaining its current diversity and complexity. This chapter discusses the emergence of EAP, dispels various myths, compares EAP with other English language teaching contexts, and examines the major influences on the field, before returning to its current global context and looking ahead.

Contextualization

The field of English language teaching (ELT) is diverse, global, and complex. Within the field many different sectors, approaches, and cultures coexist. These sectors include:

- general teaching English as a foreign language (known as TEFL, EFL, or ELT, i.e. English language teaching)
- teaching English as a second language (TESOL, TESL, ESOL, or ESL)
- more specialized sectors including English for specific purposes (ESP), English for science and technology (EST), English for occupational purposes (EOP), and English for academic purposes (EAP).

EAP, the focus of this book, has itself given rise to two further sub-sectors: English for general academic purposes (EGAP) and English for specific academic purposes

(ESAP). ESAP can cover a variety of types of English for specific academic and professional purposes, such as English for law, architecture, or nursing.

The fact that this very brief overview contains a dozen or so abbreviations and acronyms illustrates the diversity and complexity of the field, and the potential for confusion. The same sector can have different names. Different sectors can, in effect, have the same name. TESOL, for example, is associated with the USA and is taken to mean the teaching of English to speakers of other languages; in its northern neighbour, Canada, the abbreviation for this activity is more likely to be TESL. In the UK, meanwhile, a distinction is usually made between the teaching of English to speakers of other languages who are learning it anywhere (EFL/ELT, or TESOL in some contexts such as MA programmes), and those, such as migrants, who are learning it in the target language community, for example the UK, in order to integrate into that community (ESOL or ESL). In practice, some of the names and abbreviations are used interchangeably. As the field of ELT develops, some of the names, though not necessarily the sectors, are being used less—for instance EST (English for science and technology), once the 'senior branch of ESP' (Swales 1985: *x*) is now supplanted by business English and EAP— while others represent growing sectors and are becoming more widely used and familiar (EAP).

In order to define and position EAP within its broader context of English language teaching, a brief historical overview illustrates how EAP emerged from the need to teach English language in specialized, academic contexts.

The emergence of EAP

The term 'EAP' is widely used in the field of English language teaching today. It can, however, mean different things to different people. Even within the same institution, EAP staff and management may disagree on what EAP is and, by implication, what to focus on when teaching it. There follows a brief historical account which serves to contextualize EAP and establish what it means today.

ESP and EAP

The concept of 'ESP', English for Specific Purposes, developed in different parts of the world from the early 1960s into the 1970s and 1980s and beyond. A number of countries and regions were central to this development, including the UK (particularly in the development of testing) and various other European countries, North Africa and the Middle East (with their fast-growing oil industries), countries across the Americas from Canada and the USA to Chile, various Asian countries such as Thailand, and India, where English-medium university teaching was widespread. In these early decades, much ESP and EAP activity centred on English-medium university departments around the world, in particular science and engineering departments. Certain organizations were involved in this early development, notably the British Council, who published volumes of **articles** relating to ESP and EAP, (for example Harper 1986; Chamberlain and Baumgardner 1988).

Branching out from ESP were different, broadly grouped English-for-specific-purposes sectors, notably English for science and technology (EST), English for occupational purposes (EOP) and English for academic purposes (EAP). EAP was a product of the 1970s with the rise in the number of students whose first language was not English studying at universities. The term 'EAP' appears to have been first used in 1974 by Tim Johns (Smith 2013). This phenomenon has grown steadily ever since as increasing numbers of students seek to study in English-medium institutions worldwide, particularly universities.

For a number of years, much of this EAP activity took place in the major English-speaking countries, notably the USA, Canada, the UK, Ireland, Australia, and New Zealand. In the UK, for example, EAP grew rapidly in the 1980s and 1990s as universities recruited increasingly large numbers of international students. This growth was characterized by a dominance of a few countries and regions, such as China and the Middle East. Many students had a level of English which was too low for academic study in English, as well as a limited background in academic English culture and practices. The teaching of English for academic purposes has aimed to fulfil these needs.

Increasingly, the dominance of English-medium universities in the major English-speaking countries has been challenged as English-medium departments and universities are being established globally. Major growth areas include European countries such as France, Sweden, and Spain, the Middle East, South America, Central and South-East Asia. Some countries, Turkey and Saudi Arabia for example, can count in dozens the number of recently established English-medium universities. The student growth rate in such institutions is typically very rapid.

Student needs

What ESP and EAP have in common is that they are primarily needs driven: students are learning English with a particular purpose in mind, which is identifiable and describable, and these descriptions form the basis of the ESP or EAP programme. Within ESP there are a very wide range of purposes, from learning English for business purposes (for example, to operate in a global logistics environment) through medical purposes (to be a doctor or nurse in an English-medium medical institution) to military purposes (to serve in an international peacekeeping force). Indeed, these labels themselves are over-simplifications; 'business English', for example, is itself complex and broad in **scope**.

Students in the disciplines

As its name suggests, English for academic purposes involves the teaching and learning of English language so that students can operate effectively in the disciplines, i.e. in their specific subject(s) in an academic institution, typically a university. The term 'students in the disciplines' simply refers to students who are currently following their academic programme of study; they may or may not also be studying EAP.

There is more to EAP, however. It is not so much driven by language as skills, tasks, and competences. In terms of skills, EAP certainly involves the familiar four skills of reading, writing, listening, and speaking, particularly in an integrated way. Yet there are many more skills and competences, such as critical thinking skills, study skills (which include many conventional academic skills such as **citation** and referencing), and the practice of working towards familiarization within the target academic culture. Also, EAP is concerned with the development of student autonomy and independence. The term sometimes applied to cover many of these skills and competences is 'academic literacy' or 'academic literacies'. The latter plural term is intended to convey the diverse sets of skills and competences in academic contexts in contrast to a unitary academic literacy. An academic literacies approach goes considerably beyond language alone and emphasizes academic practice in the disciplines. In almost any EAP context, language does remain a major area of focus, and language can be approached in many different ways.

EAP today typically recognizes that students plan to study or are studying in the disciplines and therefore need an approach which can help them acclimatize to their academic study in a broad sense.

The academicization of ESP

Some ESP activity has shifted from a professional orientation to an academic one. Traditionally, many ESP programmes have been geared mainly towards operating in the given specific environment, such as business and technology: there was often a practically oriented **syllabus** with plenty of functional/notional language, technical language, and communicative skills work. In many contexts this remains the standard practice, but with increasing professionalization and specialization, many students need more than such skills and language. Many students are aiming for a qualification in their field, such as a bachelor's degree in business studies, a more specialist master's degree or an MBA (Master of Business Administration). These academic aims are leading to a greater focus on academic skills and language.

While business English continues to thrive professionally in company settings, the phenomenon of academicization has resulted in a major concurrent growth in EAP. With the great popularity of business-related degree programmes, a significant proportion of EAP students are aiming to study a business-related subject; in the past, these business students might have been considered ESP rather than EAP students. In the early days, there was some confusion between English for business study (for example MBAs), which has a primarily academic focus, and English for business, which has a professional rather than an academic focus. By the 1980s, the considerable differences between these two branches of ESP were becoming clearer.

Complexity in the disciplines: the case of business students

A further level of complexity lies in the extremely wide range of subjects which students may be aiming to study. Several broad groupings of disciplines may be identified, although these can be grouped differently depending on the institution and context:

- medical sciences, including nursing
- life sciences, for example pharmacology
- engineering
- computing
- mathematics
- natural sciences, such as physics and chemistry
- professional disciplines, such as law
- social sciences, for example economics
- architecture, the built environment, urban planning
- arts, including art, music, and languages
- humanities, such as history
- education, including teacher training
- business and management
- vocational subjects, such as hospitality management.

These align to some extent with the faculty groupings of universities, although these can vary widely. Each of these broad groupings may be further divided; for example, engineering may include civil engineering, chemical engineering, computer engineering, geomatic engineering, and others, which as an engineer would be keen to point out, are very different from each other. The example of business can have a very large number of related but distinct subjects, any one of which may be what people mean when they talk about 'business students': business, management, finance, economics, human resources, logistics, international relations, development, sustainability, politics, government, marketing, training, corporate law, retail, accounting, public policy, gender, global issues, international politics, international business law, communications, organizational structures, social policy, business psychology.

As this chapter goes on to show, EAP is potentially quite broad in scope, but its limitations lie in its aims: EAP is not concerned with teaching subject content. Rather, it aims to develop key academic skills, language, and competences; students subsequently, or concurrently, learn about their specific subject including content and its associated discourse and academic practices.

Myths and realities in EAP

There are a number of myths, misunderstandings, and misconceptions about EAP. These may arise due to differing approaches or levels of experience. There may be differences in views between people working in the EAP sector and those working in other sectors. In the light of the discussion so far in this chapter, this section turns to seven of the more common myths.

Myth 1: To teach EAP is to teach subject knowledge and content

The main focus of EAP is to meet the needs of students wanting to study their discipline in English. As the discussions so far have shown, the number of disciplines is extremely large, and growing. The focus of EAP is not on the subject and the specific language of the subject itself, whether administration or zoology, but on the skills, competences, and language needed to study the subject. It is the job of the academic department, and the teachers on the programme of academic study, to teach specific items and concepts. Even after a lifetime of teaching, EAP teachers cannot possibly 'know' all the academic subjects in sufficient depth, although with experience a general sense of familiarity with certain disciplines gradually develops.

The sector primarily concerned with teaching subject knowledge and content as well as the target language is content and language integrated learning (CLIL), also known as content-based instruction (CBI). CLIL is concerned with teaching content through the target second or foreign language; it can involve any language, but is most likely to be in English, particularly in Europe, or other widely spoken languages, such as French (for example in Anglophone parts of Canada) and German. In contrast with EAP, CLIL takes place at quite young ages, in primary and secondary schools.

Myth 2: Vocabulary in EAP means a focus on subject-specific words such as scientific terms

As in the first myth, specific vocabulary learning is not a central concern of most EAP teaching. In earlier incarnations of ESP, technical and scientific vocabulary was a major focus. Vocabulary suitable for an EAP class, on the other hand, may include any core words (starting with the most frequent word, *the*), plus general academic words, such as *analyze, evaluation, conclusion, focus on, homogeneous*. These words in themselves are not 'owned' by any particular discipline; they occur across disciplines and are therefore essential for students of any discipline.

Myth 3: To study in an English-medium university you must have an extremely high level of English

The vast majority of students do not reach C2 (proficiency) level, in general ELT or EAP. Many students have not reached C1 (advanced) at the start of their English-medium programme. Depending on the context, students typically move from general English to EAP at B1 (pre-intermediate to intermediate) or B2 (upper intermediate), and work their way up towards somewhere in B2 or C1 territory before starting their studies. An increasing trend is to begin EAP at lower levels, for example from A2 (elementary) rather than B1. This is particularly the case in growing education hubs such as Turkey and the Middle East. Many degree programmes, including foundation courses, bridging degrees, and many undergraduate degrees, ask for a level somewhere around B2 or B1. In the UK, science and business often require lower scores than the arts, humanities, and law, though this is not always the case in other regions of the world. A typical target for science students in the UK might be IELTS 6.5 (B2), and 7.0 (B2/C1) for arts and humanities; the most prestigious universities may typically ask for IELTS 7.5 (C1) for law students. In short, English requirements vary quite widely, but are often not as high as might be expected.

To clarify language level descriptors, many familiar descriptors such as 'intermediate' map fairly neatly onto the Council of Europe Framework of References for Languages (CEFR) scale, approximately as follows: A1 beginner/starter; A2 elementary; B1 pre-intermediate; B1+ intermediate; B2 upper intermediate; C1 advanced; C2 proficiency.

Myth 4: EAP is dry and dull

EAP should not and need not be so, any more than studying one's chosen discipline is dry and dull. The academic world is about the study, research, and communication of ideas; EAP is every bit as communicative as general English, but in a different way. As shown in Table 1.1 on page 17, much of the communication takes place in set-piece events such as **seminars**, and through written assignments. A major challenge for EAP teachers is to make learning not just relevant but engaging and motivating.

Myth 5: EAP is basically IELTS

Again, there are, arguably, as many differences as similarities between the two. IELTS involves a flavour of academic tasks, and to a degree some of the language, but without the rigour of academic cognitive activities such as **analysis**, **evaluation**, and **synthesis**. In IELTS Writing Task 1 for instance, candidates have to describe a graphic, or more recently, more than one graphic. In EAP, such graphics would be used as part of a wider purpose, such as to provide support in written work or in a presentation. The student would search for, select, interpret, and evaluate the material. This would lead to the incorporation of parts of the referenced material into an original piece of written or spoken work. It would be synthesized with material from other **sources**. Simply describing a given graphic is by comparison quite a basic activity. Similarly, the IELTS speaking examination does not aim to replicate the kind of speaking done in academic settings.

Myth 6: EAP involves proofreading students' written work

Proofreading refers to the practice of correcting the errors and ensuring clarity in a text; this can be done either by the writer of the text or another person, such as a language teacher, peer, or editor working for a publisher. The main aims in proofreading a text or manuscript are: to eliminate language errors (by identifying and correcting them) including errors in spelling, grammar, and punctuation; to ensure clarity, by rephrasing any language which is hard to understand or ambiguous; to harmonize style, for example by rephrasing language which appears too informal or formal for the **purpose**; and to ensure accuracy in non-language areas, particularly with regard to **in-text references**, bibliographies, and any tables and graphics. Since the main aim of proofreading is to arrive at a high-quality text, the proofreader may not offer explanations and alternatives for their corrections, and so the process is not primarily developmental and pedagogical; however, for the reflective writer receiving their proofread text can be a very instructive experience.

Proofreading is not generally considered to be a core activity for EAP teachers. EAP teachers periodically raise and discuss issues surrounding proofreading, such as who should do it, whether it should be a paid-for service, and how it should be carried out. A key question in proofreading is the remit of the proofreader, and how far they should cover non-language aspects of the text such as quality of the argument and use of sources. While a major role of an EAP teacher is to read and give feedback on their students' written work, there are typically three main focuses: content, organization, and language. When giving feedback on content and organization, the focus is on aspects such as the strength of the ideas, how they are presented, the coherence of the argument, and use of academic sources. The work on language may involve identifying typical errors and giving an indication of the type of error and perhaps how to correct it. Students will then work on these errors themselves, rather than relying on their teacher to correct them, and the students' revised texts can then be checked for accuracy. Ultimately, then, EAP teaching aims to foster students' proofreading skills as far as possible, rather than the teacher providing a proofreading service for their students.

Myth 7: EAP is objective rather than subjective

Academic texts have been described as '**objective**' rather than '**subjective**' (for example Clanchy and Ballard (1981: 74, and 1992; also cited in Jordan 1997: 244), but this statement is overgeneralized and highly misleading. The academic world is both objective and subjective. It is objective in the sense that it searches for and transfers knowledge, and this knowledge needs to be in some sense **validated**. Research needs to be replicated in different contexts in order to yield similar results. However, different **interpretations** and evaluative **responses** are highly valued and essential to the dissemination of ideas and research. Such interpretations may be responses to objective **evidence**, but by their nature they are subjective: one person's interpretation or evaluation of the same evidence may differ from another's. A significant part of critical thinking is subjective and carried out by 'subjects' or people. None of the following examples of academic thought is an objective '**fact**': a **theory** of learning; the assessment of the impact of a historical event or medical trauma; a policy response to a crisis. There is subjectivity in all of these. Academic practice is concerned with relations between objective phenomena, such as the findings of a piece of research, and subjective responses, such as interpretation and evaluation. It is important to bear in mind that these responses need to be grounded in evidence rather than seemingly plucked out of the air.

Differences between EAP and general ELT

The discussion of myths and realities in the previous section highlights a number of important differences between EAP and other ELT contexts. These influences have contributed to the particular nature of EAP, which despite many commonalities is in many respects quite distinct from general ELT. This section examines some of the differences between the two teaching contexts.

Although the teacher moving from general English language teaching contexts into EAP has a great deal to offer, they do need to adapt to the specific context of EAP. Many established EAP teachers regard themselves as operating in a distinctly different teaching and learning environment, an environment which is not always fully understood by teachers in other contexts. By its nature, 'general' ELT is usually broadly based and generalized, while EAP tends to be more specific. This observation has many implications, which are discussed in this section. It is a useful discussion partly because, as pointed out above, in practice a majority of EAP teachers probably started out teaching general English and/or business English. The transition into the possibly unfamiliar new context can lead to the teacher feeling disorientated and lacking in sufficient skills and confidence.

Many significant differences exist between the two broad contexts of general ELT and EAP. Large numbers of students of English start learning at increasingly young ages; teaching young learners has been a major growth area in ELT since the 1990s. These students have years of learning English ahead of them. With EAP, on the other hand, time is typically limited, and proficiency targets are often ambitious.

If general English is often broad in focus with long time scales and targets based around general language proficiency, EAP has an academic focus. It aims to develop students' skills and language to a target level of proficiency while developing academic literacies. EAP has traditionally been defined by needs. In practice these can be fairly generic, in other words applicable to a wide range of academic settings. A key component of such needs is the target level of English. While this may be the easiest to quantify, usually being a number such as a particular test score, the more academic needs are also essential. In an ideal scenario, students' needs would be carefully analyzed and described by means of a needs analysis. In simple terms this might result, for example, in a group of scientists being identified as needing to learn how to write a lab report, a group of architects to plan posters and legends for models, and a set of literature students to write a critique; although in reality the results of such a needs analysis would be more detailed and complex. In practice, however, students are often placed together more by language level than discipline. The number of disciplines is very broad and often very specialized, and so to organize students by both discipline and language level would require a very large institution to be economically viable.

Critical thinking

Critical thinking is one of the major distinctions between general ELT and EAP. To engage with the academic world, critical thinking skills are vital; by implication they are at the heart of EAP. BALEAP, the UK-based forum for EAP professionals, has prepared a descriptive framework for EAP teachers: the BALEAP competency framework for teachers of English for academic purposes (2008). As stated in this framework, EAP teachers need to 'understand the role of critical thinking in academic contexts and will employ tasks, processes and interactions that require students to demonstrate critical thinking skills' (BALEAP 2008). When reading a text, EAP students need to learn to understand what it is saying. In doing so, they can ask questions such as:

- What is the writer's main argument?
- How relevant and reliable is the evidence that the writer presents in support of their argument?
- What is their **stance**, and what meanings lie implicit in the text?
- What weaknesses are there in the material?

Questions such as these should become second nature, and need to be part of EAP materials from B1 (from pre-intermediate to intermediate) or even A2 (elementary) levels upwards. These questions are not prominent in the treatment of texts in general English language coursebooks, but to have **validity**, EAP materials need to be designed around the development of critical thinking. The concept of critical thinking in EAP is dealt with in greater depth in Chapter 5.

Curriculum and syllabus

In many ELT contexts, the syllabus might be independently described, but from the teacher's perspective it may simply be the coursebook. In these contexts, the teacher works through the chosen coursebook in a given amount of time, supplementing with other materials as necessary. General English coursebooks tend to be based around the four skills plus a language syllabus which is traditionally separated out into grammar, vocabulary, and some aspects of phonology, including pronunciation and intonation. In the most popular coursebooks, grammar tends to be verb-phrase driven: the units in the coursebook systematically work through the various tense/aspect/**modal verb** possibilities. The supporting student grammar books typically reflect this; the bestselling ones devote an extraordinary amount of space to verbs with up to half the material based around the verb phrase. As Chapter 4 illustrates, this heavy focus on verbs is seriously misaligned when applied to EAP (indeed it is also misaligned when applied to general English contexts). To mirror this emphasis on verbs would be a very inefficient use of time: it would crowd out the syllabus and lead to insufficient coverage of more important language. EAP syllabuses tend to be skills driven and/or task driven, with a focus on integration of skills. Language is vital but, as in other ESP contexts, is often presented on a 'need-to-know' basis to support the skills work. Crucially, EAP grammar should primarily be built not around the verb phrase but around the **noun phrase**. Noun phrases are described and analyzed in Chapter 4.

General ELT courses are often open-ended, with students progressing over a long time, using multiple-level coursebook series, to their ultimate level of proficiency. In EAP contexts, time is a pressing constraint, with limited time for quite ambitious target aims. Students typically need to progress to a known target such as a specific IELTS score to meet their conditional university requirement. To this end, as Alexander (2010) has pointed out, EAP focuses on content: how to plan, organize, and write an essay, for example; in contrast, general ELT has a much stronger focus on **delivery**: how to teach—and how students will learn—a particular language item or skill.

Topics and vocabulary

Further differences between general ELT contexts and EAP may be found in the coverage and treatment of topics and vocabulary.

Topics

EAP topics and their coverage can frequently be cognitively challenging. Topics may include areas such as human behaviour, transport, energy, and the environment. To a significant extent, topics are student generated: in some contexts, the students can be empowered to develop topics to focus on, which they can relate to their discipline. In general ELT, topics need to have broad appeal, be reasonably accessible, and as far as many published materials are concerned, not too controversial. Choices in popular coursebooks include such topics as 'family', 'leisure', 'personality', 'appearances', 'cultural differences', 'people', 'travel', and traditionally, 'literature'. Significantly, such topics are covered in little depth. Students may compare differences related to the topic and respond to these differences, but not in a rigorously critical way. In EAP, after some contextualization a topic tends to be narrowed down and focused on in more depth, from different **perspectives**, and with a critical approach. These crucial differences are examined in more detail in subsequent chapters, particularly the chapters on the four skills, Chapters 6–9.

Vocabulary

Related to topic is vocabulary. In general ELT, vocabulary is likely to be topic driven. If the topic of the day is 'personality', for example, the students can expect to see carefully graded related vocabulary: a selection of adjectives to describe personality; some nouns conceptualizing different personality types; and perhaps some other language, including verbs and idiomatic expressions. In EAP, meanwhile, relevant topic-based vocabulary may of course be learned, but there tends to be a focus on more **generic language**. This language is widely used across all academic subjects. It is not subject specific and cannot be traced back to one discipline. Examples from this particular paragraph might include: 'related to', 'describe', 'conceptualizing', 'types', 'perhaps', 'In [EAP] meanwhile', 'may of course be [learned]', 'there tends to be', 'focus on', 'This [language] is widely used across'. Clearly, these items are frequent and potentially useful in any discipline. The **content words** in brackets are adaptable to any discipline. In addition, some of these items comprise several words.

These items reflect how language is used, not as endlessly created, brand new sequences of individual words, but as formulaic units or 'chunks' of language which can be reused. Such language has been the subject of various studies, including Wray (2002) and Biber et al. (1999). Another major area of vocabulary for study in EAP is notional language, the language used to talk about relations such as time, space, and causality, for example: '*since* the fall of communism' [time], 'mainly *in* the northern hemisphere' [space], and '*as a result of* inadequate protein intake' [causality]. In these examples, the notional language is based around the prepositions in italics, which normally come first in their phrase; content words feed in to the structures to express specific content.

Texts

In general ELT coursebooks, texts are of general interest and are chosen to fit in with the topic or theme of the unit. They may be selected from quite a wide variety of sources, for example newspaper and magazine articles, webpages and internet texts, letters, or, more traditionally, English literature. With some texts it is unclear where they are sourced from; they may be written especially for the coursebook or adapted as a pastiche from a variety of sources. Indeed, whatever the source, texts are widely adapted to refine the level and edit out challenging language. In the contents pages of a general English coursebook, the reading texts are normally presented by their title rather than by the type of text. To supplement the coursebook, teachers may choose their own texts from wherever they wish.

EAP texts may also be chosen for their topic. Another major consideration applies, however. The type of text, or **genre**, is of great importance. Apart from newspaper and magazine articles, which are not central to EAP though they may sometimes be used, students in the EAP classroom are likely to find themselves reading genres such as textbooks, **journal articles**, **abstracts**, reports, summaries, essays, critiques, and **literature reviews**. Chapter 3 explores the nature of texts in the EAP classroom.

Assessments, tests, and examinations

English language teaching works with a wide range of tests and examinations, including those from the Cambridge English suite: Key (KET), Preliminary (PET), First (FCE), Advanced (CAE), and Proficiency (CPE). Other global tests include IELTS, TOEFL, and TOEIC. Trinity College London has large numbers of candidates in its English grade examinations.

There is a belief among many EAP teachers that success in general English tests and examinations does not necessarily mean that students have the right skills, language, and competence in academic literacies to study successfully in the disciplines. Although some general English tests (for example CAE) may be accepted in some academic institutions, growing demand has led to the development of more academic tests. There is a preference among universities for the three academic English tests, namely IELTS, TOEFL, and the PTE (Pearson Test of English), academic version.

Further discussion of assessments, testing, and examinations is given in Chapter 11.

Global reach

ELT is a global industry, with distinct local variations in approach. As part of this broad enterprise, EAP is capitalizing on global challenges, recognizing that tertiary educational institutions worldwide are increasingly using English as the medium of instruction. In a parallel development, EAP is moving both up and down the academic hierarchy, with graduate students and **academic staff** around the world increasingly expected to teach partially or wholly in English, and the other end of the hierarchy, secondary school students who are preparing for their academic study in English.

At its core, academic discourse is arguably more globalized than other types of discourse, such as some fiction and journalistic writing. As Biber et al. point out, 'academic prose, and to a lesser extent fiction, can be regarded as 'global', in that they are typically written for an international audience with relatively little influence from the national dialect of the author' (Biber et al.1999: 16). This is particularly noticeable in academic journals, which have global reach.

Teaching and learning

This book aims to discuss key teaching and learning issues related to EAP. Certain differences can be noted, which can lead into the realm of generalization. In general ELT contexts, much of the motivation is teacher led; in EAP, the stakes can be high and students can be very self motivated. In both general ELT and EAP, the student body may consist of students of many nationalities and learning types, but in EAP students are more likely to be working towards a clearly defined goal, with students all aspiring to academic independence and a degree of autonomy. If in general ELT students react to material presented by the teacher through the learning materials (especially the coursebook), in EAP students will have to contribute material, particularly relating to their written work, which is frequently based on their discipline. As for the teachers, many EAP teachers started out teaching general ELT. In the process they may have done or be working towards higher-level qualifications themselves, such as MA degrees. EAP modules are increasingly common in MA TESOL degrees; dedicated 'EAP' MA programmes are very gradually beginning to emerge. As for the diplomas, the Cambridge DELTA has a possibility for EAP specialization. In the general ELT classroom, key differences between multinational students are based around culture and language. These differences certainly exist in EAP, but the most important difference is arguably disciplinary: what subjects the students are planning to study.

The focus of EAP

It is also important to note another main focus of EAP. When students are in the disciplines, i.e. studying their chosen subject through the medium of English, a major focus is knowledge. Put simply, they are assessed mainly on their knowledge of the subject. This is not to say that students in the disciplines have to merely memorize facts, rather that their assessments require them to demonstrate and process knowledge in the field by responding critically to given questions and assignments. This means, for example, that students have to select, synthesize, analyze, and evaluate knowledge. These academic practices are grounded in knowledge.

In EAP the primary focus is not the delivery of disciplinary knowledge. Because EAP is grounded in English language teaching, EAP students are not expected to develop and display subject knowledge. Neither do students need to demonstrate explicit knowledge of the English language through, for instance, its grammatical systems. Rather, students need to be able to access and process information through texts (written and spoken) in English. In other words, they need to demonstrate that they can communicate in English in an academic setting, and function effectively as students in the disciplines. The focus is the development of skills and competences which reflect academic practices in the disciplines. In developing these, language development is essential, but it is the means to an end rather than the end itself. In texts, meanings are conveyed through language: language is the vehicle for meaning. Students need to engage with meanings in texts through skills and activities, such as identifying the main points in a text and working out the author's stance. Ultimately, EAP assessments are based around skills and meanings rather than either knowledge or the demonstration of discrete language items.

Similarities between EAP and general ELT

Despite the identification of many differences in the previous section, there are many similarities between EAP and general ELT. If a communicative approach has dominated in English language teaching in many contexts since the 1970s, a rather different form of communication prevails in EAP. Similarly, many other methods, approaches, and practices may be found in EAP contexts. These include task-based learning, collaborative learning, and a learner-centred approach. Differences certainly exist across disciplines, but the amount and type of communication students have to do in academic contexts is considerable, as Table 1.1 indicates.

Nature of activity	Examples
Interaction	Working with other students to establish and maintain everyday relationships Giving and responding to advice, feedback, and approaches to a task
Discussion	Discussing and critiquing a **proposition** in a 'set-piece' event, such as a seminar Talking with peers about how to approach a piece of coursework
Collaboration	Working on a given assignment or group project Conducting a piece of research
Virtual	Communicating in general and academic communication through email, virtual learning environments (VLEs), etc. Maintaining online communication via social media, **blogs**, etc.
Management	Updating tutors on progress and negotiating submission of work Dealing with support staff and administration for general living needs
Presentation	Giving a presentation, poster presentation, or delivering a paper Presenting in a seminar
Persuasion	Presenting an argument in an essay Critiquing and responding to other students and academic staff

Table 1.1   Selected communication activities in EAP

The examples in this table illustrate the varied nature and potential complexity of communicative activities. The student has to deal with peers and stakeholders at different levels and with varying degrees of formality and specialism.

For newly practising and established EAP teachers alike, a familiarity and understanding of communicative language teaching is highly valued. As with general ELT teachers, key skills for the EAP teacher include: planning and organizational skills; creative skills and techniques; language analysis; communication and presentation skills; understanding of student behaviour, motivation, and psychology; and classroom management skills. Related to some of these skills, it is also vital for EAP teachers to understand and respond to their students' needs, difficulties, and learning styles.

EAP and other specialized English contexts

The previous sections have explored similarities and differences between EAP and general English language teaching contexts. It is also necessary to establish the differences between the major branches of EAP, i.e. EGAP ('general' EAP) and ESAP ('specific' EAP), other ESP contexts, and content and language integrated learning (CLIL). CLIL refers to the practice of learning both subject content and the target second or foreign language in an integrated way: the subject teacher (for example, mathematics teacher) delivers the content through the target language (for example, English). CLIL is concerned with nearly all the features in the first column of Table 1.2 (apart from its lack of a professional focus), although its type of academic language is different from that of all the others due to the age of the learners. Most significantly, unlike the other types of teaching, CLIL is focused on content, and as a result is heavily focused on the assessment of subject content: to be successful, students need to demonstrate subject knowledge.

Table 1.2 draws together those features which are common and divergent among general ELT, EGAP, ESAP, and ESP.

Content and coverage	General ELT	EGAP	ESAP	ESP
Core language (i.e. grammatical words such as determiners and prepositions; c.2,000 highest-frequency **lexical words**)	●	●	●	●
Academic language (i.e. generic academic language used across disciplines)		●	●	○
Subject-specific language (i.e. the language of the subject, such as law or mathematics)			●	●
General functional language/skills (e.g. giving directions)	●			○
Academic context-specific functional language/skills (e.g. referring to graphics)		●	●	○
Professional context-specific functional skills/language (e.g. relating to business/aviation)				●
Authentic subject-specific texts		●	●	●
Assessments based on language and skills	●	●	●	●
Assessment of content (i.e. subject knowledge)				

Table 1.2   Comparisons between the aims of general ELT, EGAP, ESAP, and ESP
Key: ● essential   ○ possible

Given its cell-based nature, this table presents a simplified picture of its content; in reality of course the boundaries are less sharply defined. However, it remains a useful analysis of what EAP prioritizes and how it relates to other English language teaching contexts, and can serve as a very useful basis for further discussion in local contexts.

In order to describe and characterize EAP more fully, the following section provides an account the major influences on the field since the 1960s.

Influences on EAP

There have been a number of significant influences on EAP in the decades since its emergence in the 1960s. Some of these are quite major influences, others less so. The extent of these influences may vary across EAP contexts. They include the following:

- general English language teaching
- register analysis
- study skills
- genre analysis
- systemic functional linguistics
- American second language composition
- critical EAP
- academic literacies
- writing in the disciplines
- other influences, such as corpora

In any language teaching context, to understand their particular language teaching methodology, a teacher needs a degree of familiarity with the major approaches and methods in language teaching. A useful account of the major ELT approaches and methods is given in Richards and Rogers (2001). Similarly, an understanding of the influences discussed in this section is useful in order to gain a deeper understanding of EAP: the practices in any EAP context will be informed by principles and characteristics drawn from these practices, research traditions, and schools of thought. Each of the influences outlined in this section has its own complexities and requires a certain amount of knowledge and time to understand. The aim of this section is to give an overview of the influences on EAP so that the EAP teacher can learn to position their own practice with reference to the influences.

These influences have emerged from different contexts both within and outside EAP. As these contexts are associated with different practices, research traditions, and students, they do not represent either a linear progression or discrete theoretical approaches. Rather, they have informed and influenced the practice of EAP today with varying degrees of interconnectedness and variation. This section briefly discusses each in turn.

General English Language Teaching (ELT)

One of the greatest influences on EAP has been general English Language Teaching. One reason for this is simply that many EAP teachers started out in 'general' ELT or other branches of ESP, such as business English, and they brought their methodologies and teaching and language skills with them. Also, EAP itself is part of this larger teaching field, so it is bound to be influenced by it.

Unlike many of the influences on EAP discussed in this section, which have arisen at various times since the 1960s, the influence of ELT has unavoidably always been present, if not always acknowledged. Perhaps the most significant contributions of ELT have been communicative language teaching and task-based learning. It is possible that the practice of teaching language communicatively through learning tasks arose independently in ESP and EAP due to the specific nature of their learning contexts, for example giving an oral presentation and participating in a seminar. Nevertheless, if only through the practice of large numbers of EAP teachers who have also taught in general ELT contexts, teaching methodologies in EAP show the influences of ELT methodologies, such as the communicative approach. Within the communicative approach, task-based learning (TBL) in particular has had a strong methodological influence on EAP, with its typical structure around sequences of texts and tasks.

Register analysis

Register analysis came to prominence in the 1960s with a focus on language. It aimed to identify specific linguistic structures and features through the analysis of selected texts. Register refers to 'a variety of language defined according to its use in social situations' (Crystal 2003: 393). Examples of registers include a technical manual for operating machinery and a popular science article in a magazine for non-experts. Essentially, register analysis is a scientific study based on quantitative methods: the systematic analysis of a selection of texts within a particular register. In this sense, it was a precursor to corpus analysis. Jordan (1997: 228) traces the practice back to the work of West, with his 1936 analysis of texts totalling five million words which led to his *General Service List of English Words* (West 1953). *The General Service List* includes 2,000 frequent words and remains influential today, notably through its relation to Coxhead's *Academic Word List* (Coxhead 2000), which is discussed in Chapter 4. Researchers including Halliday and Ewer also contributed to register analysis.

Various examples of language structures and uses typical of academic English were identified through register analysis. These include, initial purpose **clauses** to frame new information in a sentence, such as 'To begin to understand these causes …' and conditionals with the present tense in both clauses to express universal truths and phenomena, for example 'If alcohol is heated to 78°C, it boils' (Swales 1971: 35). In a register analysis of a three-million word corpus of scientific texts, Ewer and Hughes-Davies (1971, cited in Jordan 1997: 229) identified other language items, such as *-ing* forms used to replace a finite relative clause. These are frequently employed in scientific writing to reduce the word count and/or avoid stating when the event took place. Other items include nominalized forms, which are covered in Chapter 4. An example of a nominalized form, taken from a contemporary textbook for students of physical and engineering sciences, gives the sentence 'Pumps which are driven by wind are sometimes used for raising water', which can be reduced to 'Wind-driven pumps are sometimes used for raising water' (Swales 1971: 137).

Descriptions of items such as these formed the basis of many ESP and EAP materials in the 1960s and 1970s. Clearly, the items represent sentence-based forms or structures rather than other phenomena, such as defining and arguing, which are variously known as 'rhetorical functions', 'academic functions', and most recently 'essential elements'. These are presented in detail in Chapters 3 and 5.

Study skills

Partly as a reaction to the relatively narrow linguistic focus of register analysis, the practice of study skills grew in the 1970s and 1980s. The term 'study skills' appears to have been first used in the UK in 1975 by Candlin et al. in a British Council paper (Candlin et al. 1975 in Jordan 1997: 1). As the study skills movement grew, major publishers developed resources, such as the *Collins Study Skills Serie*s (cited in Jordan 1997: 1). For many practitioners in the field, study skills became indistinguishable from EAP.

Jordan (1997: 6–7) elaborates on and exemplifies study skills in some detail, mapping out specific situations such as lectures and research, in which students practise specific study skills such as listening and note-taking in a lecture (Jordan 1997: 6) Further examples of study skills in this analysis include the following:

- asking for clarification in a lecture or talk
- agreeing and disagreeing in a seminar or tutorial
- understanding instructions in a practical laboratory session
- summarizing and paraphrasing in private study reading
- using a dictionary effectively in the library
- planning, writing drafts, and revising an essay or report
- conducting interviews in research
- preparing and revising for examinations.

Additional skills are given, such as time management, logical thinking, and using computers/word processors (Jordan 1997: 7–8).

These activities underline the essentially practical and functional nature of study skills. They are identifiable and describable, and sometimes technical, for example 'using a library catalogue (subject and author) on cards, microfiche and computer' (Jordan 1997: 7). Study skills such as these formed the basis of many EAP syllabuses from the 1970s, and in many contexts continue to do so.

As some of Jordan's descriptions show, many of these study skills are rooted in the pre-internet age, and obviously need updating to utilize newer technologies. Hyland interprets study skills slightly differently, emphasizing the 'common reasoning and interpreting processes underlying communication which help us to understand discourse' (Hyland 2006: 18). Furthermore, due to their shift away from language, study skills are broadly appropriate for speakers of English as a first language.

More recently, the emphasis on study skills has been questioned. Hyland, for instance, points out that, informed by considerable research, the skills in a study skills approach are 'more complex than first thought' (Hyland 2006: 19).

Genre analysis

Research into academic genres, notably by Swales (1990 and 2004b), has had a great influence on EAP materials and practice, particularly since the early 1990s. In Swales' definition (1990: 58), 'genre' refers to 'a class of communicative events' which involve members of specific discourse communities. In practice, genres are widely taken to mean text types which are informed by their audience (i.e. members of the discourse community they are written for) and communicative purpose (for example to present the results of a piece of research). Swales' definition of genre (1990: 45–58) stresses the complexity of genre and purpose and warns against a 'facile classification' of purpose based on such evidence as linguistic analysis alone (Swales 1990: 46). Genre, then, is situated in a specific context, such as a discourse community, with people who have a depth of knowledge about how to communicate and the conventions associated with this communication.

An example of a 'product' of research into genre analysis is the CaRS (Create a Research Space) model which is used in **research article** introductions (Swales, 1990: 141). This is based on the analysis of a large number of such articles and is intended to serve as a description to guide the academic writer. The CaRS model is presented in Chapter 7.

Various other influences from genre analysis have made their way into EAP materials. For example, the problem-solution text structure, based on early work by Winter and developed by Hoey (1983: 31–106), is widely used in academic writing and EAP coursebooks (for example Swales and Feak 2004: 14ff; Hamp-Lyons and Heasley 2006: 119ff; and de Chazal and Moore 2013: 158–161).

The influence of genre on EAP continues to be recognized. Bruce, for example, argues that genre should play a central role in EAP courses (see Bruce, 2013: 25–31). Approaches to the teaching of academic writing are discussed further in Chapter 7.

Systemic functional linguistics

Systemic functional linguistics (SFL) is the term given by Halliday in the 1970s to a description of language which is functionally driven. SFL probably enjoys the greatest exposure and application in the country in which it was developed, Australia. The main characteristics of SFL have been summarized by Coffin and Donohue (2012: 64ff) as follows:

• a focus on analyzing texts in context, which involves analyzing their linguistic forms as well as the wider socio-cultural and ideological meanings of the text

- a theory of language which highlights the relationship between language, text, and context
- a broad scope which seeks to explain how people use language to express meanings, and to understand the relationship between language and society
- a strategic tool to respond to language-related issues in a wide range of contexts, including academic contexts.

One aspect of the agenda of SFL is to address perceived inequalities in how different people are able to construct meaning (Coffin and Donohue 2012: 72). For example, a student is less likely to be able to write a well-structured report compared with their lecturer; conversely, the student may be more proficient in constructing a social media text, such as a tweet. SFL is seen as a tool that this student could use to construct a more effective report. The SFL theory has been described as a 'democratic literacy pedagogy' which is 'subversive' (Martin 2011: 35 in Coffin and Donohue 2012: 64ff).

SFL has influenced EAP mainly through its application in analyzing texts; in this sense it compares with other work (for example, by Swales) in genre analysis, although the theories and motivations underpinning these approaches are different.

American second-language composition

North America has for a long time had two flourishing but largely separate traditions of academic writing. These fall across first language/second language (L1/L2) lines, with one tradition of first language (L1) composition writing, which engages with ideological and critical issues, standing in opposition to the other, namely second language (L2) writing, which is largely concerned with the technical and linguistic aspects of writing informed by applied linguistics research. The latter practice, American second-language composition, is largely practised in North America (Bruce, 2011: 11); in other contexts this L1/L2 distinction is not as prominent. The situation in the USA is however quite diverse, and in some senses, such as the concern in first language (L1) composition of helping undergraduates 'find their voice', there are similarities with general ELT.

These different approaches have been highlighted by Santos (1992). The American second-language composition approach has become known as the 'accommodationist' approach. In short, this approach aims to enable students to produce the kinds of texts that their departments require, but does not encourage them to be critical of their wider position in **the academy**; in this way they can be 'accommodated' into their academic context. Santos has stated that education can only proceed on a non-ideological basis, although as Bruce (2011: 12) points out that this is seemingly incompatible with the nature of American second-language (L2) composition, given its inevitable location with American culture and the values associated with this culture.

Critical EAP

Critical EAP (CEAP) stands in explicit opposition to the accommodationist approach outlined above. Thus the two positions, accommodationist and critical, tend to be seen as polarities and dichotomies. Bruce (2008) warns against conducting educational debates in such stark terms, and positions his favoured genre approach between the two (Bruce 2008: 10 and 2011: 10–14).

Critical EAP is most associated with Benesch in the USA, and Pennycook in Australia. Benesch (2009) describes critical EAP in the following way:

> Critical EAP widens the lens of academic purposes to take the sociopolitical context of teaching and learning into account. This is not to say that CEAP overlooks on-the-ground requirements of academic genres and classroom interactions but, rather, that they are explored in relation to EAP students' and teachers' complex and overlapping social identities: class, race, gender, ethnicity, age and so on. Critical EAP considers hierarchical arrangements in the societies and institutions in which EAP takes place, examining power relations and their respected reciprocal relationship to the various players and materials involved. This social turn necessitates a reckoning with contemporary globalization and its possible effects on the institutions and classrooms in which EAP is carried out.
>
> (Benesch 2009: 81)

In other words, Benesch sees students potentially as challengers of power relations and roles within their educational and national/global context. Other researchers have also argued for a more critical pedagogy in EAP, for example Cotton (2009: 20), who invites the EAP practitioner to question their whole approach:

> Criticisms of EAP practice provoke greater self-reflexivity and raise questions which EAP lecturers may need to ask themselves. Do I ignore the political dimensions of my practice? Do I promote acceptance of different varieties of English? Do I perpetuate the 'deficit' model of the NNS [non-native speaker] learner? Do I pay insufficient attention to sociocultural elements in language learning? Is my classroom practice appropriate in my context and for my learners?
>
> (Cotton 2009: 20)

These views are echoed and expressed in practical terms by Hannam, a UK-based EAP teacher, who writes: 'A critical teacher is likely to be engaged with debates and discussions going on in the world at a socio-political level and to feel enthused by finding out what their students might think' (Hannam 2012: 18). It is significant that she writes this in the IATEFL (International Association of Teachers of English as a Foreign Language) publication *Voices*, which is aimed at practising teachers of English, only a minority of whom teach EAP. For practitioners such as Hannam who support a critical EAP approach, part of the role of the EAP teacher is to create a learning environment in which students not only learn to think critically but also put 'some of those thoughts into action by creating a transformative classroom which may also influence change outside the educational environment' (ibid.). In this article Hannam goes on to offer examples of critical practice, which include:

- using newspaper articles to present contentious issues of the day
- considering how the passive can be used to remove agency (i.e. by avoiding stating who did the action) in cases of atrocities
- language choices in public contexts, such as the term 'customer' in UK railways.

Critical EAP and Critical Discourse Analysis

Critical EAP, then, goes beyond critical thinking related to objective sources such as texts into much broader areas including hierarchies in the educational establishment and power relations in the world, potentially without limits. In this respect it is closely related to critical discourse analysis (CDA). The background to CDA is that there is much that is hidden, or not immediately obvious, in texts. As Paltridge argues, 'the **norms** and values which underlie texts are often "out of sight" rather than overtly stated' (Paltridge 2012: 186). Rather more boldly, Rogers (2004: 6 in Paltridge 2012: 186) states that discourses are 'always socially, politically, racially and economically loaded'. Essentially, CDA is concerned with issues such as these, and the reader is expected to question, for example, how ideologies are expressed through discourse.

Academic literacies

The term 'academic literacies', as distinct from 'academic literacy' (which is generally taken to mean the skills needed for academic study), was first used in the 1990s, and Lea and Street (1998, 1999, 2000) are the researchers most associated with the movement. Academic literacies emerged in the UK through research into tertiary educational practices. It draws mainly on **ethnographic** research and **case studies**. Other researchers have emphasized the importance of an academic literacies approach. For example, Ann Johns, based in the USA, promotes a broad and inclusive view of literacies which moves beyond the skills of reading and writing into areas such as content, languages, practices, and 'strategies for understanding, discussing, organizing, and producing texts'; in this way the processes and wider experiences of the writer are foregrounded (Johns 1997: 2).

Lea and Street (2000, in Hyland 2006: 119–123) offer the following as characteristics of the academic literacies approach, which:

- draws on selected methodologies from the study skills approach and what Lea and Street call 'academic socialization', but is positioned at the top of this 'hierarchy'
- is situated in the broad institutional and epistemological (i.e. related to how knowledge is constructed) context
- is broader in scope than what they describe as the 'atomistic' skills and language covered in the study skills approach

- takes a broader view of skills than in the academic socialization approach, which sees the tutors' role as being to 'inculcate' students into their new culture
- sees literacies as social practices, i.e. 'something people do, an activity rather than a cognitive ability in people's heads' (Hyland 2006: 118)
- views student writing and learning 'as issues at the level of epistemology and identities rather than skill or socialization' (Lea and Street 2000, in Hyland, 2006: 120)
- sees literacy as involving various communicative practices including genres, fields, and disciplines
- emphasizes identities and meanings
- recognizes that students need to engage with their department and institution to work out meanings and academic practices.

Lea and Street identify three important themes in their research (Lea and Street, 2000, in Lea and Stierer: 45–6). First, they argue that students' lack of skills should not be dealt with through a learning support unit, as this approach is based on a belief that knowledge can be transferred; rather, they emphasize an approach in which students' knowledge is 'mediated or constructed through writing practices' (ibid.). Second, supported by their research, they emphasize the identity of the student over the acquisition of a set of skills. Their third theme is concerned with the increasingly modular nature of university courses, and the implications of this for student writing (ibid.).

It is worth noting that the main proponents of academic literacies, Lea and Street, do not work in EAP (Hyland 2006: 118), and that comprehensive pedagogies for their approach have not yet been developed (Tribble and Wingate 2011). Tribble and Wingate also suggest that the proponents of academic literacies 'may not be not fully aware of the theoretical and pedagogical contribution that Genre/EAP has made to the field'. They also point out that research in academic literacies is based mainly on ethnographic research and small-scale case studies, and is geared towards 'non-traditional' students (i.e. those coming from backgrounds whose family members rarely or never went to university in the past) rather than more mainstream English language students (ibid.).

An academic-literacies-informed approach is likely to be more effective in an in-sessional rather than a pre-sessional context (these contexts are clarified in Chapter 2). In an in-sessional context, students are already studying in their discipline and can therefore develop their identity as members of the academy in an informed way. Given disciplinary variation and the diverse nature of the academy, teaching and learning materials are likely to be locally developed in an academic literacies approach.

Writing in the disciplines

The 'writing in the disciplines' (WiD) approach originated in the USA, and is based on research into teaching practice in tertiary institutions. It grew from the American tradition of college/university writing classes, which originally began in response to a perceived need: these writing programmes can be traced back to the nineteenth century with the establishment of such a programme at Harvard University in 1874 (Deane and O'Neill 2011: 5).

Essentially, as its name suggests, students develop and practise their writing in their discipline rather than in conventional dedicated English classes, such as composition classes. It is closely related to 'writing across the **curriculum**' (WAC); indeed, the terms are sometimes used interchangeably. Both approaches aim to integrate students into their specific discourse communities (Deane and O'Neill 2011: 15). A major benefit of these approaches is the proximity of student and discipline which enables students to learn at first hand how their specific discipline operates.

Other influences

Other influences on EAP may also be identified. Benesch states several influences in broad terms: linguistics; applied linguistics; sociolinguistics; communicative language teaching; writing across the curriculum; learning theory; and genre studies (Benesch 2001: 4). She also states that due to its practical nature, EAP is 'responsive to the complexities of institutions, teaching, and learning in local contexts' (ibid.), thereby implying that a wide range of influences continue to be experienced in the field.

One further influence is the use of corpora. Corpus-based research has informed EAP materials, for example through Coxhead's (2000) *Academic Word List,* and through language descriptions like *The Longman Grammar of Spoken and Written English* (Biber, Johansson, Leech, Conrad, and Finegan, 1999) and various other work by Biber and others, which offer detailed descriptions of a wide range of grammatical and lexical phenomena in written academic texts. These are considered, where appropriate, in other chapters, such as in the analysis of evaluative language in Table 5.5, Chapter 5. Apart from corpora, various other technologies have impacted on EAP. These are discussed further in Chapter 12.

In addition to the influences discussed in this section, there are further issues which affect EAP practice, notably the general–specific distinction (i.e. EGAP–ESAP), and the global–local distinction. These are discussed in Chapter 2. There are also a number of practical approaches in developing EAP programmes and materials. These are examined in Chapter 10, which brings together the influences, issues, and approaches within a framework for developing EAP materials.

Influences on EAP: divergence or reconciliation?

To gain widespread familiarity and acceptance in EAP practice, an idea, theory, practice, or research-informed pedagogy needs to be effectively disseminated. EAP teachers need to be persuaded that it has something useful to offer. In reality, the occasional conference presentation and research paper on a new theory may gain the attention of some practitioners, but to gain traction in widespread EAP practice, the theory needs to find its way into the materials that EAP teachers use. Effectively this means that the theory needs to gain the attention of publishers, perhaps through materials writers and authors who can persuade the publishers that the new theoretical approach can translate into saleable published materials. Once these approaches are embedded into materials that are widely used, the theory can be said to be widely adopted in practice.

The influences discussed in this section exhibit a significant degree of heterogeneity in academic, cultural, ethnographic, geographical, historical, linguistic, methodological, practical, and theoretical terms. This heterogeneity suggests the potential for divergent practices to become entrenched in different local and global contexts. Yet it does not have to be so. EAP teachers can be empowered to develop their own approaches in their local context, drawing on what works best from the schools of thought and research traditions that have influenced the field.

EAP as an emerging global phenomenon

This final section in Chapter 1 looks ahead, and in doing so suggests that the prospects for EAP are very encouraging. The number of students studying in English is growing, as UNESCO (United Nations Educational, Scientific and Cultural Organization) statistics show:

- In 2010, at least 3.6 million students were enrolled in tertiary education abroad, compared with 2 million in 2000.

- Major regional sources of international students include East Asia, the Pacific, many Arab countries, certain African countries, such as Nigeria, and Europe.

- Major country destinations for international students include the USA, UK, Australia, Canada, France, and Japan.

- Students from Central Asia and sub-Saharan Africa are the most mobile in the world in proportion to their populations.

- Regional education hubs are emerging, such as South Africa, France, the Gulf, and South-East Asia.

(Adapted from the Education Pages. UNESCO institute for statistics, <http://www.uis.unesco.org/Education/Pages/international-student-flow-viz.aspx> accessed 17 August 2013.)

In a global context, English is rapidly becoming a key basic skill. Professionals need key skills such as computing skills and language skills in order to operate both locally and globally. Initially this English language skill was needed for business and international relations; more recently it has emerged as a need for academic study. The majority of academic discourse and publishing, from textbooks, online materials through to journals, is in English. The field of EAP has grown to serve the needs of increasingly mobile students around the world. EAP teachers can respond by keeping up with the field, gaining in professionalism, and being adaptable and open to new opportunities. With greater experience, these opportunities can grow: from teaching EAP in an institution to training EAP teachers globally; from writing individual lessons to writing syllabuses, courses and published materials; from influencing a class of EAP students to influencing a wider aspect of the field such as a university department of academics who need to switch their language of instruction to English.

EAP has the potential and power to be transformative. EAP teachers can be empowered to influence their local context through transforming their students' lives in terms of their academic and future professional outcomes. They can also influence the wider academic environment in a more global context, through such activities as fostering sound academic practices like intellectual honesty and originality, and producing and making available high quality teaching and learning materials, which can be accessed and used globally. In a sense, EAP teachers are ambassadors for academic institutions and countries, in that they are often their students' first port of call when arriving at a new academic institution, and through the significant amount of time they spend with students. Knowingly or unknowingly, this time spent is a time of cultural as well as academic exchange, with EAP teachers privileged to learn about the students' learning and wider culture, and the students positioned to adapt and assimilate to their target academic culture in which English is the most visible differentiator from their own.

EAP teachers can shape the field of EAP in which they work. They have the potential to lead rather than follow, to question rather than accept, and to offer positive proposals for change rather than only criticizing the negative aspects of their context. Through these processes, which involve influencing people, many of whom will themselves become influential, EAP teachers can cascade their impacts across ever-wider contexts throughout the world.

Conclusion

The opening chapter of this book has positioned EAP within the wider context of English language teaching, and highlighted differences between these teaching contexts. These discussions have brought out important differences with regard to the major influences on these respective fields, and in their purpose, methodologies, and materials. EAP is highly focused in that it exists to serve a large and growing number of students' academic needs in English worldwide. It is closely connected to the world of the academic disciplines, while typically being separate from it: EAP is normally not taught by subject teachers but by dedicated EAP professionals who frequently work in separate departments or institutions. Just as academic discourse is global rather than dialectic, EAP is global in scope, though it also has many local and regional variations and interpretations. In order to build up a more complete picture of the field of EAP, the remaining chapters in the book make reference to familiar English language teaching concerns, such as language and skills, to work through the key aspects of EAP today.

Further reading

There are a number of dedicated EAP books available, which can be divided broadly into those that are more theoretical, and those that are more practically oriented. As titles are not repeated in subsequent 'Further reading' sections, these are given here only, but are nonetheless relevant to many other chapters in this book. The dates of publication and their titles give an indication of their currency and scope.

In addition, there are innumerable other sources for EAP, notably articles in the dedicated journal, the *Journal of English for Academic Purposes* (JEAP), as well as selected articles in other journals, such as *English for Specific Purposes, Journal of Second Language Writing, TESOL Quarterly*, and the *English Language Teaching Journal*. Journals dedicated to EAP and ESP are also published in particular countries, notably *Iberica* in Spain and *The ESPecialist* in Brazil. New journals continue to launch in which EAP articles are published, such as the *Journal of Second Language Teaching and Research*.

More theoretical EAP titles

Bruce, I. 2011. *Theory and Concepts of English for Academic Purposes*. Basingstoke: Palgrave Macmillan.

Flowerdew, J. and **M. Peacock.** 2001. *Research Perspectives on English for Academic Purposes*. Cambridge: Cambridge University Press.

Hyland, K. 2006. *English for Academic Purposes: an advanced resource book*. Abingdon: Routledge.

More practically-oriented EAP titles

Alexander, O., S. Argent and **J. Spencer.** 2008. *EAP Essentials: A teacher's guide to principles and practice*. Reading, UK: Garnet Education.

Jordan, R. R. 1997. *English for Academic Purposes: a guide and resource book for teachers*. Cambridge: Cambridge University Press.

McCarter, S. and **P. Jakes.** 2009. *Uncovering EAP: How to Teach Academic Writing and Reading*. Oxford: Macmillan.

2 TEACHING AND LEARNING

EAP students as resources of knowledge and experience

The discussion of the context of EAP in Chapter 1 shows that the field is complex and diverse. EAP teachers need to be able both to navigate their way through their own EAP context and guide their students through it. Those teachers moving into EAP from other ELT contexts can be confident that they have a lot to offer, and, using good learning materials, should find success provided they develop a sound working knowledge of EAP.

Most importantly, EAP teachers need to put their students at the heart of their practice. In a 'deficit' approach, EAP students are seen as lacking academic skills and language, particularly in academic writing. This view can inadvertently play down what students already know by focusing on what they do not know; in this way students are merely recipients of remedial work.

In contrast to this construction of EAP, it is possible to see EAP students as 'resources'. Typically adults or young adults, EAP students are likely to have had at least ten years of education, and a considerable amount of wider experience which could include their interests and perhaps professional experience. Their education probably included a considerable amount of time spent learning English. With regard to their chosen discipline, every student is different, but they are likely to have at least a basic understanding of and interest in what they plan to study or are already studying. Given these observations, it can be highly productive to view EAP students as potentially rich resources of knowledge and experience. In doing so, EAP teachers can offer tasks which draw on this knowledge and experience in a communicative setting, and EAP students can build on their knowledge and experience through tasks and projects which aim to develop independence. Above all, students are positioned at the centre of EAP practice.

This chapter explores the learning context and discusses major issues in teaching and learning. This discussion then broadens into the wider academic context, in order to clarify what students are aiming at, before exploring competences for the EAP teacher based on the BALEAP (2008) competency framework.

EAP students and teachers

EAP contexts can vary widely, and each specific context is unique. Given this, and the likelihood that many contexts are in a constant state of development, EAP teachers and students need certain key skills and qualities. Adaptability, responsiveness, and responsibility are particularly useful, and as students tend to look to their EAP tutors for guidance, other vital skills and expertise are needed in areas such as methodology, critical thinking, and discourse analysis in order to develop as an effective EAP practitioner. An in-depth, specialist knowledge of disciplines is not expected or required, although an open-mindedness in exploring and learning about disciplinary texts and conventions is important. Knowledge of the wider tertiary educational context is also highly valued. Key qualities include a rigorous approach and a passion for communication. In short, EAP teachers need to develop an ability to respond to and meet their students' needs. Students, meanwhile, can be encouraged to develop an initiating and interactive approach, in which they actively search for and respond to input, resources, and feedback. A key responsibility for students is to learn more about the specific academic context they plan to study in, or are already studying in. Clearly, both teachers and students have a vital role to play in creating a supportive and effective teaching and learning environment.

Defining the teaching and learning context

As Chapter 1 shows, the purpose of EAP is to meet the needs of students planning to study, or already studying, an academic discipline through the medium of English. To a lesser but growing extent, EAP is needed for academic staff in universities (i.e. teachers, lecturers, professors, researchers) who are operating in a second or foreign language, English. Student needs are based—to varying extents—around skills, initiation into academic conventions, language, and critical thinking. The EAP teaching and learning context needs to enable these to be taught and learned as effectively as possible within given constraints, such as specific targets and time.

Time, indeed, is a key dimension in any EAP context. EAP programmes are based around the dimensions of students, level, and time. Students may be planning to study in any discipline, and have any level of English at or above the course minimum requirement. EAP courses, or programmes, are typically of fixed length, although some can be long, such as one or more academic years, and may allow students to progress from one level or course to the next. Institutional models vary, but these three variables of students, level, and time are common to all.

Pre-sessional and in-sessional programmes

In practice, many EAP contexts are traditionally divided into two broad types: **pre-sessional** and **in-sessional.**

Pre-sessional programmes

Pre-sessional programmes exist to prepare students for their future academic study. Students may already know exactly what they want to study, and have a conditional place at university. This condition is normally a statement of a specific language level in a general or 'academic' English examination that the student needs to gain. There can be further conditions, for example high-ranking universities may ask for a particular score on a critical thinking test, such as the Cambridge Thinking Skills Assessment (TSA). Alternatively, the student might be less sure about where they are going in terms of their choice of subject and university, and while they are working this out, want to improve their level of English in an EAP context. In all cases, they are aiming to study wholly or mainly through English. Pre-sessional programmes are frequently full time, with perhaps 15–20 hours of classroom time, plus independent study. They are normally of fixed length, such as four, eight, or 12 weeks, or a longer period of up to a year or more.

Traditionally, pre-sessional programmes have centred around tertiary institutions such as universities, but increasingly EAP is offered to students in private language schools (PLSs) as well as to older students (for example aged 16+) in secondary schools. These students are typically working towards their school exit exams, which often function in addition as university entrance exams. These may be national examinations or international ones, such as the International Baccalaureate (IB) or the UK-based A-levels.

It is worth noting here that while university degree programmes are generally offered in one particular language, in some regions the degree may be taught partly in the language of the country of the university, for example Czech, and partly in English. In this case, a pre-sessional course is still perfectly appropriate, but an in-sessional programme might be more likely.

Variants of pre-sessional programmes include pre-foundation, pre-undergraduate, and pre-masters programmes. As the name suggests, the latter are targeted at graduate students who are planning to embark on a master's programme. Pre-foundation students are typically younger, 17 or 18, and much less familiarity with academic practices can be assumed.

The main aims of pre-sessional programmes are built around developing academic and language skills, which in practice relate to wider cultural aspects and raising cultural awareness. This cultural development involves such aspects as the institutional culture of the university or other educational establishment, the culture of the location (i.e. the city and country), academic culture, and 'softer' cultural skills, such as interacting with people from different cultures.

In-sessional programmes

In-sessional programmes take place alongside the students' subject, so they are part time. Their main aim is to support and develop students' competences in academic culture, language, and skills. Many of the students attending in-sessional courses are required to do so because their English language proficiency level is felt to be not quite high enough, or they are seen to be struggling in their degree programme. Alternatively, students may themselves choose to attend an in-sessional programme. Although in-sessional programmes may focus on the four skills, academic writing is typically the main focus. Again, time is limited and it is in their writing that students' English and academic level is most visible, and on which they are most frequently assessed. One advantage of in-sessional over pre-sessional programmes is that because the students are already studying their subjects, they are often able to identify their needs quite accurately, and have some useful materials to contribute in order to meet these needs. These materials may take the form of an essay with the comments and feedback of the subject tutor, and specific core textbooks to be read. Such materials are extremely useful for the EAP teacher to see, and can be developed into learning materials as well as used to inform the classroom approach.

An in-sessional model adopted in some universities is based around centres such as writing hubs. Students can access these whenever they need help with their academic tasks. In such models, there is likely to be a focus on meeting students' specific needs on a one-to-one or small-group basis, and the EAP teachers working in these learning centres can respond and assist within a student-led approach. In terms of efficiency, given the much larger number of undergraduates in most institutions, drop-in learning centres may be more associated with postgraduate students.

As this section has shown, there are various differences between pre-sessional and in-sessional programmes, such as in the likely amount of time per week students spend with EAP teachers. However, it is worth emphasizing that most principles and issues discussed in this book are of relevance to both pre-sessional and in-sessional contexts.

Issues in EAP teaching and learning

Chapter 1 looks at the major influences on the field of EAP. This section presents and discusses two important issues which inform EAP teaching and learning: the general–specific debate, and the global–local distinction. Issues such as these are relevant in EAP because they influence methodologies and learning materials. Understanding these issues can help EAP teachers to position their practice in an informed and principled way.

General–specific

The general–specific debate refers to the two approaches to EAP practice: EGAP (English for general academic purposes) and ESAP (English for specific academic purposes). This section discusses these approaches at some length in order to illustrate how different approaches can inform and empower the EAP teacher in their own practice. Many of the ideas and themes in the EGAP/ESAP discussion are also relevant to other issues and practices discussed throughout this book.

The development of EAP into these two distinctions took hold in the 1990s with a movement towards greater specificity in EAP. Contemporary practitioners including Jordan, Blue, and Hyland contributed to the development and scope of the movement through their publications (for example Jordan 1997: 141ff and 228ff). Subsequently, EAP practitioners such as Alexander, Argent and Spencer have contextualized the issue, for example through their observation that most EAP contexts are of necessity general (Alexander et al. 2008: 26) and their argument that 'it is ultimately the students' responsibility to deal with subject specificity' (ibid.). Hyland (2006: 9ff) casts the EGAP/ESAP distinction as one of the four 'conceptions and controversies' in EAP. Bruce also places the EGAP/ESAP distinction in the opening chapter of his methodology book (Bruce 2011: 4ff). The theme has come up regularly in the *Journal of English for Academic Purposes* since its launch in 2002, for example the article by Liu, Chang, Yang, and Sun, who found discrepancies in student perceptions of their needs and wants in EGAP/ESAP contexts (Liu et al. 2011).

In terms of EAP teaching contexts, the main aim of most pre-sessional and in-sessional programmes is to develop students' academic skills and language so that they can function effectively in the disciplines. Such programmes may operate at different levels of specificity. What this means is that they may be quite focused on a specific discipline. This can be at discipline or department level (for example pharmacology) or more likely at the higher level of faculty (for example life sciences). Alternatively, and in practice more frequently, such programmes are general in scope. General EAP contexts are characterized by the breadth and perhaps unpredictability of students' disciplines. A general EAP class may comprise students, for example, of business, law, pharmacy, psychology, economics, engineering, and urban planning. A key question affecting general versus specific contexts is the extent to which academic skills and language—whether vocabulary or critical thinking skills—apply across disciplines or only in specific disciplines.

Arguments for and against an ESAP approach

A key researcher and proponent of the EGAP/ESAP distinction, arguing in favour of ESAP, is Hyland. His main arguments are built on a small but growing body of research which emphasizes differences rather than commonalities. Much of this research is based around corpus analyses which show differences in the distribution of specific linguistic features across disciplines and genres. Hyland's (2011: 13) argument cited research of this type by Biber (1988) and Halliday (1989). The work of the latter researchers, and others such as Carter and McCarthy (2006) provide evidence of differences in language features such as **nominalization** across genres. Hyland's defence of his specific **position** is expressed in the following **quotation**, in which he argues against what he terms a 'common core' EGAP approach:

> We can dispute the view that teaching specialist discourses relegates EAP to the bottom of the academic ladder. In fact the opposite is true. The notion of a common core assumes there is a single overarching literacy and that the language used in university study is only slightly different from that found in the home and school. From this perspective, then, academic literacy can be taught to students as a set of discrete, value-free rules and technical skills usable in any situation and taught by relatively unskilled staff in special units isolated from the teaching of disciplinary competences. It therefore implies that students' difficulties with 'academic English' are simply a deficit of literacy skills created by poor schooling or lazy students which can be rectified in a few English classes. EAP then becomes a Band-aid measure to fix up deficiencies. In contrast, an ESAP view recognizes the complexities of engaging in the specific literacies of the disciplines and the specialized professional competences of those who understand and teach those literacies.
>
> (Hyland 2006: 12)

Hyland's arguments appear to equate general EAP teaching with a deficit approach in which students are taught without reference to wider academic contexts. The widespread practice of EAP teaching and learning in which academic and cultural values play an integral part provides evidence to the contrary, however. Furthermore, according to Bruce (2011: 6), Hyland's work appears to be based on insufficient evidence:

> Hyland's studies show that academic texts from different subject areas differ in the use of these linguistic or citational features [for example **hedges**, use of 'I' and 'we']. However, the strength of his argument for specificity rests on the extent to which these researched features of academic texts, of themselves, can be said to operationalize the wider phenomenon of academic subject discourses realized in texts. While the range of elements investigated in such studies is probably too small to achieve this operationalization, this research, nevertheless, appears to provide partial evidence for the case for disciplinary specificity.
>
> (Bruce 2011: 6)

In this analysis, Bruce expresses a degree of scepticism over Hyland's **claim**; in other words, a description of different language features is not sufficient in itself to support an ESAP approach.

Arguments for and against an EGAP approach

An alternative, EGAP approach has been articulated by various researchers and practitioners including Feak, based at the University of Michigan in the USA. Feak has argued for a general approach based on her ethnographic research at Michigan (Feak 2011). Feak identifies disciplinary differences as a major source of challenge for students, even when the disciplines are apparently closely related such as anthropology and sociology. She notes an increasing trend towards interdisciplinarity (Feak 2011: 35–37), which refers to the practice of students taking courses and building their degree programmes and research practices from different departments and faculties. Moreover, research is increasingly interdisciplinary. For example medical research can take place through an interdisciplinary approach in which researchers and practitioners in different fields (e.g. from the medical, social, life, and natural sciences) can collaborate on a research project, and this principle of interdisciplinarity can apply to many other disciplines and types of research. Feak's solution is to shift the responsibility of navigating the way through the disciplines onto the student. Thus, EAP students need to work out the conventions of their discipline(s), and act as informant to the EAP teacher (Feak 2011: 42). The Michigan approach is to accommodate students from all disciplines onto their writing programmes 'from the hard sciences to the humanities, thus allowing for the raising of interdisciplinary awareness' (ibid.: 43). In summary, Feak is arguing for an interdisciplinary approach rather than a discipline-specific one:

> Advanced academic literacy courses [...] should not put us in the position of acting as substitutes or surrogates for content advisors; that is not our role to play. Such classes may perhaps require us to relinquish the idea that we must know in advance what our students need, and that we need to have the disciplinary content expertise before we can offer courses that achieve the level of specificity that fills the gaps in students' understanding of academic discourse.

> (Feak 2011: 42–43)

However, an EGAP approach such as that advocated by Feak has been argued against by Hyland:

> The importance of disciplinary specificity in academic literacy education is not new: Peter Strevens highlighted it as a defining feature of ESP in the early 1980s, for example, but there are still voices who deny the value of this kind of instruction, and instead argue for the teaching of general academic skills.

> (Hyland 2011:14)

In this argument, Hyland divides the argument, situating Strevens on one side, and others implicitly on the wrong side of the argument: as 'voices' who 'still ... deny the value' of an ESAP approach.

Comparing EGAP and ESAP approaches

Table 2.1 offers a comparison of the two approaches based on different aspects related to disciplines and the wider academic context. Many of these points are based on and adapted from a forum article on this topic (de Chazal 2013b) in the *Journal of Second Language Teaching and Research*.

Criteria:	ESAP (specific)	EGAP (general)
Discipline choice	Assumes that students know what they want to study, and stick to their choice	Can accommodate students' changing discipline choices
Discipline specificity	By its nature, ESAP aims to meet students' distinct and very specific disciplinary needs	EGAP aims to equip students with sufficient generic academic skills, language, and knowledge to enable them develop greater specificity through independent learning and investigation
Multiple disciplines	Better suited to a single discipline rather than a multidisciplinary context	Well suited to meeting students' needs in a multidisciplinary/inter-disciplinary context
Division of disciplines in an EAP cohort	Effective ESAP delivery depends on EAP provision within discipline-specific classes, however small these classes may be	Aims to facilitate effective EAP learning through mixed-discipline classes, i.e. with students from any disciplines
Discipline knowledge	Requires EAP teachers to have an in-depth knowledge of discourse and academic practices of their students' specific discipline(s)	Requires EAP teachers to have a general knowledge of academic practices, with an emphasis on widely-applicable academic language, skills, and knowledge; specific knowledge can be uneven
Disciplinary conventions	Assumes that specific characteristics and conventions within a discipline can be isolated, as they need to be identified and described	Academic conventions, skills, and language which can cover a wide range of disciplines need to be identified and described
Responsibility for acquiring disciplinary knowledge	The EAP teacher is likely to have to acquire detailed familiarity with the discipline, through processes such as needs analysis	Both the EAP teacher and the EAP student are responsible for investigating and constructing knowledge of academic practices
Interdisciplinary knowledge construction	In-depth knowledge of the student's discipline is prioritized over wider knowledge of academic practices in other disciplines	Enables students from many disciplines to communicate and construct knowledge from these disciplines
EAP materials	Favours the development of discipline- and context-specific EAP materials, written locally and based on needs analysis	Enables the use of commercially available EAP materials, which have broad applicability
Students' professions	Focuses on the immediate demands of disciplinary study rather than future professional needs, which may develop unpredictably	Also focused on meeting student's academic needs, but able to accommodate more unpredictable future professional needs

Table 2.1   A comparison of ESAP and EGAP approaches in practice

In connection with the point in the final row of the table, it has been noted that 'you could make a manager out of an engineer, but you couldn't make an engineer out of a manager' (Brown, Lauder, and Ashton 2011: 30). This point was made in the context of certain South-East Asian countries whose governments have been encouraging core subjects such as the STEM (science, technology, engineering, mathematics) subjects, in the belief that students studying these can become engineers and scientists—and eventually managers if necessary—but that students studying management cannot become engineers and scientists. By analogy, this is an argument against an ESAP approach, as too great a focus on one discipline, such as engineering, does not take account of the possibility of the EAP student eventually becoming a manager. Students studying a more general EAP programme, meanwhile, can enjoy a broader context of study which can include texts and students from many disciplines. The latter approach is akin to the liberal arts tradition. General EAP enables teachers to raise their rhetorical consciousness across a wide, unpredictable, and evolving range of disciplines.

Education and training

Widdowson (1983 in Dudley-Evans and St John 1998: 42) sees the EGAP/ESAP distinction as one of education and training respectively. In this analysis, education is concerned with 'a general capacity or set of procedures to cope with a wide range of needs' (Dudley-Evans and St John 1998: 42), while training 'involves the development of certain skills and familiarity with specific schemata' (ibid.). Dudley-Evans and St John disagree with this analysis, arguing that an ESAP approach is equally concerned with education, the main difference being that ESAP means a focus on the identifiable tasks that students will have to carry out (ibid.).

Practicalities

There are also a number of practical difficulties with an ESAP approach. Even where it is possible to run courses for specific groups of students, there can often be a striking lack of homogeneity among them. For example, a pre-sessional **cohort** of 100 students could be divided into different classes based around discipline or faculty area. Classes with fewer than a dozen or so students are likely to be uneconomic to run, so with this group eight classes are possible. This might mean classes for each of the following: business, economics, law, humanities, science, engineering, architecture, and medicine. Even a quick glance at these divisions suggests heterogeneity rather than homogeneity. The teacher of the medicine class, for instance, might be met with students of molecular medicine, pharmacy, sports science, pet psychology, dentistry, cardiology, clinical research, genetics, immunology, psychology, business/management, and biomedical engineering. This may look like a peculiar list, but it has happened (de Chazal 2013b). On closer questioning, it is revealed that the business/management student is focused on the gerontology sector as a business opportunity, while the biomedical engineering student plans to do research into new drugs; both have requested to be part of the medicine class rather than any of the others. For the course director, student requests such as these have to be reconciled with pedagogical and practical considerations.

Still on the practical level, further issues surround the students and their needs. Traditionally, as with all ESP/EAP programmes, a needs analysis is ideally carried out in advance to determine the needs of a particular group of students, using a model by Munby (1978) or a later model, such as Tomlinson (2011). In reality, the needs analysis is more likely to take the form of questions and discussions at the start of the course, meaning that there is little time to prepare a body of subject-oriented materials. In the example given above, the students articulated surprisingly diverse needs. This situation was partly due to the age range and educational level of the students: from pre-undergraduates to postgraduate researchers. Not only were their targets different, but also their starting-level. They were on different trajectories.

Increasing the pre-sessional cohort to several hundred students may appear to alleviate these challenges. However, in practice the difficulties remain simply because of the large number of specific disciplines available. Also, where courses are promoted as being discipline-specific, there is growing scope for a mismatch in expectations. Some students may expect a closely related and familiar learning context made up of other students in their field, and a teacher with in-depth knowledge of this field. In reality this is unlikely to be possible.

Pedagogy

These considerations ignore a further pedagogical perspective. Ultimately, all disciplines can be connected, and a student from a particular discipline can always learn from students of other disciplines. An EAP context is, in many ways, an ideal forum for interactive, interdisciplinary learning experiences. Traditionally, some universities have emphasized a broad education, encouraged by events such as lectures and societies for all students, and joint honours and liberal arts degrees where students study across traditional discipline and faculty boundaries.

Relatively recently in the development of universities, but now the prevailing model, degree programmes have become closely defined and increasingly specialized. Course titles include such disciplines as specific as 'Analysis and design of structures for fire, blast and earthquakes'. Paradoxically, such specificity requires an understanding of many broader, potentially related subjects, such as engineering, psychology, geography, business, finance, and law. The latter three may be relevant because design issues take place in a world driven by business and finance within legal and political frameworks.

A further important trend is the emergence, or more accurately re-emergence, of interdisciplinary study. Increasingly, students may be required to study two or more subjects within or across faculties, which has has long been the case in the USA. An additional language might also be required. In short, students of any discipline can benefit greatly from those of potentially any other. The essentially communicative context of EAP enables such learning.

This discussion points towards EGAP working more effectively than ESAP in many contexts, especially pre-sessional programmes. ESAP programmes are likely to be better suited to in-sessional programmes, where students' more specific needs can be addressed. To take the ESAP argument to its logical end might result in EAP groups of just one or two students, an outcome that is not only economically but pedagogically unsound. Essentially, the argument boils down to whether similarities or differences are seen to predominate. EAP programmes tend to focus on commonalities, with the understanding that a class on referencing, for example, is relevant to all students' needs, even though referencing conventions vary across disciplines and, for that matter, within disciplines. As a result, students become aware of different academic conventions, and learn to adapt accordingly. Given the unpredictable nature of students' future needs, adaptation, as stated at the start of this chapter, is an essential skill for students and teachers alike.

Global–local

Related to the general–specific debate is the extent to which a given EAP context is global, in terms of its outlook, scope, applicability, materials, teachers, student body, and language. These factors can vary enormously depending on the location and management of the teaching and learning context.

The issue of language is a question closely related to the English as a *lingua franca* movement (for example Jenkins 2007 and 2009), and the notion of English as an international language (EIL). The implication of research into different varieties of English is which to choose. The EAP teacher can certainly choose to focus on one particular variety of English; alternatively, they can work with multiple varieties of English in their curriculum and classroom. These can include both written and spoken texts: written texts published in different varieties (for example British, American, or local varieties such as Indian English); and spoken varieties including recordings of first language (L1) and second language (L2) speakers from different contexts, as well as the varieties of English of the students themselves.

The global nature of academic contexts

In some senses, the academic world is extraordinary global. As Biber et al. (1999: 16) point out, unlike other registers, academic prose can be considered global, i.e. written for and read by an international audience with little of the local or author dialect. The other registers in Biber et al.'s research refer to fiction, news, and conversation. To illustrate this phenomenon, it is worth noting that the most prestigious and frequently cited academic journals are global with respect to their audience, contributors, and application. A leading journal in cardiovascular health or heart surgery, for example, is available globally through university and professional libraries, subscriptions, and with possible limitations on access, via the internet. Thus it can be read widely, while drawing contributions from researchers and practitioners in potentially any country. Its aims include disseminating sound research and good practice, and the editorial board and readers (people in the field who read papers submitted to determine whether these can be published) are likely to be drawn from many countries. While the content of the journal may be local, such as research into a particular community in a specific country, the implications of this research lie far beyond its immediate context.

Apart from higher levels, such as EAP teaching for researchers who want to publish their work, the aim of most EAP programmes is not to teach students how to write for such journals, but depending on the syllabus and the students' graduate level, to read them and cite them in their own writing.

The implication of this example of academic journals is how far to go globally when planning and delivering EAP courses. The choice of text is one element of this: whether to choose locally produced texts, including articles and textbooks, or more global texts, such as textbooks written for a wide international audience. Further implications include the choice of materials, such as coursebooks or materials written in house; teaching methodologies; and culture. In some contexts, topics may be restricted; for example, in some Middle Eastern countries, topics such as evolution may be proscribed.

This discussion logically comes back round to student needs. If some of the students on the EAP programme aim to study and/or work globally, and engage with global issues, then clearly this programme should be global in outlook and not be restricted to very local materials, topics, and pedagogy.

Characteristics of core teaching and learning contexts

Depending on the specific situation, there can be different teaching and learning contexts: the university as an institution; the students' department(s) where they will study or are studying; the EAP environment, which may be a university language centre or private language school or another type of school.

In an institution as complex as a university, from the students' perspective a major challenge is working out what to do—what is required and expected—and how to go about doing it. In principle, this applies to both EAP students and students in the disciplines. Academic staff in the disciplines and EAP teachers can, with varying degrees of confidence, identify what their students need to do in terms of their assignments, participation in the course, and assessments. For students, though, it can be quite challenging to assemble this knowledge. As for working out how to go about achieving what needs to be done, while students may have little idea, academic staff may have surprisingly little to say about it. For instance, they might make general comments like 'This student's writing needs to be clearer', but this in itself does not tell the student very much. This student may well ask: 'What do you mean? Why is it unclear? Show me some examples. How can I make it clearer? Who can help me?'

A key player in helping students is of course the EAP teacher. There will always be constraints and limits, but the EAP teacher should be well placed to make a significant difference to their students' prospects in terms of language and skills as well as in broader areas such as university culture and expectations.

The following sections explore various characteristics of the EAP context, and consider the roles of the student and EAP teacher in relation to these. As noted earlier, each academic context can be considered to be in a sense unique; however, there are a great many commonalities among them, one of which is the sense of 'shock'.

Three shocks: culture, language, and academic

For students embarking on a course of study in English in an unfamiliar university setting, a number of 'shocks' can await them. Three kinds of shock have been identified: culture, language, and academic (Ryan 2012). The extent to which these shocks impact on students' lives will vary widely. Culture shock will not be an issue in cases where student are studying in their own country, but can present significant challenges for those students moving to an unfamiliar country. Language shock will depend on the students' level of English, and can express itself in different ways, such as through the amount of unknown vocabulary in the texts that students have to read. Academic shock refers to the wider academic environment, and its unfamiliar practices and characteristics, such as academic conventions in writing, **plagiarism**, the amount of reading that has to be done, and navigating the physical and virtual university environment. From the perspective of the student who has perhaps just left high school, academic shock may well be the greatest on account of its unexpected and unpredictable nature.

Academic honesty and plagiarism

All participants in an academic community are expected to show academic honesty. This means essentially that students, teachers, and academics alike should be clear that the work they are presenting, either publicly through publications, or as part of a course as assignments and assessments, is their own except where other people's work is cited. In this spirit of honesty, all parties are expected to acknowledge other people's influence and work wherever necessary, in written and spoken texts.

Plagiarism is associated mainly with academic practice, and refers to the dishonest practice of gaining credit for work which is presented as the student's own, but which is not entirely their own. This work may be part of a piece of coursework or an assessment, and the plagiarized material in it may be unclearly or incorrectly referenced, or not referenced at all. The exact definitions (and penalties) associated with plagiarism vary across—and within—institutions and cultures.

Dishonest practices in general and plagiarism in particular are widely recognized and widely discussed problems. Plagiarism invariably has a negative connotation, which can be traced back to its Latin origins to yield its core meaning of stealing and theft (Marsh 2007: 31). Since the emergence of the internet as a vast source of readily accessible material, academic dishonesty has been easier for students to practise, and for the same reason, easier to detect: academic staff can access the same internet resources as their students. Without clear chronological evidence it is not possible to say whether academic dishonesty is increasing, although many argue that it is (for example Whitley and Keith-Speigel 2002: 3). Another researcher reports an overall synthesis of **opinions** that plagiarism is increasing, then proceeds to question this (Sutherland-Smith 2008: 9–19).

Students, academic staff, and EAP teachers all have a responsibility to become familiar with the concept of plagiarism, and to work out how this relates to their particular context. Many institutions publish their policy online, which can be a useful resource to facilitate such familiarization. All parties need to understand both the practices which constitute plagiarism and the penalties for it. Plagiarism is such an important issue that it should be an integral part of their EAP programme. The issues surrounding it need to be explicitly presented and discussed.

Originality

There are times when the language used to talk about plagiarism can become suggestive of criminal activity ('students charged with plagiarism'; 'the offence'). To avoid plagiarism, Marsh (2007: 91 103) promotes positive teaching of academic practice, particularly through the use of handbooks of academic writing, which clearly spell out the conventions.

An alternative to the negative message of plagiarism is the positive notion of originality. By encouraging students to draw on their individuality and ideas, the notion of originality can be fostered. EAP teachers can point out that originality does not have to entail new research, but can simply be an individual response or idea based on existing work. On many master's programmes, evidence of original thought is explicitly stated or implicitly understood, as in the following advice in an MA handbook aimed at postgraduate students:

> Originality is highly desirable, but often hard to achieve in course assignments. Much of what you say, especially in exercises, will inevitably be based on books or lectures—and indeed there is no harm in that, provided that you acknowledge the source of your inspiration where relevant. However, to guarantee a grade A mark, especially in essays or projects, you must show genuine originality. This can be achieved in a variety of ways. If you do a full project where you gather some data yourself *[…]* there is inevitably a new element in that, even if the question being researched is a familiar one, no-one can have gathered and analysed exactly that data before *[…]* Purely discursive essays can be a harder medium to show originality in. We are looking for originality in the way ideas are brought together in new ways, and even for new ideas themselves.

> (Scholfield 1990: 37)

These guidelines express both advice to students and the expectations of the lecturers. They are designed to be informative and supportive, and helpfully spell out the positive message of promoting originality rather than a negative one of avoiding the offence of plagiarism.

The starting-point for originality and ideas is the student's **criticality** and evaluation. These crucial characteristics apply to students at all academic levels, and are explored further in Chapter 5.

Other aspects of teaching and learning

There are many further aspects of teaching and learning, which include the following:

- culture, affect, and intelligence
- teaching and learning styles
- independence and collaboration
- motivation
- expectations
- methodology
- feedback

These are considered throughout the book and are integrated into the relevant chapters as appropriate.

Specialist EAP teaching contexts

The observations in the previous section apply generally across a wide range of teaching and learning contexts. In addition to the 'core' contexts assumed in the previous section, a number of 'niche' or specialist EAP contexts have been emerging in recent years. These include contexts at both ends of the academic scale, namely academic and research staff at universities, and students at high school who have not yet started university: 'secondary EAP'.

Academic staff in the disciplines

Given the dominant and growing position of English as the language of publication and dissemination of academic research, academic staff are under increasing pressure to publish and present their research in English. Higher-level students, particularly PhD and research students, are also frequently encouraged or required to publish in English. Hyland identifies two 'principal audiences' in writing for international journals: 'the community of scholars who will read the finished paper and hopefully cite it and use it in their own research; and the journal gatekeepers who will judge the paper as ready for publication' (Hyland 2012: 4). This means that writers have to carefully consider these two audiences when writing: firstly the 'gatekeepers' who are the editors and reviewers of the texts; and secondly, if successful in gaining acceptance, the readership of the journal.

Academic publishing in English

The growing phenomenon of academic publication in English has a number of implications, which can apply to academic staff of any first language including English. In Swales' analysis, a more useful distinction than the traditional native/

non-native speaker classification is that of academic experience (Swales 2004b: 56). For instance, in an English-medium university a well-educated student with English as their second language is in many respects better positioned to succeed academically than a student whose first language is English but who has a lower level of education.

Table 2.2 presents an analysis of the main challenges facing academics wishing to publish in English for an international audience.

Factor	Explanation
Language	Academic staff can face significant challenges in communicating in English (i.e. writing for academic journals and presenting at academic conferences and events). These challenges can relate to grammar, vocabulary, accuracy, style and phraseology, and (in spoken genres such as presentations) phonology.
Culture	To publish successfully, academic staff need to become familiar with the academic and wider culture of academic publishing in English in general and that of their chosen journal in particular. Cultural aspects include the requirements and expectations of the publishers (including the editorial staff who select the articles for publication) and the audience of the journal(s) in question.
Competition	Depending on the journal, acceptance rates can be very low, i.e. rejection rates can be very high, due to intense global competition by potential writers, who are under pressure to publish.
Practice	Journals generally expect to be the sole recipient of an article for publication, meaning that authors have to wait for a decision; if rejected, the article can then be submitted to another journal, in a process taking potentially months or years. During this time the research may become dated.
Professional	Publication in prestigious journals is increasingly tied to an individual's professional development, e.g. academic staff have to show evidence of such publication for tenure and promotion. Also, university rankings are typically based on departmental publication records, which are in effect used as proxy for quality of teaching.

Table 2.2   Challenges in publishing in English for an international audience

Table 2.2 shows that challenges for the academic research staff go considerably beyond language alone. For those staff who have not had to learn or use English until later in their professional lives, language will present the most time-consuming challenge to address. Yet they will also have to deal with the global realities of academic publishing.

Academic journals as global standard

Publishing in academic journals has resulted in a highly competitive market in which academics and researchers are competing for international exposure, and by extension, a higher profile, status, promotion, and remuneration. In many contexts, these goals can only be achieved through publication in the most prestigious journals.

Long-established prestigious journals such as *Nature* (first published in 1869) and *The Lancet* (founded in 1823) now rank alongside vast numbers of journal titles. The highly-influential Institute for Scientific Information (ISI) index includes about 8,000 journals, in addition to other genres such as essays and book series (ISI 2013). There are many more journals in existence, and their number is constantly growing; this growth has been estimated at an annualized rate of 3.46% since the year 1800 (Mabe 2003). The ISI index probably includes fewer than half of all the journals currently being published, and its influence is such that these journals, and in particular the much smaller number of very high ranking journals (such as *Nature* and *The Lancet*) remain a prime target for academics and researchers. An analysis by ISI showed that just 150 journals account for 50% of citations, while the highest-ranking 2000 titles account for 80% of published articles and 95% of cited articles (ISI 2013).

Teaching EAP to academics and researchers

The teaching of EAP to academic staff and researchers who need to publish in English is a niche activity which is beginning to attract wider attention. An early conference on this branch of EAP was held in 2007 at the University of La Laguna, Tenerife, which led to a special issue of the *Journal of English for Academic Purposes* in 2008. The editors state that English for Research Publication Purposes (ERPP) 'can be thought of as a branch of EAP addressing the concerns of professional researchers and post-graduate students who need to publish in **peer-reviewed** international journals' (Cargill and Burgess 2008: 75).

Secondary EAP

Teaching pre-university students, i.e. students still at high school, is the other niche area of EAP activity discussed in this section. Many students aged about 16–18 who are studying at high school hope to go on to study at university. These students may currently be studying for their country's national exams, or international exams such as A-levels and International Baccalaureate, which are used for school exit and university admission.

This area of EAP has been called 'secondary EAP' (Johns and Snow 2006: 251). In a special issue of the *Journal of English for Academic Purposes* dedicated to academic English in secondary schools, Johns and Snow identify one 'pervasive argument' in secondary EAP, namely that '*deep learning* [authors' original italics] of content, interwoven with the disciplinary constructs and the language that supports them, is essential to effective teaching across the curriculum' (Johns and Snow 2006: 252).

Students' engagement with content—and their construction of meaning—is a major concern of all but one of the six research articles in this special issue.

Teaching EAP to secondary-school students

This is a trend which can be viewed as being at the lower end of the academic hierarchy from the perspectives of students' ages, experience, and familiarity with the academy. However, an alternative view is that this sector is potentially the most influential and valuable, akin to pre-service teacher training which has the potential to shape trainees' outlooks and methodologies throughout their careers. In contrast, when beginning the teaching of EAP at postgraduate (and undergraduate) levels, which is where EAP first emerged, the students have already gone far in their academic career without the benefits in knowledge and skills that EAP teaching brings. In this sense, then, teaching EAP to younger age groups can be very valuable and efficient. Early ESP/EAP materials exist which were explicitly aimed at secondary-school students, for example Swales' (1971) *Writing Scientific English*, which is written partly for secondary-school students specializing in science.

There are various benefits for these students to gain a working knowledge of academic skills and practice (for example how to use sources in academic writing) before they start university:

- Knowledge and skills: many universities do not explicitly teach academic skills, and may simply assume that students will already have this knowledge or gain it independently—which may or may not happen effectively.

- Time and efficiency: academic skills can take a considerable amount of time to learn, and students who have a working knowledge before they start their studies will be at an advantage as time is freed up to focus on other academic work, such as reading.

- Progress and profile: students who appear more familiar with academic practices at the start of their university study may catch the attention of peers and academic staff, potentially leading to a positive cycle of confidence, improvement, skills-building, and greater academic success.

It seems likely that a form of EAP will make major inroads into the secondary-school sector, particular with higher-achieving and more ambitious student groups. This development of EAP will require more specific teaching and learning materials, which are discussed in more detail in Chapter 10.

In order to facilitate the development of their students' academic success in their specific context, EAP teachers need to have certain skills, knowledge, and competences.

Teacher competences: the BALEAP competency framework

For the EAP teacher to operate effectively, they need to be competent in the relevant skills and knowledge. For example, they need an understanding of how universities work in terms of their conventions, communication of knowledge, and policies. BALEAP, the UK-based professional association which supports the development of EAP practitioners, has published a comprehensive and increasingly influential framework for EAP teachers, the *Competency Framework for Teachers of English for Academic Purposes* (BALEAP 2008).

As its title states, it is aimed at teachers, who are positioned as being central to the EAP context. The framework seeks to map out the core teacher competences, which are designed to translate into effective student learning. It is useful to use this framework as a starting-point in describing the teaching and learning context as it informs all key areas within the four broad contexts of the field of EAP: academic practice; EAP students; curriculum development; and programme implementation. While most EAP teachers would probably be challenged to demonstrate a high level of competence across all eleven areas, the framework serves as a valuable description of target knowledge and ability which they can aim for.

There follows a brief extract from the framework with summary and **commentary** relating to each of the eleven competences, in order to understand more fully the scope of the EAP teaching context from the perspective of the teacher. There are also suggestions for how the competences can be achieved.

1 Academic contexts

The first four competences relate to academic practice. The first competence sets out how the EAP teacher needs to develop an understanding of the academic context in which they work. It is summarized as follows (BALEAP 2008: 4):

> An EAP teacher will have a reasonable knowledge of the organizational, educational and communicative policies, practices, values, and conventions of universities.

The framework elaborates on the types of knowledge this refers to, such as university assessment and policy. EAP teachers are encouraged to relate such knowledge to the materials they use, and enable their students to become familiar with university and disciplinary practices.

Various challenges exist. Universities are complex institutions, and even for those people who work in them, can take a long time to understand, particularly in terms of their culture. Nonetheless, since the aim of a university-oriented EAP programme is to enable the students to study effectively in the disciplines, knowledge of the relevant academic context, or academic contexts in general, will beneficially inform EAP teachers' materials and approach.

EAP teachers working in universities can build up links with academic and administrative staff in the disciplines, and aim to systematically extend their knowledge of the academic context by reading university bulletins, news, and information on the website.

2 Disciplinary differences

The second competence emphasizes differences between disciplines (BALEAP, 2008: 4):

> An EAP teacher will be able to recognize and explore disciplinary differences and how they influence the way knowledge is expanded and communicated.

This competence acknowledges differences, which may take the form of texts and tasks which students have to undertake, as well as differences in the culture and expectations of departments.

It may be worthwhile developing a collaborative approach to extending EAP teachers' knowledge. Each member of a teaching team can undertake to build up knowledge in a different discipline, most logically one in which some of their students aim to study in. Teachers can disseminate this knowledge among their team through processes such as informal meetings and presentations, together with written summaries and sample material relating to the discipline.

3 Academic discourse

The nature and study of academic discourse is the focus of the third BALEAP EAP teacher's competence:

> An EAP teacher will have a high level of systemic language knowledge including knowledge of discourse analysis.

This competence states explicitly that EAP teachers need to develop their analytical skills through processes such as text analysis, in order to present the language to their students. The discussions of academic language in Chapters 3, 4, 5, and 7 illustrate the complexities of academic discourse and the challenges facing the teacher. Language is approached rather differently in EAP compared with many general ELT contexts. An effective way of acquiring this knowledge is through a cycle such as the following:

- reading about the language, for instance studying noun phrases in a grammar book such as Carter and McCarthy (2006) or Biber et al. (1999)
- carrying out text analysis to see how the language is used in authentic texts
- processing this information to introduce the language areas in their EAP teaching classroom.

This three-stage approach ensures that the classroom work is based on the sound linguistic analysis of corpus-driven grammar reference books, and that EAP teachers are taking responsibility for developing their knowledge—and that of their students—through their own text analysis work.

4 Personal learning, development, and autonomy

This competence emphasizes the importance of the EAP teacher's continuing professional development (CPD) and their critical reflective practice:

> An EAP teacher will recognize the importance of applying to his or her own practice the standards expected of students and other academic staff.

Professional development can take many forms, including:

- attending and participating in staff development sessions within and outside the institution
- leading staff development sessions
- attending conferences
- giving a presentation or leading a workshop at a conference
- reading relevant books and journals, such as methodology, reference, and research publications
- writing reviews and articles for publication in institutional forums, teaching magazines, journals
- conducting research, including small-scale action research
- studying for a higher professional or research qualification, such as an MA or PhD.

It is important to emphasize the active nature of participation in professional development opportunities such as those above. For example, attending a conference is the starting point for full participation in the conference—examining new resources, asking questions in sessions, and generally networking with the other participants including other teachers, managers, and publishers. Following the event, it is highly worthwhile to summarize each session attended, and make these summaries available to colleagues or, if appropriate, to a wider audience through online forums and social media.

A motivating way of developing personal learning and development is to set personal targets. If EAP teachers themselves decide to participate in twelve professional development sessions in an academic year, they are likely to be more motivated to achieve this target, and perhaps exceed it, than if they are told to do so by their line manager. It is important to keep a record of all development in a given year, including not only formal events attended but also books read and summaries written. This process should be motivating, and the EAP teacher can track their development over a longer period of time.

5 Student needs

The next three competencies relate to EAP students. In relation to student needs, the framework states that:

> An EAP teacher will understand the requirements of the target context that students wish to enter as well as the needs of students in relation to their prior learning experiences and how these might influence their current educational expectations.

The thrust of this competence is developing greater knowledge and understanding of the students: their learning, values, culture; and their language, knowledge, and skills. The description also states that EAP teachers should gain an understanding of the two major contexts of pre-sessional and in-sessional teaching. It associates these with undergraduate and postgraduate students respectively, although in reality these distinctions may be less clear-cut.

Student needs are discussed in greater detail in Chapter 10, which looks at ways in which EAP teachers can carry out a needs analysis.

6 Student critical thinking

This competence emphasizes how 'critical thinking underpins academic practice' (BALEAP 2008: 6), and states that:

> An EAP teacher will understand the role of critical thinking in academic contexts and will employ tasks, processes and interactions that require students to demonstrate critical thinking skills.

The challenge for EAP teachers is to incorporate into their teaching materials tasks which involve critical thinking. Such tasks need to be developed through the curriculum in a staged way. Approaches and practices associated with critical thinking are discussed in Chapter 5, and critical thinking emerges in the reading tasks elaborated on in Chapter 6, and in other chapters.

7 Student autonomy

The role of EAP teachers in fostering their students' autonomy is emphasized in the seventh competence:

> An EAP teacher will understand the importance of student autonomy in academic contexts and will employ tasks, processes, and interactions that require students to work effectively in groups or independently as appropriate.

Put simply, student autonomy is the ultimate goal of EAP teaching because students' experience of EAP generally precedes their study and they may not have access to EAP teaching while they are in the disciplines. Thus the EAP teacher needs to develop skills which steadily develop their students' independence. While the two terms 'autonomy' and 'independence' are sometimes used interchangeably, a distinction is sometimes made between them, with independence being more of a physical dimension in which the student is independent of their teacher, the timetabled lesson, and the prescribed materials—as they are when doing a project. The notion of autonomy can be seen as more of a state of mind, with a student learning autonomously in any situation, including in the EAP classroom.

EAP teachers can encourage students to find answers to their own questions where feasible, for example through guided research and reading. For example, rather than standing up and explaining what plagiarism is while the students listen and take notes, the EAP teacher could develop a group task in which different students have to go out and find specific information relating to plagiarism—such as definitions of it, the university's policy relating to it, ways of avoiding it, and what academic staff think of it—based on interviews and reading about it in the library and on the university website. Each group can then report back to the whole class. In this way, students develop their autonomy in a practical and useful way, as well as learning about a key academic concept.

Student independence is raised in Chapter 7 in the description of a student-centred writing approach.

8 Syllabus and programme development

This competence and the following one relate to curriculum development. As distinct from the syllabus, the curriculum typically states the overarching purpose of the programme, the main content, and the assessment. The syllabus is the more detailed description of the content in terms of aspects such as language and skills, and the order in which these are to be covered.

Regarding syllabus development, the framework states that:

> An EAP teacher will understand the main types of language syllabus and will be able to transform a syllabus into a programme that addresses students' needs in the academic context within which the EAP course is located.

This description emphasizes the role of EAP teachers in bringing the syllabus to life in the classroom through materials which they can 'select, adapt, or create' (ibid.: 7). In this process, EAP teachers refer to their identification of student needs to inform the realization of the syllabus. These ideas are illustrated in Chapter 10.

9 Text processing and text production

The ninth competence relates closely to the third (discourse analysis), and is based around classifying and analyzing texts, informed by theories such as genre theory.

> An EAP teacher will understand approaches to text classification and discourse analysis and will be able to organize courses, units, and tasks around whole texts or text segments in ways that develop students' processing and production of spoken and written texts.

Texts and tasks are thus seen as being at the heart of the EAP syllabus. The competence description requires EAP teachers to 'identify and analyze academic genres and the functional and rhetorical features of academic texts and train students to do the same'. This approach therefore argues for students as well as teachers to be discourse analysts, a view shared by Alexander (co-author of the competency framework) and Bruce (2011: 5 and 83ff).

Aspects of text analysis and language analysis are presented in Chapters 3 and 4.

10 Teaching practices

The final two competencies relate to programme implementation. In terms of teaching practices, the framework states that:

> An EAP teacher will be familiar with the methods, practices and techniques of communicative language teaching and be able to locate these within an academic context and relate them to teaching the language and skills required by academic tasks and processes.

The framework positions communicative language teaching (CLT) at the heart of EAP methodology, a point that is discussed in Chapter 1. This CLT methodology should be familiar to those teachers who have taught in more general English language teaching contexts as well as other ESP contexts such as business English. One of the abilities required in this competence is that EAP teachers should be able to distinguish between teaching subject content (i.e. discipline knowledge), procedural content (for example ways of doing a task), and language knowledge. Other abilities call for the integration of study skills into other skills work, and the integration of technology into teaching, a point which is developed in detail in Chapter 12.

11 Assessment practices

The final competency covers assessment:

> An EAP teacher will be able to assess academic language and skills tasks using formative and summative assessment.

Formative assessment refers to ongoing assessment during the teaching programme in order to monitor students' progress and give feedback with regard to specific teaching points covered. Any shortcomings can be quickly addressed. Summative assessment typically takes place at the end of the programme, and is a means of quantifying students' proficiency across the whole syllabus which has been covered.

The role of EAP teachers is an important one, for students look to their teachers for advice and guidance on the institutional assessments and other tests they may have to take. Chapter 11 goes into detail of the three main international academic English tests: TOEFL, IELTS, and the Pearson Test of English (PTE).

At a more local level, EAP teachers need to provide ongoing assessment and feedback so that they can monitor the students' progress on the course; the students themselves also welcome access to this information. These assessments will mainly cover language and skills, including integrated skills.

Gaining confidence and competence

The BALEAP competency framework illustrates the breadth of knowledge and expertise that EAP teachers can aspire to. In order to build their competence, EAP teachers can select specific targets within one or more competence, and work out strategies to reach them, as in the examples given in the individual competences.

It needs emphasizing that the framework is the work of a committee of UK-based EAP teachers, and, in common with other texts and documents, should be challenged. There is no universal agreement that both EAP teachers and their students should become discourse analysts, for example, and issues such as these can be discussed locally. Above all, EAP teachers need to take responsibility for their professional development. Through this process they can gain in confidence and adopt roles in which they can begin to train and mentor less experienced EAP teachers.

Principles of teaching and learning

The discussion of teacher competences in this section serves to emphasize the nature of the teacher–student interface at the heart of the teaching and learning endeavour. If these are two sides of the same coin, on the one side teachers need an understanding of, for example, the role of critical thinking in underpinning academic practice (BALEAP 2008: 6); on the other, students ultimately need a similar competence.

Certainly it is the teachers' role to bring out their students' critical thinking skills. Equally, however, it is the students' role, influenced by the teachers, to work out what these skills are and how to go about developing them. What this observation illustrates is that both students and teachers have a crucial part to play. At its most fundamental and crudest level, teachers need the students economically, and the students need the teachers pedagogically. In terms of learning and teaching, both need each other. It is an inappropriate and inaccurate deficit viewpoint to state that teachers 'know' all about critical thinking, and the students are in the classroom to learn how to do it. Rather, both parties have much to learn, and can learn from each other. To differing extents, the two parties are both teachers and learners.

Competences related to EAP students are integrated into the chapters in this book. For example, the reading requirements of EAP students are elaborated on in Chapter 6.

EAP practitioners

The statements in the BALEAP competency framework, and the material in this EAP methodology book, illustrate the breadth and complexity of the field of EAP. Clearly, there is a lot for EAP teachers to learn and gain: knowledge, skills, and competences. Whatever the level of a particular EAP teacher, in terms of this knowledge and these skills and competences, and in terms of their experience and qualifications as an EAP teacher and language teacher, there is always more to absorb. Nevertheless, EAP teachers' reality is defined by where they are now, so they need to function effectively in their work today while developing professionally to function even more effectively tomorrow.

Their overarching aims can involve the following:

• developing as EAP practitioners and participants in a professional community

• developing professionally and academically

• developing through reading, writing, and research into the field of EAP.

The BALEAP competency framework is certainly a very useful target to aim for; to be an effective tool it needs to be personalized, critiqued, and integrated into each EAP teacher's practice.

Conclusion

This chapter has explored the academic context and the roles required of EAP teachers, particularly with reference to the BALEAP competency framework. The discussion has examined the key issues of general—specific and global—local approaches, which inform EAP practice. The discussions in the chapter have emphasized the role of EAP students as resources of knowledge and experience; students are the reason for the EAP enterprise and need to be positioned at the heart of it. This is as true whether the students are at the traditional 'core' of EAP activity or at one of the emerging peripheral activities of students at secondary schools and academic staff. The role of their teachers is of course a crucial one, and given appropriate expertise and continuing professional development, EAP teaching and learning can become successful and rewarding for all those involved.

Further reading

EAP titles

The theoretically and practically oriented EAP books given at the end of Chapter 1 are also highly relevant to teaching and learning.

The BALEAP competency framework

BALEAP. 2008. *BALEAP Competency Framework for Teachers of English for Academic Purposes.* BALEAP. (Available at: <www.baleap.org>)

Special issues of the Journal of English for Academic Purposes on specialist EAP teaching contexts

Cargill, C. and **S. Burgess.** 2008. *Journal of English for Academic Purposes Special Issue: English for Research Publication Purposes* 7/2.

Johns, A. and **M. A. Snow.** 2006. *Journal of English for Academic Purposes, Special issue: Academic English in secondary schools* 5/4.

3

TEXTS

Academic texts as sources of knowledge and argument

Texts from a range of contexts occupy a central place in academic practice. Texts are often thought of in terms of written texts—such as chapters in textbooks, reports, and articles—and many of these written texts also have integrated visual material. However, spoken texts, such as presentation and lecture texts, are also central to academic discourse. Texts tend to be situated in particular contexts, which this chapter will explore. It will also consider the nature and purpose of texts, with particular emphasis on texts as genres, essential elements in texts, and how texts are held together in terms of meaning and language, i.e. **cohesion**.

Texts and contexts

Texts are typically constructed, in writing or in speech, for clearly defined readers or listeners, who are known as the audience of the text, and for a particular purpose, such as to present new information on a topic. The participants in these contexts typically have clearly defined roles. For example, the audience of a university textbook on psychology essentially comprises students who are studying psychology or a related discipline. The writer(s) of the text, i.e. the textbook author(s), understand that their audience need to access the expected information in a readily navigable way, in order to increase their knowledge of the discipline and use selected parts of the content in their own work.

Texts in EAP programmes

In EAP, many texts that the students have to read may be presented as extracts in coursebooks or as photocopies of published texts. In addition, many spoken texts can be found, such as extracts from lectures, which may in turn be accompanied by written texts, such as slides and handouts. There are also the spoken texts of classroom participants (students and teachers), plus those of presenters and lecturers as well as recorded texts and the limitless resource of texts available on the internet and in resources such as libraries. Other 'texts' are constantly emerging, such as the preconceived ideas and pre-formed arguments that are in people's minds. These go on to form spoken and written texts, which can then be accessed by other people.

In short, texts are all around us, and through technology they can be instantly available, essentially without limit. What applies in the classroom also applies outside, so students are likely to be encountering texts throughout their learning in the broadest sense.

Lectures

The availability and complexity of texts can be illustrated using the familiar example of a lecture. The main text in a lecture is of course the lecturer's text, i.e. their intended material, which they deliver from any of the following: prepared notes; visuals; memory; and experience. While listening to this delivery of the core text, the student may have to deal with other texts: the texts of in-the-moment anecdotes, questions, references to current events, and responses to audience input. Given their relative spontaneity, these texts are likely to be delivered in a different way, perhaps at a different pace and level of formality and tone. Each student also has their own texts: the text which they are constructing as the lecturer's meanings are conveyed, and very probably other, unpredictable content. There are also, potentially, the texts they want to communicate within the lecture event: questions, contributions, responses.

Further texts may include external texts brought into the lecture, such as audio and video recordings, which may be the lecturer's own material, relating to their research, or more publicly available material. The texts discussed so far are spoken, but there are also the written texts of the lecturer: their slides, handouts, and references to reading material, such as textbook chapters and articles, which may have been photocopied and brought into the lecture room. Finally, there might even be apparently completely unconnected texts, such as discarded handouts from previous lectures in the room. Very possibly from different subjects, these old handouts are potentially distracting (or perhaps more interesting than the 'target' texts); the student may find intellectual stimulation in trying to understand them and relate the contents to their own subject. Listening and lectures are discussed further in Chapter 8.

This outline of one academic context illustrates the complexity of textual material that the student has to engage with. A key characteristic of many contexts is their multi-textual nature. Each student in the same context will construct their own individual narrative, based on their current competences and built up from their existing knowledge using their particular selection, understanding, and processing of the available textual material.

Texts as genres

Given the abundance, diversity, and centrality of texts, it is important for EAP teachers to develop an understanding of different types of text in order to present appropriate and varied texts for students to access. As well as being written for a particular audience and for a particular purpose, texts represent and exemplify genres, and can be seen as more, or less, prototypical examples of their genre.

Defining genre

As Chapter 1 states, research into genre has had a great impact on EAP methodology and materials, particularly since the early 1990s. The EAP practitioner and researcher most closely associated with genre since the 1980s is John Swales, who in his seminal book *Genre Analysis* (1990) defines genre in the following way:

> A genre comprises a class of communicative events, the members of which share some set of communicative purposes. These purposes are recognized by the expert members of the parent discourse community, and thereby constitute the **rationale** for the genre. This rationale shapes the schematic structure of the discourse and influences and constrains choice of content and style. […] In addition to purpose, exemplars of a genre exhibit various patterns of similarity in terms of structure, style, content and intended audience.
>
> (Swales 1990: 58)

This influential definition of genre emphasizes the interrelatedness of genre, audience, and purpose. A text is not isolated and decontextualized, but connected to and informed by other related texts, its purpose, and the expectations of its audience with regard to the structure, style, and content of the text.

Genre, audience, and purpose

Swales positions 'audience' at the top of a hierarchical representation of considerations for the academic writer (Swales 2004b: 7). He emphasizes the primacy of audience, which writers need to consider even before they write (Swales 2004b: 8). In this representation, the following considerations are interrelated: audience – purpose – organization – style – flow – presentation.

Essentially, texts do not exist in isolation, but are related to other texts which have similarities in aspects including structure, purpose, formality, style, and audience. The audience, or expected readership, of a text approaches the text with definable knowledge and expectations relating to the topic of the text. In short, texts in general are normally written for a particular audience and for a particular purpose. Academic texts tend to be written following accepted conventions such as text structure and style (genre), for a clearly defined reader profile, such as students of sociology (audience) and for a specific purpose, for example to persuade through a convincing argument. These are all closely interrelated and mutually informing.

Academic texts, moreover, tend to be situated in their discipline, and typically have notable characteristics, such as carefully defined given and new knowledge: the writer of the text believes that their audience will be familiar with given information, while new or unfamiliar information needs to be explained, defined, and exemplified. This principle applies to different genres at different levels. For example, a local newspaper published in a particular town can simply refer to the town (even if it is quite small) without needing to explain what it is or where it is, while a national newspaper would very likely add such information. This difference is explained by the audience's expected existing knowledge.

EAP students need to be familiar with the genre, audience, and purpose of a new text in order to understand how the text fits into its broader context. This information contributes to the student's understanding of important textual information, including the author's stance. Students' awareness of genre, audience, and purpose also informs how they evaluate texts, including assessing the value of a text to use in citation. These ideas are further developed in Chapters 5, 6, and 7.

Primary and secondary sources and non-academic genres

Well-established written academic genres that students are likely to encounter include textbook chapters, journal articles, reports (scientific, research, legal, review), lecture notes, critiques and reviews, summaries, essays, examination texts, case studies, dissertations, and theses. Students are more likely to read than write some of these, such as textbooks. With others, such as essays, students are more likely to write than read them.

Primary and secondary sources

In academic contexts, texts are widely used as sources. This means that the student or academic practitioner locates, reads, and selects material from source texts to use in their own work. Two main types of source text are widely recognized: **primary** and **secondary sources.** Primary sources refer mainly to those texts in which new research is first published and some other types of source; they include the following:

• research articles, i.e. journal articles in which new research is published

• original documents, such as historical documents, law reports, manuscripts and official texts, which represent the recording of knowledge at the time they were written

• works of literature, in the original language or in translation

• case studies

• non-written objects, such as artefacts and textiles.

Primary sources are highly valued as they are the closest (in time, place, and people) to the original events which they describe or express. A student's piece of work which mainly cites primary sources such as those above are likely to be assessed more favourably than one which draws only on secondary sources.

Secondary sources refer to publications which are one step removed from the original event. They include:

• textbooks, i.e. discipline-specific **expository** books which in effect select, synthesize, describe, explain, and discuss material relating to that discipline

- critical works, for example commentaries and reviews on specific work such as works of literature
- journal articles which review existing work rather than presenting new research.

A further category of source text is sometimes recognized: tertiary sources. These are texts in which the content is drawn from secondary sources, so that the material is in effect two or more steps removed from the original event. Examples include online encyclopaedias, such as Wikipedia (where many of the entries are based on information in the public domain, which is therefore likely to be secondary). In terms of reliability, primary sources are considered to be the most reliable, followed by secondary sources. Depending on the context, tertiary sources will probably not be appropriate for students to cite in their academic work, although such sources can be useful for initial information gathering.

Non-academic genres

Non-academic genres include a very wide range of texts. In some academic contexts, journalistic genres such as articles from newspapers and popular magazines can provide useful background information. However, these are not generally considered to be reliable sources in most disciplines. A journalistic text such as a newspaper article may cover the same topic as an academic article and contain some similar information, but is likely to be markedly different in terms of its rhetorical structure, depth of content, rigour, language, and ultimately its reliability as a source. Newspaper articles, for example, do not follow a conventional academic structure, i.e. moving from introduction and background through review of the topic, argument, discussion, and conclusion. In some respects, they represent the opposite, with the conclusion forming the basis of the newspaper headline. Further issues in journalistic texts include selectivity of information, any agendas of the publisher, and the prevalence of unsubstantiated opinion.

In a study tracing the development of a topic (DNA 'fingerprint' discovery) from its original presentation in the scientific journal *Nature*, through the popular science magazine *New Scientist*, to the non-specialist newspaper *The Economist*, Myers (1994) identifies important differences in organization, syntax, and vocabulary. The original scientific article is logically organized by argument, while the popular science magazine emphasizes the applications of the work and the activity of the scientists (ibid.). Finally, *The Economist* goes on to foreground the apparent problem of distinguishing between individuals. The research of the original report is presented as a solution to this problem. However, the original research actually reached its findings through 'pure' scientific research, and these results were subsequently seen as a solution to a problem (Myers, 1994). Myers' work underlines the great differences between academic writing, particularly the communication and construction of new knowledge in research articles, and journalistic writing. These differences lie not only in the audiences of the genres, but in the way the content is selected, presented, and communicated.

EAP teachers need to consider carefully the use of non-academic genres in their EAP programmes. There may be good reasons to use them as reading texts, for example with media students or for the purposes of comparing academic and journalistic texts. However, given the aims and constraints of EAP programmes, too much emphasis on such texts is unlikely to be appropriate and is ultimately unhelpful for students.

Student genres

Certain teaching contexts enable EAP teachers to determine which genres their students have to produce (i.e. write and speak) and process (i.e. read and listen to). In-sessional programmes are probably better suited to this endeavour than pre-sessional programmes because with in-sessional programmes students are simultaneously studying in their disciplines while learning EAP. In the context of in-sessional programmes, EAP teachers can ask the students and liaise with their department(s); also they can access published information, such as that on departmental websites and Learning Management Systems (**LMSs**). In other contexts such as pre-sessional and preparatory programmes, however, the students are likely to be less informed about which genres they will have to produce, and they may not yet know exactly what or where they are going to study. Although in theory EAP is a needs-driven endeavour, in practice it can be very difficult, and often infeasible, to build up a complete picture. Therefore some assumptions have to be made. These points are developed further in Chapter 10.

An added difficulty is that similar genres may be given different names in different contexts (e.g. academic departments), while different genres may be given the same name. For instance, a 'report' in the context of natural sciences typically refers to an account of research organized along conventional lines and may be significantly different from a 'report' in law, which might involve secondary rather than **primary research**, be based on cases, and be organized in a different way, and written for a different purpose, such as to challenge and critique previous legal judgments. In the latter context, there is likely to be more subjectivity.

Student written genres are discussed in more detail in Chapter 7, while Chapter 6 looks at genres which students may have to read.

Essential elements in texts

In order to enable students to produce and process the required genres, it is useful to approach texts in terms of their **essential elements**. The use of the term 'elements' reflects the physical world where a manufactured object may comprise a single element—for example copper—or more than one element —for example bronze, made of copper plus tin. Similarly, texts may be comprised partly or wholly of an essential element.

Essential elements are the major components of texts and are informed by the purpose of the text. The term 'essential element' was introduced in the *Oxford EAP* coursebook series (de Chazal and McCarter 2012). It is intended as a broad term to account for the many different types of material in academic texts (and many other types of text). An argumentative or discursive essay, for instance, is likely to be made up largely of arguments, including the main argument and supporting arguments, plus other essential elements as necessary, such as definitions, citations, and evaluation. Argument is an essential element which occurs in a very wide range of academic genres.

Many of these essential elements have attracted different labels elsewhere, for example 'functions', 'rhetorical functions', and 'academic functions' which can cover certain essential elements like definition, explanation, and cause and effect. Essential elements also include notions (for example expressing movement), cognitive activities (for example stance) and academic practices (for example citation). Essential elements in the analysis here are grounded in texts (written and spoken), and so are encountered by the reader or listener and produced by the writer or speaker. Relations between essential elements and critical thinking are elaborated on in Chapter 5.

The most frequent examples of essential elements are given in Table 3.1. These are presented alphabetically, with two selected examples for each essential element, where appropriate: first, a genre; second, part of a genre.

Table 3.1 illustrates the breadth of essential elements that students are likely to encounter and produce in texts. EAP students need to produce many of these in their writing and speaking, and process them in their reading and listening. Clearly, some are more associated with certain disciplines; for example narrative is associated with case studies in disciplines such as anthropology, linguistics, and psychology. Most, however, occur across the disciplines, and are related to the genre, audience, and purpose. Some essential elements are so closely linked as to form familiar pairings: 'cause–effect'; 'problem–solution'. Others tend to go in cycles. For example, an 'argument' is widely supported by 'evidence' and 'exemplification', which typically takes the form of 'citation', which in turn may need 'explanation', leading to 'evaluation'. In another example, the presentation of a 'problem' may be followed by a discussion on the likely 'causes' of that problem, leading to proposed 'solutions', which are then 'discussed' and 'evaluated'. Cycles like these can form the basis of a paragraph in a text, although they should not be viewed as prescriptive models to replicate uncritically.

Perhaps the most familiar pairings of essential elements in texts are the following:

• Problem–solution: developed and codified by Hoey (1983: 31–106) and influenced by the work of Winter, who used the term 'instrument–achievement relation' (Hoey 1983: 39). Sometimes known as 'Situation–Problem–Solution– Evaluation', or 'SPSE', although this lengthy description and abbreviation seems unnecessary given that all text types are likely to include contextualization (i.e. the situation) and evaluation.

Essential elements	Examples of genres/parts of genres in which these elements can occur
Analysis	Examination essay on an analysis of a specific event or phenomenon Analysis or discussion section of a report
Argument	Argument essay Presentation of an argument in a report
Cause	Journal article speculating on causes of a specific condition
Citation/evidence	Citation presented as support for an argument Part of any academic text to support, define, exemplify, or evaluate an argument
Claim/claim of centrality, occupation of a niche or gap, rationalization/ generalization	Outline and justification of the area(s) of focus in the introduction to an essay or report Statement of the writer's argument in a **thesis** statement
Classification	Classification of different types of entity/phenomena (e.g. species, behaviours) Classification as part of longer text, e.g. thesis
Comparison and contrast	Comparison essay Comparison and contrast of two systems/approaches in a report
Concession limitation	**Limitations** to findings and their applicability/scope in the conclusion to an essay or report
Connection of phenomena or ideas	Presentation of original or existing connections between phenomena or ideas in an argument
Contextualization/background information relating to time, place, and context	Background information in an introduction to a text
Critique/criticism/review	Review of a published work Literature review as part of a dissertation or thesis
Definition	Definitions in a subject-specific dictionary Discussion and proposal of definitions for the purposes of the text, e.g. dissertation
Description, e.g. of a physical or abstract entity or a natural phenomenon	Description of a site of special interest Description of an organization in a case study
Discussion	Discussion paper Discussion section of a research article
Effect	Examination essay on the effects/**associations** of a specific event or medical condition
Evaluation	Exercise/short answer evaluating a proposal Integrated evaluation in a report, essay, or review
Exemplification	Example or series of examples to support an argument in an essay

Explanation/exposition	Essay explaining the characteristics of a specific policy or approach Explanation following a citation in an article
Expression of notional meanings such as movement, relations between entities, obligation, condition, concession, purpose	Description of a space or construction Section of essay expressing concessions to an argument or theory
Expression of functional meanings such as suggesting, advising, denying	Suggestions for solutions to a problem in a presentation
Hypothesis, **prediction**, speculation	Section of a report speculating on possible causes of a problem
Interpretation, inference	Discussion section of a report
Justification, e.g. of a position	Evidence and supporting arguments for an argument in a discussion
Narrative/narration	Narrative in an ethnographic study Narrative section in a case study
Perspective	Analysis of an issue from various perspectives
Presentation of information, data, statistics, findings	Data-based text Fact-based content in a textbook chapter
Problem	Problem–solution essay Presentation of possible problems arising from a specific approach in a research paper
Process/chronological sequence of events	Process description Description of a process to illustrate a cause–effect chain in an article
Proposal, e.g. of a new idea or theory	Research proposal Proposal of a new theory or approach in an article
Qualification: expression of certainty of the message through emphasis or caution	Part of a conclusion in which the findings are hedged Section of a report emphasizing the importance of a policy
Recommendation	Recommendations section of a report
Recount/report of an experiment, case study, or research	Case study Ethnographic study Account of the research methods in a lab report
Reflection/empathy	Reflective journal Section of a research project to offer reflection on the research and writing process
Solution	Proposal of solution(s) to stated problem(s)
Stance	Statement of the speaker's stance in the introduction to a presentation
Summary	Abstract to a research article Summary of a piece of research or school of thought, reported through a citation

Table 3.1   A taxonomy of essential elements in texts with examples of genres and parts of genres in which they can occur

- Cause–effect: again discussed by Hoey (1983: 41ff), who refers to it as the 'cause–consequence relation'. As noted in the point above, causes and effects are typically evaluated, for example by appraising their significance or seriousness.
- Comparison–contrast: a very well-established text organization pattern, typically driven by a rubric such as 'Compare and contrast X and Y.'

In addition, the discursive, or argumentative, essay is perhaps the longest-established, most widely used, and familiar genre.

The familiarity of these organizational patterns has led to the essential elements themselves becoming shorthand labels for such texts; for example, EAP teachers routinely refer to 'problem-solution' texts and 'cause-and-effect' essays.

In short, essential elements form the bedrock of texts; they inform the organization of a text, and are closely related to the genre and purpose of a text. As Table 3.1 shows, texts can be comprised mainly of one essential element, such as process and case study. Most texts, however, are likely to be made up of multiple essential elements. The students need to be able to understand essential elements in order to gain an understanding of a text. EAP teachers need to use materials that develop their students' familiarity with texts.

Essential elements are further discussed in Chapter 5 in relation to the role of critical thinking.

Texts and tasks

There are many possible tasks and activities based around texts, for example researching, planning, and writing an essay. The terms 'task' and 'activity' are closely related; tasks are sometimes taken to be at the level above activities, with a single task being realized through multiple activities. EAP tasks and activities normally lead to a particular outcome, which may in turn be assessed. For example, a general English class may have a discussion on a topic. A likely reason to do this is general fluency practice arising from language input. The focus of a discussion in EAP is more likely to be part of an integrated sequence of tasks with an outcome. For example, students may have to read a text on a given topic. The reason for looking at the topic may involve an investigative question. Students could then search for further material on the topic, and summarize this.

All this work precedes the discussion. The discussion involves specific input from different students, based on their reading texts. Furthermore, the discussion is contextualized within an academic event such as a seminar which has particular expectations, etiquette, and conventions. The outcome of the discussion could be the clarification of the original question in the form of a report, summary, or essay. Alternatively, the students participating in the discussion may be assessed as part of their coursework. These possible examples show the complex nature of the task, the fact that it is planned, and that it takes place for a particular purpose, all within a limited timeframe. Tasks and activities in EAP materials are explored further in Chapter 10.

Cohesion in texts

Texts are more than the sum of the discrete language items from the language systems (vocabulary, grammar, and phonology) that make up the texts. Crucially, texts are held together through textual **cohesion**. Arguably, cohesion is one of the most important yet least understood phenomena of texts. A deeper understanding of textual cohesion can result in considerably enhanced comprehension and construction of texts.

The most influential work on cohesion was done by Halliday and Hasan in the 1970s, who define cohesion as 'part of the system of a language' which lies in the relation between two items; it is a semantic relation which is expressed through language, the lexicogrammatical system, and intonation (Halliday and Hasan 1976: 5–6). More recently, Biber et al. describe cohesion as 'the integration which is achieved between different parts of a text by various types of semantic and referential linkages' (Biber et al.1999: 42).

In a later description in a student coursebook, cohesion essentially refers to 'how a text is connected in terms of meaning and language' (de Chazal and McCarter 2012: 199). Related to but distinct from cohesion is **coherence**, which refers to 'how a text is connected in terms of meaning and ideas' (ibid.). In this sense, cohesion and coherence can be seen as two sides of the same coin in terms of meaning.

To illustrate cohesion in context, the following text is analyzed in different ways to focus on the cohesive language, based on the work of de Chazal (2011a: 127–9). There are seven main analyses. The first three of these look at 'identifiers', which 'state what something is, or what quality it has, and typically involve noun phrases' (de Chazal 2010b). This analysis downplays the obvious and intuitive area of discourse markers such as 'however', in order to show that expert texts can be constructed with minimal use of such devices. This point is developed later in this section.

This comprehensive analysis also serves to illustrate much of what is happening within a text as a whole: how meanings within a text are related; the interaction between the writer and audience of a text; the contribution of language in the construction of meaning; and the textual development of argument. Argument is examined in greater detail in the first section of Chapter 7.

Lexis

Analysis 1 illustrates how a text is made cohesive partly through lexis, that is by using words and phrases. Writers do this by using synonyms, repetition, substitution, parallel expression, and rephrasing. Other kinds of lexical cohesion include **antonyms**, **hyponyms**, and **meronyms**.

Analysis 1: Lexis

To understand life on Earth, we need to know how animals (including humans), plants, and microbes work, ultimately in terms of the molecular processes that underlie their functioning. This is the 'how' question of biology; an enormous amount of research during the last century has produced spectacular progress towards answering this question. This effort has shown that even <u>the simplest organism capable of independent existence, a bacterial cell</u>, is a machine of great complexity, with thousands of different protein molecules that act in a coordinated fashion to fulfil the functions necessary for <u>the cell</u> to survive, and to divide to produce <u>two daughter cells</u> (see Chapter 3). This complexity is even greater in higher organisms such as a fly or human being. These start life as <u>a single cell</u>, formed by the fusion of an egg and a sperm. There is then a delicately controlled series of <u>cell divisions</u>, accompanied by the differentiation of the <u>resulting cells</u> into many distinct types. The process of development eventually produces the <u>adult organism</u>, with its highly organized structure made up of different tissues and organs, and its capacity for elaborate behaviour. Our understanding of the molecular mechanisms that underlie this complexity of structure and function is rapidly expanding. Although there are still many unsolved problems, biologists are convinced that even the most complicated features of living creatures, such as human consciousness, reflect the operation of chemical and physical processes that are accessible to scientific analysis.

(Charlesworth, and Charlesworth 2003: 4)

First, the writers introduce the technical concept, a type of cell. The concept is nicely contextualized by the introductory phrase 'the simplest organism capable of independent existence'. The purpose of this is threefold: to introduce and contextualize the concept which follows ('a bacterial cell'); to offer a description and definition of the concept which briefly answers the anticipated audience question, 'What is a bacterial cell?'; and to help the reader efficiently navigate the text. These three purposes are all closely connected to cohesion. Grammatically, the whole phrase 'the simplest organism capable of independent existence, a bacterial cell' is a noun phrase, the second part of which ('a bacterial cell') is an **appositive**, in other words a different way of saying the same thing. Both parts of appositive noun phrases refer to the same thing, in order to define, exemplify, explain, or rephrase. Appositives are widely found in academic texts, and can be easily missed or misinterpreted as the comma dividing the two parts signals not separate items in a list but the same entity expressed in a different way.

Following the introduction of the concept, the writers then repeatedly refer to it again as the text progresses. To meet the needs of their description they vary the lexical pattern slightly. When first introduced, the item is 'a bacterial cell', using an indefinite determiner ('a'). Subsequently, it is referred to using definite determiners, 'the' and 'two': 'the cell' …, 'two daughter cells' …, 'the resulting cells'. When the description reverts to any cell, an indefinite determiner is used, 'a single cell', and in the plural with the zero determiner, 'cell divisions'. Further lexical content adds more information: 'bacterial', 'daughter', 'single', 'resulting'.

Synonyms, antonyms, hyponyms, and meronyms

In this description of evolution, the technical term itself normally remains constant; it would be unusual or impossible to offer synonyms for a technical term such as 'cell', while rephrasing, which would require several words, is inefficient and also unusual. Therefore it is simply repeated as many times as required. Frequent repetition of a technical term is typically related to the topic of a text: this part of the text is mainly about cells.

Examples of synonyms of general words in the text, as opposed to technical terms, include 'work' and 'functioning', and 'research' and 'effort'. These are not necessarily words with exactly the same meaning, but they are used to refer to the same thing. Examples of antonyms include 'answering this question' and 'unsolved problem'. Again, these are not necessarily exact opposites, but clearly express a contrast in meaning. Examples of hyponymous relationships in the text include 'organism' in relation to 'cell', 'fly', and 'human being'. The latter three are all examples, or types, of the first: organism is a **superordinate** of these three nouns. Finally, examples of meronyms, where lexical items are related in a 'whole to part' way (Paltridge 2012: 119) include the 'protein molecules' that make up part of the 'cell'. All these types of relations contribute to the cohesion of the text.

Metaphor

Two lexical choices are of further interest in this analysis. The choices of '*daughter* cells' and '*adult* organisms' are, technically speaking, not accurate. The cells resulting from divisions do not have a sex (and if they did presumably the cells would include both male and female), nor is the familiar term 'adult' appropriate in scientific terms in this context of cell division. These lexical choices function as **metaphors**, which are common in academic discourse, just as they are in journalism and fiction: for example, in economics and finance, money 'flows' though it is not a liquid, demand 'explodes', and rising commodity prices 'trigger' inflation. As this extract is written for a reasonably educated but non-expert audience, the choice of lexis reflects the purpose of the text. Like many academic texts, this text is written both to inform and persuade, and the writers conceive their audience as appreciating help in the form of metaphors.

Cohesive noun phrases

The second analysis highlights the **cohesive noun phrases** in the text. These refer to carefully chosen language used 'to coherently link text, by encoding (summarising, labelling, evaluating) a previous stretch of discourse, and moving the text forward (de Chazal 2011a: 127). These textual features have been discussed by a number of different writers, including Francis (1986), who uses the term 'retrospective labels', and Swales and Feak, who refer to them as '*this* + summary word' (1994 and 2004) and '*this* + noun phrase' (2000: 44ff). Swales and Feak's term '*this* + noun phrase' recognizes that this type of noun phrase is sometimes used interpretively, 'or designed to persuade the reader how to "read" the previous sentence' (Swales and Feak, 2000: 45). The later term, 'cohesive noun phrases' is intended to express the primarily cohesive function of this type of noun phrase, which covers both previous stretches of text (through anaphoric reference) and forward-looking text (through **cataphoric** reference). In a study based on research articles written by dentists whose first language was Turkish, Kafes (2008) found that these writers used considerably fewer such language devices than in articles written by writers whose first language was English.

Cohesive noun phrases are essentially short noun phrases which normally comprise a determiner or semi-determiner (for example 'this', 'such') plus a noun to express meanings such as cognition, stance, category, class, or process. The writer can carefully select an appropriate noun to express their target nuanced meaning. These structures are widely-used in managing the presentation of information in a text, particularly with regard to the 'given–new tendency' in English sentences. This tendency refers to the placing of given (i.e. known) information at the beginning of the sentence in order to contextualize the content and frame the new information, which is typically presented at the end.

Analysis 2: Cohesive noun phrases

To understand life on Earth, we need to know how animals (including humans), plants, and microbes work, ultimately in terms of the molecular processes that underlie their functioning. <u>This</u> is the 'how' question of biology; an enormous amount of research during the last century has produced spectacular progress towards answering <u>this question</u>. <u>This effort</u> has shown that even the simplest organism capable of independent existence, a bacterial cell, is a machine of great complexity, with thousands of different protein molecules that act in a coordinated fashion to fulfil the functions necessary for the cell to survive, and to divide to produce two daughter cells (see Chapter 3). <u>This complexity</u> is even greater in higher organisms such as a fly or human being. These start life as a single cell, formed by the fusion of an egg and a sperm. There is then a delicately controlled series of cell divisions, accompanied by the differentiation of the resulting cells into many distinct types. <u>The process of development</u> eventually produces the adult organism, with its highly organized structure made up of different tissues and organs, and its capacity for elaborate behaviour. <u>Our understanding</u> of the molecular mechanisms that underlie <u>this complexity of structure and function</u> is rapidly expanding. Although there are still many unsolved problems, biologists are convinced that even the most complicated features of living creatures, such as human consciousness, reflect the operation of chemical and physical processes that are accessible to scientific analysis.

The noun phrases highlighted in this analysis express the writers' careful choice of **head noun**. The statement in the first sentence is labelled a 'question' in the sentence which follows. Next, the core material of this second sentence, 'an enormous amount of research during the last century', is expressed as 'This effort' in the third sentence. As the text unfolds, the writers use further cohesive noun phrases to connect the ideas in the text, while frequently reducing them to single nouns which express various meanings.

The choice of noun is significant because it conveys to the reader how the writers are conceptualizing their material. Table 3.2 gives examples of nouns which may be used in academic texts in cohesive noun phrase structures:

Function, meaning, and connotation	Examples
Broadly neutral	question, issue, challenge, outcome, eventuality, phenomenon, discussion, result
Positive	achievement, endeavour, opportunity, solution, ambition, success
Negative	problem, failure, difficulty, controversy, uncertainty Note: 'issue' is also often intended to be negative rather than neutral
Categorizing and labelling	argument, trend, pattern, analysis, finding, condition, process, explanation, development, complexity, work, effort, research
Expressing stance	observation, standpoint, view, viewpoint, stance, position, perspective, opinion

Table 3.2   Nouns in cohesive noun phrases

Table 3.2 illustrates the significant number of nouns which can be used in cohesive noun phrases. This choice of language represents an opportunity for the writer/speaker to express a carefully nuanced meaning in their texts.

The examples in the text are of anaphoric reference, meaning that they refer back to something already mentioned. As a result, the noun phrases normally start with a definite determiner, which expresses shared knowledge (the reader/listener knows it because it has just been mentioned). In most cases these determiners are 'this' or 'the', but there is one instance of the possessive determiner 'our'. This is an example of an interactor, which is discussed further in Analysis 5.

Pronouns and determiners

Analysis 3 examines pronouns and determiners. These are used to avoid repetition of recurring nouns, and to show backward and forward (anaphoric and cataphoric) chains of reference in a text. Unlike cohesive noun phrases, pronouns and determiners are mechanical rather than creative. The writer simply chooses the correct grammatical item, pronoun (including relative pronoun) or determiner, plus an 'uncontroversial' noun phrase.

Analysis 3: Pronouns and determiners

To understand life on Earth, we need to know how animals (including humans), plants, and microbes work, ultimately in terms of the molecular processes that underlie their functioning. This is the 'how' question of biology; an enormous amount of research during the last century has produced spectacular progress towards answering this question. This effort has shown that even the simplest organism capable of independent existence, a bacterial cell, is a machine of great complexity, with thousands of different protein molecules <u>that</u> act in a coordinated fashion to fulfil the functions necessary for the cell to survive, and to divide to produce two daughter cells (see Chapter 3). This complexity is even greater in higher organisms such as a fly or human being. <u>These</u> start life as a single cell, formed by the fusion of an egg and a sperm. There is then a delicately controlled series of cell divisions, accompanied by the differentiation of the resulting cells into many distinct types. The process of development eventually produces the adult organism, with its highly organized structure made up of different tissues and organs, and its capacity for elaborate behaviour. Our understanding of the molecular mechanisms <u>that</u> underlie this complexity of structure and function is rapidly expanding. Although there are still many unsolved problems, biologists are convinced that even the most complicated features of living creatures, such as human consciousness, reflect the operation of chemical and physical processes <u>that</u> are accessible to scientific analysis.

In ELT, the type of item highlighted in this analysis has long been the staple of gap-fills and reading comprehension questions like 'What does 'it' refer to?' Apart from pronouns which only have a syntactic function such as the 'it' in 'It has been argued that', pronouns normally refer to something known, i.e. already mentioned in the text; again this is an example of anaphoric referencing. Relative pronouns tend to directly follow the noun to which they refer, e.g. 'thousands of different protein molecules <u>that</u> act in a coordinated fashion'. In this example, 'that' refers to 'thousands of different protein molecules', i.e. all the material in the noun phrase up to and including the head, and not just 'molecules'. Other pronouns can be grammatically ambiguous in their reference. As such, the second pronoun in the analysis, 'These', could refer to 'higher organisms', or a 'fly' or 'human being', although as the latter are examples of the former they are in effect the same entity. Similarly, the pair of 'its' could refer, grammatically, to 'the process of development' or 'the adult organism', again both in the preceding sentence; it is the reader's knowledge, skill, and logic which leads them to the reference intended by the writers, 'the adult organism'.

Contextualizers

Analysis 4 deals with 'contexualizers' (de Chazal 2010b and 2011a), which add circumstantial information (where, when, why, how, how much/many/often, to/for whom...); linking material; and offering freestanding stance and perspective elements. This is done by using adverbials, which as Chapter 4 discusses, are mainly prepositional phrases, adverbs, or adverbial clauses.

Analysis 4: Contextualizers

<u>To understand life on Earth</u>, we need to know how animals (<u>including humans</u>), plants, and microbes work, <u>ultimately in terms of the molecular processes that underlie their functioning</u>. This is the 'how' question of biology; an enormous

amount of research <u>during the last century</u> has produced spectacular progress towards answering this question. This effort has shown that <u>even</u> the simplest organism capable of independent existence, a bacterial cell, is a machine of great complexity, with thousands of different protein molecules that act in a coordinated fashion to fulfil the functions necessary for the cell to survive, and to divide to produce two daughter cells (see Chapter 3). This complexity is <u>even</u> greater in higher organisms <u>such as a fly or human being</u>. These start life as a single cell, formed by the fusion of an egg and a sperm. There is then a delicately controlled series of cell divisions, accompanied by the differentiation of the resulting cells into many distinct types. The process of development <u>eventually</u> produces the adult organism, with its highly organized structure made up of different tissues and organs, and its capacity for elaborate behaviour. Our understanding of the molecular mechanisms that underlie this complexity of structure and function is <u>rapidly</u> expanding. <u>Although there are still many unsolved problems</u>, biologists are convinced that <u>even</u> the most complicated features of living creatures, <u>such as human consciousness</u>, reflect the operation of chemical and physical processes that are accessible to scientific analysis.

The opening contextualizer, 'To understand life on earth', expresses the purpose of what is to follow. The contextualizers in the text express the following meanings:

- purpose ('To understand life on earth')
- examples ('including humans'; 'such as a fly or human being'; 'such as human consciousness')
- time ('during the last century')
- sequence ('then'; 'eventually')
- concession ('Although there are still many unsolved problems')
- manner ('rapidly')
- context ('ultimately in terms of the molecular processes that underlie their functioning').

The last example is introduced by the complex preposition 'in terms of', which is a prototypical example of academic language. Also highlighted in the text are three instances of 'even', which are adverbs modifying another word or phrase rather than adverbials. They express emphasis, and are variously known as 'maximizers', 'emphasizers', 'boosters', 'amplifiers', or 'intensifiers'. The contextualizers in the text serve to frame, situate, and contextualize the text and the ideas in the text, thereby contributing to textual cohesion.

Interactors

The fifth textual analysis looks at interactors. Interactors refer to the practice of 'visibly situating the text within the writer/audience context by involving and interacting with the audience, sharing experience, and offering directives including references to items outside the text (**exophoric**)' (de Chazal 2010b). This is achieved by using imperatives, inclusive language, and references to familiar agents.

Imperatives occur frequently in conversation, accounting for about 1% of all words, but are far less frequent in academic written texts, at 0.1% of words (Biber et al.1999: 221). There has also been found to be wide disciplinary variation in the types, uses, and purposes of imperatives (Swales, Ahmad, Chang, Chavez, Dressen and Seymour 1998); one purpose is to engage the reader. Biber et al. report that variations in word order achieve cohesion and emphasis. These include fronting, inversion, and the placement of direct and indirect objects, all of which are statistically significant (Biber et al. 1999: 899, 909, 926, 930). The following is an example of varying the position of direct and indirect objects: 'make their recommendations available' versus 'make available their recommendations'.

Analysis 5 Interactors

To understand life on Earth, <u>we</u> need to know how animals (including humans), plants, and microbes work, ultimately in terms of the molecular processes that underlie their functioning. This is the 'how' question of biology; an enormous amount of research during the last century has produced spectacular progress towards answering this question. This effort has shown that even the simplest organism capable of independent existence, a bacterial cell, is a machine of great complexity, with thousands of different protein molecules that act in a coordinated fashion to fulfil the functions necessary for the cell to survive, and to divide to produce two daughter cells (<u>see</u> Chapter 3). This complexity is even greater in higher organisms such as a fly or human being. These start life as a single cell, formed by the fusion of an egg and a sperm. There is then a delicately controlled series of cell divisions, accompanied by the differentiation of the resulting cells into many distinct types. The process of development eventually produces the adult organism, with its highly organized structure made up of different tissues and organs, and its capacity for elaborate behaviour. <u>Our</u> understanding of the molecular mechanisms that underlie this complexity of structure and function is rapidly expanding. Although there are still many unsolved problems, <u>biologists</u> are convinced that even the most complicated features of living creatures, such as human consciousness, reflect the operation of chemical and physical processes that are accessible to scientific analysis.

Although used relatively sparingly, this cohesive language performs the very useful function of involving the reader or audience in the argument ('we', 'Our'), directing the reader ('see Chapter 3'), and referring to agents ('biologists'). The reference to biologists is significant because the audience is aware that the writers are biologists (the title of the book is *Evolution*); the audience can therefore assume that the writers are similarly convinced by the concluding argument of the paragraph, that even complex natural features can be scientifically analyzed. The key players of reader, writer, and scientists/biologists are potentially able to come together by the end of this paragraph.

Macro-text organizers

The next analysis of the text presents macro-text organizers. These refer to the embedding of non-linguistic, navigational, and overarching devices to indicate macro-textual relations. This is done through the use of titles, headings, numbering, legends, iconic statements, and visual means. Textbooks, for example, typically have different levels of heading, which can be presented in different fonts, font sizes, and colours. Conventional sections of text, for example introductions to essays, reports, articles, and textbook chapters, can incorporate iconic statements such as thesis statements and macro-text signposting language.

Analysis 6 Macro-text organizers

Chapter 2

To understand life on Earth, we need to know how animals (including humans), plants, and microbes work, ultimately in terms of the molecular processes that underlie their functioning. This is the 'how' question of biology; an enormous amount of research during the last century has produced spectacular progress towards answering this question. This effort has shown that even the simplest organism capable of independent existence, a bacterial cell, is a machine of great complexity, with thousands of different protein molecules that act in a coordinated fashion to fulfil the functions necessary for the cell to survive, and to divide to produce two daughter cells (see Chapter 3). This complexity is even greater in higher organisms such as a fly or human being. These start life as a single cell, formed by the fusion of an egg and a sperm. There is then a delicately controlled series of cell divisions, accompanied by the differentiation of the resulting cells into many distinct types. The process of development eventually produces the adult organism, with its highly organized structure made up of different tissues and organs, and its capacity for elaborate behaviour. Our understanding of the molecular mechanisms that underlie this complexity of structure and function is rapidly expanding. Although there are still many unsolved problems, biologists are convinced that even the most complicated features of living creatures, such as human consciousness, reflect the operation of chemical and physical processes that are accessible to scientific analysis.

The macro-text organizers work across large tracts of text to help the reader navigate the whole text. Clearly, the heading 'Chapter 2' shows a sequence of chapters, confirmed by the in-text directive to 'Chapter 3'. Also, the reader can quickly gain an overview of the chapter by reading the accompanying sequence of headings, starting with 'The process of evolution'. These cohesive items are clear, due to their prominent positioning and more noticeable font. Less clear, but similarly useful, are the in-text iconic statements 'the "how" question of biology', and 'the "why" question of biology': the latter is positioned in the paragraph following the text analyzed. These statements provide both macro-level navigation and vital encoding of meaning to help the reader access the full meanings in the text.

Focusers

One further category of cohesive language can be identified, that of focusers. Focusers cover grammatical transformations from the expected default patterns such as subject–verb–object. These help to organise text and focus the reader's attention, and are achieved through the use of a number of grammatical phenomena including the following:

- fronts
- clefts
- inversion
- ellipsis
- certain uses of the passive
- 'it'/'there' structures
- coordinators, especially 'but'

These focusers are particularly associated with persuasive texts, which include much journalistic writing. There are no examples in the text on evolution analyzed above. An alternative text (Gannon 2008), given in the Appendix on page 343, can illustrate how a writer can use focusers rather than default structures. The five instances are presented below with five alternative forms. These alternative forms are 'unmarked', i.e. neutral, and probably more frequent in English. A practical task for the discourse analyst is to compare the two versions and decide which one is more appropriate for the genre and purpose.

Analysis 7: Focusers

The following textual analysis, based on the text on page 343, presents two versions for selected cohesive language in the text (the original version followed by an alternative version).

1 Original—the writer chooses the passive

The number 700,000 is often cited in articles and editorials about science, politics and economic development as an estimate of the number of scientists, technicians and engineers that the European Union will need by 2010 to keep up its current rate of growth.

Alternative version

Writers often cite the number 700,000 in articles and editorials about science, politics and economic development as an estimate of the number of scientists, technicians and engineers that the European Union will need by 2010 to keep up its current rate of growth.

2 Original—the writer chooses to front 'the problem' to give it topic status

The problem of the availability of skilled personnel worries policy-makers worldwide, who solve it in different ways.

Alternative version

Policy-makers worldwide worry about the problem of the availability of skilled personnel, and they solve it in different ways.

3 Original—the writer moves the stance adverbial from the default medial to the initial position

Clearly the demand for trained scientists and engineers is increasing worldwide.

Alternative version

The demand for trained scientists and engineers is clearly increasing worldwide.

4 Original—the writer uses an 'it' structure to emphasise the evaluative 'worthwhile'

It is therefore worthwhile to reflect on this lack of interest in science, because the projected deficit in manpower will ultimately strangle economic development and delay the process of discovery and invention.

Alternative version

Reflecting on this lack of interest in science is therefore worthwhile, because the projected deficit in manpower will ultimately strangle economic development and delay the process of discovery and invention.

5 Original—the writer fronts the evaluative 'worse still'

Worse still, the salaries of experienced researchers who reach the level of group leader or professor are rarely reported.

Alternative version

The salaries of experienced researchers who reach the level of group leader or professor are rarely reported, which is worse still.

These alternatives illustrate further structures available to the academic writer and some of the choices that are available. The choice of forms is far from mechanical and technical; there can be a subtle shift in meaning. To take the third example above, the position of 'clearly' at the start of the sentence strongly suggests the writer's stance, whereas in its 'default' medial position before the lexical verb, is more likely to convey a more objective meaning such as 'noticeably'. Importantly, the writer's choice of structure will also be influenced by the previous sentence: its structure, content, and emphasis.

Cohesion in EAP materials and assessments

These analyses show that cohesion is neither a peripheral element of a text, nor a formulaic, surface-based phenomenon added on at the end of the writing process. Like meaning, cohesion is fundamental to a text, and can draw on a potentially large pool of language. Logically, meaning should come first, then cohesion, not the other way round.

Regrettably, cohesion is widely misunderstood, or dealt with at a superficial level. Published materials and popular language tests and assessments perpetuate this practice, by sending the message through tables of language and grading of student language. Many EAP students are led to believe that through a generous sprinkling of explicit linking language they can achieve a more favourable assessment. This belief can lead to an overuse (and misuse) of overt linking language such as the sentence-initial adverbials 'therefore', 'however', and 'furthermore'. Interestingly, research has shown that the use of such linking adverbials has been steadily declining over the last two centuries (Biber and Gray, 2010: 15). In the eighteenth and nineteenth centuries, linking adverbials were used quite frequently by academic writers, whereas their use decreased rapidly in the twentieth century, during which time the use of the colon increased markedly (ibid.).

It is noteworthy that the text analyzed, clearly written by expert writers, contains almost no linking adverbials; there is one 'however' in the subsequent paragraph, which is positioned not initially in the sentence but medially, before the main verb. It is both impressive and interesting that just one linking adverbial like 'however' is needed in about 550 words of text. Included here, it is very useful, but there is no need for the repeated use of 'popular' discourse markers. The following two paragraphs of the text are given below, with the contextualizer 'however' highlighted. Meanwhile, further interesting examples of the more fundamental cohesive language from Analyses 1–6 may be identified throughout the text.

Analysis 8: 'Popular' cohesive language

At all levels, from the structure and function of a single protein molecule, to the organization of the human brain, we see many instances of adaptation: the fit of structure to function that is also apparent in machines designed by people (see Chapter 5). We also see that different species have distinctive characteristics, often clearly reflecting adaptations to the environments in which they live. These observations raise the 'why' question of biology, which concerns the processes that have caused organisms to be the way they are. Before the rise of the idea of evolution, most biologists would have answered this question by appealing to a Creator. The term *adaptation* was introduced by 18th-century British theologians, who argued that the appearance of design in the features of living creatures proves the existence of a supernatural designer. While this argument was shown to be logically flawed by the philosopher David Hume in the middle of the 18th century, it retained its hold on people's minds as long as no credible alternative had been proposed.

Evolutionary ideas provide a set of natural processes that can explain the vast diversity of living species, and the characteristics that make them so well adapted to their environment, without any appeal to supernatural intervention. These explanations extend, of course, to the origin of the human species itself, and this has made biological evolution the most controversial of scientific subjects. If the issues are approached without prejudice, however, the evidence for evolution as an historical process can be seen to be as strong as that for other long-established scientific theories, such as the atomic nature of matter (see Chapters 3 and 4). We also have a set of well-verified ideas about the causes of evolution, although, as in every healthy science, there are unsolved problems, as well as new questions that arise as more is understood (see Chapter 7).

(Charlesworth, and Charlesworth 2003: 5)

There can be considerable variation between writers on their use of overt cohesive adverbials such as 'however'. It can be challenging to construct coherent and clearly-signalled text with minimal use of such language. For the student writer in particular, using items like 'furthermore' and 'on the other hand' can help both in the construction and understanding of their argument. During the writing development process the writer can gradually learn to construct their writing using fewer instances of such structures.

More broadly, these analyses also demonstrate the highly useful skill of textual analysis, or discourse analysis, for the EAP teacher. One certainty is that there will always be new texts to encounter, and through the use of analytical techniques, readers can learn to analyze any text regardless of its content or discipline.

EAP tasks for textual cohesion

EAP teachers can encourage a deeper appreciation of cohesion through tasks such as the following, based on de Chazal (2010b):

- identify and evaluate cohesive language in text

- rewrite given texts to improve cohesion

- put back taken-out cohesive material—either 'cold', or from memory after having read a text

- collaboratively choose the best cohesive material

- match semantically similar items

- correct wrong items/improve poor items/delete superfluous items, based on a student text

- construct/improve chains of reference in a text to maximize navigational assistance for the reader.

Such tasks can be done with a degree of student autonomy appropriate to the teaching and learning context.

Independence and autonomy

Broader than independence, the notion of autonomy can usefully involve student collaboration, such as might take place in project work. An initially more teacher-centred approach could be the controlled practice of cohesion tasks using given texts. Gradually this can move into a more autonomous phase, with students noticing cohesion in texts they have searched for themselves, and actively using more subtle cohesive language in their own work. They can ask scaffolded questions such as:

- Is this cohesive item necessary?
- Is it used accurately?
- Is it creative?

Scaffolding questions such as these can gradually be 'withdrawn' as they become internalized: initially they can be displayed and then removed once they are routinely practised. Through continued integrated practice and an element of discourse analysis such as that carried out in this section, students will ultimately gain a heightened appreciation of the crucial phenomenon of cohesion in English, thereby measurably raising their language level.

Cohesion and evaluation

Like cohesion, evaluation is a vital part of academic texts, but for a different reason: while cohesion relates to how meanings are expressed through language, evaluation leads directly to the writer. The writer of a text incorporates their own evaluation in response to the main content and argument of the text. The notion of evaluation is discussed further in Chapter 5.

Conclusion

This chapter has emphasized texts as sources of knowledge and argument for students to use in their own work. In doing so, students need to reconstruct the meanings in the text and process these to use in their own written and spoken texts. Texts exist both in their 'original' contexts, in other words as genres written for clearly defined audiences and purposes, and in the EAP classroom. A major focus of text study in the EAP classroom is cohesion, together with other discourse analysis work. Since texts are made up of meaningful parts which are generally larger than individual sentences in the text, students need to identify and understand these essential elements. Through these processes, students should be enabled ultimately to work independently and understand a wide range of texts at a deep level.

Further reading

Gee, J.P. 2011. *How to do Discourse Analysis: A Toolkit*. Abingdon: Routledge.

Halliday, M. A. K. and **R. Hassan.** 1976. *Cohesion in English*. Harlow: Longman.

McCarthy, M. 1991. *Discourse Analysis for Language Teachers*. Cambridge: Cambridge University Press.

Paltridge, B. 2012. *Discourse Analysis: An Introduction 2e*. London: Bloomsbury.

Swales, J. 1990. *Genre Analysis: English in academic and research settings*. Cambridge: Cambridge University Press.

4 LANGUAGE

Academic language as agent of meaning

Given that the 'E' in 'EAP' stands for 'English', the English language is at the heart of EAP practice. Language informs the work of EAP teachers on many levels, from selecting appropriate language to express meaning in a written text to using the language of criticism to respond to ideas raised in a seminar.

As Chapter 2 discusses, an important competence of EAP teachers is to be able to systematically understand and analyze academic discourse. They also need to be able to process the language, present it, and facilitate students' learning of it. This section presents a selective overview of academic language, grounded in the descriptive work of the grammarians Quirk and his team (especially Quirk, Greenbaum, Leech, and Svartvik 1985), Huddleston and Pullum (2002), and subsequent corpus-based research which builds on the earlier work of the Quirk school, notably that of Biber and his team who wrote the *Longman Grammar of Spoken and Written English* (Biber, Johansson, Leech, Conrad and Finegan 1999); this latter work is the most heavily cited as it is offers a recent and exceptionally informative corpus-based account of academic written discourse. Leech provides continuity between the work of the Quirk and Biber schools of linguists. EAP teachers can use the information in the 1999 volume, together with the more concise and accessible *Longman Student Grammar of Spoken and Written English* (Biber, Conrad and Leech 2002) as principled sources of reference and workable descriptions of English grammar and language which can be readily applied to EAP contexts.

There are four extended analyses of language in this book. The first is the language of cohesion, covered in the account of texts in Chapter 3. Later in this current chapter, Chapter 4, the language of cause and effect is analyzed, and in Chapter 5, evaluative language is described within the context of the language of critical thinking. Finally, the language of citation is considered in the context of academic writing in Chapter 7. Further contextualized analyses of language occur throughout the book, such as that in Chapter 6 in the context of challenges in reading. This chapter examines academic language, with a particular focus on written language, so that EAP teachers can make informed choices about what language to emphasize in their classroom practice and materials.

Academic language and the EAP teacher

Mainstream EAP practice stresses the need for EAP teachers to become to some extent experts in the language and discourse analysts (for example *The BALEAP Competency Framework* 2008: 5, Alexander et al., 2008: 30ff; Bruce 2011: 83ff). In the wider context of ELT, there are others who also argue that language analysis should be central to language teaching (for example Brumfit 1991: 24–39). These arguments underpin this chapter, and indeed this book, although there are EAP practitioners and materials writers who prefer to emphasize competence in skills over competence in language.

The particular focus of this chapter is academic language, i.e. the language found in written and spoken academic discourse. Academic discourse tends to follow conventions. It is also characterized by a certain degree of formality, although this level of formality can vary considerably across texts and genres. The discussion on texts in Chapter 3 illuminated aspects of academic language in context, particularly within the crucial phenomenon of cohesion. This chapter surveys the major characteristics of academic language in context (i.e. in texts) and suggests approaches to teaching and learning such language.

Academic language is complex, potentially vast and sometimes unpredictable. It is clearly the job of EAP teachers to position language—in its broadest sense—at the heart of the teaching and learning environment. The key challenges in attempting to do this are, from the teacher's perspective, how to select, prioritize, and present the language to be learned, and from the student's perspective, how to deal with a seemingly limitless input of often unfamiliar language (particularly vocabulary) and challenging structures (grammar).

Language is to some extent the sum of the three major systems of grammar, vocabulary, and phonology. Rather than being separate, these three systems are naturally inter-related and mutually influencing. Used together, they can create infinite meaning. Language is more than the sum of the discrete parts— it encompasses meaning and discourse, style and formality, and in academic texts language is the means of expressing cognitively challenging concepts and structures, both physical and abstract. In this sense, academic language can be seen as the agent of meaning: just as chemical agents produce changes which can be used for particular purposes, words combine with other words and structures in texts to produce particular meanings. To understand academic language in its fullest sense, EAP teachers and students therefore need to understand how grammar, vocabulary, and phonology combine in texts to create meanings. Analyses of grammar and vocabulary may be a useful starting point, but EAP materials need to go beyond discrete items in order to focus on meaning. To arrive at meaning, an examination of the major characteristics of academic language is a logical starting point.

Characteristics of academic language

Academic language, including the language of both written texts (such as textbooks, essays, and dissertations) and spoken texts (for example lectures and presentations), has a number of characteristics and tendencies. Chapter 1 discusses the global nature of academic discourse identified by Biber et al. (Biber et al.1999: 16). The work of Biber and others has greatly illuminated teachers' and researchers' understanding of academic language, particularly written genres, and is referred to throughout this chapter.

As such, academic language has much in common with the language in other contexts, and as Carter and McCarthy have pointed out with regard to grammar, 'there are no special structures which are unique to academic English and never found elsewhere' (Carter and McCarthy 2006: 267). The passive voice provides a useful illustration of this: almost 25% of all finite verbs occur in the passive in written academic texts, compared with about 15% in journalistic writing and only 2% in conversation (Biber et al 1999: 476). This analysis, based on corpora of 40 million words, shows that the difference in the distribution of the passive across different genres and contexts is essentially one of frequency.

Academic language in context

There are of course further differences, such as in style and register, and an inescapable reality of academic discourse is its complexity. The following text is an abstract to a journal article and illustrates many of the characteristics of academic language, notably its complexity.

> This paper links changing global coffee markets to opportunities and vulnerabilities for sustaining small-scale farmer livelihoods in northern Nicaragua. Changing governance structures, corporate concentration, oversupply, interchangeable commodity grade beans, and low farm gate prices characterize the crisis in conventional coffee markets. In contrast, certified Fair Trade and organic are two alternative forms of specialty coffee trade and production that may offer opportunities for small-scale producers. A research team surveyed 228 farmers to measure the impact of sales on organic and Fair Trade markets. The results suggest that participation in organic and Fair Trade networks reduces farmers' livelihood vulnerability.

(Bacon, 2005: 497–511)

A major reason for the complexity of this text is its density, which results from its genre. As an abstract to a journal article, with a strict word limit (in this case 100 words), the text needs to pack in a great deal of information. As highly conventional genres written for specialist audiences, research article abstracts typically include most or all of the following information within their strict word count:

- background to the research
- rationale (i.e. the reason for the research)
- aims of the research and the text (i.e. the whole article)
- research methodology
- main findings
- main implications and conclusions.

Complex noun phrases

The only way to express this amount of conceptual information so concisely is to use complex noun phrases. In fact, most of the abstract is made up of noun phrases, which is where the complexity in the text lies. Noun phrases are analyzed in greater detail later in this chapter. The term 'noun phrase' is used throughout this book; the alternative term 'nominal group' is used in Hallidayan grammar and SFL (e.g. Halliday 1994). If the information in the text was instead delivered in an oral presentation, the likely result would use far more words, and more (shorter) sentences rather than the dense noun phrases leading to longer sentences in the abstract. It would also probably take considerably longer to present the same information than the time taken to read the abstract aloud. A presenter may choose to use rhetorical questions such as 'What do these results mean?' which they then go on to answer. In the abstract, no question forms are used. Academic texts have about 500 questions per million words, while conversation has almost 50 times that number (Biber et al. 1999: 211). Abstracts are not written to be read aloud; if they are read aloud they present major challenges in comprehension due to their density, i.e. dense use of noun phrases.

Characteristics and examples of academic language

Using examples from this text, Table 4.1 on the next page illustrates some of the major tendencies of academic language, based on the work of Biber et al. (Biber et al. 1999: 23–4; 166; 211; 835; 896ff).

Biber et al.'s account of the major tendencies in academic writing is a useful guide, but should not be seen as definitive or prescriptive. Their work has limitations. For instance, one shortcoming can be illustrated by the acceptability of contractions in some disciplines, such as philosophy, and the widespread use of 'I' and 'we' in many disciplines. Also, the corpus texts used in Biber et al.'s 1999 book are all published book extracts and research articles, so they exclude student writing and many other genres, such as conference abstracts.

This analysis based on the abstract on coffee illustrates most of the tendencies of academic writing identified by Biber et al. The complexity of the text requires relatively slow, careful reading, though the experienced academic reader will have learned how to read a large number of abstracts quickly in order to fulfil their purpose for reading. This purpose is typically not so much to assimilate the details of each abstract but, based on the information in the abstract, to determine the

Characteristics	Examples (Commentary)
Written, carefully planned, edited by author(s) and external editor(s) and revised/redrafted	(The text is clearly carefully planned, crafted and redrafted, and edited)
Based around sentences	(The whole text is made up of complete sentences)
Grammatically complete; low instance of error; long sentences, complex structures, especially noun phrases	'Changing governance structures, corporate concentration, oversupply, interchangeable commodity grade beans, and low farm gate prices characterize the crisis in conventional coffee markets'.
Morphologically complex vocabulary items	'interchangeable' (i.e. **prefix** *inter* + lexical root *change* + **suffix** *able*)
Author mostly does not refer to themselves	'This paper' (Not: 'I'/'We')
Non-interactive	'The results suggest that ...' (Not: 'See the results'/'Please refer to the results')
No contractions: full forms are virtually the only choices in academic prose	(Only full forms are used)
A strong given → new pattern	'This paper (*given/known information*) links changing global coffee markets to opportunities and vulnerabilities for sustaining small-scale farmer livelihoods in northern Nicaragua.' (*new information*)
Clauses can be adapted to fit the requirements of communication, e.g. through word order; the passive; existential *there*; clefting	(There are no examples of these phenomena in the text, as they are associated with argument and presentation of information; the abstract sticks to straightforward subject–verb–object (SVO)/subject–verb–complement (SVC) sentence patterns)
The clauses fit with the context, build a coherent text, and ease the processing for the receiver	'In contrast' (This discourse marker signposts new, contrasting information concisely)

Table 4.1   Characteristics of academic language

suitability of the article for their purpose. This purpose may be to read the full article, or parts of it, in order to develop their knowledge and possibly cite material from it in their own work.

It is important to note that while academic language clearly has a significant amount of complexity, this complexity lies not so much in sentence structure as in the structure of noun phrases. Research by Biber and Gray (2010) has identified the main areas of complexity, and relative simplicity, in academic language. Table 4.2 presents the main findings of their research.

Characteristic	Examples and explanation
Complexity and elaboration of phrases (especially noun phrases) rather than clauses	Sentence patterns are relatively straightforward, e.g. following an SVO or SVC pattern. There are notably relatively few subordinate clauses in academic writing compared with conversation. In contrast, noun phrases are complex and elaborate, as in the following example which contains multiple prepositional phrase **postmodifiers:** 'This may indeed be part of the reason for the statistical link between schizophrenia and membership in the lower socioeconomic classes.' (Example from Biber and Gray 2010: 7).
Explicitness in terms of referents in the text	Academic discourse has to be explicit in meaning, e.g. when referring to places and events (unlike conversation, which uses referents such as 'here'). However, nominalizations mean reduced explicitness, e.g. someone who manages hazardous waste → hazardous waste is managed → hazardous waste management (Example from Biber and Gray 2010: 11). Also, frequent use of prepositional phrases as postmodifiers of noun phrases means that time references are implicit rather than explicit. With **relative clauses**, time references are explicit (see example on page 98).
Tension between clarity and economy	Academic writers need to make their intended meanings clear, but they have limited space (i.e. word limits) to do so; also, expert academic readers tolerate a high level of implicitness (Biber and Gray 2010: 19).

Table 4.2   Biber and Gray's (2010) analysis of complexity, elaboration, and explicitness in academic writing

The tendencies of academic language illustrated in Tables 4.1 and 4.2 pose significant challenges for the EAP student. These challenges are discussed in an integrated way through the relevant sections in this chapter.

The following section examines vocabulary in academic texts, followed by grammar, which leads to a discussion of how vocabulary and grammar are closely connected and how they both contribute to style.

Vocabulary and grammar in academic texts

There are various characteristics associated with vocabulary and grammar in academic texts. Table 4.3 shows some of the characteristics of vocabulary identified by Biber et al. (1999: 58).

Characteristic	Examples and (explanation)
Multiple derivational affixes	'industrialization' (i.e. 'industry' + *ial* + *iz* + *ation*, giving three suffixes and four **morphemes**; the term is an abstract concept referring to the process of industry becoming more important in the economy)
Adjacent placing of words in longer structures	'changing global coffee markets ' (This sequence can be paraphrased as: 'markets' for coffee which are global and changing'— unlike many languages, the form of the words does not change according to their position in the structure)
Natural grouping into lexical bundles, defined as non-structural sequences of three or more words which occur at least ten times per million words of academic text (Biber et al.1999: 990)	'in the' + 'case'/'absence'/'form'/'presence'/ 'number'/'process'/'study' (These are frequent examples with a pattern based around 'in the X'; there are 17 different variations in the Biber et al. corpus)

Table 4.3   Characteristics of vocabulary in academic texts

Table 4.3 gives a useful insight into vocabulary in academic texts. Further aspects of vocabulary are discussed in this section.

Lexical and function words

In most grammatical analyses, words are divided into two types. Lexical words, also known as content words, include the four major **word classes** of nouns, verbs, adjectives, and adverbs. **Function words**, also known as grammatical words, comprise the remaining word classes (also known as parts of speech):

- non-lexical verbs (i.e. the primary auxiliaries *be, have* and *do*)
- modal auxiliary verbs (for example *may* and *will*)
- coordinators (i.e. *and, but, or, neither/nor*)
- subordinators (for example *if, because, when*)
- pronouns (for example *he, she, it, whose, which*)
- prepositions (for example *with, due to, in spite of, in the light of*)
- determiners (i.e. articles, demonstratives, quantifiers, possessives, numbers, fractions, percentages, and numerals)
- adverb particles (i.e. the dependent parts of phrasal verbs like *take off/on/out/in/ away*)
- other word classes and items including: *it/there*; *not*; the infinitive marker *to*; relative pronouns and adverbs; numerals (when not used as determiners); and semi-determiners (i.e. the four pairings *same, other; former, latter; last, next; certain, such*)

Interestingly, in frequency terms the proportion in academic texts of each type of word is virtually half, based on an analysis (de Chazal, 2010c) of the frequency information throughout *The Longman Grammar of Spoken and Written English*, summarized in Table 4.4.

Lexical words (51%)	Function words (49%)
Nouns 30%	Prepositions 13.8%
Adjectives 9%	Determiners 9.3%
Verbs 8%	Primary auxiliaries 5.8%
Adverbs 4%	Pronouns 3.5%
	Coordinators 3.7%
	Modal auxiliaries 1.5%
	Subordinators 1.2%
	Adverb particles 0.3%
	Other* 10%

* 'Other' includes: relativizers, i.e. relative pronouns and relative adverbs (1%), other *wh-* words, 'that', existential 'there' (0.25%), 'not' (0.35%), infinitive marker 'to', numerals (2.5%), semi-determiners (0.75%).

Table 4.4   Frequency of word classes in written academic texts

What this analysis clearly shows is the extreme prevalence of nouns in written academic texts, almost one word in three. By comparison, all verbs, including lexical, primary, and modal verbs, account for less than one word in six. In other words, there are three to four nouns for every lexical verb (Biber et al. 1999: 65). Even adjectives are slightly more frequent than lexical verbs. The analysis also shows that, for all their importance in conveying meaning, the four classes of lexical words barely outnumber function words. Of the latter, prepositions are particularly important, as are determiners. The high frequency of nouns, adjectives, prepositions, and determiners in academic texts is easily explained: they make up the bulk of most noun phrases, which in turn make up the bulk of most academic texts.

Analyzing word classes in academic texts: the case of nouns

Given the very high frequency of nouns in academic texts, it is worthwhile to examine them in some detail. It is beyond the scope of this book to analyze all the word classes and phrases in such detail. The analyses of nouns and noun phrases in this chapter serve to illustrate the importance of these structures in conveying meaning in academic texts. The frequency of nouns can be explained partly by their availability, i.e. the vast number of nouns which can potentially be used, as well as their scope in referring to the extremely wide range of physical entities and abstract concepts which are discussed in academic contexts.

High-frequency nouns

A further reason for the frequency of nouns in general is that certain nouns are commonly used. For example, the following nouns ending in *-tion* occur at least 200 times per million words, which is considered quite frequent, in the *Longman Grammar of Spoken and Written English* (LSWE) corpus:

action, addition, application, association, communication, concentration, direction, distribution, education, equation, examination, formation, infection, information, instruction, operation, organization, population, production, reaction, relation, situation, variation

(Biber et al.1999: 324)

For the EAP teacher and student, items such as these high-frequency words represent language that is useful, productive, and generative. Although corpus analysis such as that of Biber et al. can usefully inform the selection of items like this, it is advisable for students to encounter the items naturally in context. Students can develop their vocabulary in this way through extensive exposure to listening and reading texts. Table 4.5 gives an indication of the amount of time needed to achieve this.

Occurrences per million words	Speech: occurs once every	Writing: occurs once every
1,000	8.5 minutes	2.5 pages
200	42.5 minutes	12 pages
100	85 minutes	25 pages
40	200 minutes	60 pages
20	400 minutes	125 pages
10	800 minutes	250 pages

Table 4.5   Corpus-informed frequency of vocabulary items in spoken and written texts (Biber et al. 1999: 39)

Table 4.5 indicates that any of the above *-tion* words, as examples of items which occur at least 200 times per million words, will in spoken texts occur on average every 42 minutes (or less, depending on their actual frequency above the 200 times per million band). Thus in a lecture, students could expect to hear each of these two dozen *-tion* words about once. Obviously a larger sample is needed to be representative. For the linguist and discourse analyst this is where large corpora come in; depending on the topic, any of the words (for example *equation*) could occur far more frequently, but a large and balanced corpus can average out any unusual (for example discipline-specific) variations. For EAP teachers and students, using and engaging with extensive texts should result in effective development of items such as the set of *-tion* nouns above.

Such corpus-informed studies are indicative rather than comprehensive; to be comprehensive they take up an enormous amount of space; the *Longman Grammar of Spoken and Written English*, for instance, runs to over 1,200 pages, yet at that extent cannot give a comprehensive account of all academic language including vocabulary.

Core, academic, and technical vocabulary

Academic texts typically yield vocabulary that is 'core', i.e. frequent and wide-ranging, 'academic', i.e. associated with a broad range of academic contexts, and 'technical', i.e. subject-specific. Academic vocabulary is sometimes known as 'semi-technical' or 'sub-technical' vocabulary. These terms and categories are not absolute, and there is inevitably overlap between categories depending on the definitions used. Core vocabulary is often taken to mean the 2,000 most frequent words, so other items are of necessity less frequent. This means that some vocabulary items which seem academic, for example 'argument' may be on the list of core words, and therefore not on a list of academic words. A fourth category is also sometimes recognized, that of the low-frequency words (Coxhead and Nation 2001: 252). This category acknowledges the large number of vocabulary items in English, most of which are rarely encountered in any given text.

In terms of quantity, the bulk of academic texts are typically made up of core words; regardless of the discipline and subject matter these typically comprise about 70–80% of the words. Quantitatively, the remaining words are normally split roughly between academic and technical vocabulary. Estimates for the coverage of words in texts have become more accurate since the emergence of corpora, and now converge on the following proportions:

The 100 most frequent words make up about 45% of the words in most texts
The 3,000 most frequent make up 84%–85%
The 7,500 most frequent make up 92%–93%

(Rundell 2011)

Rundell interprets these statistics as follows: 'Most of the words in a <u>language</u> are rare. Most of the words in a <u>text</u> are common.' (Rundell 2011). This means that in a language such as English which contains many hundreds of thousands of words, the majority of words (if picked at random from a large dictionary) are infrequent in any given text. In contrast, in most texts, the majority of words in that text occur frequently. Nation (2006) estimates that a learner needs about 9,000 words to gain 98% coverage of a text such as a novel.

Form, function, and meaning

When interpreting a text (in reading and listening) and constructing a text (in writing and speaking), three starting-points can be identified: form, function, and meaning. These ideas go back to the work of Jesperson (1924), who argued in his article *Parts of Speech* (in Aarts, Denison, Keize, and Popova 2004: 183), that despite difficulties, 'everything should be kept in view, form, function and meaning'. This principle has been developed into learning materials which offer these three as possible starting-points in student academic writing (de Chazal 2007: 40-41). Form refers to the structure of the language, including grammar and vocabulary; examples could be single words or phrases such as noun phrases. Function refers to its grammatical function in the clause or sentence, for example subject, adverbial. Meaning simply refers to the intended meaning of this language.

To take an example from the text on coffee, the language item 'in northern Nicaragua' can be approached from any of these three starting-points. It appears at the end of the first sentence:

'This paper links changing global coffee markets to opportunities and vulnerabilities for sustaining small-scale farmer livelihoods in northern Nicaragua.'

In terms of its form, this is a prepositional phrase beginning with the frequent preposition 'in', followed by its complement 'northern Nicaragua'. In itself, the form is necessary to understand the language in its context, but not sufficient. In terms of its function, i.e. its grammatical function in the sentence, it functions as an adverbial; prepositional phrases are the most frequent adverbial structure (Biber et al. 1999: 768). In terms of meaning, it expresses the notional meaning of place or location. Taken together, all three analyses contribute to the meaning of the language item in its context.

Words, phrases, and clause elements

While a text could be analyzed at word level (for example a determiner then a noun followed by a verb) this is not particularly meaningful or useful, and does not reflect how proficient readers actually read. Words combine to form phrases, which are types of structures. The five major phrases in English are noun phrases, verb phrases, adjective phrases, adverb phrases, and prepositional phrases. A comprehensive description of each of these is beyond the scope of this book, so instead the discussion is limited to noun phrases, in the following section. This description may be seen as a sample or representative language analysis. At sentence level, EAP teachers and students can usefully focus on functional units, i.e. clause elements. These are the functional units which make up a sentence, namely subject, verb, object, adverbial, and complement. This form/function interface is complex; to give an example, the subject in a sentence (a functional unit) is often a noun phrase (a formal, or structural, unit), but subjects can be realized by other structures such as *-ing* forms. Noun phrases, meanwhile, do not only function as subjects in a sentence: they are also frequently used as objects and complements, and as parts of larger structures. In short, there is no one-to-one relation between form and function.

For further information on these grammatical areas of phrases and clause elements, it is useful to consult a language reference resource such as that in *Oxford EAP Intermediate/B1+* (de Chazal and Rogers 2013: 176-185), which is aimed primarily at EAP students, or the *Cambridge Grammar of English* (Carter and McCarthy 2006: 486-502), which is aimed primarily at English language teachers and offers a far more comprehensive analysis. For more advanced study, EAP teachers could consult the seminal *Comprehensive Grammar of the English Language* (Quirk, Greenbaum, Leech, and Svartvik, 1985) and the *Longman Grammar of Spoken and Written English* (Biber, Johansson, Leech, Conrad, and Finegan 1999).

The main purposes of studying forms (such as noun phrases) and functional units like clause elements are, from the perspective of the EAP teacher, to be able to present and teach them; and from that of the student, to effectively and accurately decode the meaning (in the texts that they read and listen to) and construct language (in the texts they read and write).

Noun phrases and nominalization

Nominalization refers to the process of forming a noun from a different word class, or forming a noun phrase from a clause (Crystal 2003: 314). In the following example, the clauses are built round the verbs 'suggest', 'participate', and 'make':

'The results suggest that wherever people participate in organic and Fair Trade networks, this can make farmers' livelihoods less vulnerable.'

The writers of the abstract on coffee (see page 85) use nominalized forms instead:

'The results suggest that participation in organic and Fair Trade networks reduces farmers' livelihood vulnerability.'

In the second (nominalized) version, the meanings associated with 'participation' and 'vulnerability' are expressed as nouns, rather than as a verb ('participate') and an adjective ('vulnerable') respectively as in the first (clausal) version. Nominalization is also associated with density of meaning and conciseness of expression, which explains why the second version contains 15 words against the 20 words of the first. To put it another way, the clausal version in this pair of examples uses a third more words than the nominalized version. If this ratio were extrapolated from one sentence to all five sentences in the abstract, the word count of the abstract would lengthen from about 100 words to about 130. This means that the writer of the abstract would not be able to express all the meanings of the published (heavily nominalized) version if they used a more clausal style. Nominalized forms are extremely prevalent in longer noun phrases, which are analyzed below.

EAP teacher competences

Chapter 2 looks at teacher competences, and the third such competence, 'academic discourse', states that an EAP teacher 'will have a high level of systemic language knowledge including knowledge of discourse analysis' (BALEAP 2008). These competences are then described in more detail, which includes the following competences:

Knowledge and understanding of:

discourse features and sub-technical vocabulary which would allow teachers to read and make sense of texts without being subject specialists:

- grammar and syntax at the level of phrase, clause and sentence
- discourse features beyond the sentence
- cohesion and coherence
- semantics and pragmatics
- approaches to text classification, for example theories of genre and text type
- Ability to:apply theories of text and discourse analysis to course organization, materials selection and development, and assessment.

(BALEAP 2008: 5)

This EAP teacher's competence description underlines the importance of being able to analyze academic discourse. The most important formal components in academic texts are noun phrases. The following section offers an analysis of noun phrases in two sample texts.

Analyzing complex noun phrases in an abstract

In order to illustrate the importance of noun phrases in academic texts, it is useful to analyze a sample text and highlight the noun phrases. The following analysis is based on the abstract on coffee on page 85 with the noun phrases underlined:

This paper links changing global coffee markets to opportunities and vulnerabilities for sustaining small-scale farmer livelihoods in northern Nicaragua. Changing governance structures, corporate concentration, oversupply, interchangeable commodity grade beans, and low farm gate prices characterize the crisis in conventional coffee markets. In contrast, certified Fair Trade and organic are two alternative forms of specialty coffee trade and production that may offer opportunities for small-scale producers. A research team surveyed 228 farmers to measure the impact of sales on organic and Fair Trade markets. The results suggest that participation in organic and Fair Trade networks reduces farmers' livelihood vulnerability.

(Bacon, C. 2005: 497)

This analysis shows at a glance how most of the text is made up of noun phrases: about 85%. Clearly, if these are removed, there are very few words remaining, mainly verbs, and very little recoverable meaning. Most of the meaning, therefore, is expressed through noun phrases. It should be noted that other texts, for instance the discussions in the body of this article on coffee, are likely to be less dense, and contain more prevalent and varied verb phrases.

Patterns in noun phrase structures

These noun phrases follow several frequently used patterns. All noun phrases contain a head noun: this is the noun around which the rest of the noun phrase structure can be built. Whenever a noun phrase is substituted for a pronoun (which takes the place of the whole noun phrase), the pronoun is selected on the basis of the head noun. For example, in the noun phrase 'changing global coffee markets', depending on its position in the sentence as subject or object, the pronoun can be 'they', 'them', or 'these' (but not 'it'). Also, the possessive determiner in this case would be 'their' (not 'its').

Typically, a noun phrase starts with a determiner where necessary, and can include words before the head noun (known as **premodifiers**) and words after (**postmodifiers**). Based on these categories, Table 4.6 analyzes selected noun phrases from the text on coffee.

Determiner	Premodification	Head noun	Postmodification
This		paper	
	changing global coffee	markets	
		opportunities and vulnerabilities	for sustaining small-scale farmer livelihoods
	interchangeable commodity grade	beans	
	low farm gate	prices	
the		crisis	in conventional coffee markets
two	alternative	forms	of speciality coffee trade and production that may offer opportunities for small-scale production
A	research	team	
228		farmers	
the		impact	of sales
		participation	in organic and Fair Trade networks
farmers'	livelihood	vulnerability	

Table 4.6   Analysis of selected noun phrases in an abstract

Analyzing noun phrases in visual form, as in Table 4.6, illustrates the opportunities for creativity and the choices made by the writer. Just one of the 12 noun phrases in this sample makes use of all the possibilities, i.e. determiner, premodification, and postmodification. The patterns to emerge reflect those in corpus analysis of noun phrases. Carter and McCarthy (2006: 324) analyze noun phrases slightly differently, with a division of postmodifiers (which they call 'post-head') into complements and postmodifiers.

Frequency of modification types in noun phrases

Based on analyses by Biber et al. (1999: 578 and 589), 42% of noun phrases in academic written texts are the 'bare' noun with or without a determiner, for example 'This paper'. The remainder are modified. Table 4.7 gives the frequencies and types of premodifier, using examples from the text on coffee analyzed in Table 4.6.

Types of modification	
No modifier: 42%	This **paper**
Premodifier: 26%	*changing global coffee* **markets**
Postmodifier: 21%	the **crisis** *in conventional coffee markets*
Both pre- and post-: 11%	two *alternative* **forms** *of speciality coffee trade*
Types of premodifier	
Noun: 29%	A *research* **team**
-ed adjective: 4%	*certified* Fair Trade
-ing adjective: 3%	*changing* global coffee **markets**
Common adjective: 64%	changing *global* coffee **markets**

Table 4.7   Frequencies of types of noun phrase modification with examples

The head nouns are given in **bold**, and types of pre- and postmodifier are italicized in the table. Even such a short text (100 words) yields examples of all the types of noun phrase modification identified by Biber et al. (1999: 578 and 589). The next section analyzes an academic text of a more narrative nature in order to provide a contrast with the dense abstract analyzed above.

Analyzing complex noun phrases in a textbook

The following text is taken from the opening chapter of a medicine textbook. It aims to give background information to set the scene for the rest of the book.

> One of the earliest pioneers of child public health, Edward Jenner (1749–1823), a Gloucester country physician, made the important observation that milkmaids who had contracted cowpox seemed to be immune from catching smallpox. Jenner inoculated a small boy, James Phepps, with cowpox material by scratching it onto his arm, and then proceeded to test his hypothesis by inoculating him with smallpox. The discovery that James was indeed protected from smallpox heralded the era of vaccination and the later development of what remains one of most successful preventative measures available to the medical profession.
>
> (Blair, Stewart-Brown, Waterston and Crowther 2010)

In comparison with the abstract on coffee, this text appears 'lighter', i.e. less dense. Unlike the abstract, it conveys its message effectively when read aloud. However, an analysis of the noun phrases in the text reveals that the text is also complex, as Table 4.8 shows.

Determiner	Premodification	Head noun	Postmodification
One of the	earliest	pioneers	of child public health, Edward Jenner (1749–1823), a Gloucestershire country physician
		milkmaids	who had contracted cowpox
a	small	boy	James Phepps
his		arm	
		him	
the		discovery	that James was indeed protected from smallpox
		vaccination	
the	later	development	of what remains one of the most successful preventative measures available to the medical profession

Table 4.8   Analysis of selected noun phrases in a textbook extract

Two of the noun phrases in the table are bare, i.e. unmodified: the pronoun 'him', and the uncountable noun 'vaccination'. The other noun phrases are more complex, with examples of defining relative clauses and, in the final example, a postmodifying structure containing both a prepositional phrase ('of what remains …') and an ellipted relative clause ('available …' i.e. 'which are available'). Also, there are examples of apposition, which is discussed below.

Using Biber et al's analysis of the frequency of postmodifiers (Biber et al. 1999: 606, 611, 619), Table 4.9 gives examples from the text on child health. There are no examples of non-finite relative clauses in this text, hence the blank lines in those sections.

Types of postmodifier	Examples from textbook extract
Prepositional phrases: 77%	the later **development** *of what remains one of the most successful preventative measures available to the medical profession*
Relative clauses: 12%, of which defining: 85%; non-defining: 15% (which, that, who, zero, where, whose*, whom, when, why)	**milkmaids** *who had contracted cowpox* one of the most successful preventative **measures** *available to the medical profession*
-ing clauses: 3%	–
-ed clauses: 3.5%	–
to- clauses: 1%	–
Appositives: 3.5%	One of the earliest pioneers of child public **health**, *Edward Jenner (1749–1823), a Gloucestershire country physician*

* 'whose': 75% of occurrences modify an inanimate head noun, for example 'Bilkent University in Ankara, whose staff have pioneered EAP teaching throughout Turkey and beyond'.

Table 4.9   Types and frequency of noun phrase postmodifying structures with examples

Once again, this table illustrates the complex nature of noun phrases in English, but also the usefulness of analyzing them to inform EAP syllabuses and materials.

Apposition

The example in the last row of the table illustrates how contextual information can be added through **apposition.** In apposition, a second noun phrase is added directly after the head noun, separated by a comma. The appositive, i.e. the second noun phrase, refers to the same entity as the head noun and adds identifying information to it. With appositives, all parts of the noun phrase, i.e. any premodification, the head, and the appositive, are analyzed as a single noun phrase. In this way, the appositive is classed as a postmodifier.

This example uses three appositives to give the pioneer's name, the dates of his life, and his provenance and profession. Another example of apposition in the text is: 'a small boy, James Phepps'. When reading appositives in texts, students need to understand that the comma does not signal a list. It needs to be emphasized that the two parts of the noun phrase refer to the same thing. In this example, the small boy mentioned is called James Phepps, and James Phepps is not a new person in a list.

Part of the opening noun phrase in the text is the sequence 'child public health' which occurs in the sequence 'One of the earliest pioneers of child public health, Edward Jenner (1749–1823), a Gloucestershire country physician'. This is an example of a noun phrase within a noun phrase. Like a Russian doll in structure, nestings of noun phrases within another noun phrase are very frequent in academic texts. The noun phrase 'child public health' is an example of the head noun being modified by both an adjective ('public') and a noun ('child'). There are also several examples of noun + noun structures in the text, for example 'country physician', and 'cowpox material'. Noun + noun structures present particular challenges for EAP students.

Discontinuity

For students, another challenge is posed by noun phrases when they become separated from the verbs they control. This has been termed 'discontinuity' (de Chazal 2010a: 96). Two reasons for this are apposition and postmodification, as in the following examples from the Edward Jenner text in which the <u>head nouns</u> are underlined and the **main verbs** they control are in bold:

One of the earliest <u>pioneers</u> of child public health, Edward Jenner (1749–1823), a Gloucester country physician, **made** the important observation that <u>milkmaids</u> who had contracted cowpox **seemed to be** immune from catching smallpox. <u>Jenner</u> **inoculated** a small boy, James Phepps, with cowpox material by scratching it onto his arm, and then **proceeded to test** his hypothesis by inoculating him with smallpox. The <u>discovery</u> that James was indeed protected from smallpox **heralded** the era of vaccination and the later development of what remains one of most successful preventative measures available to the medical profession.

Analyzed in this way, the text shows how the reader needs to work out the grammatical structures of the noun phrases in the text in order to correctly interpret the meanings expressed. In the first sentence, for instance, both modification ('of child public health') and apposition ('Edward Jenner (1749–1823), a Gloucester country physician') come between the head noun and its verb.

EAP teachers can help their students notice and deal with challenging language such as discontinuity through inclusion in EAP materials. One useful solution to the challenge is to read the text aloud: a speaker is likely to introduce variations in pitch and slight pauses at clause or phrase boundaries such as 'cowpox' and 'seemed'.

Noun + noun modification

The noun + noun pattern, i.e. a head noun premodified by a noun, is very frequent in academic texts. This phenomenon presents two challenges for EAP students: how to construct this pattern when writing/speaking; and how to understand it when reading/listening. In writing/speaking, certain combinations will work, while others will not. For instance, it is difficult to make sense of 'coat lab' (a lab where coats are researched?) while 'lab coat' is more familiar (a coat worn in a lab, i.e. a white coat). If students do not know this phrase, they may be able to come up with it, or they may produce a less concise phrase such as 'a coat for wearing in a lab'. In reading/listening, students have to reconstruct the 'missing' meaning between the two nouns. This (re)construction of meaning involves producing language (grammar and vocabulary) and world knowledge. In the 'lab coat' example, students have to supply extra grammatical and lexical material: 'a coat (which is) worn in a lab'.

It can be quite challenging for students to supply the 'missing meaning' between two nouns in noun + noun combinations. This is because there are a large number of possible meaning relations, as the following examples show:

metal trays: trays _____ metal

lab coats: coats _____ labs

law reports: reports _____ law

university management: management _____ university

government sources: sources _____ government

problem students: students _____ problem

cave man: man _____ cave

A useful task for the EAP student is to reconstruct the phrases. The first, for example, could be 'trays which are/were made of metal' or 'trays made of metal' depending on the context: in the context of an archaeological find the past tense would be more likely, whereas if it is not necessary to specify the time the latter reconstruction would work.

Biber et al. identify fifteen meaning relations in noun + noun combinations, three of which (objective, subjective, and location) are closely related, but with the relationship between the nouns reversed. These are represented in Table 4.10

together with examples. In the table, N_1 refers to the first noun in the phrase, and N_2 to the second noun.

Relation	Explanation	Examples
Composition	N_2 is made from N_1; N_2 consists of N_1	word class, iron supplement
Purpose	N_2 is for the purpose of N_1; N_2 is used for N_1	safety device, extortion plan,
Identity	N_2 has the same referent as N_1 but classifies it in terms of different attributes	consultant cardiologist, member state
Content	N_2 is about N_1; N_2 deals with N_1	currency crisis, success rate
Source	N_2 is from N_1	irrigation water, crop yield
Objective type 1	N_1 is the object of the process described in N_2	egg production, child cruelty
Objective type 2	N_2 is the object of the process described in N_1	discharge water, pilot projects
Subjective type 1	N_1 is the subject of the process described in N_2	eye movement, management buy-out
Subjective type 2	N_2 is the subject of the process described in N_1	labour force
Time	N_2 is found at the time given at N_1	summer conditions, Christmas holiday
Location type 1	N_2 is found or takes place at the location given by N_1	world literature, heart attack
Location type 2	N_1 is found or takes place at the location given by N_2	staff room, theme park
Institution	N_2 identifies an institution for N_1	insurance company, ski club
Partitive	N_2 identifies parts of N_1	family member, rifle butt
Specialization	N_1 identifies an area of specialization for the person or occupation given in N_1	finance director, management consultant

Table 4.10   Noun plus noun relations with examples (adapted from Biber et al. 1999: 590–1)

Patterns following noun phrases

Noun phrases most frequently function in the clause as subject and object. They can also be followed by two frequent types of complement clause: 'that' and 'to'. Table 4.11 gives the most frequent abstract nouns taking such clauses, based on corpus analysis by Biber et al. (1999: 649–652).

Abstract nouns taking 'that'- complement clauses	fact, idea, possibility, doubt, belief, assumption, hope, impression, suggestion, sign, conclusion, claim, ground(s), view, sense, report, notion, hypothesis, observation
Abstract nouns taking 'to' complement clauses	attempt, effort, ability, opportunity, desire, decision, plan, chance, power, right, tendency, failure, capacity, inability, commitment, determination, intention, refusal, willingness

Table 4.11   Complement clauses following abstract nouns

These examples demonstrate the case for EAP teachers presenting and EAP students learning vocabulary items together with their broader grammatical patterns, termed 'colligation' by Hoey (2005: 13).

Organizing vocabulary: academic word lists

In some ways, vocabulary learning in English language teaching (ELT), especially ESP and EAP, has had a curious history. For centuries of language teaching, seemingly decontextualized lists of words prevailed, closely associated with grammar-translation methods and influenced by the teaching of classical languages. The words on these lists were often drawn from the most influential literature of the language; for instance many Latin words were taken from the works of Caesar and English words from the great poets such as Shakespeare. In some respects the works in this literature were the precursors of today's computer-based corpora. While presented in list form, the words on these lists are usually selected from texts. From the mid twentieth century, the focus shifted towards greater utility, with an emphasis in general ELT on high-frequency words used in common topics, functions, and notions. In many ESP contexts, however, a tendency to promote technical vocabulary emerged, with more specific and restricted meanings.

Emerging academic word lists

Meanwhile, since the 1970s and 80s the consensus in EAP has been on general academic vocabulary to serve the widest possible range of disciplines. Tracing a heritage back to 1953 with the publication of West's *General Service List* (West 1953) of the then 2,000 or so most frequent and useful words (which itself was first formulated in 1936), wordlists have made a notable comeback since 2000, when Coxhead's 570-headword *Academic Word List* was published (Coxhead 2000). Such is its success that, although the title of the original article in which it was published was 'A new academic word list', it is widely referred to as '*the* academic word list', abbreviated to AWL. Further academic word lists have since emerged, notably the 930-item *Academic Keyword List* (Paquot 2010: 55ff). What these lists have in common is a general academic focus and a basis in corpora of varying sizes, which are built around authentic academic texts from a representative range of disciplines.

Issues in academic word lists

The basis and usefulness of such lists has been questioned (for example Hyland and Tse 2007). One of Hyland and Tse's arguments is that many words have distinct meanings depending on their context. They offer the examples 'convertible' and 'analysis'. A chemical analysis is different from a linguistic or psychological analysis, for example. Yet arguably there are more similarities than differences. Once the essential meaning of 'analysis' is understood, i.e. 'the detailed study or examination of something in order to understand more about it; the result of the study' (OALD, Hornby/Turnbull 2010: 48), this meaning can then be applied to a wide range of other contexts. Although a chemical analysis is physical, while a linguistic analysis is cognitive, both involve this essential process of detailed study or examination. This essential meaning covers most or all contexts in which the word 'analysis' is used.

Technically, putting texts together and analyzing the language in them has become relatively easy. However, although today's corpora may be compelling, the interpretation of the results they yield needs to be questioned. One undoubted consequence of producing lists of discrete vocabulary items detached from their provenance and context has been a quantitative focus on word-learning which often does not go deeper than the denotative meaning (i.e. the word's given meaning) and simple translation.

One further drawback of some academic word lists, including Coxhead's (2000) *Academic Word List*, is the exclusion of any lexical item which is made up of more than one word. This means the exclusion of, for instance, **prepositional verbs** (for example 'look into', 'be defined as') and complex prepositions (i.e. prepositions comprised of two or more words such as 'due to', 'in line with', 'in the light of'), all of which exist only in these multiword forms.

Criteria for organizing academic vocabulary

Linguistically, including pragmatically, any word is understood most deeply in its original authentic context. For students to learn them effectively, words need to be organized in a principled way. Statistically based organization such as relative frequency in a corpus of texts can be of some benefit to the student, although relative frequency alone is insufficient. An alternative method of organization, alphabetical, works more effectively for reference than acquisition; it is not normal to learn new words in alphabetical order. Thematic association, such as perspectives and research practices, can be more useful, although, by their nature, many academic words require an authentic context to become truly meaningful, and many themes overlap. Organization by discipline is unworkable, as by definition academic words are interdisciplinary. Grammatical organization is a possibility, but given that there are only four lexical word classes (noun, verb, adjective, and adverb), the sub-lists would be very long, and word families would of course be spread across different classes. Coxhead's *Academic Word List* is made up almost entirely of lexical words, plus one or two simple (i.e. one-word) prepositions.

Level

Language level may be an intuitive organizing principle for vocabulary, although determining the level of a word is not particularly straightforward. One reason for this is the tendency for many academic words to have general and specific meanings, for example the word 'capital':

- a city such as London and Tokyo which is normally the seat of government in a country (general meaning, which is frequently used)

- the sum of money which is invested in a business, and the root of capitalism (technical meaning used in areas such as business and politics)

- the form of a letter which starts a sentence and proper noun (widely used technical meaning, useful for language students)

- the top of a column (technical meaning, used in architecture)

- used with 'punishment' and 'offence': involving punishment by death (technical meaning used in law and politics).

With the large number of words that have both general and technical meanings, the general meanings are more frequent, and are therefore more logically placed at lower CEFR levels. In EAP, some or all of the more technical meanings need to be covered, depending on the students' disciplines.

There are online tools which can indicate, though not prescribe, the CEFR level of a word, for example English Profile (<http://www.englishprofile.org>). This tool aims to give examples of language for different CEFR levels, but it does have limitations in the number of words it covers.

Word depth

There are several further possibilities for organizing words, which can help students in different ways. First, they can be graded according to the level of linguistic and cognitive challenge. The word 'heterogeneous', for example, may appear challenging at first sight. At six syllables, it is long and it is therefore potentially challenging to work out its meaning, pronounce, and spell. However, its essential meaning (different in type or other) is perhaps less challenging than might initially appear. A closely related word in its family is the noun 'heterogeneity', which presents a similar profile of challenging versus accessible. At a deeper level, its lexical morpheme *hetero-* turns up in a number of other words including 'heterosexual' and 'heterochromatic'. A knowledge of the deeper parts of these words can help to understand newly encountered words: for example, 'chromatic' essentially means 'connected to colour', enabling the student to arrive at the meaning of 'differently coloured' for 'heterochromatic'. Further examples of 'deeply' related words have been suggested (de Chazal 2008a: 180), such as words containing *tract*, meaning pull or draw : 'contract' (draw together), 'protract' (draw out), 'extract' (pull out), and 'distract' (draw attention away from).

Other organizational categories

Another alternative criterion is the usefulness of a word. This is sometimes known as 'utility'. Assessing a word's usefulness, however, poses difficult questions: according to which criteria? useful for whom? for what purpose? A simple answer might be to use frequency as proxy for usefulness, as they are likely to be related, which goes back to the starting point.

Alternatively, a more conceptual classification could be used, such as concrete/abstract, or cognitive/practical activity. For example, 'evidence' (often concrete) versus 'theory' (abstract). Many words can be both physical/practical and cognitive, such as: 'analysis' (chemical analysis versus linguistic analysis); 'structure' (structure of a building versus structure of an argument); and 'impact' (environmental impact versus emotional impact).

Finally, at a more practical level, wordlists can be organized by topic or activity. Thus words like 'legal', 'economic', 'environmental', etc. can be grouped together as they are all related to academic disciplines or perspectives, and they are all classifying adjectives.

Challenges in organizing vocabulary

What these organizational approaches illustrate is ultimately the slippery nature of vocabulary organization. The only uncontentious system is alphabetical. Yet there is only one main reason to store words in alphabetical order: for easy reference. To be learnable, words need con*text*ualization, which calls for texts. Such texts should be carefully selected, and the approach to vocabulary learning needs to be principled. These principles lie in the current thinking that words exist not in isolation but in **collocation** (i.e. the tendency of certain words to occur frequently together) and colligation with other language on the vocabulary–grammar cline (for example Biber et al. 1999, Wray 2002, Hoey 2005). This text-informed approach is shown to be comprehensive, meaningful, and empowering. Using such an approach liberates EAP practitioners and students from lists, and ensures effective coverage of the lexis that students need to learn.

Academic word lists in context

The obvious way of illustrating the argument for the contextualization of academic vocabulary is to present and analyze the words in an academic text.

Selecting academic words from a text

The text on intelligence (given on pages 344–5) is used here as a sample text to examine academic vocabulary in context. It is also used to illustrate the extended sequence of reading tasks in Chapter 6. The original source of the text is a university textbook on sociology. Thus, it is an authentic academic text, aimed mainly at undergraduate students of any first language studying in English. This text extract has also been used in the EAP coursebook *Oxford EAP B2/Upper-intermediate* (de Chazal and McCarter 2012: 73). During the reading process, a selection of the most important academic words can emerge from the text, for example drawing from the following (based on an activity by de Chazal 2011b):

> specific   genetic   compared   associated   originated   inherited   score nature   nurture   correlate   cognitive   criticize   mathematical social essential   educational   cultural   environmental   European   explain stimulation   situation   socialization   reflect   argument   concept respectively   significantly   capacity   heredity

What connects all these words is that they occur in the text on intelligence given on pages 344–5, and they are all arguably 'academic' words. The 30 words extracted from this text are vital in contributing to the meaning of the text, and could all conceivably occur in texts from any discipline, hence the argument that they are academic. In short, they have a high utility value.

Meaningful organization of academic words

The words above from the text are presented following one of the organizing principles outlined in the section above: alphabetical. People are conditioned to expect alphabetical order to be from left to right, but they are presented here from right to left, i.e. starting with the last letter of the word rather than the first. This unfamiliar alphabetical organization clusters together related types of words, and emphasizes the importance of suffixes and endings which contribute to meaning.

For example, the classifying adjectives appear in adjacent sets:

• specific, genetic

• mathematical, social, essential, educational, cultural, environmental

Similarly, the abstract nouns are placed together, illustrating the frequent noun suffixes *-tion* and *-ity*:

• stimulation, situation, socialization

• capacity, heredity

Most predictably the adverbs are together:

• respectively, significantly

Due to the principled nature of their presentation—contextualized and grouped together—seeing the words presented in this way can greatly assist vocabulary learning.

Analyzing words using an academic vocabulary list

Returning to academic vocabulary wordlists, it is revealing to note that only a fraction of these 30 words appear on the widely used *Academic Wordlist* (AWL). Using the vocabulary analysis tool based on the AWL 'The Compleat Lexical Tutor' (<http://www.lextutor.ca>) which categorizes the words in any text fed in by the user, the 30 items actually fall equally into all five categories, as given in Table 4.12.

Category	Examples from the text on Intelligence
K1 Words (the 1,000 most frequent on West's (1953) service list)	attached, social, explain, situation, nature, respectively
K2 Words (items 1,001–2,000 on West's service list)	reflect, compared, educational, essential, argument, originated
AWL words (items on Coxhead's 570-headword academic word list)	environmental, concept, capacity, significantly, specific, cultural
Off-list words (less frequent items)	cognitive, heredity, mathematical, socialization, criticize, nurture
MED words (medical and technical words)	inherited, correlate, genetic, score, stimulation, European

Table 4.12   *Categorization of academic words in a sample text*

This analysis is interesting for various reasons. It illustrates a number of shortcomings of academic wordlists. It has been established that this set of words is related (because they occur in the same text on the same topic of intelligence), and academic (because they are used to construct meaning in a specific academic discipline—sociology—but are also used in other disciplines). Yet the breakdown into the categories above appears unpredictable and unprincipled in the following ways:

• A highly coherent set of words—the classifying adjectives 'social', 'educational', 'environmental', 'mathematical', and 'genetic'—appear in entirely different categories

• Words from the same family are in different categories: 'heredity' and 'inherited', both derived from 'heir'

• Closely associated words are in far-apart categories: the collocates 'nature' (the category of most frequent words) and 'nurture' (the least frequent)

• Word families which contain verbs related to academic practice are similarly scattered across all the categories: 'explain', 'compare', 'specify', 'criticize', and 'correlate'.

In short, wordlists may have a place in EAP vocabulary learning, but they need to be handled with great caution. Frequency is an extremely important criterion for language selection, but can get in the way of more logical classification, as some of the above examples show. A more emergent approach, which relies on carefully selected texts as sources for vocabulary, offers greater scope for contextualization and principled selection.

Implications for the exclusion of the 2000 most frequent words

One related reason for the shortcomings of some academic word lists, such as the AWL, is their exclusion of the 2000 most frequent words, i.e. those in West's 1953 *General Service List*. In contrast, the *Academic Keyword List* (Paquot 2010) makes the decision to include words from the *General Service List*. Paquot's list includes useful reporting verbs such as aim, *argue, cause, claim, effect,* and *suggest,* which are absent from the AWL (Grainger and Paquot 2009: 194). Grainger and Paquot argue that students' incomplete knowledge of verbs such as these reporting verbs is a 'serious handicap' for learners (ibid.). They go on to emphasize the importance of a detailed description of the use of such words to accompany the word lists, thereby underlining the need for contextualization.

Vocabulary and grammar: academic language

As the previous sections have suggested in their focus on vocabulary and grammar, in reality the two are intricately connected. This section could instead be titled 'Vocabulary + grammar = academic language'. Furthermore, academic language serves to express meaning, notably the meanings associated with essential elements, which are presented in Chapters 3 (in relation to texts) and 5 (in relation to critical thinking).

This section presents one of the four extended analyses of language in this book, the language of cause and effect. These language analyses show that both grammar and vocabulary are needed to construct meaning and express relations (such as cohesive relations) in a text. In pragmatic terms, vocabulary and grammar are inseparable. The latter includes areas such as **hedging** and degrees of certainty. All these areas (and various other areas) are very typical of academic discourse. As Biber et al. explain:

Syntax and lexicon are often treated as independent components of English. Analysis of real texts shows, however, that most syntactic structures tend to have an associated set of words or phrases that are frequently used with them (Biber et al. 1999: 13). As example of this is that the passive tends to be associated with certain verbs. The following verbs occur over 90% of the time in the passive in academic prose, 'be' plus:

> aligned (with), based (on), born, coupled (with), deemed, effected, entitled (to), flattened, inclined, obliged, positioned, situated, stained, subjected (to)

The following occur 70% of the time in the passive in academic prose, 'be' plus:

> approved, associated (with), attributed (to), classified (as), composed (of), confined (to), designed, diagnosed (as), distributed, documented, estimated, extracted, grouped (with), intended, labelled, linked (to/with), located (at/in), plotted, recruited, stored, transferred, viewed
>
> (Biber et al. 1999: 478–9)

Corpus research by Swales (2004a: 5ff) has produced comparable results, showing, for example that the following verbs are highly likely to occur in the passive in academic prose: 'associate', 'attach', 'derive', 'distribute', and 'connect'. Conversely, other verbs rarely occur in the passive, for example 'imply'. Examples such as these show how vocabulary and grammar are mutually informing; a further example is the language of cause and effect.

The language of cause and effect

This section investigates the language used to express cause and effect relations in English. In a text, a single item in isolation could be many things, for example a cause, a problem, a point of comparison, an effect, or simply a one-off statement. To work out what an item means, it needs to be related to something else. One of the most important endeavours in academic contexts is the research and practice of connecting and relating two or more different phenomena.

Cause and effect are very frequent types of connection. Two items may be related as cause and effect, but key questions are: how likely is it that A (the cause) will lead to B (the effect)? Is B the only effect of A? Is A the only cause of B? The answers to these crucial questions are reflected in the language. The language needed to express these connections is presented in Table 4.13. The first section of the table presents language items which express cause → effect meanings, i.e. where a cause is mentioned first, followed by its effects. The second section presents the reverse.

Cause → effect language		
Grammatical category	**Examples**	
Nouns	cause (of) reason (for) source (of)	
Noun phrases	one possible cause of B is A A is a likely reason for B A has had a profound effect on B	
Verbs	Optional auxiliary or adverbial: should may might can is likely/unlikely to typically/arguably frequently/often	Verbs in active voice: cause lead to result in account for bring about produce affect causes leads to etc.
Subordinators	so that so as to	

Adverbials: single adverbs	therefore so accordingly consequently thus hence thereby
Adverbials: prepositional phrases	as a result/as a consequence because of this for this reason/for these reasons
Adverbials: non-finite clauses	(thereby) causing/resulting in/bringing about/producing/creating… Verb in the *-ing* form, e.g. A (=situation/cause A) takes place, *raising* the temperature (=effect B)
Other expressions	which is why/the reason for B which means that which (in turn) may lead to That/This is why
Idiomatic and figurative expressions	(is/may be seen as) a precursor to give rise to pave the way for open the way for lay the foundations of/for

Effect → cause language		
Grammatical category	**Examples**	
Nouns	effect result consequence outcome impact	
Noun phrases	*an unfortunate consequence of* A is B B is *one such effect of* A *a likely result* might be B	
Verbs	Optional adverbial: typically/arguably frequently/often	Verbs in active voice: result(s) from originate as/in/from
	Auxiliary: is/are [adverbial] is/are likely to be can/could be may/might be	Verbs in passive voice: caused by produced by brought about by attributed to

Subordinators	because
	since
	as
	for
	when/if A, (then) B
	due to the fact that
	owing to the fact that
	because of the fact that
	on account of the fact that
Prepositions (complex, i.e. 2+ words; simple, i.e. 1 word)	owing to
	due to
	because of
	as a result of
	as a consequence of
	on account of
	through
Other expressions	which is one effect of A
	That/This is the result of B
	Why? To …

Expressing association	
Verb-based expressions	is associated with
	are involved (with)
	may connect with/to
	may be linked to

Table 4.13   The language of cause and effect

The language of cause and effect is an excellent example of essential elements (in this case expressing causes, effects, and associations) which yield a complex yet definable body of language. This language forms the core of a language resource for EAP students to draw on; it needs to be presented in contextualized form, i.e. in academic texts which express cause and effect relations.

Academic style

Written academic style is often said to be 'formal' (for example Clanchy and Ballard 1981: 74, and 1992, also cited in Jordan 1997: 244). However, it is not particularly accurate or helpful to describe academic texts in this way, as they can vary considerably in their level of formality. Depending on the discipline, genre, audience, and purpose, academic texts can range from formal to quite informal in style. Some researchers, including Swales and Feak (2000: 16–17) point out that academic style is becoming more informal in certain contexts.

Formal and informal style

Certain disciplines, particularly law, are associated with a higher level of formality, as the following example from a popular academic book on law illustrates:

> While lawyers and politicians habitually **venerate its merits**, reformers **bewail its inadequacies**, and sceptics **refute the law's often self-righteous espousal** of justice, liberty, and the rule of law.
>
> (Wacks, R. 2008. *Law: A Very Short Introduction*. Oxford: Oxford University Press: 2)

With language as formal (and flowery) as this, even proficient readers may need to read the sentence more than once to fully understand it. The challenging vocabulary impacts on the reader's understanding of the grammar, for example through an incorrect analysis of the sequence *reformers bewail its inadequacies* as an item in a list rather than one of the coordinated main clauses in the sentence.

In most disciplines however, language like that in bold in the example above would come across as too formal. On the whole, academic texts are neither very formal nor very informal. The following sentence is quite formal for academic text:

> '**Notwithstanding** these benefits, these research teams faced challenges.'

The following example sounds more 'standard':

> '**Despite** this development of tags, it is doubtful whether currently available satellites can accomplish the task.'

In some more **popular academic textbooks**, the style can be slightly more informal, less 'academic', or more literary:

> New York has grown by shedding its past, tearing down old neighborhoods and erecting new ones in their place, usually in a bare-faced struggle for financial gain.
>
> (Zukin, S. 2010. *Naked city: the death and life of authentic urban places*. New York: Oxford University Press: 1–3)

Occasionally, some academic texts can be quite informal and conversational in style, illustrated by the following extract from an academic textbook on visual perception:

> If you lead a sad and uninteresting life you may have this book as bedtime reading; if so, turn off the light and try looking at Figure 0.3 in your dimly lit bedroom. […] How can this be?
>
> (Snowden, R., P. Thompson and T. Troscianko, 2006. *Basic Vision: An Introduction to Visual Perception*. Oxford: Oxford University Press: 5)

This level of informality and textual interactivity is, however, somewhat marked and unusual.

Personal and impersonal styles in stating aims

When stating their aims or signposting their audience through a text, writers can choose to use a personal structure, such as the first person, *I* or *we*, for example:

> 'In this chapter **I focus on** practices involved in harnessing fortune for households; for an example, **we turn to** an event some years ago.'

A major use of *we* is literal, i.e. its use in multi-authored papers.

In a piece of research based on corpus analysis of 1.3 million words, Hyland (2002) finds significant instances of the use of self-mention through 'I' and 'we', in research articles. Hyland concludes that second language (L2) writers are less inclined to use such forms compared with the authors of published research articles. He argues that the use of 'I' and 'we' contributes to the expression of the author's identity and stance (Hyland 2002: 1091–1112).

Many academic texts are written in a more impersonal or 'objective' style which in effect avoids referring to the author(s); an abstract noun is often used instead, for example:

> '**This article analyzes** the geography of innovation in China and India; **The following sections** will argue this is the result of the continued presence of unregulated ivory markets within and near these countries.'

In reality, an article cannot 'analyze' and a section cannot 'argue': it is the authors who are analyzing and arguing, so they are in effect using these nouns to avoid using personal pronouns. It is worth noting that such use of 'objective' style does not necessarily mean that the content itself is objective; the texts are still likely to express material that is subjective.

Alternatively, the structures *it* and *there* can be used in impersonal or 'objective' style, for example:

> '**There is** no desire to share this information with others.'

This example means that 'people have no desire to share this information with others', but the author wants to avoid referring to people. Similarly, in the example:

> '**It is estimated that** daily inbound traffic would be reduced by 5 percent in New York if a toll …,'

the authors at this point avoid saying who estimated this.

Both impersonal and personal structures can be used in the same text, for example:

> '**This article analyzes** the geography of innovation in China and India. Using a tailor-made panel database for regions in these two countries, **we show that** both countries exhibit increasingly strong polarization of innovative capacity in a limited number of urban areas.'

Gender

A further aspect of academic style is the issue of gender. From a grammatical perspective, gender is a less important category in English than many other languages, as pointed out by Biber et al. (1999: 312). In their corpus analysis of the grammatical and lexical expression of gender, Biber et al. argue that gender 'is not a simple reflection of reality; rather it is to some extent a matter of convention and speaker choice and special strategies may be used to avoid gender-specific reference at all' (Biber et al.1999: 312). In other words, speakers and writers have choices. These choices include gender-specific and dual gender pronoun reference, given by Biber et al. (1999: 317) as follows:

- 'he or she' (subject), 'his or her' (possessive), and 'him or her' (object)
- 'he/she' (subject), 'his/her' (possessive), and 'him/her' (object)
- 'they' (subject), 'their' (possessive), and 'them' (object)

The first two paired choices are relatively common in academic texts (and rare in other texts), while the third option ('they', 'their', 'them') is used less, although its use is probably increasing and is the one chosen in this handbook. EAP teachers can present these forms as possibilities to use, which their students can draw from as they develop their own style and voice as writers.

Selection of language: criteria and emergence

A key question to ask when selecting language for the EAP learning context is 'What is the source of the language?' As language does not meaningfully exist in a vacuum, it has a context and a source. If the source is generally a useful one for a particular class of EAP students, or an individual EAP student, then the language in that source is potentially worth studying. In planning a syllabus for language study, language needs to be selected using criteria.

Criteria for selecting vocabulary

There are a number of approaches to the selection of language. In terms of vocabulary, the following are well-established criteria for selection:

- frequency
- familiarity
- utility
- range

The first criterion, frequency, is important simply because the most frequent words make up a larger percentage of texts, and students are more likely to encounter frequent words than infrequent ones. Helpfully, the five major learner's dictionaries published in the UK all give information on the frequency of different words (including different word classes of the same word, for example 'table' (noun) and 'table' (verb); the latter word class is considerably less frequent). These dictionaries are:

- *Oxford Advanced Learner's Dictionary* (first published in 1948)
- *Longman Dictionary of Contemporary English* (first published in 1978)
- *Collins COBUILD Advanced Dictionary* (first published in 1987)
- *«Cambridge Advanced Learner's Dictionary* (first published as *Cambridge International Dictionary of English* in 1995)
- *Macmillan English Dictionary for Advanced Learners* (first published in 2002)

All these dictionaries have had multiple editions to update their content.

The word 'table' as a noun is very frequent: it is in the most frequent 1,000 words in West's *General Service List of English Words* (1953). More recent and comprehensive information on word frequencies is given in Leech (2001). This information is drawn from their research based on the British National Corpus.

In terms of familiarity, the word 'table' is very familiar in nearly all cultures (except of course those that do not have tables). The word 'table' is also a useful word in many everyday contexts such as homes and classrooms ('Where's the dictionary?' 'It's on the table'). Finally, in an EAP context it has good range, as it can be used in specific contexts such as textbooks ('Table 4.2 illustrates …'), and certain disciplines such as geography which are concerned with the 'water table'. As a result, the word 'table' scores highly on all four selection criteria, and, along with many other such words, is therefore a good candidate for a language syllabus. As for other words which are less frequent/familiar/useful and with more limited range, these need to be weighed up on a case-by-case basis.

Criteria for selecting grammar

As for grammatical structures, arguably there are fewer established selection criteria. As pointed out in Chapter 1, grammar in many English language teaching contexts has traditionally been verb-phrase driven. The following criteria are proposed here as being relevant in an EAP context:

- frequency
- utility
- efficiency/complexity
- generatability

The first of these criteria, 'frequency', is arguably the most important. There is a difficulty, however: unlike what exists for vocabulary items, which are graded by frequency in the five major learner's dictionaries, there is no such easily accessible resource for grammatical structures. Leech (2001) cites the work of his team (Leech, Rayson and Wilson, 2001) as useful recent research into vocabulary frequencies, plus that of Biber et al. (1999) for information on the frequency of grammatical items. Various examples of the frequency of grammatical structures have been presented in this chapter, mainly based on the work of Biber et al. (1999), but at 1,200 pages this is not a manageable resource for students. An example of a frequently occurring structure is the following lexical bundle, based on the frame '(the) _____ of (the)':

the absence of	the composition of	the per cent of the;
the aim of this study	the end of	the presence of
the base of the	the role of the	the point of view of

(Selected from Biber et al. 1999: 1000–1014).

Biber et al. identify 43 variations on this lexical bundle. Lexical bundles such as this are defined as non-structural sequences of three or more words which occur ten or more times per million words, and can be regarded as lexical building blocks for extended noun phrases or prepositional phrases (Biber et al. 1999: 990–4). The percentage of words in recurrent versus non-recurrent expressions in academic writing are as follows (ibid.):

- non-recurrent sequences 79%

- three-word bundles 18%

- four-word bundles 2%

- phrasal/prepositional verbs 1%

These figures would seem to show that 80% of academic text is in effect new text as it does not recur to a statistically significant degree. Of the remaining 20%, most is made up of three-word lexical bundles such as the sequence 'in the [case]' presented in Table 4.3. Four-word lexical bundles are much rarer, such as the items 'the [end] of' the given above. The remaining language is accounted for by phrasal and prepositional verbs, although the latter are much more frequent than the former in academic discourse as unlike phrasal verbs they can express cognitive as well as physical meanings (Biber et al. 1999: 415).

Further work into lexical bundles in university teaching and textbooks found frequent instances of different semantic types, such as stance bundles—a selection of which is given below:

I don't know what …	are more likely to be …	You might want to …
I don't know if I …	you need to know …	the fact that the …
I don't want to …	It is important to …	What do you think …
I think it was …	on the other hand …	
I want you to …		

(Selected from Biber 2006a: 139–145),

Many of these can be instantly identified as being spoken (i.e. used in university teaching) rather than written; they can be selected and used in EAP materials.

As for the other criteria for selecting grammatical structures, they relate to how the writer/speaker can use them. Utility covers the usefulness of the structures, i.e. how readily the writer can use them in different contexts. The criterion of efficiency relates to how a given amount of information can be expressed using a particular structure. For example, the following noun phrase taken from the text on coffee, follows the frequent noun + prepositional phrase structure:

'the crisis in conventional coffee markets'

This structure expresses the target meaning in six words, whereas an alternative structure using a relative clause will use more words, for example:

'the crisis which is taking place in conventional coffee markets'

'the crisis which has recently been taking place in conventional coffee markets'

What the relative clause structure adds in terms of specificity of time it loses in efficiency. Given the tendency of academic assignments and publications such as journal articles to be limited in their word count, efficiency is an important criterion for the academic writer.

Finally, generatability relates to how generative a structure is. The sequence 'the [end] of the …' is highly generative, as it can express many meanings using different lexical words within the frame. The major noun phrase structures, those with postmodifying prepositional phrases and relative clauses, are also highly generative.

Idioms and journalistic language

Some language is probably best avoided. Given that EAP programmes are generally time pressured, certain language items are infrequent, have little utility value, and low generatability. Many idioms, familiar expressions and clichés come into this category: students do not need to know the meanings of items like 'It's raining cats and dogs' and 'at the end of the day'. If students encounter them then they can deal with them, but it is probably inefficient to include them in the syllabus and materials. The main category of idioms that deserve a major focus in EAP is that of prepositional verbs. The following frequently used prepositional verbs illustrate their familiarity, frequency, and utility in academic discourse:

> look at, look for, deal with, be applied to, be used in, be made of, be aimed at, send NP to, give NP to, be derived from, be divided into, obtain NP from, use NP as, refer to, be expressed in, think of, hear of, be known as, be seen as, be regarded as, be seen in, be considered as, be defined as, lead to, come from, result in, contribute to, allow for, be required for, occur in, depend on, belong to, account for, consist of, differ from, be based on, be involved in, be associated with, be related to, be included in, be composed of

(Biber et al.1999: 416–8)

In this list, the abbreviation 'NP' refers to 'noun phrase', and the inclusion of 'be' with the verb in the past participle form indicates that it is more frequently found in the passive.

An emergent approach to language selection

For EAP teachers, a practical solution to selecting language lies in a simple principle. If EAP is predicated on needs analysis, which in turn informs the choice of text, then the text should yield the language. Put simply, the language emerges from the chosen texts. This principle is the opposite approach to general EFL, where a decontextualized syllabus of discrete language items is based heavily around the content word classes of verbs, nouns, adjectives, and adverbs; and these items determine the choice of text. In EAP, on the other hand, a body of selected texts can form the starting point.

Using their knowledge of the language, together with their skills in discourse analysis, the EAP teacher can draw out language from the texts (both spoken and written) that are selected in the learning materials.

Conclusion

The discussion and analysis of language throughout this chapter illustrate three important points. First, academic language is in many ways highly complex, yet studying and analyzing it is extremely useful for EAP teachers and students. Second, it is quite limiting to simply focus on a narrow description of language. While each aspect of the analysis is potentially useful, none is in itself sufficient. Words need to be used in a grammatical and discoursal context. A grammatical analysis needs to move into wider meaning and context. Grammar and vocabulary are closely related, not distinct, and both are needed in an analysis of such aspects as meaning, context, purpose, and style. Phonology, too, is a vital component of language in spoken form, and is also an essential contributor to meaning— together with paralanguage, i.e. tone of voice, facial expression, and movement. Third, language is most fundamentally the agent of meaning in written and spoken academic discourse. Most naturally, the starting point of communication is meaning, and it is through language that people express their desired meanings. In the EAP context, students need support in finding appropriate language to communicate their ideas, and in understanding ideas in texts.

Further reading

Biber, D. 2008. *Variations across speech and writing.* Cambridge: Cambridge University Press.

Biber, D., S. Johansson, G. Leech, S. Conrad and **E. Finegan.** 1999. *Longman Grammar of Spoken and Written English.* Harlow: Longman.

Biber, D., S. Conrad, and **G. Leech.** 2002. *Longman Student Grammar of Spoken and Written English.* Harlow: Longman.

Carter, R., and **M. McCarthy.** 2006. *Cambridge Grammar of English.* Cambridge: Cambridge University Press.

Coxhead, A. 2000. 'A new academic word list.' *TESOL Quarterly* 34/2: 213–238.

Hoey, M. 2005. *Lexical Priming: a new theory of words and language*. Abingdon: Routledge.

Paquot, M. 2010. *Academic Vocabulary in Learner Writing*. London: Continuum.

Wray, A. 2002. *Formulaic language and the lexicon*. Cambridge: Cambridge University Press.

5

CRITICAL THINKING

Critical thinker as reflector and challenger

In Chapter 1 critical thinking is identified as one of the defining characteristics of EAP. This chapter illustrates the importance of critical thinking, starting with a brief investigation of the history and background to the concept of critical thinking before considering the characteristics and approaches to critical thinking and how these can work in the EAP classroom.

While critical thinking is traditionally conceived as an abstract process, naturally it cannot exist without a critical thinker and some material. In EAP, everyone needs to be a critical thinker: EAP students and their teachers need to approach texts and the ideas presented in them with a critical state of mind. As critical thinkers, they should reflect on and challenge the material they encounter, and this process of reflection will include such cognitive activities as analysis and evaluation. This chapter starts with a brief account of the history of knowledge, before moving into an investigation of critical thinking into the practice of teaching and learning it in EAP. This journey starts some 2,500 years ago with an exploration of the nature of knowledge and how people approach and construct it.

The nature of knowledge and the scientific method

Perhaps the earliest known philosopher and critical thinker whose work survives today was Confucius (who lived from 551–479 BC). He said:

> I do not open up the truth to one who is not eager to get knowledge, nor help out any one who is not anxious to explain himself. When I have presented one corner of a subject to any one, and he cannot from it learn the other three, I do not repeat my lesson.

The Analects, Jen, Humaneness, VII.8:

(<http://academic.brooklyn.cuny.edu/core9/phalsall/texts/analects.html>)

This is interpreted as Confucius encouraging his students be dedicated and take the initiative in learning, and, when presented with material, to learn to draw inferences from it (Shen 2001 in Palmer: 2). This early teaching strongly suggests a critical approach to learning and knowledge.

In the same era, but in a different part of the world, in ancient Greece, the great educational philosophers were flourishing In medicine, for example, Hippocrates (c360–470 BC) was challenging traditional irrational thinking: his 'Hippocratic oath' is still sworn by doctors in many countries today and its core principle of honesty could also apply to students and academics in the avoidance of plagiarism. As part of the same tradition, Socrates (469–399 BC), his pupil Plato (427–347 BC), and Plato's pupil Aristotle (384–322 BC) were all contributing to the development of an approach to knowledge that was reflective and questioning. Crucially, despite each philosopher's love and respect for their teacher, this approach did not exclude challenging their teachers. Aristotle, for instance, is reported to have said 'Plato is dear to me but dearer still is the truth' (Hobson 2001: 15). Socrates, meanwhile, challenged and clashed with the authorities of his day (Ehrenberg 197: 379) and in doing so 'showed remarkable courage and independence' (ibid.: 375); however, when he was eventually condemned to death by the state, Socrates did not question the verdict, but, in accordance with his philosophy of obedience to the rule of law, he carried out his own execution, by drinking the hemlock provided to him. The elegantly simple principle of Socrates, and his great legacy, is not to teach, i.e. impart information from teacher to student in the traditional sense, but to make the student think. This is done through questioning, looking for definitions, and finding truth.

The scientific method: inductivism versus falsification

It is significant that whilst these ancient philosophers from China and Greece are still venerated today and continue to influence education, there is considerable disagreement about what constitutes the true 'scientific method', i.e. the soundest approach to investigating phenomena and acquiring new knowledge. The most fundamental dichotomy is the split between inductivism versus falsification. The **inductive** method can be traced back to Sir Francis Bacon (1561–1626), a British politician and philosopher, who died during an experiment, in the age of Shakespeare (1564–1616) and Galileo (1564–1642), the Italian physicist and astronomer. Inductivism is based on induction, which starts with observations: scientists and researchers collect a large number of careful observations, based on which they can infer generalizations or make predications. For example, in the novels by Conan Doyle (a practising doctor), Sherlock Holmes uses an inductive method: he collects data first, and then theorizes, based on this data. Bacon used statements such as 'All ravens are black' and 'All swans are white' as analogies: if this bird is a swan, it must be white. This latter statement was believed to be true until the 18th century when black swans were discovered in Australia. In other words, Bacon's inductive observation was eventually refuted, or falsified, by experience.

The doctrine of falsification (as opposed to the classic inductivist approach) received general acceptance much later, pioneered by, Karl Popper (1902–1994), an Austro-British philosopher and professor at the London School of Economics. He argued against inductivism, saying that it was absurd. Popper believed that induction is, by its very nature fallible, and instead promoted conjectures and refutations: scientific research, he believed, should start with conjecture, then try to refute this, and modify it. This scientific method is known as falsification.

Approaches to knowledge: positivism and epistemology

Epistemology refers to knowledge and how it is constructed and validated. Knowledge can be built up using different means, and in academic contexts, knowledge is questioned as a part of the process of validating it, i.e. establishing its **reliability** and truth.

Today, two distinct approaches to the gathering of knowledge can be identified: the quantitative and the qualitative. In the natural sciences, the researcher is seen as objective, and uses quantitative methods to measure and then analyze data. In quantitative analysis, there is a progression from correlation through causality to generalizability: for example, in the earlier stages of research, scientists may identify a correlation between sugar consumption and the onset of diabetes. Further research reveals a causal link, i.e. high or excessive levels of sugar consumption in the diet tends to result in diabetes. From these findings, researchers are able to generalize that, among humans worldwide, diets high in sugar are a major cause of the rise in cases of diabetes. Drawing on the ideas of both Bacon and Popper, this objective approach is sometimes known as 'positivism'.

Whilst in the natural sciences the researcher should remain objective and not impact on the data, in the social sciences the researcher is seen as subjective and can both interact with and impact on the data. This is due to the qualitative nature of social science research, which uses ethnographic approaches and methods such as observation, interviews, and case studies. Results are discussed mainly through words rather than numbers. This approach is sometimes known as an epistemological approach; however, positivism is also sometimes seen as an epistemological position, which 'advocates the application of the methods of the natural sciences to the study of social reality and beyond' (Bryman and Bell 2011: 717).

These two approaches are sometimes held up as being in opposition to each other, although in practice (and in theory) this is a false dichotomy: aspects of both can be found in research across all disciplines. Academic knowledge is sometimes represented as a continuum, for example by McDonald, who places the sciences at one end, moving through the social sciences in the middle, to the humanities at the other end (McDonald 1994, in Coffin, Curry, Goodman, Hewings, Lillis and Swan 2003: 47–8). This conception is akin to a 'hard' to 'soft' gradation, with the natural sciences being empirically based, and the humanities lacking in quantitative methods (Coffin et al. 2003: 48). Such a division is a controversial one which merits critical examination.

Reflecting on and challenging sources of knowledge

The principle of approaching knowledge sceptically is central to academic practice and EAP. EAP practitioners can do this in various ways: for example, in the accommodationist approach of EAP (see Chapter 1 page 23), students learn to look for such things as assumptions and flaws in texts, and in the critical EAP approach (see also Chapter 1, page 24) students are encouraged to question the wider basis of research and the construction and presentation of knowledge. What is essential is that EAP teachers and students, as critical thinkers, reflect on and challenge the nature and sources of knowledge and how it is presented.

Bloom's taxonomy

Bloom's taxonomy (Bloom, Englebert, Furst, Hill and Krathwohl 1956) offers a helpful tool for mapping and classifying aspects of knowledge. When, in 1956, a team of educational researchers led by Benjamin S. Bloom, proposed taxonomies to cover different aspects of teaching and learning, one of these dealt with what they called the 'cognitive domain'. The most fundamental step in this taxonomy is knowledge. It has since been updated and revised by other members of the original team, notably Krathwohl. The original taxonomy is reproduced below.

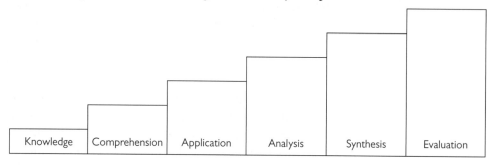

Figure 5.1   Bloom's taxonomy of the cognitive domain

Conceived in hierarchical terms, the research team isolated six key cognitive processes and presented them in ascending order of complexity. In simple terms, we start out with what we know, and learn new information ('knowledge') after which we learn to understand it effectively ('comprehension'). We can then do something with it, such as make use of it in a given situation ('application'); later we can deconstruct it and work out what its parts are and how they interrelate ('analysis'). The next stage is to deal with other sources of knowledge, repeat the process, and start selecting from the different sources and putting them together into something new and creative ('synthesis'). Finally, we critically respond to the whole by asking and answering questions relating to its reliability, validity, influence, effectiveness, and other criteria ('evaluation'). In Krathwohl's revision (Krathwohl 2002: 5ff) the final two steps are transposed, with synthesis renamed as 'create' (the nouns of the original were converted to verbs).

Bloom's taxonomy has influenced educational policy well beyond the United States where it was first conceived. With regard to this chapter, the three higher cognitive processes—analysis, synthesis (or creativity), and evaluation—are of particular relevance to critical thinking. Knowledge is fundamental and necessary, and critical thinking activities need to be based on knowledge and its understanding. To be meaningful, critical thinking needs to take place in a clear context, which can be in the form of a statement or text, perhaps with accompanying learning materials. For example, a student can synthesize information from multiple sources in different ways: they can search fairly superficially for key words relating to their topic and pick out short extracts to stitch together in their own new text; or they can identify themes in different sources which may not be explicitly related (i.e. they are not described using exactly the same key words) but which can, through argument and persuasion, be related and then brought together in their own new text. The latter scenario demonstrates a higher level of critical thinking than the former, and is equally relevant in whether the student's new text is written or spoken, such as presentations or contributions in seminars.

Critical reading and critical writing

The concept of critical thinking explored in this chapter is broad and it is important to be aware that it has a number of more restricted meanings. Critical reasoning is taken to be the application of logic to given problems and scenarios; these may take place in non-academic settings, such as business and other professional contexts. In academic contexts, two types of critical thinking with more restricted meanings can be usefully identified: critical reading and critical writing.

Wallace and Wray define critical reading as follows:

> The skill of critical reading lies in assessing the extent to which authors have provided adequate justification for the claims they make. This assessment depends partly on what the authors have communicated and partly on other relevant knowledge, experience and inference.

(Wallace and Wray 2006: 7)

This definition is intended to cover a broad range of possibilities relating to authorial justification. Wallace and Wray provide various examples in connection to this, which are things the reader can do: 'asking **critical questions** to look for a hidden agenda; establishing that there are sufficient grounds for a claim, or otherwise; identifying flaws in the author's reasoning; finding assumptions and bias; and identifying evidence that has been missed out despite its possible relevance' (Wallace and Wray 2006: 3–7).

By implication, critical writing, which follows on from critical reading, aims to ensure that claims are adequately supported, and so on. Wallace and Wray's definition for critical writing is the following:

> The skill of critical writing lies in convincing your readers to accept your claims. You achieve this through the effective communication of adequate reasons and evidence for these claims.

(Wallace and Wray 2006: 7)

Having introduced working definitions for these types of orthographically based critical thinking skills, this chapter goes on to identify ways in which critical thinking can inform a wide range of essential elements.

Critical thinking and essential elements

Critical thinking lies behind many familiar tasks and practices in EAP, and can inform how the student undertakes such tasks. The discussion in the following section uses the example of the task or practice of 'defining a term'. In order to contextualize and vitalize critical thinking it focuses on how critical thinking informs essential elements, which lie at the heart of academic practice. It is this widespread presence of critical thinking which underlines its importance throughout all aspects of academic practice.

Essential elements and critical thinking

Essential elements (which are presented and elaborated on in Chapter 3) represent the meanings expressed in written and spoken texts. For example, if the academic practitioner wants to critically compare two theories, this is likely to involve the essential elements of comparing, contrasting, discussing, and evaluating. All essential elements are informed, to some extent, by critical thinking.

Text management functions and essential elements

Text management functions are distinct from essential elements and involve constructing and managing a text. Figure 5.2 summarizes the major text management functions.

Constructing and managing the text using original input (i.e. from the writer of the text) and research input (including referencing cited material)

Ensuring cohesion:

- signposting and providing navigational material to manage the organization of a text and facilitate audience comprehension of meaning
- stating aims, for example through a thesis statement
- introducing a topic, and sequencing items within the topic
- maintaining focus
- concluding.

Figure 5.2   Text management functions

This process of management involves presenting the material that goes into the text—both original input from the writer of the text, and research input from primary and secondary sources. It is essentially the writer's responsibility to present this material clearly, cohesively (i.e. how the material in the text is connected in terms of meaning and language), and coherently (i.e. how the material in the text is connected in terms of meaning and ideas). Text management functions represent the framework and context of the text. To carry them out effectively, the writer needs to be appropriately competent in language and academic skills.

Essential elements

Essential elements refer to the major components of texts, which are informed by the purpose of the text: they are essential elements are what the writer or speaker constructs when producing their text, and the reader or listener encounters when processing it. For instance, when a writer defines a term in their text, this results in the essential element of definition in the text, which their audience will read, identify, and interpret. In practice, essential elements interface with critical thinking. Essential elements such as defining and evaluating constitute academic practice in a broad sense, and relate to aspects such as disciplinary knowledge and discourse communities. An academic practitioner needs to develop an appropriate degree of competence in producing and decoding essential elements like defining and evaluating which requires not only knowledge, skills, and language, but a degree of criticality, i.e. having a critical state of mind. For example, in defining a key concept in their field, the student (or teacher) could simply reach for the nearest dictionary and copy the definition into their text. This may be satisfactory in some contexts, but if the term is a contentious one or one that has been discussed and written about over a long period of time, then a more critical approach is called for.

Stages in producing essential elements

Table 5.1 illustrates possible stages in the academic process of defining a term, using 'culture' as an example.

Stages in the process	Practices and cognitive processes
Searching and consulting	Look up the term in one or more specialist dictionaries, e.g. a dictionary of psychology or sociology
Researching	Search for published definitions of the term in academic texts, including textbooks and journal articles, using the term as a search term (i.e. looking up the term in the index of textbooks, and using the term as the key word in electronic searches)
Comparing and contrasting	Compare, contrast, and evaluate the definitions, asking questions such as: 'What are the commonalities (i.e. specific characteristics of 'culture' that appear in most or all of the definitions)? Which definitions, or parts of definitions, seem to be particularly convincing?'
Noticing and recording	Notice and note down any significant contributors to definitions (e.g. Hofstede in the case of 'culture')
Evaluating and selecting	Select the most appropriate definitions from those found; these may include less successful ones (which can then be argued against) as well as the most convincing one(s)
Processing	Incorporate the selected definitions, suitably referenced, in the text
Integrating	Integrate original material relating to the definitions: explanation; analysis; commentary; evaluation
Evaluating and selecting	Reach a **resolution** based on the evidence offered, i.e. by identifying the most appropriate definition(s) which will then inform the discussion of the text

Table 5.1   Stages in the process of defining a term

The process outlined in Table 5.1 can of course apply to any other key concept in a discipline. The process clearly requires elements of critical thinking. The student has engaged with the target concept, carried out research based on academic texts (rather than the most convenient general dictionary or online resource such as Wikipedia), critically approached this source material through comparison, analysis, and evaluation, and selected from the material in a principled way in order to construct and inform their own text. The essential element which drives this process is defining, though other essential elements also support it, for example analyzing and evaluating.

In carrying out this process, the student has demonstrated evidence of learning through critical engagement with their subject and its **literature**. As a result, their work is likely to be far more favourably assessed than if they had uncritically pasted in a definition from a popular source.

A taxonomy of essential elements and critical thinking

Table 5.2 presents a new taxonomy of essential elements. The items in this taxonomy are synthesized and put together from widely practised essential elements in EAP and the academy. Closely related essential elements are combined, such as claiming centrality, occupying a niche, and giving a rationale; although these are seen as different 'moves' in Swales' analysis such as in his CaRS model (Swales 1990: 141), these three essential elements all relate to the practice of specifying the research area to be focused on. Each essential element is exemplified with one example. These examples are not intended to be comprehensive; they are given to illustrate possible ways in which critical thinking can inform the essential element.

Essential elements	Examples of associated critical thinking practices
Analysis	Using perspectives (e.g. cultural, ethical, environmental) to analyze an issue or proposition
Argument	Constructing a persuasive argument based on evidence, which has to be evaluated and selected
Cause	Weighing up the degree to which a phenomenon can be the cause of something else, based on strength of evidence
Citation/evidence	Searching for and evaluating supporting evidence, and determining an appropriate way of presenting this evidence—through summarizing, paraphrasing, and quoting of sources
Claim/claim of centrality/occupation of a niche or gap/rationalization/generalization	Weighing up the major movements in a field, and identifying a niche which can be successfully developed Reaching a degree of confidence to (publicly) state an argument, and being able to support and defend it
Classification	Selecting the material and determining the criteria for classifying it

Essential elements	Examples of associated critical thinking practices
Comparison and contrast	Analyzing and evaluating aspects of multiple items using appropriate criteria
Concession/limitation	Recognizing and stating limitations in the argument or research, thereby also showing awareness of other work in the field
Connection of phenomena or ideas	Determining complex connections between items, e.g. associations, thematic or theory-informed links
Contextualization/background information relating to time, place, and context	Demonstrating awareness of the wider context of the material through recognition of the most important events/theories
Critique/criticism/review	Finding flaws and weaknesses in the source material; identifying assumptions and omissions
Definition	Comparing, selecting, and evaluating different published definitions which can all support this process of analysis (i.e. comparing like with like)
Description, e.g. of a physical or abstract entity or a natural phenomenon	Identifying and selecting the key characteristics to be described; evaluating and incorporating descriptions from sources
Discussion	Locating, selecting, and synthesizing evidence to use as support in the discussion section of a report or essay
Effect	Working out the strength of a possible causal connection between two phenomena
Evaluation	Drawing on appropriate criteria to evaluate an argument, entity, proposition, stance, theory
Exemplification	Locating and selecting an appropriate example to effectively illustrate a phenomenon
Explanation/exposition	Using an appropriate analogy to explain a point
Expression of notional meanings such as movement, relations between entities, obligation, condition, concession, purpose	Explaining how different events can be related within a larger event such as a military campaign, and giving reasons why
Expression of general functional meanings such as suggesting, advising, denying	Proposing and justifying alternative approaches to achieving an objective
Hypothesis, prediction, speculation	Expressing possible scenarios based on an analysis and evaluation of existing evidence
Interpretation, inference	Constructing more concrete meaning from limited evidence using logic
Justification, e.g. of a position	Selecting relevant evidence and drawing on strength of argument to support the position
Narrative/narration	Considering the audience in presenting the narrative material

Essential elements	Examples of associated critical thinking practices
Perspective	Deciding on appropriate perspectives from which to approach and analyze an issue
Presentation of information, data, statistics, findings	Working out patterns amid complex data; emphasizing important trends while downplaying minor blips
Problem	Evaluating the seriousness of a problem, and its impact in different contexts
Process/chronological sequence of events	Drawing on descriptions in the literature to work out the chronological order of events which may be given in a different order
Proposal, e.g. of a new idea or theory	Confidently constructing a new idea or theory informed by existing work
Qualification: expression of certainty of the message through emphasis or caution	Refining and defining the material and situating it within the evidence available in the discipline; assessing how reliable/current/generalizable, etc. it is
Recommendation	Using results and other research to propose new work arising from these
Recount/report of an experiment, case study, or research	Establishing the main points in a piece of research in order to present these in the recount
Reflection/empathy	Creatively and emotionally critiquing self-/others' practice, and suggesting alternative approaches
Solution	Proposing and evaluating solutions to given problems
Stance	Formulating a stance based on wide evidence and argument
Summary	Identifying the author's stance, which may be implicit in the source text, in order to express it in the summary

Table 5.2   A taxonomy of essential elements with examples of associated critical thinking practices

Like Table 3.1 in Chapter 3, this taxonomy demonstrates the breadth of essential elements which academic practitioners, researchers, writers, and presenters have to engage with in their work. There may be instances where some of the essential elements are quite closely related or overlapping, while others are more distinct. The practices involving critical thinking in the second column constitute examples to illustrate aspects of the processes involved; they are not intended as definitions or complete descriptions.

Essential elements in language reference books

Language reference books are only infrequently organized by academic function, essential element, or meaning. Vocabulary reference books such as dictionaries are almost invariably alphabetically organized, while vocabulary practice books, such as McCarthy and O'Dell's (2008) *Academic Vocabulary in Use*, tend to be presented by topic. Grammar books tend to be organized by form (i.e. structure), although they sometimes have later sections which are meaning-driven, such as the chapter on 'The grammatical marking of stance' in Biber et al. (1999: 965–986). The earlier *Communicative Grammar of English* by Leech and Svartvik (1975) is partly organized by meaning, and in particular notion, with sections on 'place, direction and distance' and 'cause, reason and purpose'; the second half of the book, meanwhile, reverts to a structurally-driven approach. Another language reference book with a hybrid approach is *Oxford Grammar for EAP: English grammar and practice for Academic Purposes* (Paterson with Wedge 2013), which devotes about half its units to essential elements including 'comparing and contrasting' and 'arguing and persuading'; the other half are based around structures like modal verbs and noun phrases. Another recent language resource, *The Student Phrase Book: Vocabulary for Writing at University* (Godfrey 2013) is organized entirely by essential element and text management function, such as classifying and introducing a topic.

Defining the scope of critical thinking

Critical thinking has been defined in various ways, and perhaps unsurprisingly these definitions vary in what they include and exclude. This section aims to establish the criteria and characteristics of critical thinking in order to demonstrate the breadth of the concept, leading to a working definition of critical thinking.

Tasks, characteristics, and intelligences in critical thinking

A key characteristic of critical thinking is that it is independent of language; the level of a student's first or second language is not a predictor of their level of critical thinking. As Cottrell points out, 'nobody is an absolute beginner when it comes to critical thinking' (Cottrell 2005: *viii*).

In order to establish what critical thinking entails, it is useful to examine tasks, characteristics, and intelligences associated with critical thinking.

Tasks in critical thinking

Various tasks are associated with critical thinking. They centre on cognitive tasks and generally involve interaction with prompts such as texts, propositions, and different phenomena. A wide range of critical thinking activities emerge from the essential elements discussed in the previous section. The example of defining an abstract concept serves to illustrate some of the processes involved.

Many such tasks are unkeyable. In other words, a definitive key cannot be provided in advance of students doing the task. Sample answers may be possible to predict, but students can legitimately create new responses. Examples of unkeyable tasks include a comparison and critical analysis of two systems (for example legal systems) or phenomena (for example airport designs). Much of the interest of these tasks lies in their unpredictability: in carrying them out students can demonstrate original ideas such as new connections between existing phenomena, or criteria-based evaluation of the effectiveness of different systems.

The first column of Table 5.3 on page 133 presents a wide range of these activities.

Characteristics of critical thinking

Critical thinking tasks yield certain characteristics of critical thinking. Depending on who is doing the thinking, these characteristics may include a wide range of phenomena. The second column of Table 5.3 presents the main characteristics. Any of these might be present, with varying degrees of relevance, depending on the task.

In doing a task, the critical thinking student undergoes a cognitive process involving such characteristics as logic and inference, for example when constructing relations in meaning between elements in a text. In doing so, it is useful to show scepticism towards what is being presented, together with a degree of uncertainty and self-doubt. It is not always necessary for the student or teacher to be sure they are right; it is better to attempt to construct meanings and in the process make mistakes than not make this effort at all.

Chapter 6 notes that language level, as defined by criteria such as the CEFR does not correlate with cognitive level. As such, students at any level may have any level of cognitive development. Students at lower language levels like A2 should be challenged with cognitively ambitious tasks; there is no logical reason to delay these kinds of tasks until B1 and B2 (pre-intermediate to upper intermediate) or C1 (advanced).

Intelligences in critical thinking

Critical thinking may appear to be a wholly cognitive process. However, tasks requiring critical thinking may involve the full range of intelligence types. These are listed in the third column of Table 5.3.

To exemplify the necessity of bringing in multiple intelligences to the world of critical thinking, a surgeon requires not only deep knowledge and understanding of medicine. They also need great kinaesthetic skills. When carrying out an operation, unexpected difficulties may emerge which require quick thought and skilled action. Among others, then, logical and kinaesthetic intelligences are necessary. These two intelligences are inseparable as far as the surgeon's skill is concerned. In the context of an operation neither is of much use without the other. To take a different example, a conductor of an orchestra obviously requires musical intelligence, among other types. A written score is in a sense a visual set of instructions; a great conductor will interpret this and offer a degree of originality within given constraints such as which notes are played by which instruments at which time. The way they communicate all this is through movement including paralanguage, i.e. kinaesthetically.

Further examples could be suggested, described, analyzed, and elaborated on at great length; what they serve to show is the centrality of critical thinking to their work, and the breadth of intelligences required to carry out this work.

Tasks associated with critical thinking	Characteristics of critical thinking	Intelligences in critical thinking
observation	originality	logical
examination	cognition	linguistic
interpretation	inference	mathematical
analysis	logic	intrapersonal
evaluation	scepticism	spatial
synthesis	uncertainty and doubt	artistic
reasoning	making mistakes	musical
justification	state of mind	kinaesthetic
adding something	self-awareness	
making connections	reflection	
looking for analogies,	unkeyability	
patterns, weaknesses,	unpredictability	
flaws, and bias	open-endedness	
problem-solving	liberation	
	creativity	
	culture	
	affect	

Table 5.3 Tasks, characteristics, and intelligences in critical thinking

Many of the phenomena in Table 5.3 can blur and overlap, and rather than attempt discrete definitions of each one, a task based on a real text might be more illuminating. A critical question might relate to the value of evidence offered in support of an argument, or to an assumption presented in a text. Tasks are presented in the section 'Critical thinking in practice' in this chapter, below, and in Chapter 6.

Conditions and implications for critical thinking

For critical thinking to develop effectively, certain conditions are preferable. Most importantly, EAP has a crucial role to play in encouraging critical and creative thought. Teachers sometimes give discouraging responses to answers that they see as incorrect, though these answers may be very intelligent responses.

Critical thinking may benefit from creativity and imagination, depending on the task, but it is not the same as free 'blue skies thinking'. In other words, it needs to be grounded in evidence and supported by logic and rigour. Some of these conditions associated with critical thinking are listed in the first column of Table 5.4 on page 134.

Conditions of critical thinking	Implications of critical thinking
rigour	application
principle	transferability
logic	generalizability
support	limitations
focus	
use of criteria	

Table 5.4   Conditions and implications of critical thinking

When carrying out an activity involving critical thinking, a degree of rigour is desirable. An effective evaluation of a text or a set of results, for example, means systematically going through the evidence presented in the material. An unprincipled response without supporting evidence (for example 'It's really interesting') is insufficient. Consequently, rigour and principle are associated with critical thinking. So too are logic and focus: a critical mind at times needs to be a logical, focused mind. Logic involves particular skills such as recognizing false logic, drawing out analogies between two pieces of material, and inferring meaning in a text which does not state something explicitly. To carry out such activities, a degree of focus is necessary: the results will probably not emerge from a cursory glance or quick skim through a text. In identifying, for example meaning or flaws, support is required: the critical thinker needs to be able to point to what helped them reach their conclusion. Criteria are also associated with critical thinking. These criteria need to be appropriate for the task.

The discussion so far has focused on critical thinking from a range of perspectives. The next stage is to consider what critical thinking is for. In developing critical thinking skills, students can learn to apply these to other aspects of their lives, not only those related to academic contexts. Four major implications are given in the second column of Table 5.4. Through such practices, students can apply what they learn, transferring the cognitive skills to new contexts, and generalizing from the particular. In carrying out tasks, students can demonstrate the implications of their work, for example by demonstrating the degree to which a conclusion is generalizable across different contexts, and what its limitations are.

Definitions of critical thinking

Having explored the characteristics of critical thinking, this section concludes by presenting some definitions of critical thinking to build on the definitions of critical reading and writing (Wallace and Wray 2011) presented earlier in the chapter.

Many writers on the subject revisit the cognitive stages in Bloom's taxonomy in their discussions of critical thinking, for example Moon (2008), who draws together various characteristics of critical thinking including assessment of evidence, critical appraisal, reflection, understanding, analysis, synthesis, and evaluation (Moon 2008: 33–34).

Judge, Jones, and McCreery (2009: 1–2) emphasize the objective to subjective process and the necessity of providing supporting evidence:

> Critical thinking is essentially a questioning, challenging approach to knowledge and perceived wisdom. It involves examining ideas and information from an objective position and then questioning this information in the light of our own values, attitudes and personal philosophy. It is essential that within the process of critical thinking the writer substantiates the stance they have taken by providing evidence about the issue they are discussing in such a way that their judgements are seen as secure and verified.
>
> (Judge, Jones, and McCreery 2009: 1–2)

The following is a recent definition of critical thinking, proposed in 2011 and based on many of the criteria to emerge through critical thinking tasks, and those listed in Tables 5.3 and 5.4:

> Critical thinking emerges from a state of mind which is innate, yet to varying degrees nurtured, or discouraged, by environmental factors including parenting and education; critical thinking tasks challenge assumptions and make connections across entities and propositions through such processes as analysis, synthesis, evaluation – and creativity.
>
> (de Chazal 2012a: 155)

This definition encompasses two characteristics which recur in many definitions of critical thinking: analysis and evaluation. The importance of these is underlined by their breadth of coverage across the chapters of this book.

Critical thinking and critical EAP

Critical thinking and critical EAP are not the same thing, but there is a clear potential for overlap. The role of critical thinking in an accommodationist approach is likely to involve tasks such as identifying weaknesses in the writer's argument in a text. Critical EAP, however, takes a much broader view of criticality. In a critical EAP approach, an investigation of weaknesses in the writer's argument can be taken much further, for instance by looking at how the writer's perspective (for example a North American perspective) has informed and impacted on their argument. Further questions in a critical EAP approach could include why the teacher selected that particular text, and how it fits in with existing knowledge and established stances. Through such investigations, various issues emerge, including selectivity of the information presented, and the agendas of different agents.

Aspects of criticality, such as analysis, evaluation, and critiquing a writer's position in their field, are connected to the understanding and interpretation of texts at a very broad level, particularly in terms of their close association with an individual student's stance and voice.

Criticality: evaluation, stance, and voice

Chapter 3 states how the writer of a text incorporates their own evaluation in response to the main content and argument of the text, while this chapter explores critical thinking in EAP. Three key concepts related to criticality in academic writing are evaluation, stance, and voice. These related notions are essential and can enable students to produce effective academic spoken and written texts.

The concepts of evaluation, stance, and voice are much discussed in academic contexts. Further related concepts can be added: criticism, **critical response**, appreciation, assessment, appraisal, personal reaction, opinion, viewpoint, standpoint, point of view, feelings, and interpretation. Some of these have indistinguishable meanings (for example: viewpoint, standpoint, point of view), while others have a strong emotional element (for example: feeling, appreciation). The terms 'criticism' and 'critical response' are associated with academic practice, as are 'assessment' and 'appraisal'. The word 'opinion' meanwhile, is sometimes seen as not welcome in academic contexts as it suggests a lack of support in the form of evidence.

It is useful at this point to explore the essential characteristics of the central concepts of evaluation, stance, and voice. In doing so, it will become clear that all three have one important aspect in common: like the concepts in the above paragraph, they are subjective.

Evaluation

At the heart of the word 'evaluation' is 'value': to evaluate something is to make an assessment of its value. This value of something may relate to such features as its effectiveness, usefulness, reliability, generalizability, feasibility, significance, success, desirability, purpose, or certainty. In assessing the value of something, in other words evaluating it, students and teachers are essentially asking questions arising from these characteristics, for example, 'How effective is it?' 'To what extent can we rely on it?' and 'How likely is it to happen?' The answers to these questions can include: 'It is a significant development'; 'There is little doubt that its effects will be widely experienced'; and 'On balance, the scheme appears to be unworkable'.

Evaluation has been defined in different ways; indeed, the concept has attracted a number of competing terms. Hunston and Thompson (2000) report, for example, the following terms which to some extent are all used to describe evaluation or its related concepts, given with the researcher associated with them in brackets: 'affect' (Besnier); 'appraisal' (Martin); 'attitude' and **modality** (Halliday); 'connotation' (Lyons); 'evidentiality' (Chafe); 'hedging' (Hyland); and 'stance' (Biber, Johansson, Leech, Conrad and Finegan). Thompson and Hunston (2000: 5) take a combining approach, using the superordinate 'evaluation' to cover 'the expression of the speaker or writer's attitude or stance towards, viewpoint on, or feelings about the entities or propositions that he or she is talking about' (ibid.). This use of the term 'attitude' includes certainty, obligation, desirability, and other values. Modality therefore is a sub-category of evaluation. Thompson and Hunston explain that evaluation expresses a user-orientation, which means that it is the user who evaluates (ibid.). This last observation has implications for students: clearly, it is the responsibility of students to offer evaluation.

Different things can be evaluated. As Hunston and Thompson point out, the academic writer typically evaluates entities and propositions. An entity is typically expressed as a noun phrase, for example 'the impact of the global financial crisis of 2007–8 on developing countries', while a proposition is usually expressed in clausal form, for example 'The central bank should raise interest rates next year'. Propositions can broadly include ideas, proposals, hypotheses, and questions. In addition, texts are also evaluated: writers evaluate aspects of texts such as their quality, authority, reliability, intelligibility, context, partisanship, bias, balance, influence, impact, and comprehensiveness. In teaching, these aspects can be converted to familiar question forms, for example 'Is the text authoritative?' 'How reliable is it?' 'To what extent is it partisan/**biased**?' and 'Is this text suited to my purpose for using it?'

Stance

Stance is closely related to evaluation, but is associated more with broader and potentially more complex issues. For example, someone can have a stance on a major political issue or policy. A person's stance tends to take some time to develop, and may be modified in the light of new developments. Evaluative responses, in contrast, are more likely to be in response to propositions and entities raised in a text, or of the text itself, and can be formed much more quickly. Stance and evaluation are both highly valued in academic contexts, and are normally supported by evidence. As different people can evaluate the same thing in different ways, and hold different stances on the same issue, evaluation and stance are both subjective. These subjective, evidence-based responses and positions, then, are essential in constructing meaning in academic contexts.

Voice

As its name suggests, voice is unique to a writer. Evaluation and stance are major contributors to a writer's voice. Voice is also related to language: a writer selects and uses certain language to express their meaning. As the academic level increases, students should be encouraged to develop their own voice. This means that students at postgraduate levels need to develop their voice more noticeably than at many undergraduate levels.

A writer's voice also emerges through the citations they select and include in their text. The content, style, and language of citations can complement or contrast with those of the writer.

It is important to note that in certain texts the author's voice is not welcome. For example, in co-authored texts like subject-specific dictionaries and medical textbooks and manuals, the editor would not want the reader to identify the individual voice of the contributors; rather, the whole publication has its own style which the individual contributors have to follow. For certain student genres, such as a collaborative project written up as a report or poster presentation, a unified voice may be preferred to a series of distinct voices within the one text. One implication for students is the need to develop an awareness of voice in such contexts.

Criticality

These related concepts of evaluation, stance, and voice are in turn part of criticality. Criticality, a term which can be used to cover critical thinking and critical (evaluative) responses is highly valued, and expected, in academic contexts. Yet a number of researchers have commented that students' written texts frequently do not offer sufficient and appropriate critical evaluation. For example, Cotton reports that academic staff sometimes comment on an absence of critical evaluation in some international students' written work (Cotton 2004 and 2010), while Thompson and Ye (1991) report that students tend to 'introduce evaluation in a somewhat crude way'.

Cotton (2004 and 2010: 74) suggests a number of reasons to explain these tendencies. Perhaps most obviously, students may not realize the importance of criticality and the related concepts of evaluation, stance, and voice. Alternatively, students may not feel confident enough to offer their own critical evaluation. Some students may not understand what criticality entails, or how to develop critical and evaluative material. Students may not be familiar with the language used to express such criticality. In all these cases, the role of the EAP teacher is vital in promoting criticality.

Aspects of criticality such as evaluation are essentially subjective. They are also comparative: in order to evaluate something it is compared—explicitly or implicitly—to something else. Evaluation is a critical response to evidence, and distinct from many other textual functions and essential elements, including description and exemplification. Academic writers and speakers can offer their own evaluation and, through citation, report the evaluation of others.

A wide range of academic genres incorporate evaluation, for example essays, reports, and reviews. Citations are often followed by evaluation, where the writer comments on aspects of the cited material, such as its validity and credibility. Essays may integrate evaluation, while in certain genres such as reports it is presented within conventional sections. Hunston and Thompson (2000) emphasize that evaluation not only expresses the writer's opinion but also constructs and maintains relations between writer and reader, and organizes the discourse.

Critical responses such as evaluation are what make a text unique and interesting. In short, 'information is ubiquitous; a writer's stance is unique' (de Chazal 2009a: 156). Evaluation serves to illuminate the identity of the writer to the reader. The reader does this partly through their choice of evaluative language.

The language of critical thinking

In order for students to express their thoughts and ideas, they need language. This is particularly true in the area of critical thinking. Lack of language has been recognized as a barrier to critical expression (for example Cotton 2010: 74). Therefore it is important for EAP students to develop their language in this area.

Evaluative language

Cotton (2010: 74) makes the reasonable assumption that students' use of evaluative language constitutes evidence of critical evaluation. In written and spoken texts, particular language is associated with evaluation. Students need to recognize this in their reading and listening, and produce it as necessary in their writing and speaking. Key researchers (for example Hyland and Milton, 1997; Biber et al., 1999, and other research by Biber and his team, various dates; Swales and Feak, 2004; Carter and McCarthy 2006) have used corpora to identify and describe such language. Apart from the work of Hyland and Milton (1997), who use corpora of both first language (L1) and second language (L2) English speakers for comparative purposes, these researchers base their work on corpora containing mainly first language (L1) English speakers' language. Some of their findings are presented in Table 5.5 overleaf.

The table illustrates a common core of language, with some variations between different researchers who emphasize slightly different evaluative language. Students can identify these language options in texts used in EAP materials, and then select appropriate language to use in their own speaking and writing.

One approach to selecting language is to start with the familiar, more conversational language of evaluation which EAP students might generally use, and 'convert' this to language more appropriate to the target academic context. Table 5.6 presents some examples of such language.

More conversational	More academic
I think, I guess, I suppose	It seems that, It appears that, It could be argued that, I would argue that
great, brilliant, fantastic	outstanding, excellent, seminal
obviously	clearly
definitely	arguably
totally	absolutely
sadly	unfortunately
If you do that you're going to fail.	This approach is unlikely to be successful, because...

Table 5.6   From conversational to academic evaluative language

	Vocabulary	Grammar
Hyland and Milton (1997)	**Verbs**: think, appear **Adverbials**: apparently, perhaps, possible, about, certainly, indeed, probably, to a certain extent **Adjectives**: possible	**Modal verbs**: will, may, would **Verb-based structures**: I believe, It seems to me, It is certain that, It might be possible to, On balance it would seem
Biber, Johansson, Leech, Conrad, and Finegan (1999); Conrad and Biber (2000); Biber (2006b); Gray and Biber (2012)	Wide range of lexical choices including adjectives, adverbs, verbs, nouns, e.g.: **Stance nouns**: possibility, value, evidence, importance, problem, understanding, significance, validity, risk, tendency, need, failing, opportunity **Frequent predicative adjectives**: sure, right, true, wrong, difficult, different, hard, possible, impossible, aware, likely, unable, important, necessary, clear, small, available, unlikely, better, promising, appropriate, certain, obvious **Stance adverbials** (adverbs, prepositional phrases, clauses): obviously, unfortunately, to a significant/great extent, no doubt, of course, clearly, evidently, probably, surprisingly, according to X, honestly, briefly, undoubtedly, in most cases, from our perspective, most surprisingly of all, as one would expect, certainly, perhaps, in fact, generally, worse, fortunately, as may be expected, somewhat surprising, on the whole, in most cases, definitely, primarily **Modal verbs**: might be	**Lexical bundles**: are likely to be, It is (un)likely/important/(im)possible that, it is possible to, it can be seen, it is not surprising that, it may be that, it was found that **Complement clauses**: I feel that, Smith seems quite satisfied that, It is surprising that, The fact that, It is known that, We have shown that, It is clear that, Thus, we hypothesized that, Nevertheless, we propose that, This is not to imply that, We are becoming increasingly certain that, It seems fairly obvious **Adverbs modifying adjectives** (frequent collocations): more general, quite/significantly different, significantly higher, statistically different, very difficult/important/large/low **Adverbs modifying adverbs** (frequent collocations): much more, much less, almost certainly, almost entirely, very much, very often
Swales and Feak (2004); Feak and Swales (2011)	**Adjectives**: scholarly, flawed, up-to-date, innovative; impressed, interesting, important, significant, potential, excellent, state-of-the-art **Nouns**: clarity, accessibility, success, failure **Adverbs**: successfully, regrettably, nevertheless; clearly, elegantly, greatly, relatively, well **Verbs**: succeed, fail, overestimate, consider; contribute **Prepositions** despite, rather than, as opposed to	**Adverbials**: adverbs, adverbial clauses **Idiomatic expressions**: no doubt, of course, on the whole
Carter and McCarthy (2006)	**Adverbials**: apparently, arguably, evidently, partially **Prepositional phrases**: as a rule, in a sense, in principle	**Modal verbs**: must, will, should, can, could, might, may, would + lexical verb **Passive voice**: It is (reporting verb) that **Noun phrases**: There is little doubt that

Table 5.5   The language of evaluation and stance informed by corpus research

Hedging

Hedging, which refers to the academic practice and language of 'softening' statements, is closely connected to critical thinking. This is because the writer or speaker has to be aware of how their message is situated in its wider context, and how robust it is. The concept of hedging in academic discourse has been discussed at least since 1972, beginning with an article by Lakoff titled *Hedges: a study in meaning criteria and the logic of fuzzy concepts* (Lakoff 1972, cited in Swales 1990: 112). For the academic speaker or writer, situating material and stating a claim implies consideration of critical questions such as:

• How sound it its research basis?

• To what extent can its implications be generalized in other contexts?

• How successfully can its findings be defended?

To use an example of an essential element, stating a claim leads to the crucial area of hedging. Due to the uncertain nature of claims—they may be convincing but they do not (yet) enjoy 'proven' status—they should not be stated in over-confident, absolute terms. The use of such absolute terms lays the writer or speaker open to criticism which they cannot defend, because the evidence is not strong enough to support the presentation of the claim as fact. This is why academic writers need to learn how to hedge. Students can draw on the language in Table 5.5 to express their desired nuanced meaning based on the strength of their evidence. Frequently-used language includes the modal verbs, lexical verbs like 'appear; and 'seem', adjectives such as 'likely' and periphrastic expressions (i.e. comprising two or more words) such as 'seems set to' and 'is on the verge of' (de Chazal 2009b: 46–9).

Cultural implications of hedging: the case of Russian

There are cultural implications for hedging. In some cultures, a more robust style is preferred, leading to a possible reluctance to use appropriate hedging language in English. For example, it has been found that writers whose native language is Russian hedge less than average in both first language (L1) and second language (L2) (Khoch 2013). Khoch identified the following reasons and motivations for first language (L1) and second language (L2) writers to hedge:

• non-categorical nature of science

• individual style of writing

• desire to be precise

• signposting personal view

• specific research framework or method of analysis

• protection from possible criticisms

• insufficiency of evidence

• desire to look modest

- journal readership
- the role of editor.

Khoch (2013) found that among Russian writers there was a perception that a hedge like 'might' 'reduces the value of the article', and is 'unnecessary' or 'not appropriate stylistically'. Given findings like these, EAP teachers need to develop an awareness of how students from different countries and backgrounds may express themselves differently, not only in terms of language but also in terms of how they construct and view their meaning. To promote and develop their students' critical thinking, EAP teachers need to draw on a range of appropriate practical tasks.

Critical thinking in practice

As its name suggests, critical thinking is a thought process. It is essentially cognitive rather than physical, although a physical dimension may well be present in many activities involving critical thinking, as seen in the example of a musician in interpreting and communicating a score. In order to develop critical thinking in the EAP classroom, the EAP teacher needs to use appropriate materials and tasks. As Table 5.3 showed, there are many activities associated with critical thinking, and these can be incorporated into learning materials in both planned and unplanned ways.

Planned and scaffolded approaches to critical thinking

To help students develop a habit of critical thinking in their regular academic study, various approaches have been proposed. One approach is *SQ3R*, (survey, question, read, recite, review) proposed by Beard (1990) and aimed at schoolchildren.

Fairbairn and Winch (2011: 36) elaborate on this approach:

- students are first encouraged to survey the text to determine whether to read it in more detail;
- they then decide what they hope to get from the text, and how and where to find it;
- students should then use a range of reading techniques to gain knowledge from the text;
- in a test phase, students recall their learning using further techniques;
- finally, they review their learning and work out what to read next.

Scaffolded approaches like this can be very useful in the earlier development of critical practice in reading. Fairbairn and Winch go on to offer a more critical approach to reading, by adopting either an 'adversarial approach' or an 'inquisitorial approach' (Fairbairn and Winch 2011: 241). Their conception of an adversarial approach is akin to the UK/USA approach to judicial practice, where the prosecution aims to overcome the defendant's presumption of innocence while the defence aims to maintain this presumption (ibid.). In the inquisitorial approach, meanwhile, the aim is to go through the evidence to determine whether the crime took place. Applied to reading, these approaches involve identifying weaknesses in arguments (an adversarial approach), or trying to work out what they actually meant (an inquisitorial approach). In both approaches, the students is aiming to analyze and evaluate arguments (Fairbairn and Winch 2011: 241).

In another approach aimed at engaging with academic literacy, a number of interconnected strategies are combined and the role of the teacher is emphasized (Gibbons 2009: 58ff). Gibbons specifies the following strategies directed to the teacher:

- Develop academic language on the basis of what students already know, for example elicit what students know before presenting new information, and encourage personal narrative.

- Move towards complex texts rather than beginning with them; also, reading after the class rather than in preparation for the class, is more effective.

- Model the use of academic language in interactions with students.

- Talk about language: develop a **metalanguage** with students.

- Integrate language activities with content teaching .

(Gibbons 2009: 58–63)

These strategies provide useful support for the teacher, and can be put into practice using a wide variety of activities.

An unplanned 'critical thinking moment'

This chapter has established that critical thinking involves various cognitive processes; it can also been seen as a state of mind. It is useful to approach activities, such as reading texts, in a critical frame of mind, in a state of self-awareness and in a reflective way. As EAP teachers foster a critical state of mind in themselves and their students, critical thinking 'moments' can emerge unpredictably in the classroom. EAP teachers can also integrate critical thinking tasks throughout their teaching. For example, the lecture slide in Figure 5.3 was included in a university lecture for EAP students. The lecturer was from the business faculty and was speaking on entrepreneurship.

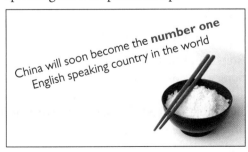

Figure 5.3   A lecture slide

The students' EAP teacher, who during the lecture was sitting in the audience with their students, decided to use the slide in the discussion following the lecture. The teacher's preliminary question was 'Should you believe everything you are told?' While most students said 'No', a minority thought the opposite, giving the answer 'Yes, because this is an academic lecture and the lecturer is the expert.' This is an example of a question in the spirit of critical EAP. This question led to an instruction to students to think of as many critical questions as possible arising from the slide. Some students found this task challenging, and struggled to think of any meaningful questions, while others thought of several. The class as a whole, and their teacher, came up with fifteen questions:

Specific critical thinking questions based on the lecture slide

- When?/How soon is 'soon'?

- Why not India?

- How do you know? (What are your sources?)

- How well will they speak English?

- Is it going to be 'Chinese English' (like we have Indian English and American English, for example)?

- Is it desirable or undesirable that this will happen? From whose perspective? Why?

- Why do/should the Chinese need/want to speak English?

- Does 'number one' mean the most speakers (quantity) or the speakers with the best English (quality)?

- Why is 'number one' printed in red? (The words 'number one' were printed in red on the original slide)

- Which country is the current 'number one'—the USA? India?

- The image—is the picture of a bowl of rice and chopsticks stereotyped? Should the image have been something else, for example a skyline view of Shanghai or a factory?

- Given that the lecture topic was entrepreneurship, why did the lecturer include this slide?

- If the statement in the slide is true, how will it affect me personally?

- What do Chinese people think about it?

- Can we do anything to stop it happening? Should we?

An interesting next step could be to invite students to discuss possible answers to their critical thinking questions. What is motivating here is that the questions are generated by that class on that day and are unique. Also, the answers are unpredictable and unkeyable. Indeed, answers to the questions may not all be found, and will involve a degree of speculation.

Benefits of unplanned critical thinking tasks

This activity illustrates several points. First, if the teacher sees critical thinking as a 'state of mind', they can exploit ordinary classroom materials and resources to develop their students' skills. They can do this in advance, as part of their lesson planning, or in the moment whenever something interesting comes up. Second, the questions raised, and in turn the answers to these questions, are unpredictable, open-ended, and unkeyable, yet demonstrate rigour in that the students need to respond to the prompt—in this case the lecturer's slide—rather than simply do a bit of 'blue-skies thinking'. In contrast with a 'teaching by numbers' context in which all answers can be keyed in advance, this critical thinking task may be seen as liberating and creative.

Third, it might not be possible to answer all the questions with much certainty: this does not matter as it is the process of coming up with the questions rather than answering the questions that is the main focus of the task. Fourth, and this is important as this is an EAP context, students are practising their English. This includes both language and skills: they are likely to be using critical language such as modals and causal language (*It could be because ...*); and they are developing their speaking and listening skills during the discussion. As with any other speaking activity, EAP teachers can monitor and note down interesting or problematic examples of student language.

Teaching implications

Given these characteristics of critical thinking, there are a number of implications for the EAP classroom. One is the degree of unpredictability: just as student responses may be unpredictable, so too may the amount of time spent. What looks like a simple task or question might legitimately take up a considerable amount of class time—far more than a comparable task in a general EFL situation. This means that other planned tasks may be displaced. EAP teachers need to find an appropriate balance between planned work, which has been carefully selected due to its importance, and more spontaneous activities. In this instance, the likely student use of modal verbs for speculation could be seen as a useful preview or review (depending on when it appears in the syllabus and **scheme of work**) of this important language area.

Perhaps the most important implication is that in practice particular students from any culture and certain students from particular cultures may not all deal with the same task to the same degree of effectiveness. This might be true for a task of any nature, whether purely language-based, skills-based, or based on a graph, for instance. Yet with regard to critical thinking tasks, culture can impact on them quite considerably. Culture includes such aspects as education and ways of viewing the world.

Students and critical thinking

In addressing such critical thinking tasks and questions, students are situating the text in the world, gaining an overview of the text, recognizing its structure and main elements, and making their own, possibly original, connections. For instance, in a text it is not always obvious what is supposed to be evidence, which is at the factual end of the fact–opinion cline, and what is the author's stance. In other words, students are beginning to interpret the text. With most texts, different readers can interpret elements of them in different ways.

Asking critical questions

Critical thinking tasks require students to ask critical questions. While some questions are very specific to a given context, many others are much more generic. The following are examples of possible generic questions for discussion in response to a reading or listening text such as a lecture:

Generic critical questions

- What is the authors' stance? How did you work this out? What language helped you do this?
- How do the examples contribute to your understanding of the text?
- How strong is the evidence which supports the writer's conclusion?
- Why has the writer selected the particular evidence and examples provided?
- What unkeyable questions are asked in the text, and what are your answers to them?
- Are there any points in the text which particularly invite you to demonstrate knowledge and offer your own personal response?
- Which arguments in the text did you like and would you use in your own written work?
- (In response to a specific point stated in the text) Is this point true or false, or are you unsure? How do you know? How can you check?

These examples of critical questions underline the generic nature of many critical thinking tasks. There are, however, potential differences in how knowledge is constructed and interpreted in different contexts and disciplines.

Communicating knowledge and ideas

In reality, knowledge and ideas are not communicated in a neutral, value-free way. They are expressed in relation to other knowledge and ideas. Table 5.7 shows factors which inform how people communicate knowledge and ideas.

Factor	Rationale
Selection	People select and limit what they want to communicate (i.e. say and/or write). In simple terms, in communicating a message people include what they want to say, and exclude what they do not want to say, or do not know.
Context	People relate knowledge to the contexts which they know, based on their schemata and knowledge of the world.
Values	People approach new knowledge and ideas in relation to their existing values and beliefs.
Language	A writer or speaker's choice of language is informed by how they view their message, and contributes to how a person interprets this message.
Disciplinary knowledge	A person situates new subject knowledge within the discipline in which they study or work.

Table 5.7   Factors informing the communication of knowledge and ideas

These factors illustrate some of the influences in how ideas are communicated and interpreted. In effect, each person is at the centre of their world, so an EAP student or teacher is liable to process and critique knowledge in a slightly different way.

Conclusion

As start of this chapter noted, critical thinking skills lie at the heart of academic life and EAP. Perhaps more than any other aspect, critical thinking differentiates EAP from general EFL. EAP materials need to encourage and develop students' critical thinking skills; EAP teachers should foster the 'state of mind' in which critical thinking moments emerge naturally in the classroom. In doing so, students will be much better prepared for their academic study. Opportunities to include elements of critical thinking in EAP teaching and learning emerge throughout this book.

Through a focus on critical thinking from a range of perspectives, this chapter has discussed what it involves, looked at a selection of tasks and language, and related the concept to EAP. Above all, the development of critical thinking skills involves a mindset, or state of mind, which challenges, investigates, questions, and looks for patterns. These observations apply both to EAP teachers and their students.

Further reading

Bloom, B.S., M.D. Engelhart, E.J. Furst, W.H. Hill, and **D.R. Krathwohl.** 1956. *Taxonomy of educational objectives: The classification of educational goals. Handbook 1: Cognitive domain.* New York: David McKay.

Cottrell, S. 2005. *Critical Thinking Skills: Developing Effective Analysis and Argument.* Basingstoke: Palgrave Macmillan.

Hunston, S. and **G. Thompson,** (Eds.). 2000. *Evaluation in Text: authorial stance and the construction of discourse.* Oxford: Oxford University Press.

Krathwohl, D. R. 2002. 'A Revision of Bloom's Taxonomy: An Overview'. *Theory into Practice* 41/ 4. Ohio: The Ohio State University.

Wallace, M. and **A. Wray.** 2011. *Critical reading and writing for postgraduates 2e.* London: Sage Publications.

6

READING

Academic reader as processor and evaluator

This chapter examines the roles of the academic reader, putting EAP students at the centre of the reading process. It follows a student-centred approach to discussion of key processes in academic reading, as illustrating what students have to do gives EAP teachers an informed base on which to construct their approaches and materials.

Reading in an academic context involves a potentially wide range of activities and cognitive processes. Fundamentally, academic reading involves understanding the text, yet this is just one stage in the wider reading process, which is driven by the reader and their purposes for reading.

Theories in reading: top-down and bottom-up

The two distinctions of top-down and bottom-up processing have been used in relation to both reading and listening. In Chapter 10, the notions of synthetic (i.e. bottom-up) and analytic (top-down) are discussed (Wilkins 1976), in the context of syllabus design. Top-down processing is associated with Goodman (Goodman 1967: 126–135 in Bruce 2011: 42), and focuses on wider contextual information, such as the authors' background and how this might inform the text. These ideas are developed further later in this chapter in the section 'Approaching and navigating texts'. In contrast, bottom-up processing starts with the words in the text and builds up meaning from this linguistic input (Gough 1972, in Bruce 2011: 142). Inevitably, an approach has been proposed which synthesizes these two processes. This approach is known as an interactive approach (Rumelhart 1977: 573–603, in Bruce 2011: 142).

Processes in academic reading

Students need to follow a number of possible stages in study processes which are centred on reading. The whole process, and each stage in it, is driven by a main aim. One possible sequence of processes, together with their aims and associated activities, is illustrated in Table 6.1.

Stage	Process and aim	Activities involving reading
1	Becoming familiar with the discipline, sub-discipline, and current area/topic of study to determine area of specialization	Reading introductory and background material, especially subject textbooks and texts recommended through reading lists
2	Dealing with a new assignment, such as a reading task or research project, to plan how to approach it	Reading and understanding the assignment including related documentation (e.g. rubrics, detailed guidelines, and samples)
3	Searching for (e.g. by using library search facilities) and locating potentially appropriate and relevant source texts to use in the assignment	Reading macro-informative parts of texts, such as titles, contents, and introductions of textbooks; and abstracts of journal articles
4	Evaluating the relevance and usefulness of potential texts by selecting, limiting, and rejecting specific texts to use in the assignment	Navigating and selectively reading extended extracts of selected texts, such as chapters in textbooks; and introduction/conclusion of journal articles, or the whole article
5	Understanding, recording, and processing relevant material in the texts selected to use in the assignment	Reading and taking notes on the selected texts, for example by identifying main and supporting arguments and authors' stance
6	Using material from the source reading texts in the assignment	Reading, reprocessing, and selecting material from the notes to integrate into the assignment

Table 6.1   Selected processes in academic reading

As with many academic processes, these stages are not entirely linear, but to some extent cyclical. For example, becoming familiar with the discipline is, of course, not something that is achieved and 'ticked off' before moving on to the next stage. It is ongoing, and as such endless: it is limited by time, and the constraints, requirements, and expectations of a particular course of study and the individual student. Similarly, the core stages of searching for and evaluating source material may well continue during other stages in the process, including the writing stage. Table 6.1 is a representation of one possible way of dealing with an academic assignment; depending on the assignment, the process might be more straightforward, or more complex. Factors affecting the different stages in the process include:

• the level of the assignment, for example undergraduate, postgraduate

• the amount of time allocated to the assignment—the example in Table 6.1 is likely to take a number of weeks

• the amount of input from the subject teachers—they may prescribe some texts and expect their students to search for others

• the assessment—work done at different stages in the process, such as first drafts, may form part of the assessment, while the range and quality of sources is also likely to be assessed, explicitly or implicitly.

As this cycle illustrates, two key roles of the academic reader are processor and evaluator. Students in the disciplines typically need to read, process, and evaluate a large amount of text. In their course of study, students are likely to have to select texts to use in their work. Text selection and reading require repeated processing and evaluation. A key factor driving this process is purpose, i.e. why students are reading this particular text.

Automaticity

As students become more proficient in their reading at a given level, there is greater potential for automaticity in processing. The phenomenon of 'automaticity' refers to the gradual development of macro-level reading skills, which through guided practice become more automatic. Following this, micro-skills associated with that skill also become automatic (Hudson 2007: 35).

Purposes in reading

There are a number of identifiable purposes in reading. For readers in general, an obvious reason is to gain knowledge. Large numbers of genres, from academic texts such as textbooks to journalistic texts such as newspapers, are informative. (Other genres are primarily for entertainment, for example novels and comics).

For EAP students in particular, an important purpose in reading is to develop skills. These skills include not only identifiable reading skills like intensive reading to work out the main points in a text, but also wider study skills like using library databases to search for texts relevant to a given assignment. Related to this idea is another purpose: to synthesize information to use in new texts. In other words, students' purpose in reading is to locate material to use in their writing or speaking. In this way, reading becomes part of a wider communicative cycle.

Through tasks such as these, students should also develop their critical thinking skills. These include key academic skills such as evaluating sources, identifying and challenging assumptions in a text, and working out the writer's stance. Critical thinking tends to be closely associated with reading, which has given rise to the term 'critical reading'. Put simply, students need to question what they read.

A further major purpose for EAP students is to develop language. Traditionally in ELT, language is presented through texts, both spoken and written. Reading is a vital means of language development for a number of reasons: the texts are likely to be authentic, so natural language patterns (for example syntax patterns and collocation) will be prominent; students are exposed to language in a meaningful context; and given their likely need to access information in the text, students might be more motivated to work out and discover new meanings independently—which is a powerful way of learning.

Finally, two further purposes in reading for EAP students may be identified, which indeed apply to students generally. One is to be assessed. The other is because they are told to. Students generally are required to read prescribed texts, and often to find additional texts, and reading texts typically forms an important part of assessments.

This section has argued for the purpose-driven nature of reading, with the reader as processor and evaluator. These roles represent a significant challenge for EAP students.

Challenges in reading

In their academic reading, students face a number of challenges, from multiple perspectives. In identifying these challenges, EAP teachers can understand effectively what their students need to do in academic reading and find appropriate materials to achieve this.

Analyzing reading challenges

The most obvious challenge for EAP students in reading is frequently identified as vocabulary. Nuttall, for example, argues that an insufficient vocabulary is the most serious challenge facing the second language (L2) reader (Nuttall 2005: 62ff). Her solution is for students to read much more (ibid.). Certainly vocabulary represents a very major challenge in reading, but it is not the only challenge. Table 6.2 categorizes and exemplifies vocabulary and some of the other challenges in reading that face EAP students.

Nature of challenge	Examples
Linguistic	Vocabulary load, including specialist vocabulary Grammatical complexity, especially complex noun phrases and some syntactic patterns
Non-linguistic	Graphics, charts, visuals, statistics
Cognitive	Density and complexity of information Ideas and concepts
Academic	Purpose and method of reading
Social, cultural, and psychological challenges	Analogy, metaphor, application
Knowledge-based (schemata) challenges	Understanding, interpreting, and situating the meaning in the world

Table 6.2   Challenges in reading

Challenges facing students reading a sample text

The short text extract from an ecology textbook (including the accompanying graphic) in Figure 6.1 illustrates many of the reading challenges described in Table 6.2; these are examined in detail below.

Assumptions by the authors of a text

The textbook is aimed mainly at undergraduate and postgraduate students, and as with many textbooks, the authors make certain assumptions. Foremost among these assumptions is a certain familiarity of context and content: for a student from a poor region in a developing country, the notions of 'stability' and 'sustainability' may concern basic security (freedom from violence and war) and survival (local food and water production), rather than the global environmental questions intended by the authors. There is also the assumption that students will know what is meant by 'political practice': what this is, how it relates to ecological theory, and how it affects ecosystems.

The question of how many species are needed for an ecosystem to function is critical, both to ecological theory and to political practice. Perhaps we could afford to be unconcerned about species going extinct if their ecosystems continued to work in their absence. If ecosystem services were unaffected by their loss we might be able to live without some species and the economic argument for protecting large and talismanic species would be weaker.

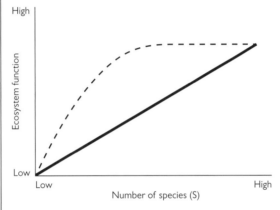

Figure 9.17   *Functional redundancy in ecological communities.*

If every species is important in maintaining some ecological function then we would expect a linear relationship between S and the process (the solid line). If, instead, some species are more important—that is other species are to some degree redundant—the ecological function will not decline linearly as each species is lost (the broken line).'

(Beeby, A. and A. Brennan, (2008). *First Ecology: ecological principles and environmental issues 3e.* Oxford: Oxford University Press: 345)

Figure 6.1   *Reading text*

Linguistic, cultural, and psychological challenges

As far as language is concerned, the text may initially seem to be reasonably accessible for B1/2 students aiming to study ecology, although one unusual word jumps out: 'talismanic'. This is likely to prove difficult to understand. The OALD (2010) definition of 'an object that is thought to have magic powers and to bring good luck' does not help much: what kinds of species have magic powers? The point is that the word is being used not literally but metaphorically. Depending on the student's culture, the species in question could be anything from aardvarks to zebras. This exploration of one word in the text has led to issues of culture and world knowledge. A useful piece of advice for students would be to either try to work out the meaning of the word 'talismanic', or ignore it. The essential meaning is retained with either of the following interpretations: 'protecting large and important species'; 'protecting large species', so the word 'talismanic' can be ignored.

To investigate language in terms of grammar, the complexity of some of the noun phrases is potentially challenging. For example, the opening clause uses a single complex noun phrase as its grammatical subject, underlined: 'The question of how many species are needed for an ecosystem to function is critical'. There are several nouns within this noun phrase (question, species, ecosystem), but the student needs to identify the head noun in order to understand what is 'critical', i.e. 'question' (it is helpful that 'critical' collocates with 'question'). The sentence structure, on the other hand, is straightforward: subject–verb–complement. This phenomenon, i.e. complexity of phrase and relative simplicity of clause, is typical of academic discourse, as Biber and Gray (2010) argue, and is elaborated on in Chapter 4. Their research finds that the main complexity in academic discourse lies in its use of complex noun phrases and nominalized forms; the structure of clauses and sentences (for example through the use of subordination) is significantly less complex than other types of discourse, such as conversation (Biber and Gray 2010).

Further uses of language relate to social and psychological perspectives. While the first sentence is objective in style, the second is subjective due to the use of 'we'. This is intriguing in pragmatic terms, as the student needs to establish who 'we' refers to: the authors of the text (i.e. Beeby and Brennan), or in keeping with the use of 'we' in many scientific papers, both the authors and their audience. If the latter, is the audience supposed to include all students of ecology (i.e. the intended audience of the book), or academics and students generally, or perhaps the whole of humanity? For the student reading the text, they may or may not be consciously concerned about the proposition in the text, i.e. the extinction of species. This student might feel that 'we' is an invitation, or an expectation, to become concerned. In this analysis, it is not the most difficult word in the text, 'talismanic', which is most challenging (it can simply be ignored), but one of the simplest, 'we'.

Non-linguistic, cognitive, and academic challenges

The non-linguistic parts of the text also present challenges. The graph may appear quite simple, yet in conjunction with the accompanying text, the content requires considerable cognitive processing. Basic mathematical familiarity is assumed, and students have to connect and interpret the linguistic content in the legend, i.e. the description and commentary accompanying the graph, and relate this to the graph itself. In this sample text, the commentary is particularly challenging given the hypothetical nature of the content, expressed by language including *if*, *would*, and *will*.

As for academic challenges, students need an understanding of what is in the text (the main points, etc.), how to read it, and what to do with the content.

Reading speed and reading load

What this short text extract does not show is the reading load expected of many students in the disciplines. While the reading load can vary enormously depending on the discipline and specific context, including the institution and the country, in many disciplines and contexts a great deal of reading is expected. Given the limited time available, and fast pace of many degree programmes, particularly master's programmes, which in the UK are typically one year compared with the two or more years required in many continental European countries, reading speed is also critical. It is useful to quantify the amount of reading expected by establishing how much, in pages, students on a particular course need to read, and in what timeframe.

Advising students on their reading speed and reading load

There are a number of ways in which EAP teachers can assist and advise their students to deal with their reading load once they are studying in the disciplines. Clearly an improved reading speed should translate into faster coverage of the reading to be done. The suggestions in Table 6.3 can all contribute to improving students' reading speed.

Reading speed can be improved considerably by addressing the challenges discussed in Table 6.2 and this section, leading to improvements including extending language proficiency and technique. These improvements, in turn, can help students to deal with their reading load.

These purposes and challenges in reading demonstrate several points: the breadth of possible reasons for reading and outcomes arising; the potential complexities involved in reading; the frequent interrelatedness of reading to other skills; and the centrality of reading for EAP students. Reading in an EAP context should be purpose driven with clear outcomes. The questions and challenges raised in this section are explored in the following three sections, which deal respectively with the student's role in the EAP reading text, how they read, and why they read.

The EAP reading context

The EAP reading context ideally puts students at the heart of the reading process. In their academic discipline, students are likely to read a range of genres which can include textbooks, reference resources (including online resources), abstracts, journal articles, reports, conference papers, critiques/reviews, instructions, summaries, case studies, posters, handouts, and other student texts such as essays, theses, and dissertations. EAP students are also likely to have to read coursebooks. As well as identifying *what* they are reading, students also need to understand *why* they are reading.

Criteria	Advice
Purpose	Establish why you are reading (for example, to find specific material on two topics that can be related) and constantly keep this purpose in mind. Reading for a specific assignment can enable very focused reading, which is likely to be more effective and memorable than general reading for no particular purpose.
Prioritization	Work out/find out what is most important, and read that first; if you have a reading list and work through it in alphabetical order you are unlikely to reach the end (and the last item in the alphabet may be the most interesting).
Selection	Read selectively rather than working through a whole book or article. Once you have established the relevance of a book to your topic, spend a few minutes identifying the chapters which are particularly relevant and interesting. Focus on these and miss out the remaining chapters.
Order	Read some texts in non-linear order to suit your purpose for reading. For instance, in a research article read the background to the research first to establish whether it is relevant to your context and work; if so, go to the results section, then if necessary go back to look at the methods section and forward to the discussion section as appropriate for your needs.
Technique	Match your reading technique to your purpose. For example, if you want to know how a term is defined, locate definitions and discussions relating to these. Relevant techniques here could include scanning, skimming, and then reading in more detail.
Adaptation	Constantly adapt what you read and how you read, as you read. If a promising chapter in a book turns out to be of limited interest and relevance, stop reading it and find something else to read. Just because you have started reading something does not mean you have to finish it.
Output	Crucially, make sure you have some output for your input. Reading actively, i.e. making brief notes while reading, should greatly enhance your reading effectiveness – this reflects your purpose for reading and can make reading more memorable. These notes also serve as a permanent record of your reading.
Experimentation	Try reading multiple reading texts of similar lengths and genres (e.g. abstracts or the first two pages of a textbook chapter). Note down the time taken to read each text and compare and evaluate your performance: is your reading speed improving over time? What difficulties can you identify and how can you overcome these?
Record	Keep a record of what you read, preferably in electronic form. This record should include the full reference of the text (i.e. author, date, title, place of publication and publisher/volume and issue number for articles) which you will need whenever you cite the text in your own work. Also add page numbers where relevant, in order to find the material you need at a later date, and use in the in-text reference where appropriate. Personalize your reading record by adding the dates you read the text, and your responses to it. (This point is developed further in the sub-section 'Keeping track of source texts' below.)
Practice	Maintain a good pace of reading. Reading in English regularly, preferably every day, can result in greater reading coverage and improvement in speed, as well as language development.

Table 6.3   Student-centred advice for dealing with reading speed and reading load

Student awareness of academic reading

A familiar notion in English language teaching is that of different ways of reading. Depending on the purpose and task, students may choose to read in different ways.

Terminology and ways of reading

For many teachers, and therefore students, four main ways of reading are widely recognized: intensive reading, extensive reading, skimming, and scanning. Such terms, however, are not necessarily helpful or intuitive in themselves. In reality, it can be more helpful and authentic to say 'Note down the publication details of the text' rather than 'Scan the imprint page to find the publication details'. Similarly, participants in an academic context are more likely to ask 'What's the main point?' than 'Skim the text to find out the main point'. The reading sub-skills of skimming and scanning may be taking place, but the focus is on the task, which is likely to involve a complex and varied suite of skills than just one (such as skimming). As Bruce points out, the pedagogy of focusing on sub-skills such as skimming and scanning 'reflects a particular view of the reading skill that may not necessarily take account of all the areas of knowledge that converge while processing and deriving discourses from academic texts' (Bruce 2011: 140). In other words, academic reading involves a complex set of processes, and it is more effective and realistic to focus on the reading outcome and task rather than using metalinguistic terms like 'skim' and 'scan'.

Raising awareness of reading

A practical starting point with EAP students is to raise awareness of their reading. Students may lack awareness of what and how they read, and the questionnaire in Figure 6.2 is designed to stimulate reflection and discussion on students' reading, with a view to developing their reading skills.

Reading habits

1. How long do you spend reading (in any language) on a typical day?
2. Where and how do you find the texts that you read?
3. Which languages do you read texts in?
4. What do you like reading in English?
5. What do you like reading in other languages?
6. What difficulties do you have in reading in English?
7. What can you do to be a better reader in English?
8. What are your aims in reading for this academic year?
9. What do you think of reading? Do you like it?
10. How do you read? What is your reading speed? Which kinds of materials to you read more quickly, and more slowly? Why?
11. Do you consider yourself to be a good reader? Do others?
12. What have you read in the last seven days/month/academic year?

Figure 6.2   A reading questionnaire

These questions bring out a number of important issues relating to reading: frequency and length of time spent reading (question 1); searching for texts (question 2); the different genres students read in their first language and in English (questions 3, 4, and 5); challenges, such as language, text organization, content and ideas (question 6); encouraging strategies for improvement, and setting goals (questions 7 and 8); attitudes to reading (question 9); process, style, and speed (question 10); self-evaluation, and evaluation by others (question 11); and finally a general survey question to quantify recent reading (question 12).

The answers to the questionnaire lead to a key characteristic of academic reading: **authenticity.**

Authenticity

Authenticity is widely taken to mean using authentic texts in learning materials, i.e. texts which have not been adapted. The scope of authenticity can be widened to include tasks and contexts. Thus authenticity can be said to refer to authentic texts, tasks, and contexts. For example, an authentic use of a published text is to identify main points in the text and reprocess these to incorporate into a new student text, following appropriate academic conventions such as referencing. The notion of authenticity is discussed further in Chapter 10.

In terms of level, in its original context a text has its own level (language and cognitive level), and the level of its intended audience. In the EAP classroom, an 'authentic' text has no such level until it is used for a particular purpose.

Level

In language teaching in general, level is generally taken to mean language level. Thus a student's level in a particular language may be described as 'high B1' or 'intermediate'. Typical reasons for assessing a student and assigning them a level are to place them in an appropriate class with appropriate learning materials, and to establish whether they have reached a target level. If a student is currently at high B1 and their target level is high B2, or upper intermediate, then they can be given an appropriate block of time and classes with a view to reaching their target. Once they are subsequently assessed and found to be at high B2, they are in the position of having reached their target and able to move on to the next phase of their studies.

In EAP contexts, however, the notion of level needs to be extended to include cognitive level.

Cognitive level

Chapter 5 explores critical thinking and how it relates to EAP. Cognitive dimensions in EAP reading classes include critical activities, such as working out assumptions and the author's stance in a text.

A student's cognitive level relates to their ability to understand and process information, as well as the speed in which they can do so and the progress they tend to make over a given period of time. These abilities are connected to a number of factors including their intelligence, learning styles, and educational background. In English language teaching generally, notions such as a student's cognitive level and their intelligence tend to be treated very carefully, or avoided. The general ELT literature does not strongly focus on notions such as a student's intelligence level, even if teachers in staffrooms often do discuss them, for example when reporting their students' difficulties or ease in grasping particular concepts. Nevertheless, in EAP contexts cognitive level is relevant because EAP students are normally planning to study an academic discipline in English, the entry requirements of which usually include achievement in relevant subject examinations (such as mathematics, etc.). As EAP courses need to reflect, to some extent, the realities of academic study in the disciplines, the course materials will entail a degree of cognitive challenge.

With the productive skills of writing and speaking, clearly the level of the student's text is broadly indicative of their language level. To put this the other way around, the student's language level can be ascertained by analyzing a sample of their writing or speaking, whether through a formal assessment or more informally in the classroom. With the receptive skills of reading and listening, however, this correlation of output text and language level does not apply: the level, both linguistic and cognitive, of a reading or listening text being used in an EAP classroom does not necessarily indicate the level of the students. Depending on the objective of the lesson and provided appropriately staged tasks are planned, a text at any level could be used with students of any level. For instance, a selection of journal abstracts, which characteristically are linguistically very dense, could be used at a lower level, say B1, with a manageable task, such as identifying the key words in the text. These key words, which generally represent specific concepts, are frequently given at the end of abstracts, so they can easily be checked.

Likewise, there may be no correlation between a student's language level and their cognitive level. For example, a student may be educated to a high level in their first language, but be of a low level in English. This implies that a text can be used which makes, for example, 'intermediate' demands in language terms but 'advanced' demands in cognitive terms.

Input and output

By definition, if a skill is 'receptive' it represents something going on in the student's head, i.e. it is cognitive, so the EAP teacher cannot ascertain the student's level unless they also produce some output. This output may take the form of closed tasks, such as multiple-choice questions in a test, or open tasks, such as noting down specific information given in the text. The student's level can then be assessed through their output to the receptive skill input. Figure 6.3 illustrates these options.

> **Written input** → spoken output, for example oral summary, personal response
> → written output, for example written summary, notes
>
> **Spoken input** → spoken output, for example oral response to instruction, interaction such as a discussion
>
> → written output, for example note-taking from a lecture or talk, written summary

Figure 6.3   Input to output options

These examples show how the input and output can involve different skills. They also show some possibilities for varying the skills in the EAP classroom, as well as for assessing the skills. In order to develop the skills which relate to reading, students need to learn how to approach and navigate texts.

Approaching and navigating texts

This section examines ways of working with texts in the EAP classroom based on a coherent sequence of tasks. The whole sequence is made up of twelve tasks and activities, which enable a principled and student-centred approach to academic reading. The first five, dealt with in this section, lead to the point at which students can access the deeper meaning of a text, which is then investigated in the following section.

The twelve tasks are presented in a logical sequence, which amounts to a resource bank which can be selectively accessed according to specific needs. This task sequence is intended to illustrate a principled approach to EAP reading, and one which EAP teachers can respond to, critique, and personalize. EAP teachers can develop their own approach to teaching reading by selecting, adapting, and supplementing the tasks to suit their own specific teaching contexts.

The twelve tasks in the sequence are as follows:

1 navigating and positioning a text using publication details
2 genre, audience, and purpose
3 selecting a text and a text extract
4 context and essential elements
5 perspective
6 meaning
7 stance
8 citation
9 language
10 critical thinking and evaluation
11 personal response and reflection
12 next steps and independence

The sequence of tasks are illustrated and rationalized from the standpoint of the EAP student.

Navigating and positioning a text using publication details

The reading process in Table 6.1 of this chapter shows that a key reading activity involves navigating a whole text, such as textbook or journal article. These two genres are the most frequently cited source texts, and typically make up a major part of students' reading in the disciplines. A number of stages need to take place in the process of navigating and positioning a text. The starting point is the information relating to the publication itself.

Using publication details

With books, a logical starting point is the information and images on the cover and imprint page. Students need to notice the information relating to the publication: title; author(s); publisher; date and place of publication. As such, this information is outside the main body of the book, i.e. the core chapters, and is summarized on the imprint page. Noticing these publication details should become the first activity when encountering a new text. Some of the benefits of doing so can be seen in Table 6.4.

Publication details	Purpose
Title	to contextualize the publication in the discipline, and determine its scope and limitations
Author(s)	to situate the author(s) in the discipline, and recognize their relevant prominence and contribution to the discipline
Date of publication	to determine the currency of a text, i.e. how current/up to date it is
Publisher	to situate the publisher in the discipline, and assess their relevant prominence and contribution to the discipline
Place of publication (books)	to position the publication in the world

Table 6.4   Using publication details

Table 6.4 shows how students can use the publication details of a text as the first step in situating and evaluating the whole text. The importance of evaluation may need emphasizing, for in some cultures and contexts books are widely considered to be authoritative and trustworthy. In reality, academic texts are not entirely factual and absolutely reliable: they contain, to varying degrees, selectivity, subjectivity, and assumptions. By building up their familiarity with major publishers and authors in their discipline, students can both build their wider discipline knowledge, and begin the process of evaluating their sources.

A useful task is for students to go to the institution library, where possible, and do a rough quantitative survey of the books in their discipline. Each discipline, such as medicine, has a limited number of publishers who account for most of the available titles; by noticing these, students can see which publishers to look out for. Students can do the same for authors, though an electronic search might be more feasible. There are related questions of the reliability and trustworthiness of particular authors and publishers, which students need to become aware of as they develop their critical thinking. For journal articles, students can see which journals are subscribed to by the institution (online and, traditionally, in print); these partly reflect the recommendations of the subject lecturers and should therefore be a good guide of which ones are important. Departments may also recommend specific journal titles. Given the thousands of journals available, this narrowing of possibilities is very helpful.

Noticing the publication details should become second nature for EAP students. The next step is to carefully record this information, in order to keep track of source texts.

Keeping track of source texts

There are a number of reasons for keeping track of source texts. If students are going to use material from the text in their own work (written or spoken), they will need the full publication details to provide the reference. If they are *not* going to use the source at this time, students will have a record of it to refer to later. It is good practice to periodically look through records of source texts, to increase familiarity with the most prominent authors and those texts that seem to be most cited. Keeping a record of source texts can also motivate students: they can see the number of texts they have located, evaluated, and selectively read. Additionally, looking through the **references sections** of high-quality texts can be very useful in establishing prominent writers in the field.

To keep a careful record, students need to adopt a system. This may take the form of a spreadsheet, such as Excel, which can be adapted and personalized with space for notes on the source text. Alternatively there is dedicated software available, such as 'EndNote' (which has to be purchased) and 'Mendeley' (which is free to use).

Even though it is not required in a reference, it is beneficial for students to also record the genres of the texts they find. An awareness of genre can contribute to deeper understanding of the text, and ensure an appropriate balance of different genres to suit the purpose for reading.

Genre, audience, and purpose

The notion of genre is discussed in Chapters 1 and 3; the latter chapter emphasizes that texts do not exist in isolation, but are related to other texts which have similarities in aspects including structure, purpose, formality, style, and audience. A reader of a text approaches their text with both their individual knowledge and aims, as well as expectations which the writer of the text was in a position to predict.

It is useful for EAP students to work out the genre, audience, and purpose of a new text to situate the text in the discipline and its wider context (de Chazal 2005: 89). This understanding informs the students' depth of engagement with the text.

The following three-part question can be used to elicit this information: 'What is the genre, who is it written for, and why is it written?'

Selecting a text and a text extract

This section approaches the selection of texts, again from the perspective of the student. Searching for source texts can be a complicated process, and is discussed in detail on page 60. Suppose an EAP student is to give a presentation on the effects of education on a person's intelligence. They need to start by building on their existing knowledge of the topic and finding out some background information. Then they will need to find relevant source material to use in their presentation, including this background information to contextualize the topic, plus more detailed, research-based information. This means locating suitable reliable source texts. Following the approach outlined in Table 6.1 and in this sub-section, the student locates a university textbook to start reading around the subject.

The student has decided to use a textbook on sociology because it discusses many wider issues around the topic, including education and culture, as well as some useful texts on the topic of intelligence itself. The student records the publication details for this text as follows:

Title: *Sociology* (fourth edition)

Author(s): Fulcher, J. and J. Scott

Date of publication: 2011.

Publisher: Oxford University Press.

Place of publication: Oxford, UK.

In terms of the genre, audience, and purpose of the text, the student notes down related information as follows:

Genre: (an extract from) a university textbook.

Audience: students of sociology and, to some extent, related social science subjects such as economics, geography, anthropology, psychology, business studies.

Purpose: to present and explain information, while offering integrated commentary, analysis, and evaluation.

Having worked out the above information, the student can proceed and find appropriate parts of the book to read. They need to navigate the whole publication effectively to find relevant texts.

Navigating the whole text

After noting the publication details and genre, audience, and purpose, the next stage is to explore further aspects of the publication to locate suitable extracts to use, which can yield a rich amount of relevant information. These aspects may include some or all of the features given in Table 6.5; not all publications will have all these features, while some will have more.

Text feature	Purpose
Contents	to work out the scope and limitations of the whole text, and establish which specific areas are covered in depth
Index	to see which specific points/concepts are covered, or omitted
Chapter/section headings and sub-headings	after selecting one or more chapters of potential interest, to see how the topic is developed, and see how the material is organized
Non-linguistic elements, e.g. graphics, photos, diagrams, maps	to assess the level of non-text support in explaining and illustrating the material, and to quickly learn important points without reading much text
References section/ Bibliography/Further reading	to establish which key authors and texts are used in the publication, and to find further reading opportunities
Other features	• **glossary**: to scan for known/new technical terms and learn new meanings • **text inserts,** e.g. case studies: to extend existing knowledge in an accessible and digestible way • **back cover blurb**: to establish who the publication is primarily aimed at • **other resources**, e.g. website links: to follow up and learn

Table 6.5   Navigating text features

Students can use the information in Table 6.5 to assess the extent to which the whole text is useful for their own purpose, for example to find information for a presentation or to write a research essay. In doing so, they practise a range of different reading skills with clear outcomes. Having chosen their textbook in this way, students navigate through it and decide on a particular text which appears to suit their purpose

A sample text

A sample text, an extract from a sociology textbook (Fulcher, J. and J. Scott. *Sociology 4e*. Oxford: Oxford University Press: 731–2), about the nature of intelligence is presented on page 345 in order to illustrate and exemplify the navigational items in Table 6.5. The relevant material is too lengthy to reproduce here in full, but can be summarized as follows:

Contents: the extract appears in Part 5: *'Production, inequalities, and social divisions'*.

Index: the extract is listed in the index under the entries 'biology and inequality', 'biology and intelligence', 'education and intelligence', 'inequality', 'intelligence', 'intelligence test/IQ', 'poverty – deserved and undeserved', and 'race and intelligence'.

Chapter/section headings and sub-headings: the extract appears in Part 5: *'Production, inequalities, and social divisions'* → *Chapter 18 'Inequality, poverty, and wealth'* → *first section* → *'Understanding social inequality'* → *third subsection 'Poverty, intelligence, and heredity'*.

Non-linguistic elements: none on the first page on which the extract appears, but the second page contains a text insert on IQ with accompanying figure, a graph showing a bell curve.

References section/Bibliography/Further reading: the references to Galton and Spearman are not listed in the index, but are given in the Bibliography.

Other features:

• The core terms in the text, for example 'intelligence', 'heredity', are not given in the Glossary, but peripheral terms are, for example 'culture'.

• The extract is accompanied by a related colour-tinted text insert on IQ in a corner of the page.

• The back-cover blurb prominently states that the textbook 'provides sociology students with an engaging, lively and clear introduction to all the main areas in sociology'.

• Accompanying the book is an online resource centre for students and lecturers.

Searching for and locating this information in the publication should be useful, interesting, and relevant to the student's needs. EAP teachers can devise tasks to encourage students to make connections between the information they find, for example by noticing how the place of publication (Oxford, UK) informs the content of the chapter, which arguably is written from a western perspective.

Regarding genre, audience, and purpose, the statement in the back-cover blurb of this publication informs the reader of the target audience: 'provides sociology students with an engaging, lively and clear introduction to all the main areas in sociology'. It may be worth pointing out to students that they should not rely on blurbs alone, as they are obviously persuasive and aimed at selling the book.

The student's next stage in the reading process is to read the text to contextualize it.

Context and essential elements

So far the student has purposefully navigated the text, noted the publication details, identified the genre, audience, and purpose, and selected a text extract to read in detail. The student now needs to contextualize their text. The words 'text' and 'context' are derived from the same word: the Latin *textus,* meaning structure, which in turn is from *textere*, to weave. This knowledge illuminates the relatedness of the two terms: metaphorically texts are woven into a structure using material taken from and connected to other texts and their wider context.

Essential elements

Essential elements (discussed in more detail in Chapters 3 and 5) refer to the large parts which make up the bulk of academic texts, such as argument, comparison, and evaluation. There are only a limited number of essential elements, and the major ones among them tend to recur across a wide range of academic genres.

An understanding of the essential elements in a text can help students work out how a text extract is related to its publication. This question can be used: 'How does the text fit into its publication?' The EAP teacher can present this and the other questions in this section for their students to work with.

There is significant amount of information for students to process. This includes background and contextual information in the text extract, which students need to relate to other information they have already discovered. This process will enable students to work out how and where the material in the text is positioned in terms of such aspects as time, place, topic, discipline, theories, and perspectives. Contextual information is not always obvious or intuitive; the topic of the sample text, 'intelligence', could be contextualized in many alternative ways to way in which it is positioned in this textbook, which is as follows:

Context in the textbook: Sociology → *Production, inequalities, and social divisions → Inequality, poverty, and wealth → Understanding social inequality → Poverty, intelligence, and heredity.*

Context in the text: Sociology → *historical background of where intelligence comes from → questioning the assumptions of genetic basis for intelligence → arguments against these assumptions → critical analysis of IQ tests → concluding arguments for the complex basis of intelligence.*

Essential elements: description/citation of a theory → *analysis → argument → evaluation*

Perspective

Closely related to context is **perspective**. Perspective refers to the ways people look at the world. It covers aspects of the world such as economic, political, environmental, medical, technical, historical, ethical, and many others. Figure 6.4 illustrates many of the most frequently-used perspectives. Perspective (for example economic) is often aligned to academic discipline (economics). As such, perspective is associated with objectivity and analysis. A related by subtly different conception of perspective is used by Feak and Swales (2009: 14–15), whereby an author can be said to have a perspective in relation to an issue, notably positive, neutral, or negative. This realization of perspective can be used as a category to organize the literature in a field (ibid.). Creme and Lea (2008: 26–27) also emphasize the importance of perspective in discussing and analyzing an issue. They argue that students need to identify relevant perspectives in order to approach an assignment in an appropriate way (ibid.).

Approaching a topic or issue through perspectives such as environmental and geographical is a powerful way of organizing thought and argument. Chapter 7 explores how perspective can be used as a tool for analysis and development of ideas in writing. The perspectives in a text are also connected to the context and purpose of the text—any academic text will include certain perspectives and exclude others.

In language terms, perspectives are typically expressed by classifying adjectives (*-al*), which are generally ungradable, i.e. it is unusual to say 'very medical' or 'absolutely geographical', for example. Nearly all perspective adjectives can form *-ly* adverbs, for example 'economically', as well as nouns, for example 'the economy'. Perspectives can be explicitly stated, i.e. the key word is used in the text, or implicit, i.e. understood from the content itself.

> historical   ethical   aesthetic   geographical   technological   business
> scientific   medical   genetic   technical   ethnographic   sociological   biological
> environmental   epidemiological   ethnographic   religious   social   linguistic
> philosophical   economic   financial   educational   political   logistical
> behavioural   psychological   commercial   physical   ideological   ecological
> legal   chemical   military   intellectual   artistic   musical   cultural   moral
> logical   sexual   mathematical   global

Figure 6.4   Perspectives

As with any academic text, the sample text contains a number of perspectives, which can be briefly analyzed as follows, with illustrative language from the text in brackets:

Perspectives:

- historical (*nineteenth and twentieth centuries*)
- genetic (*heredity, nature, inherited, genes, genetically, genetic*)
- societal (*social inequalities, material inequalities, social disadvantage, socialization*)
- environmental (*environment, nurture, surroundings, the first few years of life, later life, parental support*)
- mathematical (*statistician, mathematical, spatial*)
- cognitive (*intelligence, cognitive, intellectual, ability, brain function, capacity, skills, understanding, understandings*)
- linguistic (*linguistic, verbal*)
- musical (*musical*)
- research/academic (*accurately measured, measures, correlate, associated with, performance, effect, IQ, studies*)
- educational (*education, learn, tests, examinations, pre-school, primary, schooling*)
- cultural (*culturally biased, Western, culture, cross-cultural, cultural support*); geographical (*American, European, East Asians, North Americans*)

These perspectives illustrate how a relatively short, accessible text can be broad in scope. The analysis should be quite straightforward for students, and can be done even if the students' language level is somewhat lower (for example B1) than the audience of the text (B2/C1). The question to ask is simply: 'What are the main perspectives in the text?'

Perspective and purpose

One purpose of analyzing a text in this way is to illustrate how writers of a text draw on different perspectives to inform their content, and in particular their argument.

Very frequently, academic texts of similar length can have a dozen or so perspectives, which serve the purpose of the particular text: in this case the purpose is to offer a brief description of historical arguments for the genetic basis of intelligence before arguing against these and reaching a measured conclusion. This division neatly illustrates the objective/subjective distinction which is discussed in Chapters 1 and 5: the first half of the text on intelligence is mainly objective (in that it offers a historical account of the topic) while the second half is mainly subjective (in that it evaluates the theories presented in the first half of the text). It is important for the EAP student to realize this, and the implication that other accounts of the issue (the nature/nurture debate) are likely to differ. Different people (or 'subjects') may evaluate the same thing in different ways, so evaluation is subjective.

The contextualization and analysis of perspective lead naturally to the deeper meaning of the text.

Investigating meaning in texts

Having reached the point at which the student can access the meaning of the text, this section focuses on meaning, stance, citation, language, critical thinking, personal response, and independence.

Meaning

This sequence of tasks has now reached the stage which is widely considered to be the point of reading: to work out, understand, and process meaning in a text. Although the multi-stage build-up to this point might seem rather elaborate, it is worth emphasizing that skilled academic readers go through these stages automatically and quite quickly. The stages are important in building up the meaning of the text, and illustrate how meaning is not a narrow construct but a broad one, based on consideration of how the published text fits in to its wider academic and cultural context. These considerations relate particularly to critical approaches to reading and processing information.

Different readers approach texts and work out meaning in different ways. Early in the development of a student as academic reader, meaning can be built up first at paragraph level, then at text level: essentially a 'bottom-up' approach, which can also be described as 'synthetic' (Wilkins, 1976) and 'atomistic' (Bruce 2011). More proficient readers can adopt a more holistic 'top-down', or 'analytic' (Wilkins 1976) approach. Questions such as the following can be used: 'What are the main point(s), and the conclusion? How is the argument developed?'

Another technique for gaining an overview of a text is to use paragraphs as stepping stones through the text; in this way the student can focus on **topic sentences** and concluding sentences of paragraphs. However, this does not work neatly in all texts as the meaning in paragraphs can be expressed in many different ways by different writers.

Depending on the student's level, a useful starting point in working out the meaning of a text is to differentiate between main points and supporting points in a text. Typically, a paragraph has a main point, together with supporting points in the form of examples and evidence which may be cited or the author's own. The main point can often be found in one (or two) sentences in the paragraph, which can then be extracted and stripped down to its essentials as in the following, based on the sample text:

Main points and conclusion:

- Paragraph 1: The argument of heredity versus the environment emerged in the 19th and 20th centuries.

- Paragraph 2: These theories led to the development of IQ tests (tests to measure general intelligence).

- Paragraph 3: Arguments linking inherited intelligence to social disadvantage rest on three assumptions.

- Paragraph 4: These assumptions are highly questionable.

- Paragraph 5: IQ tests are flawed and culturally biased.

- Paragraph 6: Intelligence is a complex process, heavily influenced by environmental factors.

The 'conclusion' of the text is essentially the main point of the final paragraph, six. During this stage of working out meaning, there is no particularly compelling reason for the student to use entirely new language; they can express the main points by extracting language from the text, particularly phrases and parts of sentences. They can use more of their own language to reprocess the meaning further in a later stage. Given that these main points carry the essential meaning of the text, the remainder of the text constitutes such elements as the following:

- support and exemplification—for example 'Mathematical and verbal intelligence, for example, are not perfectly associated with one another'.

- explanation—for example 'Essentially the arguments are concerned with the extent to which intelligence is inherited … or formed through a person's life and their surroundings'.

- background information—for example 'Various attempts have been made to explain where intelligence comes from'.

Summarizing meaning

Summarizing the essential meaning in a text is a core academic skill. An essential element in academic texts is citation, through which meaning is summarized;

likewise, students need to summarize meaning from the texts they read in order to incorporate it into their own written and spoken texts. Students can use their notes on the text to write a summary of the text. A summary needs to be a coherent text, and so requires a reference to the source text. Based on the main points only, the sample text can be effectively summarized quite briefly, in about 70 words.

Two sample summaries follow; the first is based on a high B2 level student who had followed the sequence of tasks in this section, and carefully constructed their summary. Minor surface errors are corrected in order to focus on the summary itself.

Summary 1

In their text 'Intelligence: heredity versus environment', Fulcher and Scott (2011: 731–2) trace the development of major theories of intelligence. They argue against 19th-century theories that general intelligence is essentially genetic, proposing instead a more balanced view which recognizes the importance of environmental factors such as education in determining a person's level of intelligence. The authors also question the validity and reliability of general intelligence, or IQ, tests.

The summary above shows what is achievable for a B2+ EAP student who has followed the sequence of tasks in this section. It is revealing to contrast this summary with one by a student in the same class of a similar level who has not worked through these tasks, as below:

Summary 2

This article is about intelligence and discusses different aspects of intelligence. It refers to historical views of intelligence (linguistic, mathematical, spatial, musical, etc.), as well as IQ tests which test intelligence. I think it is a very interesting text.

Summary 1 correctly includes a reference to the source text. As Summary 2 has no such reference, it does not stand as complete text; the audience will not know what 'this article' refers to. Both summaries are concise and clear, but Summary 2 is not complete: while Summary 1 includes the main points of the source text, Summary 2 does not. Instead, it gives the topic of the source text and details such as the listing of types of intelligence, but these are unnecessary and inappropriate in a summary. Finally, Summary 2 adds the student's own evaluation at the end, which is also inappropriate for a summary because it is not part of the original text being summarized.

Writing a summary can serve a number of useful purposes:

- to assist the student in the process of understanding the text, especially in identifying the main points
- to provide tangible evidence for their teacher that the student has understood the text effectively; or, in the case of flawed summaries, understood the text less well
- to serve as a record of the text and its main meaning
- to use, as a citation, in a new written or spoken text, for example as part of a literature review or as supporting evidence

- to use as a revision aid when recalling and consolidating knowledge for an examination.

Finally, since a written summary can be seen as a product, it can be read by others (students and the teacher) in the EAP classroom. Thus it usefully addresses the issue of reading being an essentially cognitive—and therefore in effect 'invisible'—activity by providing tangible evidence of effective reading.

In addition to identifying the main points of a text, another crucial aspect is to work out the author's **stance**.

Stance

Stance refers to how the writer or speaker stands in relation to a notion such as a theory, issue, argument, school of thought, or proposition. There are several examples of these from the text, for example: 'General intelligence is a cognitive ability that underlies all other specific forms of intelligence'; and 'General intelligence … can be accurately measured by IQ tests'. As different people can adopt different stances on the same notion, stance is inherently subjective.

Stance and evaluation

As discussed in Chapter 5, stance is closely related to evaluation, but is a more formalized concept. A stance is not something that is instantly adopted; rather, it is something that is carefully considered and refined over a period of time. A wider range of things can be evaluated, such as ideas and physical entities, and also less formalized notions like how effectively a person delivered their presentation. Also, entities such as a proposed design for a new public building or a work of art can be evaluated, where the term 'stance' would probably not be used. Furthermore, comparison and contrast (for example between specific aspects of different countries) typically leads to evaluation.

When reading an academic text, students need to identify the writer's stance. This may be stated very clearly, or be more implicit and so harder to work out. As the meaning of a text is expressed through language, this language is a useful starting point in working out stance. At surface level, students need to become familiar with the language of stance, such as the adverbials 'clearly', 'blatantly', 'effectively'. The following examples of evaluative language (underlined) from the last three paragraphs in the sample text are key to working out the author's stance:

Each of these assumptions <u>can be questioned</u>. The concept of general intelligence <u>has been heavily criticized</u>, and <u>there is no agreement that</u> there is any such common factor behind particular abilities. Mathematical and verbal intelligence, for example, <u>are not perfectly associated with</u> one another. <u>It may be more useful to regard</u> intelligence <u>as</u> a set of intellectual capacities <u>rather than</u> a single one. Even if it is allowed that general intelligence exists, <u>however, there is the problem of</u> how it is to be measured.

<u>Many have questioned the value of</u> the IQ score <u>as</u> a measure of intelligence. Tests have been shown to be <u>culturally biased</u> towards Western (American and European)

culture and, within this, towards white, middle-class men. The cultural differences that shape the ability to perform in the tests <u>do not necessarily reflect</u> any differences in intelligence. More fundamentally, perhaps, <u>there are doubts about whether</u> performance in pencil-and-paper tests can be <u>a proper measure</u> of a person's ability to perform in 'real' situations. <u>Indeed, there are wider doubts about whether</u> performance in A-level, degree, or other examinations is <u>an adequate measure of</u> a person's understanding of a subject or ability to apply it in real-life situations.

Intelligence is a complex process that brings together numerous aspects of brain function, and <u>doubts have been raised about</u> its genetic basis. It is inherited not as a fixed quantity but as a capacity to learn the kinds of skills and understandings that make up a particular ability. The realization of this capacity depends on the stimulation that is received in the first few years of life and, to a much lesser extent, in later life. It has been found that pre-school, primary socialization is <u>critical</u> in raising or lowering measured intelligence. Formal education can have a continuing, if smaller, effect, and educational action programmes <u>can significantly raise</u> the IQ of children who enter them with <u>relatively low</u> IQ. Cross-cultural studies have shown that <u>the relatively high</u> IQ of East Asians, <u>as compared with</u> North Americans, is due to the length and type of schooling, the extent of parental support, and the cultural support for disciplined work.

This analysis shows that evaluative language is both lexical and grammatical, i.e. it uses both meaningful vocabulary (for example 'adequate') as well as grammatical structures (for example 'regard X as Y rather than Z'). Although the language underlined is evaluative, students need to be aware that it does not all express the authors' stance. Some of the evaluative language, for example 'has been heavily criticized', and 'there is no agreement that', is used to report arguments by others, so it does not necessarily represent the stance of the authors of this text. The choices of language form in these cases, i.e. the passive and 'there' structure, are objective in the sense that they are not linked to a subject (person). However, the similarly objective structure 'It may be more useful to regard' is used to express the authors' stance. The evaluative language is intricately connected to the author's argument in this text, so the reader needs to follow the argument to identify the writer's stance. Language, then, is a key to working out stance, but the reader needs to go beyond the surface and more deeply into the meaning and context. The question for students to ask is: 'What is the writer's stance?' In the case of the authors' stance in the sample text, Fulcher and Scott (2011: 731–2) question the genetic nature of intelligence, arguing instead that it is more complex and related to social, educational, and cultural factors.

Citation

Citation is a prototypical characteristic and essential element in academic discourse. In many general contexts, in contrast, writers and speakers can make statements and argue for them without the expectation of providing support from other sources. Citation refers to the reporting of ideas (for example research, theories, statements, arguments) from sources outside the text itself; this reported material can be by the same author and/or by others, and can be expressed using the original words (a direct quotation), through other language of a similar length (**paraphrase**), or as a brief distillation of the main points (summary).

EAP teachers need to provide noticing activities, such as identifying the type of citation, and the source, followed by working out the meaning of the citation, how it fits in with the writer's argument, and finally critically evaluating this material. Noticing activities such as these can be integrated into the EAP classroom and materials.

Students need to identify the cited material in a text and distinguish this from the author's own material, in other words work out whose ideas are whose. The reader of a text can also legitimately ask how clear the writer of the text makes this distinction.

Language

When approaching a text, it is usually most intuitive and effective to work on meaning first, and then language. It is inadvisable to look at language too comprehensively; rather, it is more helpful for students to focus on one or two aspects of language. The focus on stance above brought out evaluative language. Another useful aspect of language to look at is generic language: the language which serves to introduce meanings across disciplines. Generic language from the sample text is underlined in the following extract:

> These terms are often known as 'nature' and 'nurture'; Essentially the arguments are concerned with the extent to which intelligence is inherited; These theories led to the concept of how to measure intelligence.

Generic language can be informed by learning objectives such as for students to identify stance, perspectives, argument, comparison, citation, tentativeness, and speculation.

The language focus can be linked to cohesion, which is examined in greater detail in Chapter 3. In the sample text, the concept of 'nature' is connected through the text using the related words and phrases 'heredity', 'inherited', 'genetically', and 'fixed from birth' (looking more deeply into how words can be connected, the words 'heredity' and 'inherited' are linked through their derivation from 'heir'). Similarly, the opposing concept of 'nurture' is expressed in the text through another set of words and phrases: 'surroundings', 'social inequalities', 'education', 'cultural differences', 'culture', 'real-life situations', and 'parental support'.

Another aspect of language to focus on can be academic vocabulary arising from the text. As the examples of generic language show, such language is best presented as sequences of words, or chunks, rather than discrete words.

Alternatively, students can select their own language to investigate, guided by their EAP teachers.

Critical thinking and evaluation

Chapter 5 looks at how critical thinking is central to the EAP context. Critical thinking tasks based on reading can include the following: working out how and why the essential elements in a text are connected; looking for analogies and patterns; identifying assumptions and implicit meaning in the text; identifying the author's stance; and asking critical questions in response to the arguments presented.

By approaching each text critically, students can learn to ask specific questions based on the text. Critical questions arising from the sample text include the following:

- If we accept that IQ tests are flawed, how does this weaken the argument for general intelligence?
- Why are some questions left unasked, for instance, why are IQ tests still widely used, for example in the USA?
- If general intelligence, 'g', does not exist, why do people talk about it?
- Why are all the in-text references over 100 years old?
- Why are no references given for more recent claims, for example 'Tests have been shown to be …' By whom?
- Why is the claim in the last sentence (about the IQ of East Asians and North Americans) not evaluated?

It is important for students to evaluate the texts they read. Students can consider the text and its context, based on the criteria in Table 6.6.

Criteria	Questions
Context and currency	Where and when was the text published? Does the text build on and extend previous work in the area?
Examples	What types of examples and explanation are given in the text? How effectively do the examples and explanation support the arguments?
Information	How clearly is the information expressed in the text? How is it selected?
Level	How difficult is the language in the text? Can I fully understand the concepts and arguments in the text?
Application	How generally/specifically can the arguments and findings in the text be applied to other contexts?
Personalization	How interesting, useful, and relevant is the information in the text? How can I use the material in the text in my own work (e.g. written texts, spoken presentations)?

Table 6.6   Evaluative criteria for reading texts

These evaluative criteria show the extent to which students can engage with a text. In doing so, students are at the centre of the critical process: as with other critical responses, the questions and answers are subjective, and part of the purpose and interest lies in discussing and rationalizing different responses. Personal responses to texts are an important part of academic reading, and it can be very beneficial for students to respond and reflect on what they read.

Personal response and reflection

Like critically evaluative responses, personal reflective responses can be elicited using a series of generic questions. Figure 6.5 presents a set of reflective reading questions. These are designed to follow a reading class comprising a complete sequence of reading tasks. They aim to provide an opportunity for students to look back on the reading. While they are focused primarily on content, they can also be used to bring out language.

At first the reflective questions can be done in class, so as to enable EAP teachers to monitor. As with other reading tasks, an outcome is desirable, which means that students should note down their responses. This can lead to a discussion and comparison. By keeping a record of their responses, students can track their progress in reading.

How has the information in this text contributed to my understanding of the topic?

How might this text be interpreted in my own culture?

Can I make any predictions based on the information in the text?

What language and knowledge can I take away from this text?

How can I use aspects of the text (content/organization/structure/language) in my own writing and speaking?

What language have I learned?

What is my personal response to the text?

What can I read next?

Figure 6.5   *Reflective reading questions*

These reflective questions are designed to encourage independent learning. The increasingly independent learner can learn to formulate their own learning objectives, and achieve them.

Next steps and independence

Given the reality that EAP students are studying or preparing to study in English, eventually they will be studying in their disciplines with little or no EAP support. Therefore they need to become independent learners.

Independence

Chapter 2 argues that the ultimate goal of EAP is to enable students to work independently, with minimal language teacher guidance. Independence is closely related to autonomy; however autonomy is more internal, covering motivation, personal organization, achieving deadlines. Student independence and autonomy can be encouraged through:

- tasks which are independent of EAP teachers, the timetabled lesson, the classroom itself, and the prescribed materials
- tasks which use technology, for example internet resources, library databases, images. These tasks can be achieved with a degree of independence.
- tasks which involve collaboration with other students, for example group research projects and joint presentations.

As increasingly independent learners, students learn how to find and access texts for themselves, and use material from these in their own academic work.

Time constraints

In many teaching contexts, such as in-sessional programmes, shortage of time can present challenges. There can be limitations on both class time and the time available for independent study due to students' other academic commitments. In such contexts, EAP teachers could adopt some of the strategies in Table 6.7.

Criteria	Strategies
Needs	Be rigorous in selecting what to cover. Respond to specific, identifiable student needs such as writing a literature review rather than spending time covering less tangible areas like improving general language proficiency.
Material	Target material to specific students. Try covering more than one area per class in a workshop-style lesson in which each student is given personalized material and students work on this concurrently using the EAP teacher as a resource when required. In this way students' needs are prioritized and no student has to cover material they are already proficient in.
Independence	Find a productive balance between class work and independent study. A lot of material can be done outside the classroom, freeing up valuable class time for work which maximally utilizes the assets of the EAP teacher.
Methodology	Vary the channels of input. Present some material in a teacher-centred classroom setting, which suits many learners and reflects certain academic practices and can be highly efficient; also set up more inductive student-centred tasks for other input where students find out knowledge independently in a '**flipped classroom**' approach (see Chapter 12 for further material on this).
Time	With independent study, maximize ways of engaging students and ensuring task completion. Use materials downloadable onto their electronic devices (e.g. **smartphones, tablets**) which they can use whenever possible at times convenient to them, such as while travelling.

Criteria	Strategies
Tasks	Set multiple short tasks rather than one long task. Students may never have, for example, a block of four hours per week to complete a long task, but they can find a way to complete six 40-minute tasks—one per day.
Negotiation	Build a dialogue with the students about what to cover, when, and how. With student 'buy-in' to their learning process, they can be motivated to study and achieve more.
Balance	Prioritize the material to be covered so that if time runs out the most important work has been done. Sometimes the EAP teacher covers relatively little in the earlier stages of the programme, only to speed up as the deadlines approach; this is not an efficient way of learning as students can often be more motivated and energized at the beginning of a programme.
Pace	Set a reasonably fast pace of learning. Students may lose motivation or stop attending if the learning pace is too slow. Check learning regularly to make sure that the pace is not too fast.
Research	Ask a colleague to conduct a short action research task in which they quantify the time spent on different activities. Teacher activities could include: input of new material, giving instructions, checking learning, monitoring, explaining, exemplifying, backtracking, and digressing. Key student activities include: listening to any of the above; putting into practice new learning points; communicating with other students and the teacher; and producing new work, notably through communicative speech or writing. The action researcher can provide information on the balance between types of input and teacher/student activities. Optionally, parts of the lesson can be videoed: this can provide clear evidence of the balance of teacher/student activities.

Table 6.7   Maximizing time efficiency in EAP teaching and learning

Ideas such as those in Table 6.7 can enhance productive teaching and learning. Observation, as outlined in the final suggestion above, can be quite illuminating in terms of learning efficiency.

Conclusion

This chapter has discussed the complexities and challenges of academic reading for EAP students, and proposed an adaptable sequence of student-centred tasks for EAP teachers to approach the teaching and learning of reading in the wider academic context. These tasks bring out the multiple roles for the academic reader, which may be summed up as 'academic reader as processor and evaluator'. Student do this through a purposeful process of locating and selecting suitable texts, through navigating the whole text and the specific extract, engaging with the meaning and language in the text and the author's stance, to using material from the text in their own productive output.

In most EAP contexts, a major part of student productive output is in the form of writing, which is the subject of Chapter 7.

Further reading

Godfrey, J. 2009. *How to Use Your Reading in Your Essays*. Basingstokc: Palgravc Macmillan.

Grabe, W. and **F. Stoller.** 2002. *Teaching and Researching Reading*. Harlow: Longman.

Grabe, W. 2009. *Reading in a Second Language: Moving from Theory to Practice*. Cambridge: Cambridge University Press.

Hudson, T. 2007. *Teaching Second Language Reading*. Oxford: Oxford University Press.

Nuttall, C. 2005. *Teaching Reading Skills in a Foreign Language 3ᵉ*. Oxford: Macmillan.

7

WRITING

Academic writer as architect of meaning

Writing is widely seen as fundamental to EAP teaching and learning. Bruce, for instance, speaks for many when he states that 'writing tends to be regarded as the core skill in EAP courses' (Bruce 2011: 10). Academic writing is also widely accepted to involve a highly complex set of skills and competences, which even 'expert' writers with multiple publications can continue to improve on: given continued practice and a degree of self-criticism and reflection, a person's writing can continue to develop and improve indefinitely. This process of development will be further encouraged and enhanced by critical feedback. For EAP students, such critical feedback will mainly come from their EAP teacher(s); however feedback from their peers, including other EAP and non-EAP students, can also be invaluable. Hyland and Hyland report that in various studies, students have been found to prefer written feedback from the teacher to other forms of feedback, such as, oral feedback and feedback from peers (Leki 1991, Saito 1994, Zhang 1995, all in Hyland and Hyland 2006: 3).

Writers can also learn to critically review their own written work, which means that the role of critic is an important one. Given their position at the centre of the process, writers need to adopt a number of roles in order to write effectively. This chapter examines what and why students of EAP need to write, how they can write, and the role of EAP teachers in developing and managing their students' writing.

Meaning

An analogy to illustrate these roles is that of architect. As a starting point, an architect needs to engage and liaise with various key stakeholders in their project, from public representatives, such as planning officers, through legal teams to their clients and paymasters who are commissioning and financing the project. The architect also needs an understanding across many perspectives, such as structure, materials, construction processes, engineering possibilities, aesthetic and spatial considerations, ergonomic factors, human behaviour and psychology, economic and financial requirements, as well as legal perspectives relating to, for example, health and safety. The entire project needs to be grounded in its context, in environmental, cultural, and physical terms.

Informed by these understandings, the architect takes on, plans, and manages the project, bringing it to a point where it can be handed over to the construction team. Likewise, an academic writer has to 'project manage' complex assignments, through a process starting with the interpretation of the brief (the assignment rubric), through the sourcing, selection, and processing of texts, leading to the construction, transfer, and delivery of meaning to communicate to their audience, all expertly packaged into an original text using appropriate language. In this sense, the academic writer takes on the role of architect of meaning.

As with many EAP skills, writing is naturally about communication: the communication of such concepts as ideas, research, arguments, critical responses, and feelings.

Communication

Ideally, the starting point with productive academic discourse is having something to say. This might sound obvious, but it is nonetheless worth emphasizing to students. If students can note down the main points of what they want to communicate, however briefly (indeed the more briefly the better), these notes can form the basis of a writing plan. In order to get to the stage where they have something to say—i.e. some content—students are likely to have to carry out a considerable amount of reading, thinking, discussion and (depending on their academic level) research. Without such content, no amount of sophisticated academic language and style can disguise the fact that there is none. This implies that academic writing is not simply a matter of technical and linguistic expertise, but a broader process of building and managing meaning, knowledge and content, organizing and refining ideas, and communicating these through appropriately conventional texts. The centrality of communication is emphasized by Nesi and Gardner (2012) when they state that:

> Students need to learn how to write well, because writing is the means by which they will construct disciplinary knowledge, the main means by which they will demonstrate their attainment for assessment purposes, and, in many cases, also the means by which they will communicate with professional colleagues in years to come.

(Nesi and Gardner 2012: 3)

It is significant that Nesi and Gardner emphasize not only course assessments but also students' future communication. Such professional communication needs are often overlooked in EAP teaching, which can suffer from too specific and restricted a focus.

In its broadest sense, academic writing is about communicating ideas. Communication, though, is a very broad notion, and it is helpful to refine it. A useful and familiar starting point is description.

Description

A frequent essential element in academic texts is description. Academic writers therefore need to draw on the essential element of description to describe and present a wide range of things, such as the following:

- background information
- specific contexts and characteristics
- theories, ideas and developments
- entities, for example physical spaces and structures
- processes, systems, and procedures

Despite this widespread need for description, academic writing is not concerned with description alone. In most genres, description is a necessary support for many more critical essential elements (which are presented and exemplified in Chapters 3 and 5).

Persuasion

Certainly there is plenty of description to be found in academic texts, but if there is one overarching purpose of much academic writing, it is to persuade. It has been said that 'most argument would hope to be persuasive, but not all persuasion is argumentative' (Andrews 2010: 39). A challenge for EAP teachers is to develop their students' understanding and production of sound argument that is persuasive.

Academic writers produce many essential elements, such as descriptions of characteristics (as mentioned above), recounts of procedures, and definitions of concepts. Writers often provide description to provide necessary information and explanation relating to the topic of the text. In many genres, these essential elements, in turn, lead to the development of argument and the provision of supporting evidence and exemplification, and ultimately serve the more complex purpose of persuasion.

The importance of persuasion is stressed by Bryman and Bell (2011) in a textbook aimed at students embarking on a research project or studying a module in research methods. Managing a project is discussed later in this chapter. They make clear that reporting research and presenting conclusions are insufficient; these students are advised to be persuasive, which involves offering a convincing argument with a significant and plausible conclusion (Bryman and Bell 2011: 679). In short, persuasion is achieved primarily through argument.

Argument

In academic contexts an argument involves making a statement based on reason, logic, and evidence. The main argument in a text is typically served by smaller-scale arguments, which are known as supporting arguments. In some genres, notably the 'for and against' discursive essay (and its more interactive spoken equivalent, the debate), there may be a sense of balance in terms of space given to each side of the argument. Many academic genres, however, are argument driven. This means that one main argument is the thread that holds the text together and where most of the writer's material is directed. Opposing arguments, meanwhile, need to be recognized: the writer may state one or more opposing arguments (i.e. arguments which do not support the writer's main argument) in order to rebut, dismiss, and diminish them. The major part of the text, however, is likely to be taken up by the main argument and its supporting material.

Above all, an academic writer wants their argument to be persuasive. The writer's aim is to construct a text through which they can convince their audience through argument. To a great extent, their argument is often the reason for writing the text.

Developing an argument

One of the major challenges facing students is how to develop an argument. There have been a number of influential models which explain the structure and stages in an argument. Toulmin's *The Uses of Argument*, originally published in 1958 and updated in 2003, sets out an elaborate six-stage argument model. Described as being 'of seminal importance' (Andrews 2010: 43), Toulmin's model has been widely cited, incorporated into academic writing materials, and subsequently adapted by other researchers and practitioners. It is designed to provide a framework for testing the soundness of an argument (ibid.), and is summarized in Table 7.1.

Stage	Function
Claim	Presenting your statement which you want your audience to accept
Grounds	Offering evidence, typically through citations, to support your claim
Warrant	Giving reasons why the grounds support the claim
Backing	Providing further support for the claim, particularly by addressing related questions
Qualifier	Hedging, in order to avoid making an over-confident claim which could more easily be critiqued
Rebuttal	Dealing with counter arguments in order to show the claim in a stronger light

Table 7.1   Toulmin's argument model (based on Toulmin 1958)

Toulmin's analysis may appear complex; furthermore he divided arguments into different types. His classification of different types of arguments included analytic, analytic/substantial, conclusive/tentative, **deductive/inductive**, presumptive, quasi-syllogistic, and warrant-establishing (Toulmin, 1958). Riddle (2000: 57 in Mitchell and Andrews 2000 and Nesi and Gardner 2012: 91) expresses Toulmin's model in simpler and more familiar terms: 'SINCE x (grounds), THEN y (claim), BECAUSE z (warrant)'.

Building on this tradition of a conventionally structured argument, Booth, Colomb, and Williams (1995, 2003, and 2008) propose a more compact model: claim – reason – evidence. This model assimilates the core components of the Toulmin model, and can be summed up as:

• What am I trying to convince you of? (claim)

• Why is this convincing? (reason)

• What information and citations can I offer to support my argument? (evidence)

At the heart of models such as these is the construction of an argument. This, in turn, needs to be rationalized (i.e. its importance explained) and built on using relevant and compelling evidence in order to come across as convincing and persuasive.

The following quotation is taken from the Bryman and Bell (2011) textbook. This extract serves as a useful example of the kind of advice research students may encounter relating to argument: its importance, and what it entails.

The importance of an argument

One of the things that students can find difficult about writing up their research is the formulation of an argument. The writing-up of research should be organized around an argument that links all aspects of the research process from problem formulation, through literature review and the presentation of research methods, to the discussion and conclusion. Too often, students make a series of points without asking what the contribution of these points is to the overall argument that they are trying to present. Consider what your claim to knowledge is and try to organize your writing to support and enhance it. That will be your argument. Sometimes it is useful to think in terms of telling a story about your research and your findings. Try to avoid tangents and irrelevant material that may mean your readers will lose the thread of your argument. If you are not able to supply a clear argument, you are vulnerable to the 'so what?' question. Ask yourself: 'What is the key point or message that I want my readers to take away with them when they have finished reading my work?' if you cannot answer that question satisfactorily (and it may be worth trying it out on others), almost certainly you do not have an argument. The argument is a thread that runs through your dissertation.

(Bryman and Bell 2011: 679)

Bryman and Bell's central message that students should be able to write their argument down has been echoed by others, such as Bonnett (2001) who has developed a process in which students write first a rough one-sentence summary of their argument, and later a smooth version (Bonnett 2001: 5 and 47).

While Bryman and Bell's textbook is aimed at business research students who need to write dissertations, the key points apply to many other disciplines, levels, and genres, including certain essays. Fundamentally, students need to work out what their main message is, and how to communicate it effectively to their audience.

To some extent, the observations in this and the previous sections also apply to spoken rather than written academic texts, notably presentations and to some extent lectures. It is worthwhile now to look at other concepts related to argument.

Concepts associated with argument

The section above has shown that an argument is comprised of a number of stages. Central to these is the concept of the *claim*, which refers to the main point which the writer or speaker is trying to convince their audience of. To clarify this concept, it is useful to examine various other concepts associated with academic argument. Table 7.2 presents eight of these concepts, moving down the table towards the ones that are most highly validated (i.e. shown to be true). While theories may be widely validated, only facts can be considered to be completely validated and no longer in need of further research and evidence.

Term	Example
Idea	Huge solar panels could be developed to cover deserts like the Sahara in order to reflect the harmful rays of the sun back towards the sun.
Opinion	The governments of the world should unite against cutting and burning tropical forests.
Interpretation	The latest scientific figures on the temperature of the oceans indicate that the speed at which they are warming is increasing.
Evaluation	The latest scientific figures on the temperature of the oceans are disturbing.
Stance	A major increase in taxation linked to the carbon footprint of industry is a challenging yet workable policy proposal.
Hypothesis	A carbon tax will affect colder countries more than hotter ones.
Claim	Richer households are likely to be less affected than poorer ones by a carbon tax.
Theory	The rebound effect is when people drive further and use more fuel because they have a more efficient car.
Fact	When carbon dioxide is released into the atmosphere, the atmosphere captures more heat.

Table 7.2   Concepts associated with academic argument

These concepts and examples may all be associated with argument, but the two at the top of the table—idea and opinion—are in themselves not considered sufficiently rigorous to have a central place in many academic contexts and genres, such as argument essays. While ideas are interesting and necessary, they need further development before they can form part of an academic argument. Similarly, opinions may also be interesting, but need to be developed. Whereas an opinion may be formed in a moment based on an impulse, evaluation is associated with criteria. An evaluation may also be formed quickly, but is typically based on answers to questions such as 'How credible is the evidence?' and 'To what extent can this finding be generalized?' These represent the criteria being used in the evaluation.

In turn, a person's stance is likely to be more measured than an evaluation, and takes time to formulate. Like opinion and evaluation, stance is subjective and can include elements of personal belief, experience, and bias. People's stances related to issues such as global warming and politics are likely to be influenced by a wide range of factors including any of the following: their background, education, parenting, friends, culture, profession, business interests, and level of knowledge about the issue. In academic contexts, this level of knowledge, achieved through reading and research, is considered vital in supporting a person's stance. Interpretation is a closely related, and in some senses overlapping, concept to evaluation. Interpretation involves a consideration of the evidence and an attempt at stating what it means and implies. As with the other concepts discussed so far, it is subjective, and based on evidence. It is worth stating that any of the terms and examples in the table could be interpreted differently, as the terms (their labels and concepts) are not absolute, universally agreed, and clear-cut.

Above all, these concepts all need support. This support is likely to take the form of evidence based on research. With such support, ideas and opinions can be developed, or 'promoted', to the level of hypotheses and claims. These hypotheses and claims can then be contested, i.e. challenged, critiqued, and opposed, in a process which tests their validity and robustness. Eventually, if repeated research shows overwhelming support, a hypothesis or claim can become sufficiently validated to be considered a theory. Even in cases where scientists may consider the evidence to be extremely strong, such as in the theory of evolution, these remain theories rather than facts. A fact needs to be able to be proved in some sense, for example by research which can be replicated by different people in different contexts, or by measurement. For instance, the statement 'in the UK, Manchester is east of Edinburgh', which may appear confusing, can be proved by measuring the locations on a reliable map, in a validation process which confirms its status as a fact.

Characteristics of academic writing

This section has established that academic writing is about communication through description, persuasion, and supported argument.

An orthodox view of academic discourse

A number of researchers and practitioners have made observations about the characteristics of academic writing including academic style. For example, Clanchy and Ballard (1981: 74, and 1992, also cited in Jordan 1997: 244) present a number of characteristics based around the academic writer's approach, tone, and language. These are presented in Figure 7.1.

Characteristics of academic style

The academic writer's approach to his or her material is:

analytical		impressionistic
objective	*rather than*	subjective
intellectual		emotional
rational		polemical

The academic writer's tone is:

serious		conversational
impersonal	*rather than*	personal
formal		informal

The academic writer makes frequent use of:

passive forms of the verb
impersonal pronouns and phrases
qualifying words and phrases
complex sentence structures
specialized vocabulary

Figure 7.1   Clanchy and Ballard's (1981) characteristics of academic style (Clanchy and Ballard in Jordan 1997: 244)

These observations by Clanchy and Ballard have been widely cited, but it is necessary to respond critically rather than accept them as rules or prescriptions. In a sense, they are false dichotomies. Rather than being the distinctions or opposites presented here, the characteristics are arguably *all* necessary for the academic writer and researcher, depending on their context and purpose. Most disciplines deal with people to some extent—not only the social sciences but also many other disciplines such as medicine and civil engineering—and when interacting with people the characteristics in the column on the right are important and inevitable. Case studies, for instance, tend to have a strong personal element as they are based around people.

To take one pair of distinctions—objective versus subjective—objectivity is associated with facts, but facts constitute only a small part of academic discourse. Encyclopedias are concerned with facts, but academic genres are to a considerable extent concerned with concepts such as argument and discussion, interpretation and evaluation; these are demonstrably subjective rather than objective, as this chapter makes clear. An argument should not be considered as a fact; by their nature, arguments invite counter-arguments, and there is not normally universal agreement on one particular argument. In contrast, no one should disagree with a fact such as 'in the UK, Manchester is east of Edinburgh' once it has been validated.

Even analysis is not necessarily objective: while the analysis of a physical substance in chemistry may be objective (although it may be done in different ways), an analysis of the causes of a problem in economics may not, simply because different economists can analyze it differently and draw different conclusions from their analyses. Therefore analysis in its cognitive sense has elements of subjectivity:

different subjects (people) can analyze (and interpret, and evaluate) the same phenomenon in different ways.

Similar criticism may be levelled at Clanchy and Ballard's observations on language. Chapters 4 and 6 reported Biber and Gray's research which shows that the main complexity in academic writing lies in the phrase rather than the clause and sentence (Biber and Gray 2010). In order to determine the realities of academic writing, it is useful to go back to fundamentals.

These criticisms have been echoed by Hyland, who writes:

> Academic texts are often seen as purely impersonal, objective and informative, merely faceless descriptions of reality where words deal directly with facts. However, the persuasiveness of academic discourse does not depend upon the demonstration of absolute truth, empirical evidence or flawless logic. Texts are the result of actions of socially situated writers and are persuasive only when they employ social and linguistic conventions that colleagues find convincing.

(Hyland 1999: 99)

Hyland's argument underlines the nonfactual tendencies of academic writing, which are by implication essentially subjective. He also emphasizes the need for effective persuasion.

Realities of academic writing

Earlier chapters have established that academic texts are clustered around describable genres which in turn are written for definable audiences and particular purposes. An academic text is situated in a social academic context, and this context has accepted conventions in terms of style and structure as well as language. Many other characteristics are expected. For instance, the length of a piece of writing may be prescribed, and specific aspects of knowledge assumed. An academic text shows terms of understanding which are shared, such as how previous knowledge is acknowledged and extended.

The audience of an academic text is to some extent inseparable from the text, as the writer of the text creates a profile of their audience which informs their writing. Audiences have their own expectations of the text, and in turn are expected to respond critically to the text. Audiences of academic texts may expect and accommodate a degree of self-promotion by the writers of these texts.

A further crucial element of academic genres is citation. Academic writers, including student writers, are expected to include material from other relevant sources, in other words citation, to provide evidence and exemplification for their arguments. As a result, academic texts are evidence-based and referenced.

There is less tolerance for texts which do not adhere to the accepted academic conventions of citation and referencing than the features of style identified by Clanchy and Ballard above. Academic genres can vary quite considerably in terms of formality and specific features such as, for example, the use of personal pronouns, but when it comes to citation and referencing, accuracy is expected.

It is these kinds of factors that inform and shape academic texts, which, to varying degrees, include all the characteristics in Clanchy and Ballard's (1981) orthodox view of academic discourse, shown previously. The following section investigates in more detail the texts which students are expected to write.

Student writing

Student writing may take many forms, and the first challenge for EAP teachers is to determine what students will have to write.

Genres in the disciplines

Recent research by Nesi and Gardner (2012) has greatly illuminated what students are required to write in their disciplines. Their research identifies thirteen genre families, and quantifies them by academic level, i.e. undergraduate (first, second, and third years) to taught master's postgraduate level, i.e. a master's degree which is mainly taught rather than research-based. The thirteen genre families are as follows: case study; critique; design specification; empathy writing; essay; exercise; explanation; literature survey; methodology recount; narrative recount; problem question; proposal; research report. Nesi and Gardner focus on history, sociology, and engineering in this part of their research. These are presented in Table 7.3 (column 1) together with examples from specific disciplines (column 2) and their distribution in the BAWE (British Academic Written English) corpus used by Nesi and Gardner (column 3).

The research corpus comprised a total of 2,858 texts. It can be seen that certain genres are far more prevalent than others. The most popular genre family is the essay, accounting for 43.3% of the total (1,237 out of 2,858 texts). Also popular are critiques and methodology recounts, and to a slightly lesser extent, case studies. Nesi and Gardner's research also indicates how frequent such genre families occur at different academic levels (i.e. first, second, and third year undergraduate, and taught master's); some of the genres are similarly popular at all levels, but several become less frequent as the academic level rises, notably essays (Nesi and Gardner 2012: 10). Other genre families, including case studies, occur more frequently at higher academic levels (ibid.). To explain one of the less familiar genre families in the table, 'empathy writing' is a term used by Lea and Street (2000: 39, cited in Nesi and Gardner 2012: 42). It refers to genres such as newspaper articles and information leaflets which are written for non-specialist audiences.

The table also shows one genre family can be expressed in different genres depending on the discipline. A research report, for example, can take the form of a long essay, dissertation, or project in different disciplines. Clearly all these genres are research based, but each one will present variations, for example in length (word count), structure and organization, and audience.

Genre family	Specific disciplines (history, sociology, engineering) and examples of genres	Total
Case study	engineering: company report, accident report	6.8%
Critique	history: book review; sociology: evaluation of research methods, and book review; engineering: evaluations of products, techniques, performance, systems, tools, and buildings	11.3%
Design specification	engineering: design plan	3.3%
Empathy writing	sociology: expert information for a journalist; engineering: expert advice to industry; letter; information leaflet; job application; newspaper article	1.3%
Essay	history: exposition, discussion, challenge, factorial; sociology: exposition, discussion; engineering: exposition, discussion	43.3%
Exercise	engineering: calculations, short answer	4.0%
Explanation	engineering: industry overview, system overview	7.5%
Literature survey	analytical bibliography; research methods overview; **review article**	1.2%
Methodology recount	engineering: lab report, design report	12.6%
Narrative recount	sociology: urban ethnography report, library search; engineering: reflection on team work; biography; creative writing	2.6%
Problem question	business scenario; law problem; logistics simulation question	1.4%
Proposal	sociology: research proposal; engineering: design proposal	2.7%
Research report	history: long essay; sociology: dissertation; engineering: project	2.1%
TOTAL		100%

Table 7.3   *Distribution of genre families*

(Adapted from Nesi, H. and S. Gardner. 2012: 10 and 21–57. Totals refer to the number of samples in the corpus, expressed as percentages and rounded to the nearest decimal point).

Genre, audience, and purpose

Chapter 3 considers how texts can be described as genres which share related structures and conventions, and which are closely related to their audience (the expected readers of the text) and purpose (what the text aims to achieve). Chapter 6 looks at genres which students may have to read. The genres they have to write are rather different. For example, students read textbooks but do not write them, whereas they may have to write essays but as essays are mostly unpublished, students are less likely to read them.

Essential elements

In constructing their text, students can focus on the essential elements they need to express their meanings. This process involves carrying out a wide range of skills and tasks which are driven by these essential elements.

Processes in academic writing

Writing has been described as 'the ultimate juggling act' (Stainthorp 2005). In this description Stainthorp emphasizes the psychological challenges of writing, in which the writer has to balance material in their working memory (including the phonological, visuospatial, and semantic memories) together with resources in the long-term memory (ibid.). She goes on to explain that much information processing in writing requires the intensive use of the short-term (i.e. working) memory, which has limited capacity: if demands on the short-term memory are complex, aspects of the memory may suffer (Stainthorp 2005). This is similar to the phenomenon of 'automaticity' discussed in Chapter 6 (Hudson 2007: 35).

Stainthorp also emphasizes the relevance of the 'Matthew effect' (akin to the idea that the rich get richer and the poor get poorer): the more one practises a task, the more skilled one becomes at it and the easier it gets (and the reverse, the less one practises, the less skilled one becomes). The implication is that students need to do a great deal of writing in order to become more skilled at it, especially the more automated aspects, such as spelling, which can then free up capacity in the short-term memory for higher-level cognitive processing (Stainthorp 2005). Familiarity with generic language also greatly helps students in their writing process.

Stages in the process of writing

Clearly different writers may approach and carry out a writing assignment in different ways. There are, however, certain commonalities, and many academic writing processes (although not timed examination answers) can be divided into 'pre-writing', 'while-writing', and 'post-writing' stages. These are referred to in the later section on approaches to academic writing. Possible tasks in the writing process are presented in Table 7.4.

Task in the writing process	Stage in the writing process
Read and analyze the assignment brief (e.g. essay question, project rubric)	pre-writing
Formulate ideas arising from the assignment brief	pre-writing
Decide on which perspectives to inform the analysis of the topic	pre-writing
Search for and read source texts to find further ideas and material	pre-writing
Read sample texts from the same genre, e.g. from previous students on the programme or in the discipline	pre-writing/while-writing
Discuss and develop ideas with peers (i.e. other students)	pre-writing/while-writing
Search for further source texts to research the topic in greater detail	pre-writing
While reading, critically evaluate the sources selected, and identify and record supporting evidence and examples to use in the written text	pre-writing
Organize the above material into a coherent organizational framework	pre-writing/while-writing
Monitor the material, adding new material and deleting non-core material	pre-writing/while-writing
Refine and narrow down the material	pre-writing

Task in the writing process	Stage in the writing process
Write the introduction to the text	while-writing
Write sections/paragraphs of the text, gradually building up the main body of the text	while-writing
Complete the writing of the body of the text	while-writing
Write the conclusion to the text	while-writing
Critically read what you have written to check the logic, and rewrite as necessary	post-writing
Respond to tutor feedback following marking/assessment of the text	post-writing
Incorporate feedback points into subsequent writing assignments	post-writing

Table 7.4   Processes in writing

The number and complexity of these processes illustrates the challenges facing EAP students. A useful and supportive way of addressing such challenges is through the use of sample texts. EAP teachers can collect and store sample texts from students, and use these (anonymously or otherwise) with their permission. Current students can read and analyze the sample texts.

The following section offers a descriptive analysis of the essay. As with other descriptions, this should not be approached as a prescription but as a guideline and scaffold for students' own essays.

Writing essays

Of all the academic genres, the essay is perhaps the most strongly associated with undergraduate student writing. The word 'essay' is derived from the French word *essayer,* meaning 'to try': the essay retains a connotation of an attempt at writing on a given topic which is less prestigious than longer, more accomplished student texts such as dissertations. Many other academic genres such as articles and papers, which tend to be written for publication, are written predominantly by academic staff and research students rather than undergraduate students. Because they tend not to be published, essays may not be easy to find. If students want to read sample essays to help them write their own, they might struggle to find samples other than those written by other students (present and past) in the institution, or online samples of highly variable quality.

As the research of Nesi and Gardner (2012) demonstrates, the essay retains a strong position in student writing, particularly at undergraduate level. It is therefore useful to propose a structure and guidelines for an undergraduate student essay. Table 7.5 illustrates such a structure. It is important to note that this is not intended as a model, prescription, or formula; rather, it simply puts together some characteristics for each part of the essay— introduction, main body, conclusion— which may be useful for teaching and learning. The amount of detail included will depend on the type and length of the essay and its context, and further elements can be added.

The thesis statement

A key part of an essay is the thesis statement. Types and styles of thesis statement vary across countries and contexts, and the term can mean different things to different people. In broad terms a thesis statement expresses the purpose of the text, and may include any of the following aspects:

- the rationale/reason for writing the text, i.e. its main purpose and aim
- the main argument(s) or claim(s) made in the text, which are related to the purpose of the text
- any limitations, for example cautions regarding the claim, or limitations in scope
- optionally, the main organization of the text, i.e. what is to be covered first, subsequently, etc.
- optionally, the conclusion (the conclusion is stated up front in a deductive style text, as opposed to being unstated/allowed to emerge in an inductive style).

Most or all these aspects are likely to be covered in the introduction to the essay, with certain aspects expressed through the thesis statement. However, the inclusion of a thesis statement need not be taken as a prescription, and many successful essays may not have an identifiable thesis statement. There are disciplinary differences in this regard. By the end of the introduction, however, the audience is likely to expect to be clear about most or all of the aspects listed above. Creme and Lea (2008: 97–98) emphasize the personal aspect of a thesis statement, arguing that students can express their own unique thoughts in their thesis statement. In this sense, it is useful for both writer and reader: arriving at a thesis statement enables the student to clarify their thoughts, while for the reader it facilitates their understanding of the essay (ibid.).

INTRODUCTION (c.10–15% of total text)

Contextualization, moving from the general to the specific
- Optionally, an initial opening statement to gain the reader's interest (sometimes known as a 'hook')
- Contextualization and background: brief descriptive background material to situate the topic (time, place, context) and orientate the audience
- Sub-topics, perspectives, and focus: refinement of the topic through limitation, based on a number of perspectives to approach and analyze the topic
- Rationale: an explanation of the reason for writing the essay, for example to offer a new approach to a question, or (for research essays) to occupy a gap in the research
- Optionally, citations drawn from the core literature to support the approach and rationale
- Definition: definition and/or explanation of any central technical terms/concepts

The Thesis Statement/statement of purpose
- An explicit limitation and definition of the topic and focus, plus a statement of the purpose of the essay, indicating exactly what is to be included and excluded.
- A statement of the main argument of the essay plus the writer's stance, optionally stating the conclusion.
- A brief reference to items in the section above, for example the rationale.
- A brief guide through the organizational structure of the essay, e.g. 'This essay firstly examines the extent to which the differences in the educational systems of Italy and the UK are accounted for by cultural and historical rather than political factors, and goes on to evaluate the impact of these factors.'

BODY (c.80%)

Macro function

To address the thesis through a logical division of ideas, through a macro organizational structure such as:
– discussion (discursive/argumentative)
– comparison and contrast (comparative)
– cause – effect
– problem – solution
– classification
– chronology, including: historical or developmental; process; case study; narrative

Micro function

To support the macro function, drawing on a number of essential elements, e.g:
analysis; argument; case; cause; citation; comparison/contrast; definition; description; discussion; effect; evaluation; evidence; exemplification; explanation; problem; proposal; process; recount; reflection; solution; summary.

Organization into paragraphs

Each main point or idea can be developed in one paragraph. The paragraph may explicitly state the topic of the paragraph through a topic sentence, and/or may sum up the main point in a concluding sentence. The main point is developed through appropriate essential elements such as argument, citation, explanation, and evaluation.

CONCLUSION (c.5–10%)

Concluding Statements

A restatement/summary of the main point(s) of the essay, relating back coherently to the title, the material stated in the introduction, especially the thesis statement, and through the body of the essay.
– A summary of suggested reasons, solutions, or explanations for the response to the thesis, i.e. the conclusion.
– A summary/restatement of the writer's stance in relation to the question discussed.

Looking ahead

Proposals and recommendations for further work, thought, or research in the target area.

Table 7.5   Sample essay structure

This description of the essay genre can serve as a deductive framework to support students' writing. In this function, the description serves as a scaffold which students can use and then remove as they become more proficient. Scaffolds are also widely used in other major student genres at postgraduate levels, articles and reports. The framework can be adapted to suit local needs. For example, the five paragraph essay is widely practised in the USA; this essay type has an introduction, three main body paragraphs to develop the argument, and a conclusion.

Writing reports

Reports are a core genre in many academic contexts, and they can be subdivided into more specific genres such as research reports and law reports. While the detail of reports varies, reports are characterized by their conventional structure, which broadly follows an objective → subjective pattern: methodology and an account of the research (more objective) is followed by interpretation, evaluation, and recommendations (more subjective). In order to write a report successfully, students need to know how their audience (their teacher and anyone else who is likely to read it) expects it to be structured. This structure needs to be made clear.

The CaRS (Create a Research Space) model developed by Swales is mentioned briefly in Chapter 1 in the context of genre analysis, and is an influential tool for writers of research reports. The model covers article introductions. It is essentially a description based on Swales' analysis of 180 research articles, and covers three 'moves', which are akin to essential elements or rhetorical functions. Each move is comprised of a number of 'steps'. Swales' CaRS model (Swales 1990: 141) is represented as in Table 7.6.

Move 1	**Establishing a territory**		↓
	Step 1	claiming centrality	
		and/or	↓
	Step 2	making topic generalization(s)	Declining
		and/or	rhetorical
	Step 3	reviewing items of previous research	effort
Move 2	**Establishing a niche**		↓
	Step 1A	counter-claiming	
		or	↓
	Step 1B	indicating a gap	
		or	↓
	Step 1C	question-raising	Weakening
		or	knowledge
	Step 1D	continuing a tradition	claims
Move 3	**Occupying the niche**		↓
	Step 1A	outlining purposes	
		or	↓
	Step 1B	announcing present research	Increasing
	Step 2	announcing principal findings	explicitness
	Step 3	indicating RA [Research Article] structure	

Table 7.6   A CaRS model for article introductions
(Swales 1990: 141)

This model of research articles has been influential and widely reproduced. It is worth sounding a note of caution, however. One possible drawback is that it may not account for the structure of *all* research article introductions. Some research article introductions may depart from this structure for a number of reasons including the editorial demands of the journal in which they are published. Another perhaps more serious issue relates not so much to the structure of the model itself but how it is used. There is a risk that the CaRS model (and indeed other models) may move from being a description to the prescription; in other words what was intended as a descriptive analysis to guide the writer of research papers could, and in certain contexts has, become a prescriptive model which is followed uncritically. Researchers into genre continue to stress that they are not being restrictive and 'laying down the law' but rather opening up rhetorical opportunities.

Reporting and citation

Citation is a key essential element in academic writing. Indeed, citation is a defining characteristic of academic writing and one which is rarely found in most other genres including journalistic ones. There are a number of reasons for this, informed by various perspectives.

Rationale for citations

This chapter has established that an important function of citations is to provide evidence and exemplification to support an argument. Swales (1990: 6–7) reports various theories on the function of citations in academic writing. The first three of these are widely discussed, with the remaining four attributable to individual thinkers:

- Citations are expected conventions of academic discourse.

- In acknowledging intellectual property, citations are ethical.

- Citations are a form of homage to other researchers.

- Citations operate as a system of rewards. Rather than pay other authors money for their contributions, writers 'pay' them in citations. (Ravetz, 1971, in Swales 1990: 6–7)

- Citations are tools of persuasion; by using them, writers give their statements greater authority. (Gilbert 1977, in Swales 1990: 6–7)

- Citations constitute evidence that the author qualifies as a member of their chosen discourse community; citations are used to demonstrate disciplinary familiarity. (Bavelas 1978, in Swales 1990: 6–7)

- Citations are used to create a research space for the citing author. By describing what has been done citations point the way to what has not yet been done, and so prepare the way for new research. (Swales 1990: 6–7).

These theories broadly represent the following perspectives: academic, ethical, sociological, economic, rhetorical, social, and epistemological. The breadth of these theories underlines the centrality of citation in academic discourse, and emphasizes the complexity of this essential element. Citation should not be seen as a superficial and mechanical exercise.

EAP teachers can emphasize the vital nature of citation through the following approaches:

- Appropriate materials: use EAP materials which systematically integrate work in citation and referencing, so that it becomes a natural part of EAP students' academic practice.

- Assessments in the departments: find out and bring in documents relating to assessment in some of the departments that students are planning to enter. In this way students can see and read official documentation such as assessment criteria which spells out that student work needs to include citation and referencing.

- Past EAP students/students in the disciplines: invite previous students to talk to current EAP students about citation and referencing. They can emphasize that, while it may not have been covered in their final proficiency English examination (e.g. IELTS), citation and referencing is a vital and integral part of their current academic practice.

A further point is that EAP teachers can set an example by practising their art. By writing academic texts they can familiarize themselves with academic practice, with citation at its heart, and so become more convincing teachers. EAP students tend to be very interested in seeing their teachers' academic writing, and can usefully learn from reading such texts, for example presentation summaries in **conference proceedings** publications, or previous assessed academic work such as long essays and dissertations.

The academic skills associated with citation are unlikely to be acquired simply through exposure to academic texts: they need to be systematically taught and learned. In principle, citations can serve any or all of the functions outlined in the theories above. To put into practice, this principle requires a considerable amount of detailed study.

Quotation, paraphrase, and summary

Citation can take the form of quotation, paraphrase, and summary. (Sometimes a distinction is made between direct and indirect quotation.) Having identified the material to incorporate into their text (written or spoken), the writer needs to decide how to cite it. There are reasons for and against each option, as Table 7.7 rationalizes.

Through careful teaching and learning, the core academic writing skills of reporting and citation can be acquired. The emphasis needs to be on accuracy: students need to learn that all three citation methods need to be clearly and accurately referenced, in order to avoid plagiarism.

	Reasons for	**Reasons against**
Quotation	Straightforward to do once the quotation has been identified, as there is minimal text processing Suited to short, interesting text extracts, e.g. definitions, concise explanations, rationales	Generally not well suited to longer text, and certain types of text—e.g. data, factual—are best summarized Liberal use of quotation in a student's text can be seen as lacking in the more challenging skills of paraphrase and summary
Paraphrase	Suited to short extracts where there is no particular reason to use the original words	Very difficult to do, as the text extract has to be reprocessed at lexical and grammatical levels, and incorporated syntactically and semantically into the writer's text
Summary	Summary skills can be systematically taught and learned, then widely applied Suited to texts of any length Well-aligned to the reading process, i.e. identifying the main points in a text, which in turn form the basis of a summary Very widely used in academic texts	Initially difficult to do, but becomes easier with practice Requires good reading and processing skills

Table 7.7   Quotation, paraphrase, and summary

Critiquing sources to use in writing

As Chapters 5 and 6 have argued, EAP students need to approach source material with a degree of scepticism and rigour. It is useful for students to refer to criteria and questions to help them. Examples of these are given in Figure 7.2.

1 Is the source text current, i.e. is the information recent and up-to-date?
2 Is the source text accurate and reliable, i.e. can you trust what it says?
3 Does/do the author(s) of the text have a vested interest in presenting their arguments in the text, for example are they associated with a particular 'school' or business venture such as a pharmaceutical company?
4 Does the source text offer depth and coverage, i.e. is it comprehensive and detailed?
5 Is the source text factual, i.e. does it mainly presents facts rather than stance and interpretation?
6 How clearly presented and comprehensible is the information in the source texts, i.e. can you understand it in terms of language, concepts, and ideas?
7 How generalizable is the information in the source texts, i.e. can you apply the points made to your own writing context?
8 Is the information in the source text useful, i.e. does it meet your immediate needs by offering the information that you require in your current piece of writing?

Figure 7.2   Evaluation questions for using source material in writing

The criteria for critiquing source texts can be extrapolated from the questions, as follows: 1 currency; 2 accuracy and reliability; 3 vested interest; 4 coverage; 5 objectivity; 6 presentation; 7 application; 8 utility. These criteria can be used in a wide range of other contexts, including, for example, selecting language, (discussed in Chapter 4).

Another key teaching point in citing sources is for students to avoid plagiarism, which is discussed in detail in Chapter 2.

Teaching and learning criticality in academic writing

A useful starting point for eliciting critical reactions is the language of criticality and evaluation, which is explored in some detail in Chapter 5. For example, students can make questions based on the criteria of evaluation:

- desirability → How desirable is it?
- likelihood → How likely is it to happen?
- significance → How significant is it?
- authority → What evidence can I find that this text is authoritative?

The following pedagogical practices have also been proposed (de Chazal 2009a), which are aimed at EAP teachers to encourage a critical approach in their teaching and materials:

- introduce, clarify and explain the concept of evaluation
- emphasize its centrality in academic writing
- identify and recognise evaluation in texts
- foster critical evaluative reading skills
- build up examples of evaluation in texts
- develop tasks and learning materials aimed at production

  (de Chazal 2009a: 157)

Through the use of critical questions and the development of a critical mindset, students can develop originality and academic rigour in their writing. Their critical mindset is highly applicable when engaging with source material. Through selection and incorporation of source material in their writing, EAP students can demonstrate their familiarity with their discipline and rigour of their interpretation of the assignment question. To incorporate source material, students need to use appropriate language.

The language of citation

Central to the core academic skill of citing source material in writing is language. This section looks at the language of citation, referencing, reporting, and referring to sources. In doing so, it ties in with material from the language reference section of *Oxford EAP Advanced/C1* (de Chazal and Moore 2013: 200), which organizes the language of citation according to essential elements.

Referencing systems

Related to the language of citation is the system of referencing. There are three referencing systems in widespread use:

- Author-date systems, such as APA (American Psychological Association) which is clearly-described and available as a published style guide, currently in its sixth edition (APA, 2009). Other author-date systems include MLA (Modern Language Association of America), Chicago, plus less clearly standardized systems like Harvard. In such systems, the author's surname is given in brackets next to their material which is being cited (before, in the middle of, or after it) together with the year of publication, and optionally the page number. All the in-text references then have a corresponding entry in a references section at the end of the text, which is presented in alphabetical order. Variations on author-date systems such as these are used by specific academic departments, journals, and publishers.

- Numerical systems, for example Vancouver. These systems use a superscript number for each reference, which are repeated in order in the references section of the publication (or at the end of the chapter). Thus the list of references is given in text order not alphabetical order. In texts presented in electronic form, the superscript reference can function as a direct hyperlink to its entry in the References section.

- Footnote systems, where an in-text reference is given a superscript number and a corresponding reference at the foot of the page.

It is normally the responsibility of the student to become familiar with the particular system used in their department, and in any publication they might be writing for. Confusion can arise in this age of interdisciplinary degrees where different departments use different systems.

The use of an author-date referencing system can inform the choice of language, particularly in the area of author focus and content focus, which are explained and exemplified in the following section.

Citation, referencing, reporting, and referring to sources

The essential element of citation incorporates the closely related (and in some cases effectively synonymous) academic practices of referring to sources, reporting the ideas of others, and referencing these ideas. Table 7.8 offers examples of language related to aspects of this essential element. Given the large number of reporting verbs, there are several examples for this section of the table. All the examples in the second column of Table 7.8 are taken from this chapter. The language of citation is highlighted in bold where appropriate.

Focus, type, and context	Examples (taken from this chapter)
Content focus	Citations are used to create a research space for the citing author. By describing what has been done citations point the way to what has not yet been done, and so prepare the way for new research (Swales 1990). Some of the genres are similarly popular at all levels, but several become less frequent as the academic level rises, notably essays (Nesi and Gardner 2012: 10).
Author focus	Swales (1990: 6–7) reports various theories on the function of citations in academic writing.
Reporting verbs and structures	**As** Field (2005) **argues**, writing has a strong phonological underpinning. The centrality of communication **is emphasized by** Nesi and Gardner (2012) when they **state that** … The importance of persuasion **is stressed by** Bryman and Bell (2011) in a textbook aimed at students embarking on a research project or studying a module in research methods. They **make clear that** … Riddle (2000: 57 in Nesi and Gardner 2012: 91) **expresses** Toulmin's model in familiar terms … Building on this tradition of a conventionally structured argument, Booth, Colomb, and Williams (1995, 2003, and 2008) **propose** a more compact model … **For example**, Clanchy and Ballard (1981: 74, and 1992, also **cited in** Jordan 1997: 244) **present** a number of characteristics **based around** the academic writer's approach, tone, and language.
Referring to research, arguments, theories, ideas	Toulmin's *The Uses of Argument*, originally published in 1958 and updated in 2003, **sets out** an elaborate six-stage argument model. Chapter 6 **reported Biber and Gray's research which shows that** the main complexity in academic writing lies in the phrase rather than the clause and sentence (Biber and Gray 2010). It is the realities and aspects such as these which inform the characteristics of academic texts, which to varying degrees include all the characteristics in **Clanchy and Ballard's (1981) orthodox view** of academic discourse shown previously. **Recent research by Nesi and Gardner (2012)** has greatly illuminated what students are required to write in their disciplines.
Quotation	Writing has been described as 'the ultimate juggling act' (Stainthorp 2005).
Paraphrase	Tribble (2005) **stresses** the need for students to read multiple 'exemplars' of expert writing so that students can develop a competence in prototypicality.
Summary	**As the research of Nesi and Gardner (2012) demonstrates**, the essay retains a strong position in student writing, particularly at undergraduate level.
Reference reminder language	She goes on to explain that much information processing in writing requires the intensive use of the short-term (i.e. working) memory, which has limited capacity: if demands on the short-term memory are complex, aspects of the memory may suffer (**Stainthorp 2005). Stainthorp also emphasized** the relevance of the 'Matthew effect' …

Table 7.8   The language of citation

The items in the first column are not mutually exclusive choices; for example, a content focus choice can introduce a paraphrase or summary. Academic writers can choose to present their cited material either by focusing on content (content focus), or on the author of that content (author focus). The main reason to opt for an author focus is that it is particularly significant to mention the author first in the sentence, perhaps because they are important figures in their field. Alternatively, an author focus can be appropriate when comparing and contrasting theories by different researchers. Alternative descriptions of author focus and content focus are 'integral' and 'nonintegral' respectively (Swales and Feak 2000: 130).

Reference reminder language (referred to as 'reference reminder phrases' by Godfrey 2009: 34–5) makes it clear that the same source is being referred to in a sequence of sentences. If it is not used, the reader may not be clear about where the cited material starts and ends. This lack of clarity is surprisingly frequent in published academic texts such as the following extract from a textbook:

> Arguably, a 'technopower spiral' has brought about control by a technical elite. This spiral is the result of the vast, and ever increasing, amount of information available on the Web, which has led to the invention of advanced tools to enable users to find what they are seeking and manage the flow of information. It has become increasingly difficult for ordinary users to operate according to their own values, as they are dependent on the tools created and controlled by the technical elite. These tools are constructed according to the beliefs and values of the elite and in the language it has developed (Jordan 1999: 101).

> (Fulcher, J. and J. Scott. 2011. *Sociology 4e*. Oxford: Oxford University Press: 367–8)

In this example, it is not clear where the cited material (from Jordan 1999) actually starts: is Jordan's material presented in the final sentence only, or is it the whole text, or somewhere in between? EAP teachers can point to such shortcomings and encourage their students to write with more clarity. This style of end-of-sentence citation has been called 'hanging citations' (Swales and Feak 2000: 132–135). This lack of clarity in attributing ideas is also a useful message in a critical EAP approach: to critique the presentation of material in sources, as well as material presented by the students' teachers and lecturers. Such processes are ideally suited to student-centred tasks, as students can usefully evaluate their peers' use of citation and spot any instances of lack of clarity.

Choosing tenses in citations

There are three main choices to report and express ideas from sources: the present tense; the present perfect; and the past tense. Following the reporting stage, the writer(s) may discuss and evaluate the material they have cited; in these stages further options are available, particularly the modal verbs (for example *may* and *could*) and chunks such as *is likely to*. In many contexts more than one choice is acceptable. The following observations can provide useful guidelines for reporting the ideas of others:

- **Research findings** can be reported in the past tense—or the present tense if they are seen as generalizations. (Yule 1998: 69)

- The past tense is used to narrate experiments and express procedures. (Carter and McCarthy 2006: 273–4)

- Generalizations and significant findings are typically expressed in the present tense. (Yule 1998: 69; Carter and McCarthy: 2006: 274)

- The present tense is preferred when reporting the views and work of scholars in the past. (Biber et al.1999: 465)

- The present tense is widely used in abstracts and summaries, for example 'This article looks at …'(Carter and McCarthy 2006: 273)

- The present perfect is used with certain verbs, for example 'has shown', 'have seen', 'has become', to 'imply the continuing validity of earlier findings or practices' (Biber et al. 1999: 465); and to 'emphasize current relevance or continuing debate.' (Carter and McCarthy 2006: 274)

These guidelines offer useful advice for EAP teachers and students, as well as illustrating the potential for overlap. The guidelines illustrate tendencies and constitute generalizations, for example the use of the past tense in reporting and narrative versus the present tense to emphasize the currency of the ideas. If a number of contrasting theories are seen to be current, the writer may choose the present tense to report and discuss them. Students need to be exposed to a range of texts in order to work out how the tenses can be used; these texts are more meaningful and memorable for students than the decontextualized observations above. Indeed, any of the research-based observations above may be challenged in authentic language use in texts. EAP teachers should encourage their students to notice how tenses are used, and compare these uses with other texts and the observations above, ultimately to work out for themselves how to use tenses in their own written work.

Approaches to teaching and learning academic writing

The earlier sections in this chapter, and the earlier chapters in this book, have illustrated the scope of academic writing, including areas such as essential elements, criticality, and language. This section outlines five approaches to academic writing: functional approaches; process approaches; genre-based approaches; critical literacies approaches; and academic literacies approaches. Selected aspects of these critical literary approaches are then brought together in the following section, which presents a student-centred approach to learning and teaching academic writing based on ten distinct areas.

Functional approaches

A functional approach to academic writing, also known as a 'rhetorical-functional' approach, can be traced back to the 1960s when it evolved in reaction to the prevailing emphasis on guided composition and controlled writing (Paltridge, 2001: 56). The focus of the functional approach is on whole-text essential elements such as descriptions, narratives, definitions, exemplification, classification, comparison and contrast, cause and effect, and generalizations (ibid.). Paltridge cites a number of books which follow such an approach, including Jordan's *Academic Writing Course* (in three editions 1980–1999), which is also mentioned by Jordan himself (1997: 165) in this context, and Oshima and Hogue's series of academic writing books including *Writing Academic English*, first published in 1982 and now in its fourth edition (2005). Paltridge points out that these books 'take a mostly 'product-based' approach to the teaching of academic writing' (Paltridge 2001: 56). Jordan also classes the rhetorical-functional approach as a product approach to the teaching and learning of academic writing (Jordan 1997: 165).

Process approaches

Process approaches to the teaching of writing emerged in the 1970s, in turn as a reaction to both controlled composition and the then prevailing rhetorical functional approach (Paltridge 2001: 56). Essentially, a process approach is driven by meaning rather than form, and is also a learner-centred approach in that it encourages students to take responsibility for their learning (Jordan 1997: 167). Bruce (2011: 123) points out that process approaches are rooted in the North American college writing tradition, which tends to be humanities based.

Various processes involved in writing are given in Table 7.4 on page 191. These processes underline the cyclical and iterative nature of academic writing, where, for example, the writer repeatedly returns to source material to refine and extend their argument. Also central to a process approach is feedback. Feedback on students' written work can come from their peers (other EAP students) and their EAP teachers, in the form of both spoken and written feedback. The aims of feedback are partly to offer immediate comments on the piece of writing submitted, in areas including language, structure and organization, and content; also, feedback is designed to develop students' independence so that they can gradually learn to write without it.

Paltridge (2001: 57) and Jordan (1997: 169) give examples of books which follow a mainly process approach. These include Hamp-Lyons and Heasley's *Study Writing* (first edition 1987; second edition 2006) and White and McGovern's (1994) *Writing*.

Genre-based approaches

Genre-based approaches position texts at the heart of the approach. If students have to write research reports, then research reports are used as materials, and in particular as samples, sometimes known as models, or 'exemplars' (Tribble 2005). Much research has been carried out into genres, such as that of Swales (1990) and Martin (1992). This research aims to provide descriptions of specific genres, in terms of their text structure, language, and how they relate to their wider context, in particular their audience and purpose. These descriptions can form the basis of teaching materials in which EAP students analyze and produce texts in the target genre.

Jordan (1997: 166) classes the genre-based approach as a product approach. However, while examples of the genres themselves are, in a sense, products, a genre-based approach can also focus on the process of learning writing. Paltridge (2001: 57ff) points out that genre-based approaches vary, notably in the UK and the USA on the one hand, and in Australia on the other.

Widely used students' books which follow a genre approach include Swales and Feak's *Academic Writing for Graduate Students* (first edition, 1994, second edition, 2004, third edition, 2012) and Weissberg and Buker's *Writing Up Research* (1990). As their titles state, these are aimed primarily at postgraduate students.

Critical literacy approaches

Bruce (2011: 123) summarizes critical literacy approaches to the teaching and learning of academic writing. These approaches developed in the 1980s and draws on the work of Foucault (1980, cited in Bruce 2011: 123) and Friere (1994, cited in Bruce 2011: 123), who are concerned with power structures in education and how these impact on students. As with other critical pedagogies, this critical literacy approach encourages students to question power structures, prevailing pedagogies, and the assumptions and practices of teachers.

At the present time, there do not appear to be any widely used academic writing coursebooks driven by a critical literacy approach.

Academic literacies approaches

The academic literacies approach is associated with Street and Lea, and arose in the 1990s as a response to the then widespread study skills approach to EAP and what Lea and Street (2000, in Hyland 2006: 119–123) refer to as the 'academic socialization' approach. Further details of the academic literacies approach are given in Chapter 1 in the section on Influences on EAP, page 6.

As with the critical literacies approaches, there do not appear to be any widely used published materials which follow an academic literacies approach. Such approaches tend to be more associated with in-sessional EAP teaching where students are already in the disciplines and are therefore more intimately familiar with the specific academic practices of their discipline(s).

Teaching writing using multiple approaches

As with teaching methodologies in general, EAP teachers can develop their own eclectic approach, drawing on theories and practices in the various approaches that have existed to date. For example, in a sequence of tasks students could do the following:

- read and respond to a given writing task (such as an essay question)
- analyze and deconstruct a sample text which represents an answer to that question
- focus on an aspect of academic language in that text
- develop their ideas based on source reading texts
- select material to use in their own essay
- plan and draft their essay
- collaborate with other students in reading and critically responding to each other's drafts
- revise and refine the essay into a coherent product.

One advantage of an eclectic approach like this is that students' writing can develop in a learner-centred way using methods that work from various traditions yet without uncritically following any one tradition.

Recent examples of integrated skills EAP coursebooks which draw on multiple approaches include the *Cambridge Academic English* series and the *Oxford EAP* series.

A student-centred approach to academic writing

The approach elaborated on in this section draws on multiple approaches to academic writing. It follows ten steps, and each of these are briefly explained and summarized through a series of questions. These questions are specifically for student writers (or academic writers generally) and can serve as guidelines (to enable more effective writing) and criteria (to evaluate the achievement of writing). Some of this material is adapted from the article *Ten Steps to Better Academic Writing* (de Chazal 2008b: 65ff), which proposed a series of ten steps aimed at student academic writers. This approach is designed to be student centred. As various researchers from different traditions have argued, a student-centred approach is desirable. For example, Scott (1999, in Jones, Turner and Street: 171) points out that 'the individual writer tends not to be a central focus in the theory and research relating to student writing'.

The stages represent different aspects of academic writing, and are concurrent and cyclical rather than a series of linear steps. They emphasize the responsibility of the writer, and are designed ultimately to lead to independence.

1 Genre, Audience and Purpose

In any academic writing task, students need to be clear about the genre they are writing, who their intended audience is, and why they are writing it. In surveying ELT course books, de Chazal (2006: 10–11) has found that many materials do not make these three concepts clear. In some cases the key characteristics of the genre are not clarified, and very frequently there are no sample texts of that genre for students to analyze and inform their own writing. Tribble (2005) stresses the need for students to read multiple 'exemplars' of expert writing so that students can develop a competence in prototypicality. This means that wide exposure and analysis should lead to familiarity with the examples of target genre which are seen as typical. The questions for the student writer to address are given below.

Questions for the writer

What am I writing?

Who am I writing for?

Why am I writing?

2 Structure, relevance, and coherence

The second stage focuses on the achievement of the text in relation to the task. Whether the student text is a response to a given task, assignment, or question, or whether it is a response created by the student such as a research essay, the text needs a coherent, logical structure relevant to its title. In some EAP programmes, half the marks in assessments are for language, including grammar, vocabulary, coherence, and style, and the other half for non-language features such as structure, relevance, and coherence. Other non-linguistic material includes visuals such as graphs, charts, and tables. Where included, these need to support and extend the arguments in the text.

Questions for the writer

Given the title and abstract or introduction, are the expectations of my audience likely to be met by this piece of work?

Does the material in the text develop logically and relevantly through my title, thesis statement, development, and conclusion?

Have I made the connections between material within and throughout the text clear and coherent?

Does the conclusion deal with (i.e. answer, partly answer or suggest further work) the questions raised in the title and thesis statement?

Have I set the text in context within the academic world (in the introduction) and have I taken my audience out of the context of the text and into this world at the end (in the conclusion)?

Is non-linguistic material (for example graphics and images) included where appropriate? Is it relevant and clear?

3 Content

From the perspective of the subject lecturer (rather than the EAP teacher), the content of the student text is the main focus, and carries the most weight. The content of a student's text includes their ideas and material. It also includes research, citation, and criticality, which are covered in separate sections below.

Questions for the writer

Have I offered sufficient material to address the question?

Are the essential elements (for example description, explanation) sufficiently developed to meet the aims of my text?

Does the text explore and analyze the topic from an appropriate range of perspectives?

Can my audience access my intended meaning easily and unambiguously?

4 Research

The amount of research will depend on the academic level of the student and the nature of the writing assignment. At foundation and many undergraduate levels, research is likely to take the form of **secondary research**, i.e. reading and processing the literature. At postgraduate levels, primary research is more likely. All contexts will require citation, based on the student's reading.

Questions for the writer

Have I conducted appropriate and sufficient research in order to inform the content of my text?

Is the material carefully selected and clearly presented?

Is it clear throughout the text whose idea is whose, i.e. which ideas are taken from other writers and which ideas are original (my own)?

5 Critical thinking

Critical thinking is taken to include evaluation, stance, and voice. As these are highly valued cognitive activities in academic contexts, the audience of the student text (i.e. tutors, lecturers, and assessors) typically want to see evidence of criticality.

Questions for the writer

Have I included sufficient analysis, interpretation, and evaluation?

Have I critically selected my source material in order to include high-quality citations and exclude others?

Is my individual voice beginning to emerge in the text?

6 Citation and academic conventions

Closely related to the previous two aspects are citation and academic conventions. As these areas are so central to academic writing, they need careful emphasis and clear learning materials.

Questions for the writer

Does every citation have a reference which is listed in the references section (bibliography)?

Does every item in the references section have a citation in the text?

Have I avoided plagiarism?

Have I adhered to the academic conventions expected by my institution?

Is any research clearly presented in line with the expected conventions?

7 Discourse and cohesion

This stage and the next are concerned with aspects of language. At whole-text level, the writing needs to be fairly homogenous (for example consistently formal) and appropriate to the genre, audience, and purpose. There should be sufficient, though not excessive, signposting so that the reader can navigate the text, in keeping with the writer-responsible tendency of English. This concept is expanded on in the section on writing culture, below. The text needs to be clearly connected through language, i.e. cohesive, from whole-text to sentence level.

Questions for the writer

Are the ideas and meanings in the text clearly and unambiguously connected using appropriate cohesive language?

Have I taken the responsibility to offer sufficient and clear signposting to guide my audience?

Does my text have a sense of 'flow' so that the audience can read it fluently?

8 Language

The language of the text includes the accuracy and range of vocabulary and grammar, both of which contribute to the academic style. Accuracy is important as it is generally highly valued; accuracy can include word choice, spelling, punctuation, and grammar. Range of structures and lexis is also important, as variety (as opposed to monotony and excessive repetition) is also valued. The third system of language, phonology, is also present. As Field (2005) argues, writing has a strong phonological underpinning.

Questions for the writer

Is the vocabulary and style appropriate for the genre, audience, and purpose?

Are the grammatical structures (especially phrases and clause structures) also appropriate?

Have I included a good range of vocabulary and grammar?

Have I checked my writing carefully for accuracy of language choices, punctuation, and spelling?

Have I defined concepts and abbreviations/acronyms where appropriate for my audience?

Does the text sound fluent when read aloud?

9 Culture

Given that academic writing culture varies across regions and as well as institutions and departments, students need to acclimatize and familiarize themselves with the target culture, i.e. the culture in which they are studying or planning to study. Culture is partly about the expectations of academics, and students need to learn what these are in order to maximize their academic success.

Questions for the writer

Have I consciously moved towards the target writing culture?

Does my writing meet the expectations of the audience from the target writing culture?

10 Pedagogy and independence

Above all, the purpose of EAP pedagogy is to enable independence. EAP students need to learn the language, language skills, study skills, and critical thinking skills in order to be able eventually to function independently of the teacher.

Questions for the writer

Have I maximized my opportunities in and out of the EAP classroom to learn new skills and language?

Have I interacted with my peers by offering and receiving help, and discussing my assignments?

Have I put new skills and language into practice?

Have I read, understood, and responded to feedback from tutors and peers?

Am I maximizing opportunities to read, listen, speak, and write—all of which can improve my writing?

Am I making the most of learning resources and technologies?

Is my academic writing measurably improving?

What am I doing to develop my independence as a student and a writer?

What would I ultimately like to achieve as a writer in an academic and professional context, and how can I get there?

This extended description of a student-centred approach brings out many of the issues in the teaching and learning of academic writing. It rests with the EAP teacher to develop their own teaching and learning styles within their local context.

Managing students' writing

For the EAP teacher, the stages in the previous section can form a framework to plan and assess the teaching of writing. Academic writing is a complex and challenging process, and at the heart of the process are the students, the materials, and the EAP teacher. The role of the teacher is critical in a number of respects: establishing aims and objectives; providing appropriate materials; and acting as a 'resource' to manage the process, offering input, expertise, and guidance as needed. This section briefly looks at ways of managing a student writing assignment.

Managing a writing project

Student writing assignments can take many forms. In an EAP context, the responsibility for managing a writing project rests with both the students and the teacher. The EAP teacher can offer guidelines, techniques, and expertise to enable the students to carry out the assignment. Most significantly, the students need to be able to carry out subsequent assignments with increasingly less guidance. Table 7.9 presents a number of practical suggestions for managing a student writing project.

Focus	Procedure and aims
Setting objectives	Formulate the main objective(s) for improving the students' writing skills, and align these to the assessment criteria for the assignment.
Independence	Divide the writing process into monitored writing, done in class time, and guided independent writing, done outside the class. The balance of these can shift to reflect students' growing independence.
Aspects of writing	Monitor and assess restricted aspects of the students' writing, based on the ten aspects in the section above. In this way students can focus effectively on a limited number of aspects (one or two) rather than less effectively on a more unwieldy range of aspects.
Perspectives	Elicit or give a number of perspectives (e.g. economic, technological, etc.) for students to use as the basis of analysis. Students analyze their writing topic using each perspective in turn.
Fluency	Set very short time limits (e.g. 2–3 minutes) for students to write as much as possible on a single aspect of their writing topic; this can develop their fluency as a writer as this time is spent writing, not thinking.
Collaboration	Ask students to write collaboratively rather than individually; this can add to the amount of relevant material and promote criticality.
Deadlines	For longer writing tasks, break the assignment down into multiple deadlines, e.g. five deadlines in five days/weeks. Check progress at each deadline, which should help students avoid writing their whole assignment very close to the final deadline.

Table 7.9   Managing a writing project

This table illustrates the central role played by the EAP teacher in enabling their students to deliver their writing. The role of manager is an important one, and carries with it responsibilities to enforce deadlines. This role reflects that of the academic, who also requires students to adhere to strict deadlines. It does not help if EAP students are treated too leniently in this respect; learning to write to deadlines is a vital skill, and failing to meet deadlines in their academic department can result in failure of a module or course. Understanding the importance of deadlines forms part of a student's academic development through their EAP classes.

Integrating writing with other skills

Chapter 6 presents a task cycle which offers a rationale for reading and a principled practical approach to the development of reading. This cycle of reading, in turn, takes place within more extensive cycles. In addition, Chapter 6 establishes that a major purpose of reading is to synthesize information to use in new texts, particularly written texts. In academic contexts, students mostly do not think up content for their written work from their existing knowledge alone: they need to find new sources of material to incorporate into their writing. In doing so, students also extend their knowledge.

When planning writing assignments, the EAP teacher can draw on the other skills for input and content; in this way students can integrate material from different sources (for example written texts, lectures, presentations). They will also need to correctly reference this cited material.

Overcoming challenges in writing

From the student's perspective there are likely to be specific challenges in academic writing. Various challenges have been raised throughout this chapter. Good materials are vital, as is the expertise and encouragement of the EAP teacher. One practical idea is timed writing.

Timed writing

To encourage fluency, the EAP teacher can set up a timed writing task. This can be part of an assignment they are doing, such as a paragraph. It is useful to base the timed writing on a current task, so that students can go on to approach the task more successfully. There needs to be a deadline which is enforced, perhaps ten minutes to write a paragraph, depending on the students' levels. The product of the task needs to be emphasized, for instance if it is a paragraph then one or two sentences are unacceptable. A complete paragraph, even if it is full of language mistakes, is acceptable because that is the aim of the task. This type of timed writing activity should lead to greater fluency in writing and less time 'stuck' on a single sentence.

'Writer's block'

Some students may say they cannot write or do not know what to write; this phenomenon is sometimes called 'writer's block'. However, this label can become an excuse for not producing a piece of work. The EAP teacher could give an analogy: for example, you go away on holiday and pay a gardener to look after the garden, but on returning find that the garden has not been tended and is overrun with weeds. Would you accept 'gardener's block' as an excuse? If students are to participate successfully in the academy they need a serious attitude to their study, and excuses are generally unhelpful. Practical techniques such as timed writing can be used to overcome a perceived inability to start the writing process.

Writing with the students

A useful approach to writing is to write with the students. In this approach, the EAP teacher also does the same writing task that they set for their students, following the same rubrics, timings, and deadlines, and using similar resources. This approach can work for very short essays, such as IELTS essays, and longer writing tasks such as research essays or reports.

There are a number of possible reasons for using a 'writing with the students' approach:

- Validity: by doing the same writing task, the EAP teacher is in a sense validating that task, demonstrating that it is a worthwhile task; they are also themselves being validated as competent writers.

- Quality and Feasibility: given that they are doing the task, the EAP teacher can be motivated to ensure that it is a high-quality task which works in practice.

- Materials development: in doing the task, the EAP teacher can identify areas in which the task can be improved, clarified, and developed in a subsequent revised version.

- Exemplars: the task written by the EAP teacher can serve as an exemplar for the students to learn from, analyze, and evaluate.

- Process: the process of doing the writing task shows the challenges involved, such as linguistic and research practices; this knowledge gained can help the EAP teacher empathize with their students and inform their approaches to teaching and feedback relating to the task.

This rationale for writing with the students illustrates the potential for such an approach.

Writing culture

Academic writing involves more than skills, criticality, and language. Written genres are situated in a particular culture. A student undergraduate essay, for instance, exhibits cultural properties depending on where it is written. An important concept in relation to writing culture is the notion of responsibility for writing. Hinds (1987: 143) cited in Hyland (2003: 47–8) proposed the concepts of reader and writer responsibility. This theory holds that in certain academic cultures, notably English (also sometimes known as 'Anglo-Saxon' academic culture), it is the writer who is essentially responsible for communicating effectively. In some other cultures, which Hyland exemplifies as Japanese, possibly Korean and Chinese, as well as German and Spanish, the reader is more responsible for constructing meaning from an academic text. As evidence for the writer-responsible nature of English academic writing, Hyland draws attention to the use of 'signposts' which enable the reader to navigate the text (ibid.).

This may be a useful observation, but it amounts to a generalization. One obvious shortcoming is that it puts people from whole countries or geographically proximate countries into one or other category. The increasingly globalized nature of education, characterized by the spread of internationalized curricula and international schools, is evidence against the theory. Indeed, Hinds' ideas have been critiqued, for instance by Kubota (1999) who questions the notions of cultural generalizations and creations of cultural dichotomies.

Moreover, a simple observation of so-called English/Anglo-Saxon academic writing culture can reveal a striking lack of consideration for the reader: some journal article texts are extraordinarily hard for the reader to process and understand, even in their own discipline. This may not be due to any lack of signposting, but to the density and opacity of conceptual information presented mainly in complex noun phrases. Frequent use of jargon and undefined acronyms add to the difficulty for the reader.

A useful tool for students is a questionnaire to orientate into the target writing culture.

Orientating into the writing culture

The questionnaire in Figure 7.3 can be adapted to suit a specific context. Students can respond first individually, and then discuss their responses.

1 In your last school or university, how often did you write academic texts?
2 Who do you write these texts for?
3 Which languages do you normally write in?
4 What kinds of academic texts have you written in English?
5 What kinds of academic texts do you write in other languages (for example your first language)?
6 What are the main difficulties and challenges you face in writing academic texts in English?
7 What would you most like to be able to achieve in academic writing by the end of this academic year?
8 What is your attitude towards academic writing (for example which aspects of it do you like, and what concerns do you have)?
9 How do you write your academic texts? Briefly describe your typical writing process.

10 How can you get help with this kind of writing?

11 Why do you write?

12 Do you consider yourself to be a good writer? Do others?

13 What do you think are the characteristics of academic writing in English?

14 In your experience, how is Anglo-Saxon (for example UK, USA) academic writing different from that of your own culture?

15 What do you understand by the terms: 'direct quotation'; 'paraphrase'; 'summary'?

16 How and where can you incorporate personal opinions in your writing?

Figure 7.3   An academic writing questionnaire

The student responses can then form the basis of subsequent teaching and learning materials, with a focus on comparing writing cultures and moving towards the target writing culture. In order to compare writing cultures, a degree of specificity is required. Taking into account the factors associated with writing culture, each EAP teacher and student can work out approaches to meet their needs.

Comparing writing cultures

In a paper comparing Anglo-Saxon and Japanese academic writing culture (de Chazal and Aldous 2006), ten distinctions were identified. These served as a basis for students and teachers to identify, discuss, and evaluate differences between the target Anglo-Saxon writing culture, and the students' original first language (L1) writing culture, which was Japanese. The ten distinctions were placed at each end of a cline, so that students and teachers could place their first language (L1) and second language (L2) on points on the cline. The distinctions are:

• less precise–precise

• less concrete–more concrete

• less circumlocutory–more circumlocutory

• less explicit–more explicit

• less descriptive–more descriptive

• fewer digressions–more digressions

• less analytical–more analytical

• less evaluative–more evaluative

• less contextual information–more contextual information

• less depth and more breadth–more depth and less breadth

This principle of comparison based on distinctions can work with students of any L1. This series of criteria can be adapted and used in any culture.

Conclusion

This chapter has argued for the academic writer as architect of meaning. Despite the complexity of the processes and products of academic writing, EAP teachers can facilitate success through appropriate focus on what is to be written and how. Drawing on their understanding of teaching and learning (discussed in Chapter 2), texts and language (explored in Chapters 3 and 4), critical thinking (Chapter 5), and the centrality of reading in the writing process (Chapter 6), EAP teachers and students can ensure they are all central to the process of academic writing and deliver effective results using a range of methodologies and practical approaches.

Further reading

Booth, W. C, G. G. Colomb, and **J. M. Williams.** 2008. *The Craft of Research*. Chicago: University of Chicago Press.

Creme, P. and **M. R. Lea.** 2008. *Writing at University: A guide for students 3e*. Maidenhead: Open University Press, McGraw-Hill Education.

de Chazal, E. 2008. 'Ten Steps to Better Academic Writing.' in **Krzanowski, M.** *Current Developments in English for Academic, Specific and Occupational Purposes*. Reading, UK: Garnet Education.

Godfrey, J. 2011. *Writing for University*. Basingstoke: Palgrave Macmillan.

Hyland, K. 2003. *Second Language Writing*. Cambridge: Cambridge University Press.

Hyland, K. 2004. *Genre and Second Language Writing*. Ann Arbor: University of Michigan Press.

Nesi, H. and **S**. **Gardner.** 2012. *Genres across the Disciplines: Student writing in higher education*. Cambridge: Cambridge University Press.

Swales, J. 1990. *Genre Analysis: English in academic and research settings*. Cambridge: Cambridge University Press.

Swales, J. and **C. Feak..** 2000. *English in Today's Research World: a writing guide*. Ann Arbor: University of Michigan Press.

Swales, J. and **C. Feak.** 2004. *Academic Writing for Graduate Students: essential skills and tasks 3e*. Ann Arbor: University of Michigan Press.

8

LISTENING

Academic listener as interpreter and recorder

Among EAP students and their teachers, listening is instinctively seen as an important skill to develop. Given the highly communicative nature of academic discourse and interaction with other people in academic contexts, students are generally motivated to improve their listening. Yet there has been far less research into listening (and speaking) compared with the orthographic skills of academic writing and reading. Flowerdew points to the limited amount of research into academic listening (Flowerdew 1994: 7), a view echoed by Lynch, who quotes Vandergrift as saying 'listening remains the least researched of the four skills' (Vandergrift 2006: 191 in Lynch 2011: 79) and himself points to the 'dearth of papers on academic listening' appearing in the *Journal of English for Academic Purposes* (Lynch 2011: 9). Field also observes that listening is 'undervalued' and its methodology 'little discussed, researched or challenged' (Field 2008: 1).

Such under-representation of listening in EAP research does not necessarily mean that listening is neglected in EAP practice. Listening development, in particular through lectures, is widely established as a component part of EAP programmes. However, there can sometimes be a tendency for academic writing (and reading) to dominate EAP curriculums, which can in consequence leave less time for listening (and speaking) development. In an article on EAP syllabus design for writing courses, Bruce states that EAP courses 'usually include a strong focus on the development of the writing skill' (Bruce 2005: 239).

In reality, the student in their discipline has to engage with a potentially complex range of listening input. Listening, through established events such as lectures and seminars, has long been central to the academic experience. Increasingly, listening genres such as lectures have evolved into complex, interconnected experiences. Listening in academic contexts has become cyclical, integrated, and multimodal. **Multimodality** refers to the practice of communicating through multiple channels such as written texts, audio input, images and other visual material, and video. The academic listener, whether the student in their discipline or the EAP student, needs to interpret the listening input to which they are exposed, in order to select and record the content for use in their academic study.

The cyclical, integrated, and multimodal nature of listening

Listening in academic contexts is not a discrete, isolated event; rather, it is connected to other communicative events in different ways.

The integration of listening

Key academic listening events, such as lectures, are typically integrated into broader structures. For example, work on a topic is likely to involve reading (where students read given texts, and find further texts to read), listening (with input from lectures and presentations), speaking (where students participate in seminars and more informal discussions), and writing (in which students produce a written text based on their work around the topic). This level of integration means that content is introduced and processed across different skills and with different technologies. One implication is that if a student finds listening particularly challenging, then their academic performance will be affected in other skills such as writing.

Listening as a cyclical process

Listening is cyclical in that discrete listening events constitute stages in broader cycles. Although academic discourse is characterized by distinct written and spoken genres, such as research articles and lectures, in reality related content and knowledge are transferred via a series of genres and channels. Figure 8.1 illustrates possible stages in which academic staff in a university can work on a topic to extend knowledge and use different approaches to communicate, or transfer, this knowledge.

> Carrying out new research → presenting the research at academic conferences → writing up the research for primary sources, for example academic journals → delivering the content of the research through institutional lectures → introducing the content into seminars → disseminating aspects of the research through other media, for example webcasts, videos, **MOOCs** (massive open online courses) → incorporating selected content into secondary sources, for example textbooks → synthesizing material from previous sources (journals, textbooks) into new lectures

Figure 8.1 The cyclical nature of knowledge transfer and academic listening

As with many cyclical processes, the cycle in Figure 8.1 is made up of stages, which can be concurrent as well as consecutive. The researcher or research team who carried out the original research may disseminate it through various means at different times: they may present aspects of their research to selected academics and students at their institution, and introduce content from the research into their lectures at various points in the cycle. The implications for the student are that listening is a vital way of accessing content, and is closely related to other ways of delivering content in the wider cycle of knowledge dissemination. Students are likely to be exposed to the content through lectures, other media, and seminars, as well as through written texts. They will have to engage with this content and construct knowledge around it as new knowledge is presented.

Listening as a multimodal experience

The multimodal dimension of listening derives from the increasing tendency of lectures to involve multiple texts and media. Multimodality can be defined as 'the coexistence of more than one semiotic mode within a given context' (Gibbons 2012: 8). Gibbons emphasizes that multimodality is 'an everyday reality' and 'the experience of living' (ibid.). Examples of modes could include written communication (which is verbal) and imagistic pictorial communication (imagistic) (Gibbons 2012: 9), although Gibbons acknowledges the 'slippery' nature of defining a mode, echoed by Kress (2010: 87 in Gibbons 2012: 9).

Traditionally lectures have been delivered in predominantly auditory style, with the lecturer orally presenting planned and partially-rehearsed content with some visual support. While this traditional lecture style remains widespread, more complex delivery patterns have been emerging as new technologies have developed. As well as the core oral delivery of the essential 'script', today's lectures may additionally include any of the following:

- visuals such as PowerPoint slides and other projected content

- video and/or audio content

- links to external content, for example hyperlinks to websites or video content

- realia, including objects, samples, materials, and models

- handouts with the lecture slides and/or accompanying notes, tasks, texts, bibliographies

- any other concurrent texts, for example unplanned audience contributions and questions; books, articles, pamphlets, etc. brought into the listening space.

The last point illustrates that during the delivery of the lecture other live texts may emerge, such as audience contributions, questions, and unplanned responses by the lecturer such as digressions and answers to questions. The lecture itself, given its integrated and cyclical nature discussed above, may also be closely related to further materials such as reading texts, links to other resources, and material on the LMS (Learning Management System). The lecturer may explicitly refer to these in the lecture, meaning that students need to shift their focus from the listening text (the planned lecture) to other texts. In practice, a frequent lecture or presentation style is to show a new slide (visual) which can be quite text-heavy, while talking about something not quite aligned to the slide (oral), for example an elaboration of a related point or perhaps the previous point. Alternatively, the lecturer may present the same content as the slide in a different way using rather different language. Another frequent practice is to read aloud from the slide.

These approaches present particular challenges for the listener. In constructing meaning, the student may have to deal with multiple text inputs. For the student in a lecture, this multimodality requires competences in interpreting information through multiple channels—live and recorded, written and spoken, visual and auditory, plus physical (in terms of actual texts, both written and spoken) and cognitive (in terms of the mental construction of meaning).

The discussion so far has centred strongly on lectures. Certain researchers have emphasized the lecture as the primary listening activity in EAP; for instance in Flowerdew's (1994) collection of papers on academic listening, lectures feature heavily in most of the texts.

In the cyclical, integrated, and multimodal context of academic listening, the student needs to adopt a number of roles to engage with the content.

Listening genres and the role of the academic listener

Traditionally in English language teaching, listening, together with reading, has been cast as a receptive skill. By implication it is passive. In reality, however, listening (and reading) are not simply receptive and passive. In academic contexts the student needs to engage with listening material and to some degree interact with it. As with reading texts, listening texts serve a purpose and the student needs to understand and capitalize on this purpose.

Lectures are the prototypical listening genres in academic contexts: when listening is mentioned in EAP, students and teachers tend to think of lectures. As discussed in the section above, lectures involve both spoken and written elements and can be highly multimodal and multi-textual. While lectures are very widespread in academic contexts, there are a number of other important listening genres which students need to work with in their academic study.

Listening to lectures

Lectures vary enormously across contexts including disciplines, institutions, and countries. They can vary in terms of their style, length, formality, degree of interactivity, multimodality, complexity, language, content, audience profile and size, delivery, and expectations. These characteristics also apply to lectures delivered via a recording rather than live. For instance, a lecture in one context may be delivered in a highly transactional, non-interactional style: the lecturer walks into the lecture theatre, delivers their lecture as planned, possibly reading from a script which has not changed for years, while the audience remain silent, and finally walks out at the end. In contrast, another lecture—even in the same institution, department, or programme—may be strikingly different. The lecturer may adopt a highly interactive, engaging, and familiar style, showing genuine interest in the responses of the audience. Depending on the style of the lecture, and the perceived status of the lecturer, the audience (the students) will adopt different attitudes and roles.

Despite such potentially significant differences, it is useful to identify commonalities. Typically, the lecturer is cast in the role of expert and authoritative figure in their discipline, while the students are at the stage where they are learning about their discipline. In academic institutions and the literature, certain terms express and connote this subordinate student role: novice, apprentice, learner, undergraduate, bachelor, freshman. Higher up the academic scale the terms change: master, postgraduate, researcher, doctor. (Some of these terms also reflect the male-dominated early history of tertiary education). It is also worth noting that the lecturer may also be the students' assessor, and given their likely motivation to pass the course, students in many contexts may treat their assessors with some deference.

Another characteristic feature of lectures is that they exist as an efficient vehicle for transferring knowledge. In just one hour, an expert is able to present an account of a topic to a large number of students, sometimes hundreds. This can represent the result of many years of work and experience in the field, and can include synthesis and summary of the key researchers, arguments, and controversies in the field. These latter aspects are important, as lectures are not neutral but 'value-laden discourses', as Lee argues (Lee, 2009, in Lynch, 2011). Lecturers 'certainly aim to inform, but also to evaluate and critique the source materials that they are bringing to students' attention' (ibid.). This observation underlines the need for students to develop a critical approach in lectures. Various ways of developing such a critical approach are integrated into the discussions and tasks in this chapter.

Regardless of the style and delivery, students can appreciate the value of the content. Indeed, content is key, and in EAP contexts it is advisable to focus the learning objectives on content first, then language. This idea is further developed in Chapter 6.

In the disciplines, lecturers are unlikely to closely monitor the students and their output, such as lecture notes. In EAP classrooms it is useful to do so with a view to enabling students to eventually become sufficiently independent to work without close monitoring. Students need to increase their responsibility in lectures by learning to take effective notes and follow up on key points.

Listening in other contexts

Most other academic listening contexts involve more opportunities for reciprocation than lectures. Table 8.1 illustrates selected characteristics associated with academic communicative events. These include familiar listening genres such as lectures, and other contexts in which listening forms a crucial part, such as group projects. Similar events are broadly grouped together in the first column of the table, although there is significant scope for differences in specific contexts, as the discussion of lectures has shown. The characteristics are intended as generalizable observations, and once again are likely to vary across contexts.

Communicative event	Characteristics and explanation
Lecture	Planned, partially-rehearsed content/delivery
	Frequently transactional (i.e. lecturer to students), though can be more interactive
	Long, e.g. one or two hours
	Cyclical, integrated, and multimodal
	Multiskilling required, typically listening while note-taking
	Unequal status of speaker (lecturer) and listener (student)
	Potentially very large number of students in audience

Communicative event	Characteristics and explanation
Presentation/talk/ conference paper	Highly-rehearsed content/delivery Typically two-phased: transactional delivery phase followed by interactional question phase Short to mid-length and fixed-length, e.g. 10/20/40 minutes Free-standing content, i.e. the presentation contains a complete narrative—therefore less cyclical and integrated than lectures Integrated visual/audio-visual content, e.g. slides, video, audio Conventional: participants follow institutional conventions regarding timing, question phase etiquette Optional supporting text: handouts, post-presentation summary Possibly equal status of presenter and audience, some of whom may also be presenting at the same event
Seminar/discussion	Minimally-rehearsed delivery, though content is typically prepared through pre-discussion reading/listening texts Highly interactive, with participants expected to listen, clarify, respond, and build on other participants' contributions Potentially multi-textual, with interruptions and multi-stranded discussions in one space Participants' contributions are expected and valued; lack of any contribution can be seen as unacceptable Academic: opinions are welcome, but need support from academic sources Critical: contributions can be challenged, e.g. by asking for justification and support, or identifying flaws Cumulative: arguments are built up through multiple contributions Textual: prepared texts may be brought in and referred to Style: mixture of technical and potentially quite informal language Possible visual/multimodal content in prepared seminar presentation phases Purpose-driven: e.g. to reach a resolution to a question, or to explore a topic in depth
Tutorial (undergraduate and postgraduate levels)	Content is prepared by the students, typically reading or research based Small-scale: typically limited number of tutees (e.g. 1–12, or more) Tutor roles include guiding the discussion, critiquing, and checking learning, e.g. how successfully students have understood the core texts Clear tutor/student roles: tutor as expert/assessor, though also facilitator of learning and/or counsellor, motivator, plus monitor of progress Integrated into wider learning through reference to related lectures, seminars, reading, and research Part of a linear process: tasks may be set for the next tutorial

Communicative event	Characteristics and explanation
General one-to-one meeting with tutor/course director at any level (foundation, undergraduate, postgraduate)	Initiated by the student, who is expected to ask for/offer something Short/limited in time due to time pressures of tutor/course director Informal, efficient, purpose-driven: the student expects answers/advice on their question(s), any language (formal/informal) can meet these needs with opportunities for each party to seek clarification, etc. Possible social/cultural role: the student may seek a closer professional relationship with the tutor/course director, and perhaps vice-versa, to break down barriers and set the context for future personal interaction
Specialist one-to-one meeting with supervisor (e.g. progress meeting, viva, interview) at research level	A single student plus supervisor/assessor event, each with clear roles Tutor-led/student-led, depending on event and level: student expected to initiate some discussion and have prepared material and questions Part of a series of meetings: previous meeting is reviewed, new objectives set for the next meeting OR one-off high-stakes meeting Content-driven, with a focus on academic rigour and assessment: students expected to produce ideas and arguments based on academic study, research, and thought Originality: students expected to demonstrate evidence of originality, e.g. through new research or new connections/evaluation of existing ideas Student expected to respond to critical interaction by tutor(s)/assessor(s)
Group project	Highly collaborative, interactive, and dynamic Negotiated roles and content; scope for both success and disagreement/disfunctionality in terms of the project objectives Problem-solving, including working out content and group dynamics and relationships Research-based: likely to involve reading, visiting locations and people, knowledge processing, possibly new primary research (e.g. devising a questionnaire to establish people's ideas on a topic) Outcome-driven: clearly-defined product (e.g. presentation, report) required by a given deadline Assessment: likely to be assessed—explicitly as a course assessment, or implicitly by the tutor/supervisor as part of a student's progress on a course
Informal/social interaction	Typically unplanned, unrehearsed; may have an academic focus, e.g. to discuss/clarify an academic task or topic Student-initiated, potentially democratic in terms of roles Negotiated, evolving content and focus Language and style: effective communication rather than accuracy as the primary aim Complementary: supportive of other academic work such as group projects and preparation for seminars

Table 8.1   Characteristics of academic communicative events

Table 8.1 illustrates the potentially very broad scope and heterogeneity of academic institutional events in which listening is essential. EAP teachers and students need to familiarize themselves with local academic practices as there may be wide variations in how the labels (such as 'tutorial', 'seminar', and 'lecture') are used, and how many students take part. For instance, the number of students in a 'lecture' can vary, from a very small number like half a dozen in some institutions to many hundreds. Key areas of difference between the types of listening events include formality, convention, outcomes, purpose, language, student roles and expectations, degree of rehearsal, overall importance, and relative status of the participants. A key characteristic in these academic communicative events is interactivity. Lynch uses the terms 'one-way' listening for transactional events such as lectures, and 'two-way' for reciprocal events such as seminars (Lynch 2011:79ff), which are useful as generalized descriptions of these events.

As with other academic practices, such as academic writing, there is considerable scope for local and discipline variation. A particularly important variant is academic level: the institutional expectations of a PhD student preparing for their final viva will be quite different from those of a student on a foundation course. In order to design an appropriate and effective learning environment through the selection of relevant materials, EAP teachers need to become familiar with their specific context.

This section has shown that listening in academic contexts is integrated, cyclical, and multimodal, and the academic listener has to take on multiple roles in order to engage and interact with listening texts. As a result, the challenges for the student can be very considerable.

Challenges in listening

Students face a number of different types of challenge in accessing and processing listening-based material. These challenges potentially apply to all students, including those whose first language is English. As well as language and the practical implications of real-life delivery, important factors in these challenges include: the language, educational level, and experience of the student; motivational, affective, and cultural factors; and cognitive factors.

Table 8.2 presents the main challenges in listening. Many of these are similar to the challenges in reading (see Table 6.2 on page 152), with the added complexity of the spoken language delivered live: the reader can choose the pace at which they read but the listener typically has to follow the pace set by the speaker(s).

This table outlines some of the challenges facing the listener, and underlines how these are related: while listening to live events such as lectures, the listener has to deal with the speed of delivery determined by the speaker (for example the lecturer) while also processing visual content and producing notes.

Nature of challenge	Explanation and examples
Linguistic	Phonological input: understanding the speaker's accent and pronunciation; processing the input and constructing meaning Vocabulary load, including specialist and technical (discipline-specific) vocabulary Grammatical complexity, especially complex noun phrases
Practical	Real-life delivery: coping with the speed of delivery (with recorded lectures, the listener can mitigate these difficulties by using the 'pause' facility); navigating the lecture Multi-textuality/multimodality: processing multiple texts—the lecturer's live text, audience texts (e.g. questions, contributions), visual texts and any audio-visual texts (see below)
Visual	Accompanying visuals: processing information on slides plus any audio-visual media Handouts: processing the information on handouts, including text, graphics, charts, visuals, statistics
Content	Processing the content of the listening text and relating this to known content: consolidating and extending knowledge
Cognitive	Dealing with potentially dense and complex information (ideas and concepts) and language
Academic	Method and purpose of listening: e.g. note-taking while listening to a lecture in order to produce a written record of the event
Contextual and knowledge-based	Applying the content to the student's individual context Understanding, interpreting, and situating the meaning in the world Working out what to do next, e.g. how to use the information from the listening text

Table 8.2   Challenges in academic listening

Linguistic challenges

Most obviously, many challenges in listening are presented by language.
Language challenges can be divided into the three language systems of phonology, vocabulary, and grammar, although these three are of course all closely connected. The phonological dimension has been elaborated on by Field (2008 and 2013), and is summarized in Figure 8.2.

Speech signal	Decoding
↓	Word search
Words	Parsing
↓	Meaning construction
Meaning	Discourse construction

Figure 8.2 Listening and constructing meaning (Field 2008 and 2013)

The speech signal, which is the starting point of listening, is not transmitted in phonemic form but through the various sounds of the language which are referred to technically using terms such as fricatives and plosives. It is the listener who converts these sounds into phonemes, and from phonemes into words. Similarly, words are separated out by the listener, as there are usually no gaps (i.e. pauses) between spoken words, unlike printed words on the page or screen. The next stage for the listener is to convert words into meaning. This whole process involves a series of cognitive stages for the listener: decoding sounds and matching them into known words; searching for words appropriate to the context (this involves such cognitive activities as disambiguating homophones like 'floor' and 'flaw'); working out the grammar of the utterance, known as parsing; constructing meaning; and constructing discourse (Field 2008 and 2013).

Regardless of their first language, the student can draw on their education to help them access content.

Analyzing the challenges in a lecture extract

The following extract is taken from a lecture by George Pope, honorary senior clinical lecturer at the University of Oxford. It is an authentic lecture, used in the EAP coursebook *Oxford EAP C1/Advanced* (de Chazal and Moore 2013: 30–1 and 232) and represents an example of the type of lecture students need to listen to and understand in the disciplines. The lecture is intended for a non-expert audience, which means that people of a reasonable level of education can expect to understand most or all of it.

The extract represents the first three and a half minutes of the lecture and illustrates some of the listening challenges discussed above, which are elaborated on in the commentary below.

[shows slide 1]

Good afternoon, my name is George Pope, I'm a consultant physician working in the John Radcliffe Hospital in Oxford and an honour–honorary senior clinical lecturer in the University of Oxford and I have the privilege today of talking to you about stroke, an extremely exciting field of medicine evolving over the last 100 years and very, very quickly evolving over the last 10 years. So if I'd like to just go, go through the outline of my talk

[shows slide 2]

which really looks at introducing stroke and how important a stroke is in our population for patients and for society, how, what is a stroke, and try and go through some outline of giving you an understanding of what it means to have a stroke, the making of the diagnosis from the physicians' point of view, the classification which is relevant to the prognosis and the impact on, of, of stroke on people. I'd then like to go on to talk about the primary prevention, or the treatment strategy which is three-fold, primary prevention, secondary prevention, and the very exciting acute treatment which has now emerged over the past ten years as I've said, with thrombolysis and hemicraniectomy; thrombolysis is the use of clot-busting agents and hemicraniectomy is the use of surgical procedures to relieve pressure in the brain, both exclusive treatments that are restricted to a very select population of stroke patients.

So if I can go through some of the facts to begin, these people you may recognize, Elizabeth Taylor, Sharon Stone, Dudley, all have had strokes, and the list is long, and why is it long? Well, every two seconds, somebody in the world has a stroke, and every six seconds, somebody in the world dies from a stroke. That leaves 5.8 million lives per year lost to stroke, and this is information coming from the World Health Report in 2007, the Geneva Report.

[shows slide 4]

Furthermore, it's the third commonest cause of death, with a third of strokes being fatal; one in six people in the world will have a stroke in their lifetime, it's unlikely to get through life without knowing somebody, a first-degree relative or very close friend, who will not have a stroke. It is commoner than the combination of AIDS, TB, and malaria; one in six as I've said will have a recurrence. This is even more relevant in our current environment where our population is ageing; the risk of having a stroke is increased significantly by the–, as one ages, and we are living in an ageing population and

[shows slide 5]

this is some data published by Professor Rothwell in the Lancet in 2005, which shows the increased prevalence of vascular disease, especially stroke, with age. In the EU population, the over-65 group will increase by 2050, it is estimated by Social Trends Office for National Statistics, to be 29% of the population that'll be over 65 years of age.

(de Chazal and Moore 2013: 130–1 and 232)

Linguistic challenges

Linguistic challenges start with the delivery of the lecture, which of course cannot be experienced from the transcript alone. There will be challenges related to aspects such as the speed of delivery, the lecturer's pronunciation, and local conditions including background noise. The language itself, seen in the transcript above, presents challenges including the following:

• False starts and repetitions, for example 'an honour–honorary'

• Unnecessary words, for example 'So if I'd like to just go, go': the lecturer does not add a main clause following the subordinator 'if', so the listener may be primed to expect something which does not happen

• Although clearly signposted at the outset, the sequence flagged up by the words 'the outline of my talk' is very long with multiple items: 'So if I'd like to just go, go through the outline of my talk which really looks at introducing stroke and how important a stroke is in our population for patients and for society, how, what is a stroke, and try and go through some outline of giving you an understanding of what it means to have a stroke, the making of the diagnosis from the physicians' point of view, the classification which is relevant to the prognosis and the impact on, of, of stroke on people…'

- Run-on sentences with multiple clauses giving cumulative information, as in the example above

- Technical terms which can be difficult to hear, understand, pronounce, and spell—for example 'hemicraniectomy', 'thrombolysis'

- Words with dependent prepositions which express specific relational meanings, for example 'the impact on', 'of', 'of stroke on people'

- Embedded references to items mentioned before/after in the text, for example 'as I've said', which is embedded in the noun phrase in the example below

- Complex/convoluted structures such as noun phrases, for example 'the very exciting acute treatment which has now emerged over the past ten years as I've said with thrombolysis and hemicraniectomy'

- Abbreviations and acronyms, which are probably familiar but may remain unclear to the listener as they are undefined by the lecturer, for example 'AIDS', 'EU', 'TB'

Other challenges

Apart from language, various other challenges exist. Culturally, students may be entirely unfamiliar with the three people mentioned by the lecturer, introduced as 'these people you may recognize, Elizabeth Taylor, Sharon Stone, Dudley' and accompanied by their pictures. Some students may react by feeling inadequate that they do not recognize these people, or by pretending that they do. In terms of content and knowledge, the lecturer makes other references to organizations including the *World Health Report*, the *Geneva Report*, and the medical journal *The Lancet*; students may react to these in similar ways. Also, the lecturer makes an important evaluative point in the second paragraph: 'This is even more relevant in our current environment where our population is ageing'. This inclusive language ('our population') can occur frequently in lectures. However, a mixed nationality audience is likely given the popularity of the discipline (medicine) among both first language (L1) and second language (L2) students. Such language suggests that everyone in the lecture space 'belongs' to this population, despite the likelihood of some students coming from countries whose populations are not ageing so significantly.

In terms of cognitive processing, the lecture offers challenges through its references to statistics. While the numbers may be straightforward, their notional references are diverse:

- 5.8 million lives (quantity)

- 2007 (year/date)

- third commonest (sequence)

- a first-degree relative (idiomatic use, i.e. close family member)

- one in six (proportion, which the listener can convert to a fraction or percentage)

- the over-65 group (age, though no explicit reference is given to age at this first mention)
- 29% of the population that'll be over 65 years of age (proportion of a population of a given age, expressed as a percentage and defined using a postmodified noun phrase)

In each instance, the listener has to identify and process both the number and its referent (where stated), and work out the notional meaning given in brackets above. Traditionally, many listening examinations (both general and academic) require students to identify and note down numbers, and students are often naturally inclined to write down such information while listening. One possible pitfall of doing so is that students may miss other information. Arguably the single most important point of the second part of this extract is that the European population is ageing and the risk of stroke increases with age. Interestingly, the lecturer does not state explicitly the obvious implication of these two observations, namely that the European population is at an increasing risk of stroke. This syllogism requires critical thinking to process, and is a good example of students having to construct meaning while listening, based on information presented by the speaker.

Visual challenges are presented by the inclusion of five slides during this three-and-a-half minute extract, equating to an average of one slide every 40 seconds or so. The five slides contain a total of about 200 words, and include many different font styles and sizes, images, graphs, abbreviations, statistical information, symbols, and references. Clearly this all adds a further cognitive processing load while students are listening to the lecturer. Some lecturers/presenters stop speaking to allow their audience to read the slides, but many do not. Meanwhile, some read out some or all of the text on the slides using the same words, while others paraphrase and perhaps elaborate on this text. Such variations in delivery styles add to the challenges facing the students.

In terms of academic considerations and responding to the lecture, the student would be well-advised to focus on meaning, notably the main point of the second paragraph, rather than attempting to note down the minutiae of supporting detail, such as the statistical information in the points above. Less useful still are the cultural references to stroke victims (Elizabeth Taylor, etc.); these are essentially irrelevant from a medical perspective. An important part of listening development is learning to work out what *not* to note down, in tandem with learning what is important to focus on and note down. In a standard lecture of an academic hour (typically 50 minutes), to attempt to write almost everything the lecturer says would be impractical, misguided, and physically and mentally exhausting. The full lecture from which the extract is taken is 43 minutes and contains 6,100 words, equating to an average delivery rate of about 142 words per minute. Even to write a tenth of what the lecturer says means writing 600 words. It is therefore vital for students to focus on main meanings rather than exhaustive detail. Although many examinations such as IELTS and the higher examinations in the Cambridge suite (Advanced and Proficiency) do prioritize primary meaning over minor details, some English language listening examinations may test the latter rather than the former.

In-text support

Balanced against these challenges are items in the text which can be helpful to the listener, such as the following:

- Familiar and logical organization of the material, for example personal introduction, statement of aims, definition of technical terms

- Signposting language, for example 'I'd like to just go, go through the outline of my talk'

- Other cohesive language including explicit references to items mentioned before/after in the text, for example 'the treatment strategy which is three-fold', 'primary prevention', 'secondary prevention',' the very exciting acute treatment': the phrase 'three-fold' primes the listener to expect three items to be mentioned

- Definitions, for example 'thrombolysis is the use of clot-busting agents'

- Rephrasing, for example 'the primary prevention, or the treatment strategy'; one danger however with this appositive is that students may interpret the two items as separate items in a list, whereas they appear to refer to the same thing

- Familiar whole-text structure: the problem-solution text structure is widespread in academic texts and EAP materials. Students should be primed to expect the situation and problem outlined in this lecture extract to be followed by material offering solution(s) and evaluation, which in fact it is.

Although the student listening to academic texts such as lectures faces many challenges, it is worth focusing on this type of support which is given in many lectures. This focus should help build students' confidence and competence in academic listening, thereby shifting the balance in favour of the known and familiar rather than the unknown and the challenging.

Skills and competencies in academic listening

In order to operate effectively in an academic listening context, students need to develop a number of interrelated skills and competences.

The BALEAP 'can-do' framework

BALEAP have developed a competency framework for EAP students in order to inform syllabus design and materials writing (BALEAP 2013). The framework clarifies the distinction between the academic context and academic discourse, and offers specific competencies for each of these, together with exemplification and ideas for further development.

Academic context

The academic context refers to 'the academic practices, values and conventions [and] the cognitive capacity and metacognitive strategies required to cope with courses in this environment' (BALEAP 2013); in other words how people (students and teachers/professors) behave in their academic context, and what they need to do so. Academic discourse, discussed below, is given similar prominence. The clear implication for EAP teachers and course designers is that both skills (practical and cognitive) and language are vital components in academic listening development. The document goes on to state four specific competencies required for such development (BALEAP, 2013):

- Adopt a critical stance to information provided in lectures
- Use lecture extension materials to support understanding
- Cope with different lecturing styles
- Recognize allusions to recent events (UK/Euro-centric).

These competences place the responsibility for accessing and processing the content with the student. The adoption of a critical stance is particularly important: the implication is that, despite the authority of the lecturer, students should not uncritically believe everything they hear. The competency relating to lecture extension materials underlines the cyclical, integrated, and multimodal nature of lectures. Similarly, the competences recognize the reality of variation in lecturer style. Depending on the context, the final point may present considerable, or insignificant, cultural challenges.

In order to develop these competences, students need to be able to do a number of things (BALEAP, 2013):

- Produce appropriate notes for the lecture or talk
- Annotate PowerPoint slides for a critical response
- Compare listening to a lecture with pre-/post-reading to see which strategy works best
- Identify the lecturer's purpose (for example information giving/applying concepts/challenging students) and lecture style (for example monologue/interactive)
- Exemplify why/how lecturers might introduce recent events into their lectures
- Identify relevant sources for current events reporting in their own disciplines or more generally.

These practices illustrate the extent to which students need to actively respond to the lecture or talk; academic listening is not simply passive. The purpose for listening should inform the student's responses. For instance, if the lecture is part of a core series of introductory lectures on a major topic in their discipline, the student should engage with the material, relate it to the other work (for example reading and writing) they are doing on that topic, and critically respond to the ideas and arguments raised in the listening (and other) input. Part of the engagement with the material involves selecting and recording the content: writing appropriate notes, for example.

Academic discourse

Related to the academic context, academic discourse concerns 'language knowledge and a student's ability to mobilise appropriate language in response to the demands of a specific academic context' (ibid.). This aim shows the need for students not only to understand what they hear but be able to communicate it to others. The framework gives the following specific competencies relating to academic discourse in listening (BALEAP 2013):

* Understand rapid, colloquial 'lecture speech'
* Cope with different lecturing styles (this relates to both the academic context and academic discourse)
* Understand unfamiliar non-native accents
* Understand lengthy preambles
* Understand sufficient content to allow for engagement with topic (speed of comprehension and assimilation of information).

These competences reflect some of the challenges discussed earlier in this chapter. EAP teachers can develop their students' competences through the following practices (BALEAP 2013):

* Provide a series of real academic lectures
* Record group problem-solving activity; transcribe extracts; analyze successful and unsuccessful communication
* Provide staged tasks to raise awareness of different aspects of cognitive load, for example listening with and without note-taking; responding critically to monitor their own comprehension.

These ideas demonstrate the benefits of purposeful text and language analysis. It is useful to encourage students to talk about their challenges in listening both in relation to their own language and skills, and in terms of the input. Culturally, some students may be uncomfortable critiquing the delivery of a lecture. The EAP teacher can emphasize that it can be legitimate to identify points of challenge and confusion in a lecture (including its language, delivery, and content), and these points can be seen as distinct from criticizing the lecturer personally.

Discipline-related skills

Two further contexts are given in the BALEAP framework. The first covers discipline-related skills, which 'relate to recognizing and exploring students' disciplines and how they influence the way knowledge is expanded and communicated' (BALEAP 2013). Some of these relate back to those concerned with the academic context, outlined above. The discipline-related skills require students to:

- Understand sufficient content to allow for engagement with topic (speed of comprehension and assimilation of information)
- Understand sufficient content to detect lapses in understanding
- Follow mathematical problems
- Recognize allusions to recent events (UK/Euro-centric)

The student needs to determine which of these are relevant to their own needs; for instance, 'following mathematical problems' may be entirely irrelevant.

Practical skills

These relate to the specific skills which are appropriate to postgraduate study. They cover the following:

- Assimilate information and take full and effective notes
- Take notes sufficiently quickly to record appropriate detail
- Use lecture extension materials to support understanding

These practical skills emphasize the productive requirements of listening to lectures: students need to record the information they are interpreting. To fulfill these, the EAP teacher needs access to good materials which are built round lectures.

In order for students to develop their listening skills, and in particular listening to lectures, a potentially vast range of resources is available.

Listening resources

Public or open lectures frequently take place in universities and around their towns and cities. Such lectures are open to wider groups than lectures for specific courses, meaning that students and/or the general public are able to attend. Depending on the local context these lectures may take the form of an established format, such as lunch-hour or evening lectures which could be from any discipline, or be based around a theme or organization (for example scientific, public policy). Lectures of this type are typically designed to be accessible to the non-expert. This makes them ideal for students of any discipline, who can be encouraged to relate and apply aspects of the content to their own discipline.

Many lectures are recorded and made available online, resulting in a rich and growing source of high-quality lectures which are accessible to all students via the internet.

Lecture resources

New resources are constantly emerging. A selection of some useful established resources is given below.

A major emerging resource are MOOCs (massive open online courses). These resources tend to be built up by universities, their departments or individual lecturers/researchers, or other organizations such as publishers. Often, lectures in MOOCs are edited down to 'consumable' lengths of around 10 minutes. Many have accompanying transcripts, for example Coursera, edX, Udacity.

In some universities, the EAP teaching units have been investing in open-access resources, for example the UK-based University of Reading, which offers lectures through its self-access centre for language learning. These lectures are designed for independent study use rather than as an academic resource to cite in a paper. In the USA, the OpenYale project offers lectures with open licences which are free to use and have accompanying transcripts.

The University of Oxford has a major project showcasing lectures by the university's academics: the OpenSpires project. This is also openly licenced, and many lectures are on quite topical subjects.

At the University of Michigan in the USA, the MICASE (Michigan Corpus of Academic Spoken English) offers a large number of attributes to filter the selection of lectures and lecturers. Filter choices include: the level of the speaker (for example junior faculty, researcher); their language status (i.e. native or non-native speaker of English) and their first language (from Arabic to Vietnamese); speech event (with a number of potentially relevant options including dissertation defence and large and small lectures); academic division (traditionally known as faculty, for example arts and humanities, health); academic discipline (with many options from anthropology to nuclear engineering); participant level (for example mixed undergraduates, senior faculty); and finally a five-scale interactivity rating (from highly interactive to highly monologic).

Hosted by the University of Warwick in the UK, the British Academic Spoken English (BASE) corpus offers transcripts of lectures (without the lectures themselves), which can be a useful resource for text analysis.

TED (Technology, Education, Design) has grown rapidly and represents an exceptional resource of highly stimulating lectures. Viewers can select whether to watch with the accompanying transcript, which can benefit their listening development through exposure to simultaneous listening and reading. It should be pointed out, however, that students who have watched mainly TED lectures prior to their disciplinary study might feel disappointment at the delivery style of some of the more traditional departmental lectures.

Other resources include YouTube (which being so enormous represents challenges in searching, focus, and standards), iTunes and iTunes U, plus many other websites.

Resources such as these can be used in a variety of ways as core or supplementary resources to develop EAP students' competence and skill in academic listening. Further technologies and resources in EAP are discussed in Chapter 12.

Developing listening skills and competencies

Given the central position of listening in academic contexts, the development of students' general and academic listening skills is typically a major focus of EAP programmes. In both practical and pedagogical terms it is useful and efficient for students to develop their listening independently, in conjunction with in-class work. This development is greatly facilitated by the abundance of appropriate resources, such as the online lectures referred to in the previous section.

Developing listening in the classroom

Classroom-based listening development enables the EAP teacher to manage and monitor their students' listening in a defined environment. A useful model is to focus intensively in the classroom on a carefully selected listening text (using video or audio, or delivered live) with accompanying tasks; assess all students' effectiveness in task achievement; and then provide further resources and tasks targeted at students for independent study. Ideally these should be individualized to some extent through language/delivery, content, and task.

Typically, a listening-based lesson falls into three phases: before listening (preparation); while listening (practice); and after listening (development or extension). Table 8.3 gives examples of activities for each stage. To maximize the use of classroom time and student independence, some of the before and after listening tasks can take place outside the classroom. It is advisable to focus on a limited number of tasks in each stage rather than go for an exhaustive approach. The tasks can be negotiated with the students to enhance purpose and motivation.

Phase	Tasks
Before listening	Read a text related to the lecture topic, e.g. textbook extract; discuss/summarize the text Search for web-based and library-based resources related to the topic, including other lectures Study any pre-lecture handouts and material on the university LMS
While listening	Note down main points in the lecture using a range of language, visuals, abbreviations, and symbols Annotate printouts of slides with additional points made by the lecturer Work in groups, each student listening for and noting down different material, e.g. the lecturer's stance, their main arguments, statistical support, citations and references to other material, perspectives, definitions, anecdote, an aspect of language; then reconvene and compare Listen critically to identify weaknesses, assumptions, unsupported claims, controversial statements, irrelevant material Note down aspects of the lecture liked and disliked, giving reasons Think of and write down questions to ask the lecturer arising directly from the lecture content

Phase	Tasks
After listening	Critically evaluate aspect(s) of the lecture, giving examples, e.g. delivery, timing, content, interest, visual support, achievement of stated aims, lecturer's knowledge and authority
	Compare and evaluate the treatment of the topic in the lecture and the texts/resources found before listening
	Process lecture notes into new text, e.g. summary, presentation to new audience who did not listen to the lecture
	Analyze and evaluate accompanying lecture materials, e.g. handouts, slides, online support
	Evaluate aspects of the lecture/lecturer, e.g. delivery, language, content
	Select and incorporate material from the lecture, correctly referenced, in a new written or spoken text
	Go through all the new information, i.e. previously unknown content, arising from the whole lecture experience including before and while listening texts, and identify and evaluate the effectiveness of learning
	Compare and evaluate aspect(s) of the lecture with other lecture(s) on a similar topic
Before and/or after listening	Research the lecturer: their areas of specialism, publications, and stances on relevant issues
	Locate items in lecturer's bibliography, to practise searching skills
	Read items in lecturer's bibliography—collaboratively (e.g. one item each, then feed back to group) or independently, to practise reading
	Search for further material related to the lecture topic, including texts and lectures

Table 8.3   Phases and tasks in academic listening

The suggested tasks in Table 8.3 show some of the possibilities for engaging effectively with lectures in the EAP classroom. Most of these tasks can also be done independently using given or guided resources such as those mentioned in the section on listening resources above.

Developing independent listening

EAP students can develop their listening in a number of ways. A representative selection of practical techniques is presented in Table 8.4.

Aspect	Practice/Procedure
Resources	EAP students can broaden their range of listening input through introduction and familiarization with listening resources, particularly online resources.
Negotiation	EAP teachers and students can discuss and agree on a plan for listening development.
Schedules	The negotiation can lead to a schedule covering specific listening resources, dates, and minimum material to cover.
Responsibility	EAP teachers can ask each student to locate at least one listening resource per week (just as they might have to find a new reading text), and report back on what they have found with an outcome.

Outcomes	Each student keeps a CPD-style (Continuing Professional Development) record, or learning diary. This covers what they have listened to including access details (url/reference) plus responses to selected listening events. These records and responses can include notes, critical and reflective responses, and summaries. EAP teachers can look at these outcomes and use them as a basis for formative teaching, i.e. to inform future teaching and learning materials.
Collaboration	Listening need not be a solitary activity, and students can work together by, for example, listening to the same material and discussing it, and listening to separate material on the same topic and comparing it. Students can also work in groups on listening projects, e.g. to piece together information on a topic based on multiple texts including listening texts.
Virtual	EAP students can use the LMS as an interactive resource to communicate and discuss what they have listened to, and respond to input by other students.

Table 8.4   Techniques for developing independent listening

Table 8.4 offers a range of possible approaches to foster the development of independent listening. Two particularly important aspects are negotiation and responsibility: with student involvement and commitment, they are more likely to undertake the tasks and produce meaningful outcomes.

A degree of independent listening development alongside classroom-based work is desirable for a number of reasons. First, the students in a given class are highly likely to have different needs arising from differences in such areas as level, pace of learning, and target listening requirement. Second, class time is often limited, and independent work can significantly increase the pace of learning over a given period of time (this observation naturally applies to all the language skills). Third, listening development is ideally suited to independent study, given today's technologies and resources such as online lectures with optional transcripts which can be paused and reviewed as required. Finally, an individualized approach can accommodate a variety of learning needs and styles in a much more responsive way than the lockstep (i.e. where all participants are 'in step' due to the nature of the input) methodology of the classroom.

Conclusion

This chapter has elaborated on the roles of the academic listener as interpreter and recorder. For any success in listening to be attained, the student has to understand the input to some extent. This in itself is a complex and challenging process. Given the limitations of the human memory, EAP teachers need to use tasks which require the student to record part of what they listen to. By effectively understanding and interpreting their input, EAP students are well-placed to record the points relevant to their purpose. An increasingly wide range of resources and technologies is available to enable students to access appropriate listening texts with a degree of independence, and process them in various ways.

Further reading

Field, J. 2008. *Listening in the Language Classroom.* Cambridge: Cambridge University Press.

Field, J. (ed.). 2011. *Journal of English for Academic Purposes Special Issue: Listening in EAP* 10/2.

Flowerdew, J. (ed.). 1994. *Academic Listening: Research perspectives.* Cambridge: Cambridge University Press.

Flowerdew, J. 2005. *Second Language Listening.* Cambridge: Cambridge University Press.

Lynch, T. 2009. *Teaching Second Language Listening: A guide to evaluating, adapting, and creating tasks for listening in the language classroom.* Oxford: Oxford University Press.

9

SPEAKING

Academic speaker as reporter and persuader

Participants in academic contexts—students, teachers, lecturers, professors, researchers —need good speaking skills, as well as listening skills, to function effectively. They need to be able to communicate their message effectively in a wide range of situations and, crucially, persuade and convince their audience. Academic speakers need to be persuasive through interactions such as the following, which may take place in a variety of events such as seminars, discussions, and presentations:

• formulating and expressing arguments

• presenting and responding to critical analysis

• responding to and building on the arguments of others

• asking convincing questions arising from the contributions of others

• reporting their reading and research

• presenting a **case** or recounting an experiment

• expressing their stance on an issue.

All of the above are meaning-driven interactions—in other words the speaker starts with the meaning and content which they want to communicate. They all also involve a degree of interaction with their audience. If speakers in the disciplines do these things, then EAP students need to do them too: in short, all participants in academic contexts need to be effective speakers, communicators, and persuaders. Previous chapters have examined the different types of spoken communication common in academic intercourse (listed in Chapter 1 in Table 1.1, page 17) and the critical responses highly valued in academic contexts (discussed in Chapter 5). This chapter examines the roles of the academic speaker, first by looking at opportunities, challenges, and competences in speaking and then moving on to discuss what is required of EAP students in two key speaking events: seminars and presentations.

The role of speaking in academic contexts

As with academic listening, there is far less published research on academic speaking compared with academic writing and reading. For example, in a meta-analysis of academic listening published in *The Journal of English for Academic Purposes*, only about 10% of the articles in that journal over a nine-year period addressed listening and/or speaking, compared to about 54% for writing (Lynch 2011: 80). In the applied linguistics textbook *English for Academic Purposes: an advanced resource book* (Hyland 2006), none of the articles or chapters focus specifically on speaking, nor does 'speaking' feature in the subject index of the book, although in some articles references are made to spoken genres such as student presentations. Again, the main areas of focus are on theories informing the teaching of reading and writing in an EAP context.

Academic events centred on speaking include seminars, tutorials, and presentations. The characteristics of these and other events are elaborated on in Table 9.1 below. The term 'seminar' is frequently used for an academic discussion which is likely to involve preparation such as reading by the participants (students and seminar leader), an interactive approach where contributions from all participants are expected and valued, and an outcome. Tutorials also involve discussion, but are different from seminars in that they are likely to involve more teaching input from the tutor and generally have fewer students than seminars. There may also be an element of implicit assessment in tutorials: the tutorial enables the tutees to demonstrate their knowledge and understanding of the topic. In tutorials, the tutor is not simply delivering knowledge, but facilitating the students' (sometimes known as 'tutees') engagement with the topic through discussion and responses to questions.

In practice, then, there is considerable potential, indeed necessity, for students to speak in academic contexts, and the role of the EAP teacher is crucial in maximizing opportunities for student speaking. In order to do so, the EAP teacher needs to provide appropriate resources, materials, input, feedback, and the space for students to develop as effective communicators and persuaders in a wide range of situations.

Speaking as both a central and peripheral activity

Speaking can be said to occupy both a central and a peripheral role in academic contexts and EAP teaching. While reading and writing are often thought of as the core skill areas within academic discourse, and therefore the main areas of focus in many EAP programmes, many ideas are also conveyed through speaking. Speaking plays a central role through discussion of content and ideas arising from reading and research, and through communication of these in set-piece academic events like seminars, discussions, and presentations. For subject teachers, i.e. lecturers and professors, a significant amount of content is typically delivered through lectures.

Speaking can also be seen as more peripheral—but nonetheless very important—in that it can take place in almost any academic context. For example, while from the student's perspective lectures mainly involve listening, the ability (including the confidence) to ask questions in lectures can be very productive. More informal interactions are widespread, such as talking about a class and working out how to do a new assignment. In academic writing, speaking may also not be viewed as a central activity, but it is nonetheless very important in this process.

In EAP contexts, many tasks and activities which involve speaking can be built around other skills, such as referring to the content of a lecture in a subsequent seminar or tutorial. Also, many opportunities for speaking naturally arise from other skills work. For example, an academic writing class does not need to be an exclusively heads-down environment: the EAP teacher can encourage and build in tasks where students present their arguments and work in progress. Such opportunities are ideal for constructive critical interaction and the development of ideas, which in turn can result in higher-quality writing.

Furthermore, depending on the local context, more informal speaking contexts can be extremely important. Students need to function effectively in their wider context, which can involve speaking with peers whose first language is different to their own, and interacting with teaching and administrative staff. If they are in an English-speaking country, students will need to speak in English to function in that context. This also applies to some extent in countries where English is not the main first language but is widely spoken; for example international students who are studying in countries like the Netherlands (whether or not they also speak Dutch) can expect to be able to speak English in the wider community.

The place of other languages in spoken interaction

An interesting phenomenon is the practice of switching between languages, known as 'code-switching', within a single discussion. This can happen when a group of students who share a language, for example Chinese, are studying together informally. The discourse and most text input in their discipline, for example economics, is in English, and during the discussion the students are collaboratively reviewing and clarifying their learning using both their first language (L1), Chinese, and their second language (L2), English. Students are likely to use English when discussing the technical content including statistics, and switch back and forth into Chinese for material such as explanations and personal responses. Such communicative events play a key role in the development and realization of students' learning. This practice illustrates how a student's first language remains vitally important in an English-medium academic context, and that in such contexts English need not dominate or be exclusively used in all situations at the expense of students' first languages.

Speaking, listening, and interaction

Academic speaking and listening can be seen as two sides of the oral communication coin. While the audience in a presentation are listening, the presenter is speaking; as the speaker in a seminar is putting forward their argument, the other participants are listening and preparing their responses. These contexts underline the inseparability of listening and speaking in a communicative context such as EAP. It is not helpful to give the message that, of the oral/aural skills, listening is receptive and passive, and only speaking is productive. Chapter 8 shows that even a lecture, which may traditionally be viewed as transactional, can be part of a much more interactive communicative cycle.

The cyclical and integrated nature of speaking

Just as listening is essentially cyclical and integrated, as discussed in Chapter 8, so too is speaking in academic contexts. Clearly, many events and situations are highly interactive, for example discussions and seminars. Presentations are also interactive rather than only transactional, in that the presenter has to engage with their audience throughout, respond to any questions, and perhaps follow up their presentation with further discussion. Much of the input for a presentation is likely to be in the form of both written texts (for example source texts, conference proceedings) and spoken texts (for example other presentations and lectures); all of which illustrates the highly integrated nature of speaking contexts.

Interruption

A further, culturally-based characteristic of listening and speaking events is the widespread practice of interruption. In some cultures, such as Japanese, interrupting a speaker, especially if they are viewed as high-status like a teacher, can be frowned upon. From a western perspective, interrupting is widely considered to be normal practice: journalists interrupt the politicians they are interviewing on television and radio, and students interrupt other students (and their teacher) while they are speaking in a seminar. Depending on the context, it can also be perfectly acceptable to interrupt a presenter or lecturer to ask a question or make a contribution. This phenomenon of interruption further underlines the integrated nature of speaking and listening; while listening in many contexts, the student may be preparing to speak.

EAP programmes need to reflect these realities by providing meaningful, interactive communicative tasks aimed at developing students' speaking (and other) skills in an academic context.

Speaking opportunities in academic contexts

Different speaking-based communicative events, such as presentations and seminars, require specific skills and language, so the EAP teacher needs to provide appropriate learning materials. Reflecting the closely-related nature of speaking and listening, Table 9.1 presents an overview of student speaking roles using the same communicative events introduced in Chapter 8, Table 8.1 (page 222). The second column of the table outlines the main characteristics and some of the implications and opportunities for speaking in such events.

Communicative event	Characteristics, implications, and opportunities for speaking
Lecture	Input: heavily listening oriented, possibly with some opportunities for student contributions within the lecture Lecturer expectations: any student questions are expected to be based on points arising from the lecture, e.g. clarifications, additional contributions, critical questions Follow-up: good potential for further work, e.g. discussions arising from the lecture topic and arguments, reprocessing of content such as oral summary of the lecture to a peer
Presentation/talk/ conference paper	Expectations: high audience expectations of the presenter and their authority due to the highly rehearsed nature of the delivery and relatively high-profile (compared with seminar contributions) of the event Clarity: emphasis on clear delivery including enunciation of key terms; appropriate volume to reach the whole audience; appropriate pace and variation of pace; intelligibility expected throughout Responsiveness to audience: via their feedback through body language and questions; through direct responses to audience questions Consideration of audience: through selection of content; building on and extending what they know Criticality: academic audiences expect presentations to offer arguments, analysis, and new content supported by evidence, rather than description alone Visuals: integration of supporting visuals, which need to be clearly referred to and commented on Convention: the audience expects the speaker to follow institutional conventions, e.g. regarding timing and question phase etiquette Support: the audience may expect the presenter to provide support, e.g. handouts, links to relevant resources, a post-presentation summary
Seminar/Discussion	Spontaneity: offering in-discussion contributions and questions Content and knowledge: contributing original content arising from preparation and reading, and extending knowledge through engagement with other participants' contributions Influence: opportunity for students to impress their tutor/seminar leader through their contributions Language and skills development: trying out new language including functional language like asking for clarification Criticality: critiquing the arguments and ideas of other participants, and asking and answering critical questions Integration: referring to source texts including lectures, Academic: developing academic credibility through rigorous responses (i.e. supported by sound evidence) and questioning Community: being part of and building an academic community through exchange and discussion of ideas

Communicative event	Characteristics, implications, and opportunities for speaking
Tutorial (undergraduate and postgraduate levels)	Initiative: initiating contributions and questions; offering and exploring new ideas Responsiveness: answering questions from the tutor Assessment: potentially favourably influencing the tutor, who is typically also in the role of assessor Interactivity: adding and critiquing other participants' (tutees and tutor) contributions; Academic: referring to sources; critiquing source material Exploration: proposing new ideas, which may be instantly critiqued, in a supportive small-scale environment Collegiality: developing closer professional/academic relations with peers (other tutees) and the tutor
General one-to-one meeting with tutor/ course director at any level (foundation, undergraduate, postgraduate)	Initiative: predicting problems and asking for help before/as they arise Needs driven: asking for practical guidance and support as needed Practicality: managing personal study through interaction with the tutor/course director Social/cultural role: becoming more familiar with the tutor/course director through occasional drop-in attendance at one-to-one meetings
Specialist one-to-one meeting with supervisor (e.g. progress meeting, viva, interview) at research level	Problem-solving: gaining valuable guidance (e.g. in formulating a research question or methodology) and resources (e.g. in providing useful source texts) from the tutor/ supervisor Reporting: recounting recent reading, research, and the development of the research question Initiative and responsiveness: opening up new discussions; answering the supervisor/ assessor questions Clarification and endorsement: seeking answers to specific questions, with the aim of gaining the supervisor's endorsement of the direction of the research Assessment: demonstrating through criticality and updating of progress that the student is meeting the requirements and expectations of the programme or research Academic community: gaining greater acceptance into the specific academic community through dissemination of the work Future work: using the current research as a basis for possible future work such as presentation of the work at conferences, writing research papers, carrying out new related research projects Networking: using the academic staff as contacts for possible collaboration in the field

Communicative event	Characteristics, implications, and opportunities for speaking
Group project	Collaboration: contributing ideas, reading, and research as part of a team focused on the same outcome Interactive: working with a group/team, and potentially liaising with other groups and academic staff Negotiation: persuading peers of the strength and validity of an approach, while conceding points where their argument prevails Problem-solving: working out content and group dynamics and relationships Research: reading, visiting locations and people, knowledge processing, possibly new primary research (e.g. devising a written or spoken questionnaire to establish people's ideas on a topic) Outcome driven: contributing to a clearly-defined product such as a presentation or report required by a given deadline Assessment: influencing positively a course assessment
Informal/social interaction	Needs driven: interacting with peers through informal social gatherings and networks, enabling more effective learning through processes such as seeking clarification and discussing projects Socio-cultural: becoming more familiar with the academic and local culture Personal: developing friendships and relationships with peers (other students) and other people in their wider networks Language: achieving effective communication on potentially challenging topics, e.g. a new concept being covered on the course Support: discussing and clarifying other academic work such as group projects and preparation for seminars

Table 9.1   Speaking opportunities in academic communicative events

Table 9.1 illustrates the considerable potential for learning opportunities in these spoken academic communicative events, as well as indicating the potential for complexity in aspects such as language, socio-cultural aspects, and assessments.

Expectations and disciplinary variations

All the spoken academic communicative events in Table 9.1 offer opportunities for students to develop their language and skills, as well as to initiate discussions and conversations. The information in the second column represents potential characteristics and opportunities offered by the academic communicative events; the realities in specific contexts are likely to vary. In reality, the EAP teacher's knowledge of their students' specific discipline in their target institution is unlikely to be comprehensive. It is important to try and establish the major characteristics and components of their study, however, in order to work out which communicative events to include on the EAP programme.

Designing the speaking component in EAP programmes

Depending on the specific context, these characteristics and opportunities can be used as targets. In formulating EAP programmes and learning outcomes, the EAP teacher and syllabus designer can identify which items are relevant to their students' needs. Given any time constraints in the length of EAP programmes, the EAP teacher can 'triage' the items, by deciding which ones are:

• essential: these items need to be covered

• important/useful: these items should/could be covered if there is time

• peripheral/irrelevant: these items should not be included.

In this process, the EAP teacher can prioritize core items. For example, if the EAP team (teachers, course directors, managers) establish that presentations form part of the assessment for students in their discipline, then presentations should be included for students on an EAP programme. Presentations, therefore, should be integral to the curriculum and covered in the syllabus, with sufficient time and resources to achieve the required standard. If, for example, students in their discipline do not have to participate in research-based meetings with a supervisor, this should be excluded. Approaches to designing syllabuses and writing materials are discussed further in Chapter 10.

Student competencies in speaking

Chapter 2 offers an overview of the competencies expected of EAP teachers, based on the BALEAP (2008) Competency Framework. BALEAP's work has led to the development of a new framework aimed at what students need to do: 'The BALEAP Can Do Framework for EAP syllabus design and assessment' (BALEAP, 2013). This framework is divided into four sections based on the four skills of writing, speaking, reading, and listening, and is aimed at postgraduate students within a UK context. The extent to which these competences can be applied in other contexts depends on the requirements and expectations of the specific context in question. Table 9.2 presents selected competences and examples taken from the framework.

Specific competences (for the student)	Examples of practice (for the EAP teacher to introduce)
Academic context relates to: the academic practices, values and conventions; the cognitive capacity and metacognitive strategies required to cope with courses in this environment (i.e. UK postgraduate)	
General approach Demonstrate critical thinking Work independently as well as collaboratively Understand value of group tasks Take part in group work using enquiry-based learning approach Take part in group work analyzing and solving problems Tell other people when they are wrong Interact with native speakers Introduce cultural insights	Group presentations to encourage collaboration, assessed by tutor, evaluated by group Introduce a western-based cultural concept to be critically reviewed from students' own viewpoints Introduce/review problem-solving language
Group competencies Take part in group discussion (and socializing) Engage fully in discussion rather than providing superficial contribution Debate and communicate/share thoughts and feelings Engage in peer review	Analyze video footage of seminar interaction to identify 1 interactional language, 2 content bearing discourse, 3 body language (culturally defined/common to many cultures) Use reflective tasks (writing) to elicit student responses to group work, both to identify difficulties in engagement and to practise the communication of thoughts and feelings
Individual competences Demonstrate high level presentation skills Select appropriate detail and limit content of presentations Expand on what is written on slides Present without over-reliance on PowerPoint	Provide input session on how to deliver effective oral presentations, covering: research and preparation; presentation techniques; oral delivery and language skills Practise 1–3 minute stand-up talks to promote greater confidence and fluency with no aids
Supplementary competences Apply critical thinking skills in supervision context Interact effectively with supervisor (acknowledging problems) Develop and maintain an independent stance while engaging effectively with supervisor Engage in 'Socration'* dialogue with supervisors Ask for advice and feedback Respond to advice and feedback Challenge a lecturer	Identify the appropriate mode of address when speaking or writing to lecturers—discuss email conventions/spoken conventions e.g. use of 'teacher', 'sir', titles etc. Set up staged seminar with prepared roles (person who challenges/agrees/disagrees/seeks clarification…). The seminar input/stimulus can be an academic reading text and students are given time to write their questions/statements after reading and prior to the seminar. Students then conduct the seminar taking on the roles given with the teacher chairing (or another student as confidence increases).

Academic discourse relates to: language knowledge and a student's ability to mobilize appropriate language in response to the demands of a specific academic context.	
General/language specific Ask for clarification Ask/respond to questions (seminar/lecture situations) Show disagreement Tell other people when they are wrong Communicate effectively, e.g. asking for things; giving orders; selling a product	Encourage the asking of questions at the end of guest lectures and presentations and provide input on question types—practice this in class with recorded/live lectures or extracts
Group competences Co-operate and take part in group work in a lab environment Take part in group work analyzing and solving problems Co-operate and complete group tasks (on time) Involve other participants in group work Report on group tasks Contribute to discussion in seminars Engage fully in discussion rather than providing superficial contribution Take part in group discussion Challenge other members of the group	Group project: PREPARATION • Put students into groups, choose or allocate topic to research and write about: teacher sets word limit and gives further guidance depending on group level • Students discuss work to be done; how to divide up; possible issues • Groups write up discussion and post on wiki/blog • Teacher comments on reports and makes suggestions/gives more direction Group project: PRODUCTION • Write up project • Report on progress each week on the wiki/blog; ask questions on a more regular basis (teacher monitors) • Final presentation—presentation itself can be divided up into sections, but students should be prepared to talk about any section, not just one part that they have particularly prepared POST ACTIVITY • Students write reflective text on what they have learned about group work
Individual competences Demonstrate high-level presentation skills Select appropriate detail/limit presentation content Interact effectively with supervisor (acknowledging problems) Develop and maintain an independent stance while engaging effectively with supervisor Engage in 'Socration' dialogue with supervisors Ask for/respond to advice and feedback Challenge a lecturer	Practise group and individual oral presentations and assess formally using an assessment template that evidences the importance of all the different areas that make an effective presentation (research and preparation, presentation techniques, oral delivery and language skills etc.

Discipline-related skills relate to: recognizing and exploring students' disciplines and how they influence the way knowledge is expanded and communicated.	
Communicate effectively: e.g. asking for things; giving orders; selling a product Co-operate and take part in group work in a lab environment Challenge a lecturer	
Practical skills relate to the skills specifically appropriate to postgraduate study.	
Demonstrate high-level presentation skills Select appropriate detail and limit content of presentations Present without over-reliance on PowerPoint	

* 'Socration' is an alternative term (used by some academic staff) to the term 'Socratic', i.e. relating to the teaching of Socrates (see Chapter 5).

Table 9.2   Student competences in speaking with selected examples of practice based on the BALEAP (2013) Can Do Framework

The competences and suggested tasks presented in this framework provide a solid basis for speaking skills development in the EAP classroom. EAP teachers need to interpret the competences and adapt them for their local situation. For instance, as Chapter 8 notes, it may not be appropriate to 'challenge a lecturer' in certain contexts. Certain competences reflect the western perspective from which they emerge (the contributors to the framework are based in UK universities), for example 'engage in 'Socration' dialogue with supervisors'. This particular tradition can be traced back to the practice of Socrates, mentioned at the start of Chapter 5.

The framework emphasizes the skills and language discussed earlier in this chapter, notably those associated with group interaction, participating in seminars, and giving presentations. A very useful activity for EAP teachers is to develop further tasks (like those in the second column of the table) aimed at building those competences most applicable to their local context.

What the framework also illustrates are lecturers' high expectations of students, which can present many challenges.

Challenges in speaking

As with the other skills, speaking in academic contexts can present many challenges for students. Among these challenges are: language (phonology, grammar, vocabulary); intelligibility; understanding the message; culture; expectations; and affective factors such as personality, confidence, and learning styles. Table 9.3 presents selected challenges in speaking for students in academic contexts.

Nature of challenge	Explanation
Practical	Initiative: working out what to say, and when and how to say it Pragmatic: coping with the speed of interaction with the other speaker(s), and understanding their message
Linguistic	Language (grammar and vocabulary): finding appropriate language to convey the meaning Phonology: producing an intelligible utterance Functional/notional: finding appropriate language to interact, e.g. ask for clarification, express a quantity
Content and knowledge	Ideas: coming up with sufficient good-quality ideas to express
Cognitive/affective	Development: understanding, processing, and building on the ideas of other people in the academic spoken communicative event Personality: speaking when having to rather than wanting to; gaining confidence in speaking in public settings
Academic	Community: establishing oneself as part of an academic community, which implies certain levels of knowledge, skills, and engagement Assessment: managing and producing material that is assessed, e.g. a presentation
Textual	Multi-textuality/multimodality: presenting and referring to other texts, e.g. visuals in a presentation, graphs in a text, other audio-visual texts Intertextual: relating and synthesizing information and meaning across different spoken and written sources
Contextual and knowledge-based	Applying the content of the spoken interaction to the student's individual context Understanding, interpreting, and situating the meaning in the world Working out what to do next, e.g. how to use the information from the interaction

Table 9.3   Challenges in speaking in academic contexts

The challenges in Table 9.3 point to the breadth and complexity facing the student. Given the interactive nature of speaking, some challenges are similar to those facing the listener, as outlined in Table 8.2 in Chapter 8 (page 225). There are further challenges in speaking, notably in the nature of practical, cognitive, and affective terms. The EAP teacher needs to be sensitive to all these potential challenges, and work towards identifying which ones are particularly relevant to their students' needs.

While there are many commonalities among groups of students, each student is of course a different person, and so may face their own distinct challenges. Factors influencing these potentially heterogeneous challenges can include culture, language, personality, level (language, cognitive, academic), educational background, needs, and expectations. Some cultures are perceived as being more 'oral' than others; for instance Arabic-speaking cultures are often viewed as producing students whose speaking is more fluent and accurate than their writing. However, such observations, though potentially useful, amount to generalizations and exceptions to these generalizations (if they are indeed viable) can always be found.

There are a number of prototypical academic communicative events, including seminars, discussions, and presentations. Students need different skills and language to operate effectively in such events, and the EAP teacher needs to provide appropriate academic speaking tasks and learning materials.

In response to these challenges, it is necessary for EAP teachers to facilitate the development of their students' speaking skills. Bruce (2011: 188) reports on the importance of repetition in developing students' speaking skills. Through repetition and practice of relevant speaking tasks, notably speaking in lectures, interacting in groups, and giving oral presentations, students can internalize their competence relating to such tasks. In this way, students can develop the accuracy of their output (Bruce 2011: 188).

Two major areas in which EAP students can develop their speaking skills are presentations, covered later in this chapter, and seminars and discussions.

Seminars and discussions

Seminars and discussions form an integral part of learning and teaching in the disciplines. Seminars are likely to be formalized, timetabled academic events which facilitate the dissemination and discussion of knowledge and ideas. Indeed, the words 'seminar' and 'disseminate' are derived from the same root, and so suggest that a major function of the seminar is to enable ideas to be raised, discussed, and through this process spread out to a wider audience. Discussions are more general in scope and not limited to academic contexts, although in practice the terms 'seminar' and 'discussion' are sometimes used interchangeably or together as in 'seminar discussion'.

These events enable students to progress in their learning through the contribution and exploration of ideas. Seminars and discussions also enable subject-teachers to monitor and assess learning. These roles are reflected in EAP contexts, where seminars and discussions primarily facilitate the development of students' skills and language.

Evaluating speaking competence

A useful starting-point in an EAP programme is to establish students' current level of skills and language, and equally importantly their perception of these. A short evaluative questionnaire can be used to establish students' perceptions, such as that presented in Table 9.4, taken from the opening unit of a B2 EAP coursebook (de Chazal and McCarter 2012: 8).

		Always	Usually	Sometimes	Never
1	I can speak confidently in a group discussion.				
2	I can think of something interesting to say.				
3	I can find the right language to express my ideas.				
4	I can use grammar accurately.				
5	I prepare for a discussion by reading and thinking about ideas.				
6	I speak clearly and people usually understand me.				
7	I can respond intelligently to other people's ideas.				

Table 9.4   Evaluating speaking: a questionnaire for students

As they are expressed in straightforward language, these statements are accessible for students and can form the basis of discussion and awareness-raising about language, practice, and affective factors such as confidence. The next step is to build on these areas through practice in the EAP classroom, leading to independent work outside the classroom.

Participating in seminars

A key aspect of seminars and academic discussions concerns knowledge: students are generally expected to prepare for the seminar by reading something on the topic and developing their ideas to bring to the seminar. Thus an important characteristic of seminars is preparation: students contribute ideas they have already started reading about, rather than spontaneously coming up with points without some basis in existing knowledge.

Seminar preparation in EAP programmes needs to reflect these realities. Figure 9.1 shows a possible cycle in preparing for and conducting a seminar in the disciplines. This cycle can be adapted to form the basis of seminar skills work in an EAP programme.

Preparation
Engage with the topic of the seminar → (Find and) read source texts related to the seminar topic → Formulate responses to the text(s)

The seminar
Clarify the topic or question: its meaning and parameters → Contribute relevant points, possibly including arguments supported by evidence → Interact with other participants through responding to and critiquing/building on their responses → Reach a conclusion or resolution to the question(s) raised in the seminar

Follow-up
Follow up interesting and important points raised in the seminar
Carry out further reading based on texts cited in the seminar
Incorporate ideas from the seminar into new written and spoken texts

---

Figure 9.1   Sample EAP seminar skills task cycle

Students can engage with the seminar topic by first checking their understanding of the topic or question, and then noting down any initial points. Source texts can include secondary sources, such as textbook extracts (for example chapters on the seminar topic) and critical texts, such as articles or reviews related to the topic or question to be discussed. Primary sources may also be cited in the seminar, such as research articles. At the earlier stages in a student's academic career, such as foundation and undergraduate levels, texts are more likely to be secondary sources and may be provided by the subject teacher/seminar leader. At higher levels, from undergraduate upwards, students are more likely to be expected to find their own relevant texts. Students can prepare for the seminar individually and/or collaboratively. They need to respond to the texts, starting with developing their knowledge through an understanding of the content. Students can then critique the ideas and assumptions in the texts, and note down points such as reactions, critical questions, further related points, and opinions. Depending on the level, students may be expected to develop an argument, which they can then introduce in the seminar.

The format of the seminar will vary depending on the seminar leader and the specific context. During the seminar, the seminar leader will probably expect all students to make a contribution and respond to the contributions of other participants.

A seminar in an EAP programme can reflect the context outlined above. Additional stages and tasks can be added, such as the following:

- Language work, for example functional language such as turn-taking and interrupting, or academic language such as referring to a source text in a discussion

- Reflective work, for example self-evaluation of performance in the seminar

- Feedback, for example critical peer feedback to offer suggestions for improvement

- Action plan, for example the formulation of an individualized plan for improvement based on an aspect of the seminar such as language, participation, preparation

- Summary, i.e. writing up the main points made in the seminar in a short summary for future reference.

The tasks described in this section indicate ways in which students can approach and prepare for seminars. This preparation can greatly enhance their level of participation and success in seminars, and can form the basis of EAP materials to develop these skills.

Giving presentations

Presentations are well-established in many EAP programmes, published materials, and assessments. Two key aspects of presentations are content (what the presenter plans to say) and delivery (how they say it).

Content and delivery in presentations

Content and delivery are crucial since they form the rationale for a presentation. Also, presentations are typically judged on the quality of the material (content) and how effectively this was conveyed (delivery). Arguably, a successful presentation needs both quality content and good delivery, although in some contexts one may be favoured over the other. For example, at higher academic levels, conference participants and audiences may be more focused on content, and might not mind too much if the presenter delivers this in an unexciting way, for example by standing at a lectern and reading aloud from a carefully written paper. Increasingly, in many contexts however, conference participants and other audiences may expect the presenter to deliver in a lively and interactive way using attractive visuals. Table 9.5 offers descriptors for effective and ineffective presentations in terms of both content and delivery.

The descriptions in the table illustrate the challenges faced by the presenter, and the potential for ineffective delivery and content. In reality, most presentations are likely to fall between the two extremes of across-the-board effectiveness and comprehensive ineffectiveness. Ideally, as mentioned above, an audience would hope for both effective delivery and relevant, interesting content. An interesting question is which is the most and least desirable of the following two scenarios: engaging delivery with limited content; or poor delivery with interesting content. Presentations in teachers' and academic conferences as well as students' presentations can be indicative of how challenging it can be to succeed in both aspects. Sometimes audience feedback can be mixed, with praise mixed with criticism of certain aspects, such as appropriateness of content, effectiveness of delivery, and timing. A frequently heard criticism is that the presenter has too much content, i.e. more material than can effectively be delivered within the allotted time.

For EAP students, the challenges of the presenter can appear very daunting. For EAP teachers and programme managers, an appropriate syllabus and materials should be developed to meet the students' needs.

	Content	Delivery
Effective	The presenter: audience have confidence in the presenter's knowledge and authority on the presentation topic Relevant to audience aims and expectations; makes appropriate assumptions about what the audience knows/wants to know Situated in audience's existing knowledge, which it extends Evidence-based: informed and supported by research Original: includes some original content/new thoughts/novel connections between existing phenomena Current: content reflects up-to-date thinking and research on the topic Critical: ideas, theories, and cited work are approached critically Application: content can be applied to the audience's specific contexts, e.g. they can use material from the presentation in their work/practice Follow-up: content forms the basis of post-presentation discussion and reading/research	Comprehensible: clear explanation of the content including new and difficult concepts, taking into account the audience profile Structure and navigation: clear communication of aims and signposting of stages in the presentation Engaging: interesting and motivating delivery of content through style, language, manner, e.g. use of repetition, explanation, humour, story, movement, illustration, questions to audience Responsive: adapts to in-presentation needs, e.g. questions from the audience to clarify/backtrack/omit material Pace: appropriate speed of delivery for the content, with pauses for audience to take in new concepts Visuals: effective use of clear, relevant, attractive visuals to support content Timing: the planned content is delivered within the allotted time, allowing time for questions where appropriate
Ineffective	The authority of the presenter does not come through in the content Relevance: partial, limited, or no relevance to audience profile/interests Misaligned: does not meet audience aims and expectations Ungrounded: claims and opinions are unsupported by evidence Unoriginal: audience do not learn anything new Uncritical: ideas, theories, and cited work are unquestioningly accepted Dated: insufficient current/new content and research, reliant on older sources Lacking purpose: the content cannot easily be applied to and used in the audience's contexts Follow-up: no obvious points to take away and discuss/read up on	Incomprehensible: by the end of the presentation the audience are unclear about the main points and purpose of the presentation Unstructured: illogical/incoherent structure and/or communication of structure to audience Non-engaging: unexciting or pedestrian delivery of content without utilizing opportunities for interaction Inflexible: not responsive to audience questions/requests for clarification Pace: inappropriate pace, e.g. too fast/slow/unvaried for audience and content Visuals: not used/unclear/excessive/not referred to or elaborated on effectively Timing: either significantly under-length or timed-out, i.e. major parts of the content not delivered within allotted time slot

Table 9.5   Balancing content and delivery in an academic presentation

Formulating a presentation skills syllabus

The points in Table 9.5 can form the basis of an EAP presentation skills syllabus and subsequent assessment. The items in the syllabus should be aligned to those in the final assessment. For instance, in the EAP classroom and through independent study, students can work on the timing aspect of delivery. They can develop their skills in timing through activities including the following:

- planning an appropriate amount of material to include in the allotted time
- practising the delivery of parts of the presentation under timed conditions
- fluency activities, for example speaking on a familiar topic for one or two minutes, to develop pace of delivery
- working with visuals to balance content between spoken and written material, which can lead to efficiency of delivery

Each point in Table 9.5 can be developed using appropriate tasks and activities such as those above. The syllabus can be realized using published materials, which are widespread, materials written in-house, or a combination of both.

Stages in a presentation

The important genre of presentation needs to be practised using appropriate materials. A useful starting point is to describe and analyze the stages in a presentation, and express these as advice for the presenter, i.e. the EAP student. Table 9.6 serves as an example of a description of the stages in a presentation. The criteria for giving a presentation are given as headings in bold; they relate to targeted advice which follows—this is aimed directly at the presenter.

Introduction
Rationale
As presenter, you have a message to communicate to a specific audience, who would like to learn something new. This message can be, for example: an argument; a report on recent research; an overview of a topic/theory; an exploration of a question; an update of a work in progress (e.g. a research project); a description of an entity or proposition with evaluation. As your message is your starting point, write it down using no more than 1–3 phrases or sentences.
Stages
There are three stages involved in giving a presentation: • the planning stage • delivery, including any question phase • post-delivery Presentations benefit from advanced planning. Start planning well in advance of the delivery date, using a file to regularly add to and refine your material.

The planning stage
Audience Identify your audience. Profile them in terms of: • What they know • What you want them to know by the end of your presentation, i.e. how you plan to build on their knowledge • What they will be able to understand in the given time Most of all, audiences want to learn something *new*, presented in an interesting way, i.e. they want good content and delivery. When including information they already know, make sure you build on this by extending it. The new material may be new ideas, theories, proposals, or simply new connections between existing knowledge items.
Material Decide what you are going to say and plan an appropriate amount of material for the time available. Limit your content by assessing how relevant each piece of material is. Do not try and include too much in your presentation; presenters more frequently have too much to say rather than too little. Find ways of explaining and illustrating unknown or difficult concepts: definitions, explanations, visuals—plan the language and materials you will use. You know your presentation well, but your audience do not.
Story Visualize your presentation as a narrative or story. Like good stories, it has a beginning, middle, and end. At the beginning, aim to quickly get the audience's attention, perhaps by asking an interesting question. Make sure this is relevant and appropriate, and is delivered in a style you are comfortable with. Do not include anything that has no purpose, e.g. a warmer (i.e. activity aimed at 'warming' up the audience) for the sake of a warmer.
Title Develop a working title for your presentation; you can refine this later if necessary. From your title, develop a summary or abstract of what you intend to include and the purpose of the presentation. When you have worked on the material for the presentation itself, make sure that the material of the presentation matches the title and abstract. In other words, the title should be clear and representative of the content. If it contains something unusual, e.g. a metaphor, this should be appropriate and illuminating for the content
Research Carry out research around your topic using the resources available, e.g. university/school library, electronic resources, internet, local facilities and places, books from bookshops, media, people, etc.
Organization Organize your material. Discard any material that is not relevant, even if you have spent time finding and processing it (you may be able to use it somewhere else). Discuss your material with your tutor and other students, and people you know in your local context.

Visuals and media

Work out what visuals to use. Evaluate each visual in terms of how it can add to the communication of your message. If using PowerPoint, remember the 'golden rules': use large fonts; avoid colour clashes/light on dark; limit the number of words per slide; limit the use of animations and special effects; avoid CAPITAL LETTERS except where needed.

Incorporate other media where appropriate, e.g. hyperlinks to websites/audio/visual files. Work out what you will do if the links or connectivity fails.

Structure

Work out the structure of your presentation: like an essay or narrative, it should have a clear beginning, middle, and end. Your audience will hope for a clear beginning which sets out the aims and limits of the presentation; many audiences like to see the main areas to be covered in the presentation. Many presenters waste the first five minutes (e.g. by starting late, giving general background information which is not strictly necessary) before they make their first main point: find a way of making an important and interesting point in the first two minutes of the presentation.

Spread your main points throughout the body of your presentation; assuming your main points are all important, avoid making one main point in the first 20 minutes, and three more in the last ten minutes.

Provide appropriate navigation for your audience: ensure that your presentation is signposted so that the audience knows where you are going and how it all fits together.

Work out how to end your presentation. Perhaps throw out a provocative or stimulating question based on your material, or give an illustration to show how important your main points are in a particular application.

Recap and review

Find ways of recapping your main points, and reviewing material. Do this both before and in your conclusion. Your audience appreciate being reminded of what you consider to be your main points, so that they can take these away.

Variety

Build in some variety. This can include:

- variety of pace (speak at different speeds at different points in the presentation, pausing after main points for your audience to take in what you have just said)
- variety of input channels (such as oral/aural, visual, movement)
- variety of style (for example tell the audience something, then later ask them a question)
- visuals and other materials (e.g. audio) can also provide variety: make sure they are relevant.

Style

Develop a style which works for you; go with your strengths and avoid trying to do something you are uncomfortable with.

For your delivery, try different techniques such as reading from slides, printouts of the PowerPoint slides with annotations, cue cards, or other notes such as on-screen notes. Some presenters can speak entirely from memory, but this can be hard to achieve.

Language

The meaning in your presentation is conveyed through language. You can use a mixture of relatively informal language (e.g. 'Now I'd like to look at ...') and more academic language (e.g. 'This leads to an analysis of the major causes of ...'). Avoid speaking in very long sentences, as your audience will forget how these started. Define any technical terms and concepts which may be unfamiliar to your audience: plan in advance exactly how to do this, e.g. through citations, explanations.

Body language is also important. If possible, get yourself videoed and analyze how you stand, speak, and move.

Rehearsing

Rehearse your presentation. Do this either alone, perhaps using a mirror, or ask friend(s)/other student(s) to help you. Ask for their feedback. Focus on timing. Do not over-rehearse as a sense of spontaneity is important during your presentation.

Assessment

If your presentation forms part of an assessment, focus on the areas on which you are being assessed, e.g. content, structure and organization, language, effectiveness of delivery, use of visuals, use of academic sources, and dealing with audience questions.

Delivery

Checking

Check the equipment in the room, including your presentation notes, PowerPoint slides, hyperlinks, internet connections, projector, sound systems, slide changer, pointer. Ask for help where necessary in how to use it.

Beginning

When starting the presentation itself, introduce yourself briefly. You can add brief biodata on a slide if necessary giving your name and affiliation (e.g. the university you belong to); audience members may appreciate your contact details (e.g. email, Twitter username). Presenters are typically judged on the first few minutes of their performance, so a clear beginning is important.

Timing

Timing is vital, and poor timing can spoil a presentation, e.g. by only delivering half your material and missing out some key points. Use a clock or timer to check your timing. You can follow timings on your notes to see if you are running on time or too fast/slow. If you are going too slowly, work out what you can cut out to save time. Do not run over the allotted time. This is important as it can take both the audience's time and that of subsequent presenters.

Speaking

Aim to speak reasonably slowly, allowing pauses between points so that your audience can follow your points and arguments.

Make eye contact with the audience members, looking in different parts of the room. Do not look out of the window, at furniture, or at the projection screen.

Visuals
Allow time for your audience to read your visuals, then either put a blank screen, or the next point as appropriate.
Have a back-up plan in case the equipment does not work.

Post-delivery
Etiquette
Familiarize yourself with the etiquette around questions following presentations. After your presentation is finished, you lose a certain amount of control: you can plan what you say before deliver and while you are giving the presentation the accepted etiquette is that your audience listen. However, afterwards, during the question stage, things become a little more unpredictable. If you feel comfortable in your knowledge of your topic, you should be confident in dealing with the question stage.
Questions
Repeat clearly any questions from the audience to show that you understand and to make sure everyone at the back can hear the question. Aim for clear and brief answers, referring back to your presentation if possible. If you are unable to answer a question you can admit this; find strategies to deal with a range of question types. You can say you will get back to people later via email.
Learning
Whether or not your presentation forms part of an assessment, it is also a learning process. Make some time as soon as possible afterwards to consider what you can learn from it: • Were your aims achieved (i.e. did the audience understand your main points)? • Which parts went well? • What did not go according to plan? • What do your peers in the audience say about it? • What can you improve next time? Write down answers to these questions in order to maximize your chances of remembering. Think of each presentation as a part of a developmental process and you will keep on improving.

Table 9.6   Giving a presentation

This table offers a framework for teaching and learning presentations in an EAP context. The next stage to consider is the assessment of the presentation.

Evaluating and assessing presentations

Students need to know how they will be assessed on their presentations. The most transparent way of doing this is to develop an assessment criteria document. This gives the criteria on which students are assessed and the weighting for each set of criteria. The value of such a document is that students can understand what they have to do, and their teachers can be clear on the basis of assessment. Table 9.7 presents the main areas in which students can be assessed in presentations, together with some of the related specific criteria.

Assessment area	Criteria
Delivery	Awareness of audience; timing; pace; pronunciation; fluency; body language; clarity; variety
Content	Appropriacy of content to aims; clear argument or exposition of content; balance of content within the presentation; appropriate analysis, exemplification, and evaluation of the material; interest of content for the audience
Organization	Clarity of organization; structure of the presentation; signposting for the audience
Language	Range, sophistication, and accuracy of language (grammar, vocabulary, style)
Academic conventions	Appropriate and accurate references to source material
Materials	Visuals (e.g. PowerPoint slides); handouts; any other, e.g. use of audio, websites, or realia
Questions	Dealing with audience questions following the presentation

Table 9.7   An assessment criteria framework for presentations

The weighting for each of these assessment areas and criteria can be determined locally depending on factors such as the stage and aims of the EAP programme. For example, language may make up a significant proportion of the available marks at lower levels.

Each area and criteria also needs to be related to a marking system. This can be based around percentages or other numerical categories (for example marks out of five or ten), letter grades (A, B, C, etc.), descriptive bands (for example: excellent, very good, good, satisfactory, poor), or another system.

Evaluating a presentation during its development

One technique for evaluating a presentation is to closely analyze a section of the presentation, particularly the opening section. This technique is well-suited to a presentation in development. A useful section length is about 20%, i.e. a two-minute section in a ten-minute presentation, or a five-minute section in a 20–30 minute presentation. As in other contexts, for example an article, book, or TV programme, a participant typically evaluates the interest and usefulness of these quite quickly, in the first few minutes of listening or reading. With presentations, the person evaluating should note down all the main points made by the presenter(s) in the first 20% section.

A 'main point' may be defined in different ways depending on the genre and context. With presentations, a main point could be a piece of information relating to the topic of the presentation, or the presenter's evaluation of a concept. As the audience in a presentation legitimately expects to learn something new and potentially be able to apply it to their own situation, a 'main point' could be taken to mean something that is new to them.

In evaluating a presentation, the audience, or selected members of the audience, note down main points in the section in focus (for example the first three minutes of the presentation). The next stage is a feedback stage in which the participants can first compare their notes on the main points, and then discuss whether the points noted are sufficient, and made sufficiently clearly, for this section of the presentation.

This '20% analysis' can be extremely useful in determining the effectiveness of a presentation. If, as is surprisingly often the case, no useful main points are made in the first few minutes or so, then the presenter can return to their presentation plan and rework it accordingly.

Poster presentations

A variation on the presentation is the poster presentation. Poster presentations are becoming increasingly popular at conferences and events at universities such as open days and theme-based departmental occasions. The posters need to be free-standing, i.e. they should be comprehensible as complete texts in their own right (unlike the visual dimension to an oral presentation, which in isolation may offer very limited content). Characteristically there are timetabled slots when the presenter(s), i.e. the person or people who produced the poster, are available to briefly present the main points on the poster and answer audience questions. Thus there is a potentially high degree of interactivity, as audience members can ask for clarification or discussion about points arising from the poster itself.

Other speaking contexts

This chapter has focused mainly on the two widely-used speaking events of seminars and presentations. As given in Table 9.1 there are other opportunities for students to speak, including tutorials, interaction with other students (for example in group projects), and meetings with tutors and supervisors.

Interacting with students and others/informal speaking contexts

There can be many opportunities for less formal speaking. These can include group projects, and social interactions like negotiating and planning an event or informally discussing coursework. Those EAP teachers who have a background in general English language teaching should be well-placed to facilitate these. They can develop tasks and activities which are both useful and fun. Techniques could include role-plays, simulations, information gap activities, scenarios, and mazes. The language can cover functional language such as suggesting and disagreeing, much of which can also be used in more formal speaking settings.

One-to-one interactions: tutorials, office hours, and meetings

In the more formal interactions with academic staff, in many contexts students need to adopt an initiating approach. EAP teachers can encourage students by responding positively to any ideas and initiatives, and in the developmental stages of their education, ask students to prepare questions to ask. This kind of preparation should be habit-forming, so that students can then naturally ask questions without being prompted.

The focus of office hours and meetings with supervisors is mainly the academic work in progress (though it can also cover more personal and administrative aspects). To develop in this area, students need to engage quite deeply with their discipline and the subject areas they are studying. The EAP teacher can build tasks related to the possible stages in a student–supervisor meeting such as those given in Table 9.8.

Stage	Focus, aim, and activity
Welcoming and introducing	Supervisor and student exchange greetings and set out the aims of the meeting.
Briefing	The student updates the supervisor on progress made since the last meeting.
Critiquing	The supervisor responds to the briefing by asking clarification questions and critical questions based on the material.
Exploration and analysis	The student offers a more detailed investigation of the material they have been working on. This may involve working with a framework to analyze and evaluate the material.
Setting targets and conclusion	The student proposes work to be done for the following meeting, and the supervisor and student agree on this.

Table 9.8   Stages in a student–supervisor meeting

These stages can form a workable framework for developing materials in this speaking area. As with other formal speaking events such as speaking in seminars, there is a strong emphasis on reading and preparation.

Conclusion

This chapter has analyzed the major areas of student speaking in an academic context: seminars/discussions, and presentations. These analyses illustrate the roles of the academic speaker as reporter and persuader. In preparation for a seminar, for example, students are expected to report on what they have read, researched, and considered whilst in preparing for a presentation, they need to provide evidence of wider reading around the topic. In both these contexts, students need to be able to put forward their views and develop a stance in a persuasive way and—as with other academic practices—these processes involve critical thinking. To help their students progress, EAP teachers need both to incorporate speaking throughout the curriculum and also to encourage students to maximize their participation in the more informal speaking opportunities which are widespread in the wider academic context. It is through such participation and engagement across the whole spectrum of academic activity that students will develop as confident and effective speakers.

Further reading

BALEAP. 2013. *BALEAP Can Do Framework for EAP syllabus design and assessment. BALEAP.* Available at: <www.baleap.org.uk>

Guse, J. 2011. *Communicative Activities for EAP.* Cambridge: Cambridge University Press.

Reinhart, S. M. 2002. *Giving Academic Presentations.* Ann Arbor: University of Michigan Press.

10 MATERIALS

EAP materials as objective-driven tasks leading to independence

EAP materials are distinct from more general English language teaching materials in that they aim to meet the clearly defined needs of students planning to study in English. Whilst a general ELT coursebook might present a lesson based around talking about the weather, there would be little point to this in an EAP context: it would take valuable lesson time away from more pressing needs. A defining characteristic of effective EAP materials is that they are informed by the identifiable needs of students studying in English and their learning objectives. There are also other typical characteristics of EAP materials, notably the use of authentic texts, and their task-based nature. Further characteristics arise as a result of choices by the materials writer. These choices are discussed in this chapter, and include the extent to which skills such as reading and writing are treated separately, or integrated. Ultimately, EAP students need be able to work independently of a language teacher; once they are studying in the disciplines they may no longer have access to EAP teachers.

Many EAP teachers want or need to write materials for the students in their specific context. There can be compelling reasons to do so, relating to their students' needs and the availability and appropriateness of published materials. Of themselves, EAP materials are not so much 'good' or 'bad' as appropriate or inappropriate for the needs of a particular group of students. Establishing the needs of a group of students will greatly inform the choice of materials, through the selection of published materials and the writing of new materials.

This chapter considers the role of needs analysis in EAP, and the formulation of the curriculum, syllabus, and schemes of work. A central section of the chapter brings together the influences on EAP presented in Chapter 1 and the issues in EAP discussed in Chapter 2, together with a set of practical approaches for EAP teachers to relate to their local context. In this way EAP can become a personalized theory-informed practice, and EAP materials can be seen as objective-driven tasks leading to student independence. The chapter also discusses the nature of authenticity and the roles of published materials.

A needs-driven approach to writing EAP materials

Like other types of ESP, EAP is widely accepted to be a highly needs driven branch of English language teaching (for example Strevens 1988, in Flowerdew and Peacock 2001: 13). Arguably, all ELT is driven by needs to some extent, although these needs can be based on future assumptions (such as the likelihood of having to use English for work later in life) rather than immediately identifiable needs (such as the need to be able to begin an academic programme of study in English in three months' time). If a context is not needs driven, this simply suggests that the students do not (yet) know why they are studying English, and they are likely to be younger. The process of identifying students' needs is not necessarily a straightforward one: it can be extremely comprehensive, resource intensive, and time-consuming; alternatively if done more superficially it can be quite quick and manageable.

Parameters informing a needs analysis

Any needs analysis should take account of the EAP teaching context, particularly with reference to its parameters, which include the following:

- length: time available for the whole EAP programme(s)

- timings: time available for EAP classes on a daily and weekly basis

- resources: rooms, equipment, technology, facilities, access to services including libraries

- staff: profile including experience of the EAP teaching staff who will deliver the programme

- management: institutional management of EAP programmes within the teaching unit (for example language centre, language school)

- wider institutional support: how the EAP provision is positioned in the university, if relevant, and how it is supported, including its funding. EAP provision may be funded directly and self-supporting through the fees charged for programmes, or block-funded through a system such as 'top-slicing' an amount of money per year from a university budget.

These parameters demonstrate the importance of undertaking a needs analysis which takes into account the target situation.

A needs analysis cycle

Figure 10.1 illustrates a comprehensive approach to needs analysis, including the follow-on stages of skills and language analysis and materials writing.

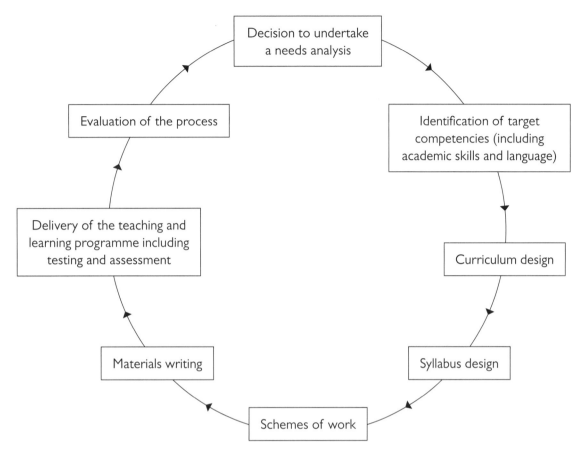

Figure 10.1   The process of writing EAP materials: a needs analysis cycle

The cycle in Figure 10.1 represents a comprehensive needs analysis, which starts with the data-gathering stage of identifying students' needs. This can be done by EAP teachers, and/or management and administrative staff, using a variety of instruments.

Instruments and informants in needs analysis

In order to carry out a needs analysis, a number of instruments are available as choices. Instruments refer to the methods of gathering information relevant to the target situation. For example, it may be possible when planning an EAP programme for the EAP teacher to access the department(s) in which their students plan to study. The EAP teacher can then ask and discuss specific questions with some of the academic staff who teach on the programme, and use a questionnaire to establish the views of staff and students. This EAP teacher is using interviews and questionnaires as needs analysis instruments, and subject staff and students as their informants, i.e. the people who yield the information. Table 10.1 shows the main instruments available (first column), with further detail on possible informants and processes (second column).

Instruments	Informants and processes
Interviews Discussions Focus groups	Setting up and conducting discussions/semi-structured interviews/focus groups with informants including any or all of the following: • students currently on the target academic programme(s), i.e. the course which the EAP cohort plan to follow (e.g. BSc in pharmacology) • academic staff including any clinical staff teaching on the programme • past students, i.e. those who have graduated from the programme • selected employers of students who graduate from the programme (e.g. pharmaceutical companies) • official bodies, such as government agencies, ministries, and regulatory bodies • sponsors (i.e. those who are paying for the student to study), including governments and parents
Questionnaires	Developing and carrying out questionnaires for use with the same informants as above
Observations	Setting up and observing students on the target programme in their learning settings such as lectures, seminars, lab work, field trips, tutorials, conferences, and social events
Researching publications	Sourcing, reading, and summarizing information relating to the programme, such as: • university prospectuses • websites and LMSs • items on the programme reading lists, including textbooks and articles
Researching student writing	Reading and analyzing selected written texts by students on the target programme, e.g. essays, reports
Researching assessments	Analyzing assessments, including any oral examinations and coursework, which are used as assessments on the target programme; also any tests and examinations that the EAP students need to pass before gaining admission to the programme

Table 10.1   Instruments, informants, and processes in needs analysis

The information in Table 10.1 illustrates the potentially broad scope and large scale of a comprehensive needs analysis in EAP. A team of people are needed to set up and carry out such research, and they need to build up good connections and networks with the various agents and informants involved. Processing and disseminating the information collected can take a considerable amount of time and resources. In short, such a comprehensive needs analysis can be very time-consuming, expensive, and difficult to achieve.

In terms of global EAP practice, such comprehensive needs analyses are carried out relatively rarely; in other words a majority of EAP programmes are planned and delivered on the basis that the students are studying or planning to study through the medium of English, together with varying amounts of supporting evidence from any of the sources and methods in Table 10.1. In practice, EAP teachers and management tend to build up their own profile of their students' needs over a period of time and with reference to the available resources and people. From a research perspective, this evidence is essentially anecdotal rather than principled and rigorous. The likely gaps in this knowledge may be filled with assumptions and guesswork, plus any further investigations based on existing contacts.

Current students

Perhaps the most important group of informants is missing from Table 10.1: the EAP students. For any programme to work, the needs and wants of the current students must also be considered: unlike students in the disciplines they may not know exactly what they need, but the EAP course is for them. Their needs and wants may include any of the following:

- any examinations (for example IELTS, PTE, TOEFL) with target scores to gain entry into the disciplines
- expectations of the EAP programme, including expected teaching styles, learning materials, and assessments
- specific skills and language they need or want to learn.

The students may be profiled using information such as the following:

- age, gender, languages (first and other)
- current level of English
- educational background and qualifications
- experience, including professional, academic, and personal
- learning styles, for example visual, preference for being directed, autonomous
- any other relevant information.

Due to their powerful washback effects, the students' examination targets can frequently be the main driver of the EAP programme at the expense of covering a broader range of academic skills. EAP teachers may be in a position to influence the EAP programme, and introduce a broader range of tasks than those covered in the entry examination. They can be supported in this endeavour by inviting past students and other informants to talk to the current EAP group. Many current EAP students will listen positively to a message from a past student, such as: 'Even though it wasn't covered in my IELTS exam, I really appreciated learning how to write a research essay on my EAP course, as on my course we have to write one every month and this is how we are assessed.'

Other methods for collecting needs analysis data

Jordan outlines a number of methods of collecting data for needs analysis. These include the following:

> advance documentation; language test (in home country and/or on entry); self-assessment; observation in class and monitoring; class progress test (and error analysis); surveys: profile (questionnaires); structured interview; learner diaries/journals; case study; end-of-course test; evaluation/feedback (questionnaires; discussion); follow-up investigations; and previous research

Jordan (1997: 30–39)

This range of methods appears so wide-ranging that the EAP teacher as needs analyst may feel overwhelmed (Jordan 1997: 38). Jordan also acknowledges that circumstances vary, and no single approach can work in all contexts (ibid.).

Current and target situations

The next stage in the needs analysis process is to compare the current students' profile with the profile in their target situation. Put simply, this means identifying what they know now, and what they need to know. This implies a gap to filled, or metaphorically a bridge to be crossed or built. This gap has led to the notion of a 'deficit': the perception that current students are deficient in certain language and skills. This notion of 'deficit' is raised in Chapter 2 in the context of student knowledge.

Issues and implications in needs analysis

There are various issues and implications in a needs-driven approach to EAP materials writing. Although it can be extremely useful and enlightening, problems can result. Table 10.2 illustrates some of these issues arising from a reliance on needs analysis to inform EAP curriculum design and materials writing.

Issues	Explanation and implications
Practicalities	Conducting a needs analysis is potentially very time-consuming and expensive, and requires considerable expertise. As a result, in many contexts it is not feasible.
Multidisciplinarity and interdisciplinarity	Due to the emerging trend of interdisciplinary study and modular degree programmes, many students are taking courses in different disciplines, e.g. business and law; also, liberal arts degrees (common in the USA, and beginning to emerge in the UK) are interdisciplinary. In such programmes, the student has to synthesize the knowledge and thought from the different disciplines they have chosen. A concurrent and related trend is multidisciplinarity, i.e. degree programmes which draw on teaching from different disciplines, e.g. a biosciences-based programme which incorporates teaching and research from other sciences (e.g. physics, chemistry), mathematics, engineering, and computing. In multidisciplinary degrees, academic staff from several disciplines contribute their expertise to the particular programme. By implication, these students' needs cannot be so narrowly defined compared with a single discipline such as law.
Predictions and expectations	While some students know exactly what and where they want to study, and stick to their plans, many others are either unsure, or change their plans due to their developing knowledge, preferences, and market realities. Therefore, their current EAP programme needs to accommodate different options.
Developments in the disciplines	In an age of rapid change, disciplines and specific programmes are liable to change from one year to the next, in terms of types of assignment, assessments, and teaching methods. For example, there may be a shift away from live lectures to recorded lectures, which require different listening skills. This means that the results of a needs analysis this year may not be **valid** next year.

Professional needs	Even if their discipline needs are known and identifiable, students' future professional needs cannot be accurately predicted.
	Many professions have multiple routes to entry, e.g. to practise law in some countries professional qualifications are needed but not necessarily a degree in law, so, for example, a student of history may become a lawyer.
	Also, within professions different responsibilities may arise, such as human resource management, which might not be considered central to that profession.
	To some extent, EAP teaching needs to consider the future professional needs of students, but realistically can only do this through focusing on generic or widely useful skills such as professional communication skills.

Table 10.2   Issues and implications in needs analysis

These implications demonstrate some of the challenges involved in carrying out a successful needs analysis. The purpose of a needs analysis is to inform the learning curriculum, which leads in turn to the development of the syllabus and schemes of work.

Curriculum, syllabus, and schemes of work

The three terms of curriculum, syllabus, and schemes of work reflect the increasing level of detail in the work to be covered:

- Curriculum: states the overall aims of the programme; the main content; the forms of assessment

- Syllabus: states the order in which the content is to be covered; both curriculum and syllabus can state the methodological approaches to be followed

- Schemes of work: describe the realization of the syllabus in detail including the learning outcomes for each item of the syllabus, suggested materials and ways of teaching the items, specific dates and times, balance of time, resources, and assessments

In practice, the terms 'curriculum' and 'syllabus' are sometimes used interchangeably. The most practical documents for EAP teachers are the schemes of work, as these specify the level of detail required to deliver, i.e. teach, the curriculum.

A syllabus can be organized in a number of ways. Traditionally, many English language syllabuses have been structurally driven, i.e. organized by grammar item. Alternatives to grammar include the other language systems of vocabulary and phonology. In the 1970s functional/notional approaches were fashionable (see Wilkins 1976 and Munby 1978). Examples of functions and notions include asking for directions and explaining where something is located. Other approaches of that time include situational (where the syllabus is built round situations such as 'at the bank'), topic based, and thematic. A variation on the functional approach is the rhetorical functions approach outlined in Chapters 1 and 7. Following these complex descriptions and models for syllabus design, coursebooks were developed which aimed to accommodate multiple syllabus strands, for example the *Cambridge English Course* (Swan and Walter 1984), which explicitly integrated lexical, structural, phonological, thematic, functional, notional, situation, and skills strands within its communicative syllabus (Swan and Walter 1984: *vii*). More recently, published coursebooks generally have opted for a more straightforward approach, favouring a limited number of strands such as skills, grammar, and vocabulary.

Preferred organizing principles for an EAP syllabus include any or all of the following:

- skills

- genres

- tasks

- language, including grammar, vocabulary, and phonology

- discourse

- essential elements, such as cause and effect, problem and solution.

Several of these can co-exist in a syllabus or programme, but it is unrealistic for the programme to be led by all of them at once. For example, in a genre-based approach a series of appropriate texts can be selected, and tasks developed; language will form an integral part of this but is more likely to emerge from the texts than form the criteria for text selection. In other words, language does not have to be the main syllabus driver in EAP courses.

Schemes of work are typically developed within the EAP team, including programme directors and some or all of the EAP teachers. The schemes of work are normally presented in a clear format which states the aims, items to be covered (e.g. skills, language, essential elements), weekly development, materials, resources available, and assessments.

Approaches in EAP programmes and materials

As well as the results of any needs analysis, the course development and materials writing processes are also informed by the EAP practitioner's theoretical approach to learning and teaching. This section explores several key areas which inform the approach to curriculum and syllabus design. These are presented as distinctions or polarities, in order to set the parameters in which local EAP course directors and teachers can position their teaching programme.

Situating materials in theory and practice

In order to write materials, the EAP practitioner needs some understanding of the major influences in the field, which are introduced and discussed in Chapter 1, together with the issues of 'general–specific' and 'global–local' discussed in Chapter 2. In addition, there are a number of further considerations in approaching course design, such as the extent to which the programme is driven by a particular English language examination. These approaches are presented in this section, and then considered alongside the influences and issues of Chapters 1 and 2 within a new framework for the EAP materials writer. The approaches are based on those given in a presentation for the British Council entitled *Putting EAP into practice* (de Chazal, 2012b). As with any learning materials, EAP materials are bound to be situated, in practical and theoretical terms, in relation to a number of concepts.

Exam-focused versus independent

The primary goal of EAP programmes is to enable students to function effectively in their chosen field(s) of study which are taught and learned in English. However, this is typically conditional on achieving a particular score on an English test. Since success in this test is one of the student's aims, the EAP programme should recognize this and incorporate test preparation into the curriculum. This leads to a question of balance: how far the EAP programme should be geared towards the test versus focusing on what lies beyond the test, i.e. the needs of English-medium study in the disciplines, and a possible consideration of future professional needs such as professional writing needs.

An EAP programme that makes no concessions to any English language test may be described as 'independent' in that it exists independently of any test, but it cannot be considered complete if students on it are not prepared for such an important test as university entry. The opposite polarity is a programme which only serves a particular test to the point of excluding any skill, language or academic practice which is not tested. A good example of such a practice is citation and referencing: the international English language tests (discussed in Chapter 11) do not assess this, whereas an institution's pre-sessional exit test may do so.

A challenge for EAP programme directors is to ensure standardization and fairness across a large programme such as a pre-sessional. If some teaching staff veer too far in one direction (towards too much exam preparation at the expense of other academic work, or the reverse), this can lead to problems including negative student feedback and poor results.

In short, the balance of exam focus and independence needs to be discussed and codified in the EAP curriculum. This process of discussion and negotiation of content applies to all the distinctions in this section.

Discrete versus integrated

The discrete/integrated tension refers to the extent to which the four skills (reading, writing, listening, and speaking), language, and critical thinking are integrated in the EAP curriculum. In a programme which is highly discrete, separate classes can cover areas such as writing, reading, grammar, vocabulary, speaking, critical thinking, and study skills (e.g. using a dictionary). An extremely integrated approach would see every class labelled 'integrated' on the timetable. One problem with the latter approach is ensuring balance and standardization: at a late stage in the course it may be noticed that in one or two classes there has been insufficient coverage of, for instance, listening.

In an integrated model, a clear main learning outcome can be specified. This is likely to be based around one skill, such as writing, and involve other skills, language, and critical thinking. For example, writing an introduction (where the main skill and learning outcome is writing) can involve the following cycle:

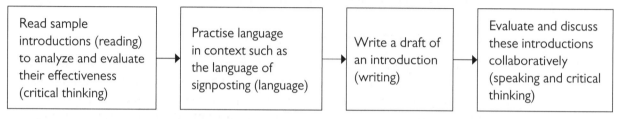

Figure 10.2   Writing an introduction

An integrated model is advocated by Bruce in which he states that 'any learning focus on language used in academic contexts should examine linguistic elements as they are integrated within texts and their discoursal settings' (Bruce 2011: 83). Alexander et al. broadly concur, stating that 'some key abilities are best developed as integral features of tasks and texts throughout the course rather than as separate lessons' (Alexander et al. 2008: 87).

Directed versus autonomous

The ultimate aim of EAP is develop a student's independence to the extent that they can study independently of an EAP teacher. There are different possible approaches to achieving this. Again, there is a question of balance: how far should the students' learning be directed and prescribed, and at what stage in the programme? An obvious answer is to gradually decrease such directedness, and increase tasks which require an element of independent learning. A key notion in this process is the sense of responsibility: if students can gain an early sense of responsibility, then this should facilitate and accelerate the process towards greater autonomy.

Tasks in the earlier stages of such development need to include sufficient staging, scaffolding, and support. This means the integration of carefully planned, sequenced tasks which ideally present one new thing at a time in a step-by-step approach. Support can take the form of such aids and resources as sample texts for students to analyze, targeted feedback, and glossaries to help with authentic reading texts.

Finally, this distinction can inform the amount of class time in the EAP programme. Some EAP programmes can be very intensive, with 20 or more hours of taught class time. This may be appropriate at earlier stages and lower levels, but at higher levels the heavy classroom load may leave the student with limited time and motivation left for their own language and academic development and research, especially reading and writing.

Corpus-driven versus emergent

This distinction refers to the materials themselves: are they based on or informed by a corpus, or does the vocabulary and grammar emerge through the texts?

Some published materials state that they are based on language informed by corpus analysis. Such analysis may involve vocabulary or grammar. An example of a vocabulary resource informed by corpus research is Coxhead's *Academic Word List* (2000). Other corpora are developed by publishers and used in certain materials they publish. One feature of language items derived from corpora is that they are decontextualized: the user does not see the word in its wider textual context. This decontextualization is not an issue for UK-published learner's dictionaries, which are corpus-based, but may be problematic if used in skills books.

An alternative to a corpus-driven approach is an emergent approach, in which language is brought out in the texts chosen for study: first the texts, then the language. A drawback with this approach is that certain language items may 'slip through the net' and not feature in a course as they are absent from the texts covered. However, if students are taught how to approach and process texts in general (as opposed to a sequence of individual texts), they can be equipped to deal with new language as it arises in their future studies.

Functional versus analytical

One view of ESP and EAP teaching is that students need to use texts for a particular purpose and do not need to analyze the texts. For instance, students may need to evaluate the ideas in a text; a functional approach would get straight to the point and not look at wider textual features such as where and how the ideas are presented and what language is used to express them. This approach is particularly widespread in ESP contexts such as business English.

In an analytical approach, student analysis of texts and discourse is seen as a necessary aim. Indeed, such an aim is stated in the BALEAP Competency Framework (2008: 5), and supported by writers such as Alexander et al. (2008: 30ff) and Bruce (2011: 83ff).

It is important to note that while some EAP teachers may be applied linguists through their qualifications and training, it is not the role of EAP to turn students into applied linguists. In other words, discourse analysis should not go too far and should be purpose driven. A simple question to ask is, 'How does this student analysis of the text contribute to their own work?'

Synthetic versus analytic

This distinction is related to the previous one. The notions of synthetic and analytic were proposed by Wilkins (1976). Essentially, in a synthetic syllabus discrete language items are isolated and presented in a sequenced way, for example the present tense, the past tense, the present perfect. This approach is termed 'synthetic' because the students have to synthesize the information, i.e. assemble all the parts into a meaningful whole.

In an analytic approach, language emerges (on a 'need-to-know' basis), and the syllabus can be organized in different ways, such as by essential element, general function/notion, or skill. The role of the students in an analytic approach is to analyze the language as it is used in the texts they work with.

These two approaches are echoed in the corpus-driven/emergent distinctions discussed above. The more intuitive terms 'bottom-up' and 'top-down' are essentially synonymous with the terms synthetic and analytic respectively in this learning context. Bruce sums up Wilkins' conception of a synthetic syllabus as having an 'atomistic nature and artificiality' (Bruce 2005: 241). Again this distinction needs to be discussed locally in order to determine an appropriate balance.

Influences, issues, and approaches

Table 10.3 draws together the influences presented in Chapter 1, the issues discussed in Chapter 2, plus the approaches outlined above. The first column presents a selection of questions based on these discussions for the materials writer to consider and address. One question is suggested for each influence; the discussion of these influences in Chapter 1 can yield further questions.

Influences	Sample questions for the EAP materials writer
English language teaching	What aspects of general ELT methodology can we use in our EAP context?
Register analysis	Which discrete grammatical and lexical items are appropriate to include in our syllabus?
Study skills	Which study skills should we prioritize, and to what extent can these be used to organize our syllabus?
Genre analysis	What genres will our students need to study, and which ones should we select and prioritize for study and transferrable analysis?
Systemic functional linguistics	How are our selected texts situated in the disciplines in socio-cultural terms, and to what extent should we highlight these ideologies in our materials?
American second language (L2) composition	Will our students expect and be satisfied with a pragmatic approach to become familiar with academic genres and practices, e.g. through text-analysis and reconstruction?
Critical EAP	To what extent is it appropriate and desirable to develop a critical awareness of students' wider context, e.g. by questioning values and assumptions in educational and professional settings?
Academic literacies	Should we enable and encourage our students to develop their academic identities through engagement and participation in their disciplines?
Writing in the disciplines	Should we carry out our teaching in collaboration with academic staff in the disciplines, or if possible entirely in the disciplines?

Issues	Sample questions for the EAP materials writer
General – specific	What generic (i.e. applicable and transferrable across disciplines) skills and language do students need to learn?
	Which genres (e.g. essays, reports) do students need to be able to produce, and in what context(s) (e.g. scientific report, law report)?
	What discipline-specific concepts and terms do students need to learn?
	What are the main commonalities in the student group (e.g. related disciplines, English exams to be taken)?
	What are the main differences in the student group (examples as above), and how far can these be accommodated?
	Can and should we teach our students in discipline-specific classes using discipline-specific (i.e. non-generic) materials?
Global – local	Is the EAP programme derived from and grounded in the local institutional context, i.e. highly focused on students' local needs?
	Does the EAP programme have a global orientation, e.g. through a focus on international journals?
	Which 'English' is used, e.g. the English of any or all the texts selected, or a specific variety of English, e.g. British, American, English as an International Language (EIL)?
	What balance should we aim to strike concerning local and global needs and expectations?

Approaches	Sample questions for the EAP materials writer
Exam-focused – independent	Which examinations do students have to take to gain entry into the disciplines?
	What are the expectations of students regarding the balance of time spent on exam preparation versus other academic work?
	What do students need to learn to become effective independent learners after the EAP programme?
	How far should the EAP materials be independent of any exam?
Discrete – integrated	Should the four skills be focused on separately, or should they be partly or wholly integrated?
	Should the language systems (grammar, vocabulary, phonology) be studied separately, or integrated?
	How far should language be integrated into skills work?
	Should critical thinking be integrated, or focused on separately?
	Should exam-focused work be covered separately, or integrated?
	Should skills (and language) be assessed discretely, or partly or wholly integrated?

Directed – autonomous	To what extent should students be directed in their study, i.e. through given materials and deadlines? How far, and at what stage in the programme, should independent study tasks be introduced? What is the target balance between core/prescribed materials and negotiated/individualized content?
Corpus-informed – emergent	Should the language and materials be informed by corpora, e.g. through systematic coverage of vocabulary lists? Should the language (vocabulary and grammar) emerge from the texts and tasks covered in the classroom?
Functional – analytical	Are the texts used for a particular academic purpose, e.g. for students to select and extract information to use in their writing (functional)? Are the texts used as models for student discourse analysis (analytical)?
Synthetic – analytic	Is the syllabus based on a bottom-up, cumulative, step-by-step approach, building on discrete language and skills development (synthetic)? Is the syllabus based on a top-down tasks and texts (analytic)?

Table 10.3   Influences, issues, and approaches: questions for the materials writer

The questions in Table 10.3 indicate the broad context of writing EAP materials in academic, linguistic, practical, and socio-political terms. Arguably it is not possible to produce materials in an EAP programme which are not explicitly or implicitly informed by the concerns raised in these questions. Thus in order to position their curriculum, the EAP materials writer in a particular context needs to develop an awareness, and formulate a stance, relating to these influences, issues, and approaches.

Teaching versus test-based materials

EAP materials should be balanced in terms of what they teach (and by implication what students are expected to learn), and how they test this. If there is an imbalance, learning is likely to be adversely affected. An excessive focus on test-based materials (for example test-based tasks like multiple choice, and exam practice using past papers) is likely to develop competence in the target test at the expense of other competences including wider language and skills development. Conversely, insufficient focus on testing risks leaving students underprepared for the exams they have to take. Testing and assessment also covers ongoing learning, so a balanced programme needs to include regular assessment of learning, for example using progress tests. Assessments are discussed further in Chapter 11.

A responsive approach

As an alternative to the traditional needs analysis approach, a more responsive approach to EAP programme design can be used in some contexts, particularly in-sessionals. This responsive approach recognizes that students will study, or are studying, in an English-medium academic context, but does not attempt to identify all the needs in advance. Rather, such an approach is to a significant extent student led, and is predicated on the responsibility of the individual student. Each student investigates their discipline, guided by their EAP teacher(s). Feak (2011) offers a rationale for this when she describes the Michigan academic writing model: EAP teachers are not disciplinary experts; students are the informants for working out what goes on in their discipline(s); and EAP teachers should not act as 'substitutes or surrogates for content advisors' (Feak 2011: 41). As discussed in Chapter 2, her approach 'may perhaps require us to relinquish the idea that we must know in advance what our students need, and that we need to have the disciplinary content expertise before we can offer courses that achieve the level of specificity that fills the gaps in students' understanding of academic discourse' (Feak 2011: 42–43).

Thus the responsibility is shared between the EAP teacher as facilitator and the student as investigator of their disciplinary practices. Both parties can embark on this process without detailed knowledge or preconceptions about what the student needs to do in the disciplines.

Writing materials

Writing high-quality EAP materials can be a time-consuming, challenging, but highly rewarding endeavour. A key feature of EAP materials is the use of authentic texts.

Authenticity

At its most familiar and fundamental, authenticity is concerned with using authentic source texts for teaching purposes. Authentic texts are not originally written for language teaching but for another purpose, and they have not been adapted: difficult language (vocabulary and grammar) has not been simplified; selected small parts of the text have not been cut out (although the text itself may well be an extract from a longer text); and the order of the text has not been changed.

Authenticity of context, task, and purpose

While the notion of authenticity might today be taken as the norm, this has not always been the case. Hutchinson and Waters (1987: 158–160) reported on the then controversial shift away from the use of composed texts, widely used in the 1960s and 1970s, towards the more widespread use of authentic texts in the 1980s. In defining 'authenticity' as 'taken from the target situation and, therefore, not originally constructed for language teaching purposes' (ibid.: 159), they identify a contradiction: authenticity resides in the text *within its intended context*. Authenticity, then, is not so much a characteristic of a discrete text which can be imported into the language classroom for its new audience of language learners; rather, it is a considerably broader phenomenon related to its intended context, audience, and purpose.

Fifteen years later Hyland picked up on purpose. In the context of teaching academic writing, he emphasized the importance of situating writing tasks 'in meaningful contexts with authentic purposes' (Hyland 2003: 27). By focusing on this authenticity of text, task, context, and purpose, the broader objective of enabling students to engage with their multiple challenges can be addressed.

Using authentic sources

Current thinking in EAP emphasizes the importance of authenticity. Alexander, Argent, and Spencer, for example, point out that the use of authentic materials is not only essential but 'intrinsically motivating for students' (Alexander, Argent and Spencer 2008: 20). Grellet's observation in 1981 that teachers 'should grade exercises rather than texts' (Grellet 1981: 8) has influenced materials writers in a wide range of ELT contexts since that date. Seminal research by Swales (Swales 1990; Swales and Feak 2004) maps out the rhetorical structure of academic texts such as research papers as scaffolds for students to produce their own work. Swales argues that texts as genres exist at the heart of communication among members and audiences within particular discourse communities (Swales 1990: 58). A major aim of students is to gradually acclimatize and integrate into the discourse community of their discipline. An added level of complexity is the (re-emergent) tendency towards interdisciplinarity, meaning that students may have to engage with two or more distinct target disciplines, for example business and law. These considerations imply that, somehow, appropriate and motivating texts need to be found and integrated into learning materials. For the EAP teacher, a challenge is to locate such texts for their classes which have varying degrees of discipline heterogeneity.

If there is a key to successfully using authentic sources with students, it lies in engagement. Students *and teachers* need to engage with the selected texts and tasks within a context that involves a degree of meaningful communication.

Engagement

In keeping with the needs-driven nature of EAP (for example Bruce 2011: 4–7), an authentic approach would lead to the selection of texts which students need to be able to read: those used in their disciplines. Clearly, while certain genres are more prevalent in particular disciplines, there is one genre which is near-universal in its reach: the textbook. Whether aimed at sixth-form (secondary school students aged 16–18), undergraduates, or postgraduates, textbooks offer scope for widespread use in EAP contexts. Undergraduate textbooks can work successfully at B2 level and above, and with appropriate support, at B1. International Baccalaureate (IB) textbooks are readily accessible at B1, while General Certificate of Secondary Education (GCSE) textbooks can be used at A2. Such genres can provide useful and motivating opportunities to develop carefully staged and scaffolded tasks to serve appropriate learning objectives.

Authenticity of task

An example of such a task sequence at B1 is for students to identify the topic, purpose, and main idea in an IB text extract, leading to a process of locating and noting down specific detail relating to the topic to use in a short written summary or spoken presentation; finally students can respond to the content of the text and relate aspects of it to their own knowledge and discipline. Eventually, through interaction with their EAP teachers as interested non-experts and their subject teachers as experts, students can synthesize knowledge and construct new meanings through written and spoken work.

Authenticity underpins this initial task sequence in that the text, context, audience, and purpose are reasonably well aligned: the IB textbook is written for students aged 16–18 who are studying a number of subjects (thereby addressing interdisciplinary needs) in order to develop both their knowledge and their language and skills. Knowledge development is the primary aim, but language is also relevant because IB students, regardless of their first language, are still learning technical language and generic language which is interdisciplinary (for example 'may result in', 'is concerned with').

In doing the tasks, students and teachers engage with the content through such activities as building on existing knowledge, critically evaluating the content and its presentation in the text, and reprocessing parts of the content for a new productive purpose. To extend the task sequence, and its authenticity, students can conduct guided searches for new texts to replicate the classroom tasks and reprocess the content for their audience, i.e. their peers and their teacher, in their own way. A high degree of authenticity might mean the selection of a published textbook by an individual student for their specific purpose, with the student also selecting the extracts to use, and why and how to use these extracts. This process encourages the student to navigate the resources available, such as a library, and the whole selected text by using the cover, contents, index, headings, fonts, graphics, and other features of an authentic text. A task sequence based on these features is presented in Chapter 6.

Authenticity of context

In this way, authenticity can relate not only to text, but to context, audience, task, and purpose. More broadly, authenticity is concerned with academic culture and can translate into authentic shared learning experiences. Starting with repeated practice in carefully scaffolded task sequences, students can go on to develop their language and become more familiar with their academic context and related cultures. By collaborating on tasks with other international students, they can gradually acclimatize with respect to their discipline, the wider institution, and the still wider global academic community. The ultimate purpose, during and after their academic programme, is the development of their own independence: gaining independence of their teacher, class time, and prescribed materials. Authentic texts, tasks, and contexts contribute to this development.

Authenticity and level

In its original context a text has both its own level (in terms of language and cognitive level) and the level of its intended audience. In the EAP classroom, an authentic text has no such level until it is used for a particular purpose. The notion of level is explored further in Chapter 6.

Using authentic texts in EAP materials

As noted in Chapter 3, texts are ubiquitous. In order to be incorporated into EAP materials, these texts need to be carefully selected and processed into effective learning materials. This processing typically involves constructing tasks around the texts, rather than adapting and rewriting the texts themselves. EAP materials should reflect academic contexts, where 'texts, skills, and tasks are naturally integrated, and we should aim for authenticity of all of these where possible' (de Chazal 2013a: 166).

Related issues around using texts are addressed later in this chapter, including task types, purpose and outcomes in tasks, finding sources, and involving students in materials selection.

Formulating learning objectives

EAP materials need to have clear learning objectives in order to be purposeful, as well as to be situated in the broader curriculum. Learning objectives refer to the explicit main outcome(s) of a given lesson or unit. These can be expressed as competencies in skills and/or language. They need to be focused rather than broad or vague. For example, 'read academic textbooks' may be an appropriate aim for an EAP curriculum, but the learning objectives for a lesson (whether one, two, or three hours) need to be more clearly defined, for example 'read an extract from a university textbook and identify the main points in the text to form the basis of a summary'. Writing a summary can then form the basis of a subsequent learning objective.

Efficiency is crucial. As outlined in Chapters 1 and 2, unlike some ELT programmes, the time available on EAP programmes tends to be limited rather than open-ended, which means that time needs to be carefully accounted for. By implication EAP programmes cannot focus on everything. Nor of course can one lesson focus on everything. If a text is used in class, the purpose for using it should be clear. Using the example learning objective above, the tasks leading towards this outcome should be clear and focused. It is perfectly possible to approach the text differently, and certainly more comprehensively. For instance, students could do any of the following: predict the content of the text; talk about the theme and how it fits in with the world; answer a battery of comprehension questions; work on the meanings of the unknown words in the text; manipulate vocabulary items to form different words in their family; analyze some of the grammatical features; do further related grammar exercises; react personally to the text; discuss the issues arising; write a critical response; and many other tasks. Any of these may be valid at some point, but to attempt too much in one class detracts from the main aim.

Formulating tasks

Learning objectives such as those discussed above need to be realized through a carefully staged sequence of tasks. This book refers to 'tasks' many times throughout the 12 chapters. In a brief survey of definitions of 'task', Willis and Willis (2007: 12) identify the core characteristics of a task in language teaching: a classroom activity with a focus on *meaning* and *outcome*. In short, a task should be driven by meaning and should be meaningful for the student, and lead to an outcome such as a product or resolution.

Tasks are needed in order to realize the learning objective, and they contribute to it in a cumulative way. In order to realize a given learning objective, several tasks may be needed. Each task constitutes a necessary stage in the realization of the whole learning objective, and each task is connected to the adjacent task.

Although very open tasks may work in some contexts, particularly with a very experienced teacher who can support the students' learning during the task, they run the risk of not achieving their aim. For example, suppose that the learning objective is for students to be able to write an introduction to an essay. This objective should be refined according to the syllabus, with further specification on how long the introduction should be, what it should contain, which essay question it should answer, and other points. A very open task might ask students to come up with what they know about introductions, then decide what to put in their introduction, and finally to write it. However, this may not be a particularly efficient way of learning and may demotivate some students. Students benefit from clear input and guidance. For this learning objective, such guidance may take the form of:

- suggested stages in introductions (for example background information, thesis statement) to identify which are seen as necessary

- an essay question with accompanying sample introductions for students to analyze their component parts (i.e. what stages they contain) and overall structure (i.e. macro to micro)

- clarification of key stages in introductions, such as the rationale for writing the essay—this can be done deductively through controlled input

- some language input which students can immediately use in their writing, for example signposting language

- a staged writing task, perhaps with parts of the introduction already given

- comparative and evaluative tasks using given criteria and based around sample introductions and students' own introductions.

These tasks should build on and extend students' previous/recent work on the EAP programme. Figure 10.3 gives a sample task sequence for the learning objective stated.

Learning objective:

For students to be able to read an extract from a university textbook and summarize the main points in the text

Sample task sequence:

Task 1: Gaining an overview of a textbook extract: students identify the topic of the text and the main perspectives covered in the text

Task 2: Identifying the main points in a text: using the first part of the text, students decide whether given items are main points or supporting points/examples; in the second part of the text students identify the main points in each paragraph

Task 3: Reading and evaluating a summary: students read a given summary based on the first part of the text, and evaluate it using given criteria/questions such as 'Does the summary include all the main points in the text?'

Task 4: Summarizing the main points using appropriate language: students reprocess the main points they identified from the second part of the text by combining them and expressing them more briefly using their own language

Task 5: Writing a complete summary: students incorporate the material from the summary given in Task 3 together with their reprocessed material in Task 4 to write a complete summary (including a reference to the source text, and the main points)

Task 6: Evaluating summaries: students evaluate their own summary using the criteria given in Task 3, then read and evaluate other students' summaries using the same criteria, offering critical feedback and suggestions for improvement (language and content).

Figure 10.3   Sample task sequence for a learning objective

This sample learning objective and task sequence can be situated in the broader curriculum in a number of ways. These are given in Table 10.4.

Aims and benefits of sample learning objective	Processes and tasks through which these aims are achieved
Supporting students	The use of a given summary as a sample Given evaluative criteria which students can use independently in other contexts
Introducing new skills and competences	Guided writing of a summary Utilizing and extending students' existing language and skills
Encouraging collaboration and critical thinking	Critical evaluation of the final communicative task through both their own and other students' summaries
Engaging with authentic texts and tasks	Repeated practice and extension
Integrating skills, language, and critical thinking	Working in an authentic academic context using an appropriate learning objective
Supporting subsequent learning objectives	Enabling students to do a specific skill, i.e. summarizing a text, which they will later use when incorporating source material in their own writing

Table 10.4   Situating learning objectives in the curriculum

The information in Table 10.4 underlines the importance of formulating learning objectives prior to writing materials.

Writing a summary

A traditional way of gauging the extent to which students understand a text is to ask them to do a series of comprehension questions based on the text. The comprehension questions generally cover both meaning and language. They can take quite a long time to write. Perhaps the most straightforward demonstration of understanding a text, however, is simply to ask students to write a very short summary of the text. This summary should be as short as possible: an introductory sentence which gives the reference to the original text and a brief overview of the topic, focus, and scope of the text; a second sentence summing up the main argument; and if necessary a final sentence adding something extra such as a major issue, question, evaluation, or implication that is contained in the source text. The students' summaries serve as products of the learning process which can be readily assessed to check the effectiveness of learning.

Task types

Task types (also known as exercise types or activity types) are the individual tasks which can combine into more elaborate cycles to realize learning objectives. Two familiar examples are gap-fill tasks (i.e. where students fill in the gaps in sentences or in a text using given items or items which they have to think of), and ranking tasks (i.e. where students put in order a set of given items using either given criteria or their own criteria). There are a great many different task types, and these can broadly be divided into two categories: test-based tasks, and developmental tasks (also known as learning-based, or open tasks).

Test-based task types

Examples of major task types associated with testing and assessment include:

- gap-fill tasks
- multiple-choice tasks
- matching tasks
- other, more productive, task types such as sentence completion.

These task types, together with many variations, are the staple of language tests as well as many classroom materials.

Developmental task types

There are many more 'open' or developmental task types. They can include any of the more test-oriented task types above when these are used in a more learning-centred and possibly communicative way. For example, students could decide which language item can complete a sentence or text (gap-fill) with respect to different meanings, for example shifts in authorial stance. Students can then compare and evaluate their selections, explaining why they chose them and how they affect meaning. Other task types such as ranking can be used in a similar way. A wide range of task types have been integrated into the practical language, critical thinking, and skills material throughout Chapters 4 to 9.

Many other types include more direct tasks, such as actually writing a whole text or a paragraph, rather than competing one by filling in gaps.

Challenges in writing materials

Although writing materials is a 'characteristic feature of ESP in practice' (Hutchinson and Waters, 1987: 106), there are many challenges in writing high-quality materials. Hutchinson and Waters point out that just because you can teach does not mean you can write your own materials, offering the analogy that actors mostly do not write their own plays (ibid.). In recognition of the challenges facing the materials writer, they go so far as to say that materials writing is best done only as a 'last resort' assuming other options are unavailable (Hutchinson and Waters 1987: 125).

The materials writer faces challenges arising from the stages presented in this chapter, namely assessing students' needs, formulating learning objectives, sourcing appropriate authentic texts, developing these texts and/or using them as a basis for fulfilling the learning objectives, and presenting the materials in a coherent and attractive way. As any teacher can recall from their experience in writing the materials and preparing for a formal observed lesson, to write good materials which can withstand critical analysis typically takes far longer than the length of time they take up in the classroom. By implication, to write the materials to cover a whole programme such as a pre-sessional course is a very major undertaking which may require a team of materials writers. Even then, regrettably, the resulting materials may not work as effectively as their designers and writers may have hoped. For these materials to work, they need to be:

- relevant, i.e. based on the academic needs of the intended students
- applicable, which means that the students can readily apply the skills and language in the materials to their own contexts
- defined, i.e. with clearly-defined learning outcomes
- comprehensible, both in terms of the level (language and cognitive) and content (texts, and tasks)
- clear, in terms of the specific aims of the material, i.e. the materials should make clear to students why they are doing these tasks and what they can learn from them
- interesting, for example through the selection of texts and tasks that are intrinsically interesting for these students; this reflects the interest in their chosen discipline that can be assumed
- varied, i.e. offering a variety of topics, genres, task types and activities
- motivating, through the materials' connection to the students' contexts and lives

- accurate, i.e. with correctly-referenced source texts, and accurate spelling, punctuation, and use of language throughout (this normally requires proofreading by the materials writer plus someone else)
- attractive, i.e. cleanly and clearly presented, incorporating any visuals where appropriate.

If these criteria are not well met, the resulting materials are likely to be unsuccessful in a number of important areas, leading to less effective learning.

As an alternative to writing materials, or as a supplementary resource, an increasingly wide range of published materials is available.

Using published materials

Published materials can be very useful either in a supplementary role or as the basis for the programme itself. The choice of published materials has increased enormously since the turn of the millennium, and the major ELT publishers offer a selection based around skills, language, and integrated skills from their UK, American, Canadian, and Australian catalogues, plus many other materials from a number of other countries.

Benefits of using published materials

There are a number of potential benefits in using published materials. Table 10.5 lists some of these.

Factor	Rationale
Appropriateness	Published materials can be selected from the comprehensive range to meet specific needs.
Practicality	The widespread availability of published materials means the materials for a new course can be provided at short notice.
Quality	Publishers invest in authors, market research, technologies (e.g. corpora), reader feedback, design, and production to ensure high-quality materials.
Features	Published materials can include features which can be challenging to produce locally, e.g. lessons built round authentic lectures and student presentations, and accompanying digital material.
Time	Writing materials is time-consuming, and requires expertise and resources; using published materials saves time.
Quality control	In large-scale teaching operations, i.e. when many EAP teachers are following a similar programme (such as a pre-sessional programme), the adoption of a coursebook can introduce a standard which the programme managers can monitor for quality control purposes.
Academic community	Users of the materials, both teachers and students, can develop as an academic community using the principles and discourse in the materials, as opposed to a more fragmentary approach in which different student and teacher groups are using different materials.

Table 10.5   Benefits of using published materials

Table 10.5 shows some of the benefits of using published materials. In selecting and using them, it is important first to evaluate their suitability for the purpose.

Evaluating EAP materials

EAP teachers and programme directors can evaluate both published and locally written materials before, during, and after use. Some of the needs analysis instruments in Table 10.1 can be used, including interviews, discussions, and questionnaires with users (students, teachers, course directors, subject teachers), together with an analysis of the materials themselves. While some aspects of the evaluation are objective, such as the number of pages and units of a particular book, many are subjective and therefore are likely to vary across different users. It is advisable to involve a larger rather than a restricted number of users in order to gain a balanced overall picture.

Table 10.6 presents a 10-point range of criteria to use in evaluating published materials. These can be added to and adapted for use in evaluating locally-written materials. The responses of different evaluators can be recorded in column 2.

Criteria/features	Responses
1 Title, author(s)	
2 Publisher, date, number of pages, price, position in series, other components, e.g. Teacher's Book, audio/visual material, digital content	
3 Stated level, target market, intended users	
4 Printing (one colour/full colour); images	
5 Content, approach and organization: e.g. number and length of units, language coverage, student/ teacher roles	
6 Features of the book, e.g. listening transcripts, learning objectives	
7 Relevance to needs	
8 Successful content/positive points	
9 Shortcomings/negative points	
10 Recommendations	

Table 10.6   Criteria for evaluating published EAP materials

There are a number of benefits of using a questionnaire-based approach for evaluating materials. One is that the evaluation can be conducted in a principled and rigorous way by a team of people who are all working from the same criteria. Another is that this adoption of a principled approach constitutes a record for wider and future reference: teachers and programme managers can subsequently consult such records when selecting materials. In this way an anecdotal, ephemeral process can be avoided.

Conclusion

This chapter has explored needs analysis in EAP as a starting-point to developing appropriate materials and informing the curriculum, syllabus, and schemes of work in a given teaching and learning context. The chapter has also considered the use of published materials, and looked at criteria for evaluating both in-house and published materials. These discussions have emphasized the nature and role of authenticity in EAP materials in both texts and tasks. In this chapter, EAP materials have been described as objective-driven tasks leading to independence: they need to be informed by principled learning objectives, the ultimate aim of which is the development of student independence. The central part of the chapter has aimed to rationalize, consolidate, and extend the principles and practices discussed in the preceding chapters of the book, in particular by bringing together key influences, issues, and approaches in EAP with accompanying questions for the materials writer. EAP teachers, in their role as materials writers, can draw on questions such as these to plan and position their curriculum and produce materials which cover skills, language, and critical thinking.

Further reading

Course design and materials development

Alexander, O. (ed.). 2007. *New Approaches to Materials Development for Language Learning: Proceedings of the 2005 joint BALEAP/SATEFL conference*. Bern: Peter Lang.

Basturkmen, H. 2010. *Developing courses in English for Specific Purposes*. Basingstoke: Palgrave Macmillan.

Tomlinson, B. (ed.). 2011. *Materials Development in Language Teaching 2e*. Cambridge: Cambridge University Press.

11 ASSESSMENT

Assessments as tools to determine academic progression

Following the exploration of EAP materials in Chapter 10, this chapter looks at EAP assessments. Assessments are taken to refer to any kinds of evaluation of students' level and performance, and range from ongoing evaluation of coursework and informal class observation to formal international tests such as IELTS. Assessment, then, is the term and concept which covers all types of test, coursework, continuous assessment, and other assessments such as observations. Essentially, assessments are tools for a particular purpose—either to collect information to provide feedback to students and inform future EAP teaching, or to determine whether students have reached an agreed level of proficiency to proceed to their next level. These two purposes are known respectively as **formative** and **summative**.

This chapter outlines the main types and purposes of assessments in EAP. A range of **low-stakes** assessments are outlined, such as observations and projects; these are considered to be low-stakes assessments because the student's progress into the disciplines is not jeopardized by a low score. The chapter goes on to focus in more detail on possibly the most predominant and **high-stakes** type: proficiency tests, i.e. those on which a student's progression depends. The chapter also explores issues in test construction and discusses the characteristics and roles of international academic tests.

Types and purposes of assessments

The terms 'assessment' and 'testing' are often spoken of as if the two activities are complementary, but tests and examinations are only one of several possible ways to evaluate a student's abilities which come under the heading of assessment. For both formative and summative purposes, assessments in the broadest sense are of major importance in academic contexts. From the student's perspective, assessments are encountered throughout their school and academic life. They regularly represent the interface, which students may see as barriers or gateways, to the next academic level. Assessments may be associated with emotions such as stress, fear, excitement, and a sense of achievement through success or disappointment through failure. Thus for the student, assessments represent stages on their academic journey to success.

From EAP teachers' perspective, their students typically start on a particular course of study with an academic record which may include reports, testimonials, certificates and transcripts of achievement, and qualifications. These may be meaningful or otherwise depending on how familiar EAP teachers are with their frames of reference and language. For example, a grade or percentage in itself is not meaningful without an understanding of its wider context: in some contexts a test score of '80%' represents an exceptionally high level of achievement, whereas in others it might be rather low. Likewise, despite the standardizing attempts of frameworks such as CEFR and organizations such as ALTE (Association of Language Testers in Europe), a judgement that a student has studied and succeeded at a particular level, for example 'intermediate', may not transfer clearly across contexts. Nevertheless, such academic records represent part or all of the resources and descriptive evidence for a student's level and abilities and institutions accept or reject students on the basis of this evidence.

Curriculum-based assessments on EAP programmes

After the arrival of their students, EAP teachers may be involved in a wide range of types of assessments, from informal classroom-based assessments to international proficiency tests. Table 11.1 presents the main types and purposes of assessments in EAP. These assessments are based on the curriculum used in the EAP programme, as opposed to being free-standing proficiency tests, which are discussed later.

The first five assessment types in the table tend to be more 'formal' and institutionally-based, while the last five are on-going through the programme and more likely to involve the EAP teacher more closely.

Depending on their purpose, these assessments may be formative and/or summative. For example, a teacher's report can be used formatively, by providing information and advice for the student to act on, as well as summatively, through its contribution to the wider suite of assessments. Teachers' reports may also be read by academic staff in the students' prospective department and admissions staff, in which case they may be used as evidence of the student's level of ability to start their academic programme.

These assessment types are based on the EAP curriculum for a specific programme. As an illustration, if one of the curriculum aims is for students to be able to write a research essay, then the placement test needs to include a writing component (although of course much simplified from the final target) so that students can be placed in the most appropriate class. Students' writing can only be determined through a writing task; a speaking task or grammar test, for example, will not yield information on their writing. The placement test result may show, for example, that the student's writing level is unexpectedly low, and much lower than their speaking and listening levels. Information on the student's writing is needed so that they can be placed in an appropriate class or programme.

Type of assessment	Purpose
Screening test (also known as an Admission test)	an initial test to determine whether a student's English level is high enough to start on the EAP programme. Those students whose English falls below the required level may be placed in a separate more general 'pre-EAP' programme
Placement test	to determine the student's level so that they can be placed in an appropriate class within the programme, or placed on another suitable programme
Diagnostic test	to identify what a student can and cannot do; also, as a check on the results of the placement test
Progress test	to check learning related to a limited period of study (e.g. a few weeks) within the programme
Achievement test	an end-of-programme test to assess how well students have learned, based on the whole syllabus for the programme of study
Coursework assessments	to contribute to the student's overall mark for the course of study, involving for example project work and independent study tasks
Assignment marks	similar to the coursework assessments, these provide an assessment of a student's performance on certain assignments or projects they have done as part of the EAP programme, and are normally based on assessment criteria
Teacher's report	to provide a detailed individual account of a student's profile for specified parties, e.g. the student and/or their sponsor; it can include aspects such as their progress, attitude to learning, participation, and achievement
In-class observation	to provide a snapshot of students' learning in an authentic classroom situation, doing specific communicative tasks which may be standardized across all classes in a cohort at the same time; the observation report is normally carried out by the class teacher and likely to be based on clear criteria which are understood by teachers and students
Class test/quiz	an informal in-class test to check recent learning relating to a few lessons or days of study

Table 11.1   Types and purposes of curriculum-based assessments in EAP

In practice, assumptions tend to be made; for instance a placement test need not involve a comprehensive sequence of tasks covering the finer points of citation and referencing, because students are unlikely to know much about this. Similarly, the other test types listed above need to be based on the curriculum. A progress test cannot measure a student's progress on what has been covered to date unless it includes that material only; if the test is based partly on material which the students have not covered, it is unfair and will not achieve its aims. The final achievement test, likewise, needs to closely reflect the material covered on the programme. Apart from achievement tests, the test types listed above are formative, which means they are intended primarily to inform (or form) subsequent teaching and learning through feedback to teachers and students.

Non-curriculum assessments

In addition, there is one major type of non-curriculum assessment: the **proficiency test**. A proficiency test is a tool to measure a student's competence in relation to certain specified criteria, and is independent of any curriculum or programme of study. This means that students can take this type of test after having studied on a wide range of programmes with different syllabuses and materials. In practice, the major proficiency tests such as IELTS have a wide range of published materials such as coursebooks and test practice books which are specifically aimed at students taking the test. It is important to note that the test (for example IELTS) is not based on these materials; rather, it is the other way round.

The three major providers of academic English tests in the international market are:

- IELTS (International English Language Testing Service), academic version
- PTE (Pearson Test of English), academic version
- TOEFL (Test of English as a Foreign Language).

These are widely accepted by academic institutions worldwide and are described and analyzed later in this chapter. The two highest level Cambridge English Examinations—Advanced (CAE) and Proficiency (CPE)—are also accepted by some institutions; however these Cambridge examinations are proficiency tests of general rather than academic English.

Achievement tests and proficiency tests are both summative: they are designed to assess, or sum up, how much students have learned, and this information, i.e. their test score, can then be used to determine whether the student is able to move on to the next stage of their academic career.

Using information from assessments

As well as evaluating the effectiveness of an individual student's learning, curriculum-based assessments serve to evaluate the broader effectiveness of the programme of study and teaching. In simple terms, the delivery of a curriculum can widely be seen as effective if a majority of the students achieve the expected level of progress. This progress can be most easily measured through appropriate assessments, such as achievement tests. At a more macro level, the assessment scores of a cohort of students can be analyzed to look for evidence of effective learning. Clearly a number of factors have to be taken into account in such a process, including the students' starting language level, the length of study, and their exit level. At a more micro level, assessment scores can be used to evaluate the learning of individual students and specific classes within the cohort, with the implication that, for example, in classes where students make less than expected progress, one explanatory factor may be the delivery of the curriculum, which largely concerns the teaching within those specific classes.

Assessments for gaining admission to a university

The university admission test can be either the EAP programme final coursework mark and/or achievement test, or an international English test. These proficiency tests are generally experienced to be the most 'high-stakes' test. There can be a great deal resting on the outcome: whether or not the student is able to proceed with their academic study; personal, family, and financial investment; and possible negative reaction and loss of face on failing to reach the target score. Students and other stakeholders are therefore likely to focus their main attention on achieving their target in their admission test, all of which impacts on EAP programmes.

Assessment strategies

A number of assessment strategies are available to the EAP teacher and institution, each of which has a different purpose. Figure 11.1 illustrates the major strategies based on the three divisions of coursework (i.e. ongoing classroom and related work based on the curriculum), testing, and the evidence of the student's prior study.

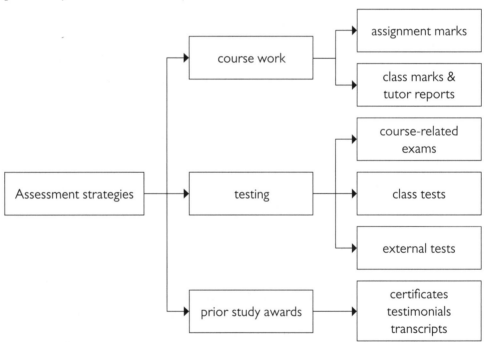

Figure 11.1   Assessment strategies

Devising and selecting assessment procedures: fitness for purpose

Chapter 10 shows that effective EAP programme design is traditionally based around the needs of the student and the study context. Similarly, assessment procedures need to be designed or selected with a clear understanding of need and purpose. The two main questions in EAP assessment are:

- What type of information is needed to build up the student's EAP profile?
- What type of decision will be based on the information obtained?

As we have seen, a key concept in terms of decision-making is that of high-stakes versus low-stakes assessments.

Example of low-stakes assessment: class placement

At the beginning of an EAP course it is necessary to decide how to allocate students to classes. As adjustments to class groupings can be made as the course progresses and as students settle in, this type of decision can be described as low stakes. For this reason, the need for accurate placement may take second place to other considerations, such as ensuring that students' first contact with the course and tutors is positive rather than stressful. The course director may wish to use a placement procedure—which also gives tutors the opportunity to answer participant questions, allay any initial concerns about the course and learn about the student's expectations, aspirations and motivation for enrolment—rather than a formal test or exam. In such cases, placement assessment might consist of information taken from informal interviews, a self-assessment questionnaire, and/ or prior study data.

Example of high-stakes assessment: admission to a degree course

Assessment of students at the end of an EAP programme is often linked to very high-stakes decisions. For example, the outcome may determine whether and what type of certificate of proficiency the student receives; this may in turn determine whether or not the student is allowed to progress onto their chosen academic programme of study such as a degree course. For such a purpose, a very robust form of assessment is required.

Assessment procedures may therefore include consideration of several sets of course assignment marks together with a final test or exam.

Issues in test construction

As suggested, tests form a major part of assessment. With the obvious exception of international English tests, all the types of tests discussed so far could in principle be developed in-house (i.e. within the EAP teaching institution) to meet the specific local needs and context. To do so, test writers need an understanding of the key issues in test construction and application, such as validity and reliability.

In the context of the purpose, effectiveness, and construction of tests, five pairs of characteristics can be identified in addition to the formative and summative distinction explained in the first section of this chapter. These issues are:

- validity and reliability
- direct and indirect tests
- objectivity and subjectivity

- discrete and integrated tests
- norm-referencing and criterion-referencing.

These issues are explored in this section before turning in the following section to how they can be applied in local EAP contexts.

Validity and reliability

From the earlier discussion on 'fitness for purpose' it can be appreciated that tests are essentially 'good' or 'bad' in terms of how far they suit the purpose for which they are being used.

Validity

A fundamental question to ask of any test is: 'To what degree is it able to measure the **trait**(s) under investigation?' 'Traits' refer to knowledge of language and skills which contribute to target performance. The technical term for this measure of a test's fitness is **construct validity**. For example, an academic English speaking test based on a one-to-one interview may have a fair degree of construct validity if used to measure a student's ability to communicate in a tutorial or even a seminar setting. However, such a speaking test would have lower construct validity if the speaking skill in question were in relation to a speaker's ability to deliver an undergraduate lecture, or to give a formal paper at a conference.

Reliability

Reliability refers to the degree to which a test is able to provide consistent results. This means that a reliable test should give a similar result when a student repeats the test or sits different versions of the test. These two situations are known by the terms 'test-retest' and 'parallel form reliability' respectively. Similarly, the test should give a similar result when different makers or scorers (also known as 'raters') assess the candidate. This is known as 'inter-marker' or 'inter-scorer reliability'.

Test item analysis can also be carried out. Item analysis refers to the 'process of statistically identifying how well the questions did their jobs, and which ones might need improvement. It includes looking at item difficulty […] and discrimination' (Carr 2011: 321). Item analysis is designed to:

- ensure that each question is unaffected by performance on another question ('knock-on effect')
- ensure that each item is at the expected level of difficulty ('difficulty index')
- look at how well each item discriminates stronger and weaker candidates ('discrimination index').

The tension between validity and reliability

Clearly, both validity and reliability are of great importance in testing. Ideally, tests would have a high degree of both validity and reliability, but there is usually a tension between them. A well-established example of the tension between validity and reliability lies in the respective merits of the direct versus indirect methods of testing.

Direct and indirect tests

The second distinction relates to the extent to which a test can be said to be direct or indirect.

Direct tests

Direct testing refers to assessment tasks that replicate 'real-life' performance as closely as possible. For example, if the skill under investigation is a student's ability to cope with lectures, a direct test would require students to take notes from a live, full-length lecture and/or to provide a written or oral summary of the lecture. Such a test can claim some construct validity: the test clearly relates broadly to the skill under investigation. Marking and interpretation of scores can also describe directly levels of skills in relation to performance, which is known as criterion-based assessment. This means that test results are in theory directly intelligible to the individual or institution making use of the results.

The challenge for the direct test approach lies in the need to minimize inconsistency in both test performance and test marking. For example, a candidates' performance may be affected by their individual background knowledge on a particular lecture topic. This knowledge, or 'schemata', can vary considerably between candidates, thereby impacting on test results. Direct tests are further vulnerable to the 'knock-on effect'. For instance, a student performing badly in note-taking is also likely to generate poor marks in a lecture summary task which relies on effective note-taking. Finally, even with the use of carefully constructed marking criteria and standardization procedures, markers tend to converge (agree on marks) only in broad terms. In other words, attempts at finer gradations of marking tend to result in low inter-marker reliability. As can be seen in the case of IELTS, direct tests therefore often use approximate marks such as bands rather than precise scores such as percentages.

The distinction between direct and indirect tests has been referred to as a 'misnomer' (Carr 2011: 13). Carr argues that direct tests are actually indirect because they assess performance (for example a student's performance in a lecture) rather than their competence (in this example their competence in listening to lectures). In reality, the assessors have to take a candidate's performance in a particular test as an indication of their competence, even though their performance is not the same as their competence (Carr 2011: 14).

Indirect tests

Indirect tests do not aim to replicate the real-life task so closely. Rather, an indirect test seeks to investigate and provide scores in relation to traits. For example, an indirect test of a student's ability to cope with lectures might be based on short recordings with multiple-choice listening comprehension items to test word stress, sentence stress, intonation, vocabulary, accent, lexis, and grammar. Items on such a test are amenable to item analysis, and a bank of items can be built up which perform well in terms of difficulty and discrimination. Such a test can be easily and reliably marked without the need to train assessors; thus it has high reliability.

However, it is somewhat less easy to establish what percentage or score on an indirect test might equal 'satisfactory performance'. This limitation is discussed in the later section in relation to the three major international tests of academic English.

Objectivity and subjectivity in testing

The issue of **'objective tests'** refers to tests where each item has one correct answer, or a limited set of correct answers. Tests with multiple-choice items fall into this category. Objective tests can be marked by non-specialists simply by using an answer key. Subjective tests, in contrast, involve answers which are not 'right' or 'wrong' but more open ended. These answers need specialist markers, and in the case of longer written texts, for example, a team of specialists markers (usually EAP teachers) and a system of first- and second-marking and standardization. Typically, objective tests are ideally suited to the skills of listening and reading, while subjective tests are widely used in writing and speaking.

Discrete and integrated tests

This distinction mirrors the 'discrete versus integrated' approach discussed in Chapter 10. Tests using discrete items present each item separately from the others. Each task in the test is unrelated, so performance in one item is not affected by that in another. In tests with integrated items, a number of items can form a sequence, meaning that success in a later item is partially dependent on success in an earlier one. In the lecture example, an integrated sequence of tasks could involve reprocessing the content of the lecture into a new text such as a summary. For students to do this, they first need to understand and note down the main points in the lecture, as these will form the basis for the summary text. If a student's notes are inadequate (even if they mostly understand the lecture content while it is being delivered), this is likely to impact negatively on their summary as they will probably forget some of the material.

The main characteristics, advantages, and disadvantages of discrete and integrated tests are given in Table 11.2, based partly on material by Carr (2011: 15–17).

The characteristics in Table 11.2 show the potential for each approach to testing, particularly in the important areas of test reliability, authenticity, and washback. These characteristics also illustrate how the distinctions in this section are related in practice. For example, a discrete test is closely related to the notion of objectivity through its ease of scoring. Integrated tests, meanwhile, are likely to be more direct.

Criteria/items	Discrete tests	Integrated tests
Language and skills items	Presented separately	Integrated through sequences of tasks
Success in an item	Probably results from competence in that item	Probably results from competence in that item *and* other connected items
Coverage	Potential for large number of items, as each item requires little space/time	Fewer items can be covered, resulting in fewer contexts (e.g. topic, situation, academic function, language use, genre, **notion**) being covered in the time available
Specific items, e.g. grammar structures	Well suited, as separately tested items are unaffected by other items covered in the test	Students can cover up any lack of knowledge in specific items by 'talking around' or 'writing around' their gaps
Authenticity	Inauthentic: real-life language use is not an unrelated set of discrete points	Relatively authentic: real-life language use involves integrated skills, where the user can use strengths to compensate for weaknesses
Scoring and reliability	Straightforward to score, with easily analyzable results	More challenging to score, requiring clear scoring rubrics and marker training (although integrated tests can be marked by computer, as with the PTE)
Interpreting scores	Straightforward: a correct item suggests competence, particularly when backed up by further similar items; and the reverse	Problematic: if a student writes a poor lecture summary, does this mean their listening or their writing is poor, or both?
Washback	The discrete nature of the test may result in a preference for discrete item practice in the curriculum and classroom, to the detriment of more authentic integrated skills and language	The more authentic integrated nature of the test has a potentially more positive washback effect, resulting in integrated skills and language work in the curriculum and classroom and a more aligned pedagogy and practice

Table 11.2   Characteristics of discrete and integrated tests

Norm-referencing and criterion-referencing

The final paired distinction in this section is based on how tests are marked and the scores interpreted. To be meaningful, the results of a test need to be compared to a point of reference. There are two possible points of reference: the other candidates who have taken the test, i.e. the whole population of test-takers; and prepared statements or standards describing achievement on the test, or criteria. These are known respectively as **norm-referencing** and **criterion-referencing**.

Where test results are **norm-referenced**, candidates know how well they did in relation to the other test-takers, who may constitute the other students in their class, their year group or institution, or all the candidates nationally or internationally. The aim is to spread candidates along a continuum or 'rank' them rather than indicate how any particular candidate is doing in absolute terms. Results are normally expressed as a **percentile score**; a candidate with a score of 80% means that they scored more highly than 80% of the other candidates. This can be a useful piece of knowledge for the EAP teacher who wishes to know how a given student is performing in relation to the others in the group. It is also intuitive: when sponsors ask how their student is doing, they may expect an answer such as 'one of the best in the class' rather than a more technical description of what they can and cannot do.

With test results that are **criterion-referenced**, in contrast, each candidate's score is expressed in relation to the published criteria for the test. In other words, the aim is to assess what candidates are able to do in relation to a task requirement rather than in relation to other candidates. Results are normally expressed as a **percentage score** rather than a percentile. For example, if a candidate managed to answer 80% of the items correctly (assuming an objective test) then their score is 80%. By contrast, if, in the same cohort, 90% of the candidates achieved accurate responses in *over* 80% of the questions asked (assuming equal weighting), then using a norm-referenced approach the candidate who scored 80% would be assigned a test score of 10%.

In reality, the boundaries between the two types of referencing can be somewhat blurred. Examination boards have traditionally adjusted the test scores on a particular cohort if the results are misaligned to previous cohorts. For instance, if in the previous ten exams an average of 15% of students scored a grade A in relation to the criteria of the test, but in the latest test only 11% achieve this, the temptation is to find a way of adjusting the boundary so that a more typical number achieve that grade. This represents the influence of norm-referencing on a criterion-referenced test.

As Hyland points out, criterion-referenced testing is well-suited to EAP, given its emphasis on what students can do (Hyland 2006: 102). In practical terms, EAP competency frameworks and 'can do' statements may be closely linked to the criteria used in the assessments.

The five paired distinctions discussed in this section all inform and impact on assessments in EAP programmes.

Assessments within EAP programmes

While externally administered international proficiency tests will always remain a major focus in EAP programmes, teachers tend to be highly involved in assessments and tests within the programme itself. A necessary stage in such in-house or local assessments is the development of assessment criteria.

Developing assessment criteria

Assessment criteria are necessary to avoid a situation where students are not fully aware of the curriculum including how they are assessed. Historically, such a situation has been surprisingly prevalent in many academic contexts, and in some contexts still persists today. In these situations, students approach an assessment without fully knowing what it covers. Such a situation arises because the contents of the curriculum have not been properly communicated, or material appears on the test which some or all students have not covered. Assessments are part of the curriculum, and assessment criteria are part of assessments: for fairness, students should know what they are being assessed on and what their assessors are looking for.

For example, students embarking on an EAP programme for the first time may imagine that they will be assessed on language. This will certainly be the case, but is not the whole story: in their academic writing students need to consider other aspects including the content and organization of their text, and academic conventions, such as referencing. Assessment criteria explicitly state what is being assessed.

Assessment criteria are statements of achievement, and need to be developed alongside the development of the curriculum and syllabus. They influence both the materials and the assessments. In order to develop assessment criteria for a particular skill, the learning objectives need to be taken into account. For example, assessment criteria can be based on the descriptions of the extreme positions 'successful' and 'unsuccessful' in Table 9.5 on page 255 in the context of giving a presentation. Extracts from these descriptions include:

- Critical: ideas, theories, and cited work are approached critically

- Uncritical: ideas, theories, and cited work are unquestioningly accepted

These descriptions can be worked up and expanded to produce criteria such as the set of marking criteria illustrated in Figure 11.2, which is based on five bands expressed as letter grades:

Grade A: The student uses ideas and theories from sources in a highly critical way, by commenting on aspects such as their validity and applicability.

Grade B: The student uses ideas and theories from sources and mostly critiques this material.

Grade C: The student incorporates source material and shows some evidence of critically examining this material.

Grade D: The student makes use of source material, but mostly uses it uncritically.

Grade E (fail): The student uses source material uncritically/The student does not use source material.

Figure 11.2 Marking criteria based on five bands

Areas of focus	Criteria with descriptions	Comments/Grades
The writer	The writer's voice and identity are evident There is evidence of originality of thought, ideas, and new connections and insights	
Content	The essay achieves the task in terms of: • relevance to the rubric • overall appropriacy • word count There is a clear main argument with appropriate supporting arguments, demonstrating sufficient evidence and exemplification from both primary and secondary academic sources There is a resolution to the argument and a measured summing-up of the main points Source material is approached critically and analyzed and evaluated where appropriate	
Structure	The essay is clearly and logically structured The essay is divided into paragraphs, including an introduction and conclusion, with a topic or theme for each body paragraph Headings and sub-headings are used as appropriate There is sufficient signposting for the audience, including a thesis statement which is revisited in the conclusion	
Academic conventions	Source material is correctly referenced All non-author material is cited and there is no evidence of plagiarism An accurate references section (bibliography) is included, which covers all the in-text references	
Language	There is an appropriate range and sophistication of grammatical structures and vocabulary Grammar and vocabulary are used accurately The style of the essay is appropriate for the purpose, with hedging and emphasizing where appropriate Technical aspects are correct, including spelling and punctuation The essay is cohesive, with an appropriate and accurate range of cohesive language to express micro and macro cohesion	
Presentation and visuals	The essay is attractively and accurately presented, with all prescribed components including a cover page and word count Visuals are incorporated as appropriate, and are correctly sourced	

Table 11.3   Sample assessment criteria for a research essay

These kinds of criteria can be incorporated into complete descriptions of assessment criteria for a particular skill. They need to incorporate a scoring system which is agreed on and recognized by the parties involved and the institution. A letter grade system such as that above may be used, or a numerical system such as percentage bands.

Academic writing remains a core focus of most EAP programmes and, like other skill areas, requires clear assessment criteria. Table 11.3 presents a possible set of assessment criteria for a research essay.

The criteria in Table 11.3 are divided into six main areas. These are transparent and thus helpful for all users: students, EAP teachers, university academic and registry staff, and sponsors. There is no mystery, and students can be clear about what they are aiming for, which in turn informs how they plan their study.

The third column in the table allows space for comments by the markers. These can be in the form of bands, which need a further document to specify. Often such bands are built round familiar adjectives such as:

outstanding – excellent – very good – good – satisfactory – borderline – unsatisfactory

Alternatively, letter grades, marks out of a given number (for example five or ten), or percentages may be used. However, to be meaningful, these alternatives probably need to be further developed using language like adverbs or the familiar adjectives above. The criteria can be incorporated into the marking document to produce scales of achievement, for example:

The writer's voice and identity are clearly evident

The writer's voice and identity are mostly evident

The writer's voice and identity are partially evident

The writer's voice and identity are occasionally evident

The writer's voice and identity are not evident

Finally, the EAP team (teachers and programme directors) need to decide on the balance of marks. A good starting point is to decide on how much, proportionally, to reward content, as distinct from language. In the earlier stages of an EAP programme, and at lower levels, there may be good reasons for emphasizing language over other aspects, such as content and academic conventions. Later, content is likely to form a greater proportion of the total marks, which reflects the premium placed on content by academic staff in the disciplines.

Writing low-stakes EAP tests

Even more than classroom materials, which themselves require considerable time and expertise to write as Chapter 10 argues, the writing of tests is best left to trained experts. This particularly applies to high-stakes tests such as the final achievement test, which may also serve as the university admission test for language. In countries where high-stakes assessments are open to legal challenge, it is crucial that experts write the tests. It is beyond the scope of this book to go into the writing of such tests; other language teachers' handbooks offer such expertise, such as Carr's *Designing and Analyzing Language Tests* (2011).

Collaborating on test writing

Despite the need for expert involvement in the writing of high-stakes tests, any EAP teacher can make a useful start by writing their own low-stakes assessments, such as class tests and progress tests. A workable way of doing this is to collaborate with other EAP teachers, particularly where they are following the same syllabus. If there are to be a number of such tests throughout the programme, it is probably better to collaborate on each test rather than write one test each and share these among the team. By collaborating on each test, less experienced EAP teachers can learn from those who are more experienced, who in turn can play a useful role in mentoring the former. Also, as with materials writing in general, a collaborative approach should result in better balanced products, which are not too quirky. Collaboration also enables checking and proofreading during the writing process.

Working out what to test

The most effective class tests and progress tests stick very closely to the material covered in the programme, which should be broadly similar to that described in the syllabus. There may of course be differences between what the syllabus states and what individual teachers cover, which is entirely appropriate as each EAP teacher should respond to their students' needs. If the differences in a particular class are too wide, there is a risk that the material in the syllabus will not be fully covered by the end of the programme, thereby jeopardizing the chances of that class when they come to do the final achievement test (which is likely to cover the whole cohort of any number of individual classes).

The collaborative approach described above can help ensure a balance of coverage in the assessments. For example, the EAP team may wish to assess the effectiveness of their students' learning over a two-week teaching block. Let us assume that one language focus of this period is the present perfect as used in reporting structures like 'Research by Jones has shown that …'. The class test should include such language, but too great an emphasis on the present perfect, particularly if covered through a decontextualized controlled manipulation of the form, might be inappropriate and at the expense of other, more meaningful work. Such work could include a task in which students have to identify and select relevant extracts from a given authentic text in order to use in their own written paragraph. The rubric for writing the paragraph should be very clear, and naturally lead to the use of appropriate reporting structures such as 'Research by Jones has shown that …'. In this way, the class test has validity and is direct, fairly integrated, and authentic through its use of authentic texts and tasks.

By collaborating on the marking, including the development of appropriate marking criteria, EAP teachers should be able to achieve a good level of reliability. The scores can be presented in both a norm-referenced and a criterion-referenced way: each student can be given their score as it relates to the marking criteria (criterion-referenced) and in relation to the other students in their class or group of classes (norm-referenced). The latter can be very useful for both teacher and students to assess the latter's progress or effectiveness of learning in the context of the cohort. If certain students appear to be falling behind in a particular language and/or skill area, their EAP teacher can help them by suggesting extra materials to work with independently.

Presenting low-stakes tests

There are two ways of presenting low-stakes tests. They can either be clearly timetabled and signalled in advance, so that students and EAP teachers know when they are and have time to prepare. Alternatively, tests can be carried out without notice. This element of surprise can have the advantage of militating against habitual cramming for the test by some students, and so may be a more representative assessment of the effectiveness of their learning.

One approach to tests is to integrate them into the regular programme of study. For example, if an EAP programme has a reading component involving timed reading based on authentic texts and tasks, one such iteration of the skill can be assessed. The class takes place as normal, and the EAP teacher marks the students' responses and keeps a record of their marks. This practice can be done by a larger group of classes using the same materials. In this way, a series of 'snapshots' of students' writing development can be built up and analyzed. Students can be informed about the assessments at any point, either before the tests, or at the point of delivery. In the latter case there is little likelihood that students make any special preparations. Also, the practice and pattern of integrating unannounced tests can be motivating for students and can have a beneficial effect on attendance.

Other types of low-stakes assessment

Besides classroom tests and quizzes, there are a number of other possibilities for EAP teachers to carry out low-stakes assessment of their students. Brindley and Ross identify journals, interviews, observations, projects, questionnaires, and portfolios (Brindley and Ross 2001: 153). They expand on portfolios, which are typically made up of different kinds of student writing, which may be done collaboratively (ibid.). There are issues of standardization in such an approach, and the volume of student texts leads to a considerable workload for the assessors, who are probably the EAP teachers.

This range of assessment types illustrates the possibilities available to the EAP teacher and institution. Any of them could be developed into useful tools to contribute to the overall assessment of students within the teaching institution. EAP teachers, and institutions, have limited influence on externally taken tests, notably the international academic English tests: with these, the influence is the other way around.

Influences of academic English tests

As this chapter has shown, assessments and tests play a crucial role in EAP programmes in determining students' academic progression. While EAP programmes can exist independently of particular tests, EAP students generally need to achieve a specified score on an accepted test in order to proceed with their academic study in the disciplines. While tests have a number of different types and purposes, teachers and students can have different attitudes towards these tests.

Perceptions and practicalities of academic English tests

Tests can be the driver of the EAP programme in that gaining a specific score on a specific test is sometimes the primary motivation of the student. This applies particularly to pre-sessional courses, where often (though not always) the student has to achieve a specific score in a final test. This test may be an international proficiency test, such as IELTS, or an institutional, locally written, or national achievement test. Practices vary across different contexts, including university and language school contexts, and countries.

EAP programmes in different contexts

In other contexts, however, the EAP programme can be less test driven. In-sessional programmes, for instance, can exist to meet the specific needs of a student in their discipline without the need for a final test. Alternatively, a student may be required to attend an in-sessional programme and gain a specific score in a particular test at the end of the programme.

There is also significant growth in independent (for example private language school) provision of EAP for students aiming at English-medium university study. Typically these students will exit their EAP programme by taking one of the widely accepted international examinations.

In some contexts, there has also been a growth in foundation and other lower level courses, perhaps beginning as low as A1 (starter) or A2 (elementary), which aim to bring students up to university entrance level such as B2 (upper-intermediate) over a long period of time through gradual introduction of EAP-oriented content. In this scenario, tests are likely to form gateways to the next level, for example to move from A2 to B1 (pre-intermediate to intermediate).

Tensions in short- and long-term goals

These scenarios naturally give rise to possible tensions. Given the different stakeholders and factors involved —the student, their sponsor, the EAP teacher, the institution, the department in which the student wants to study, and the test itself—there is considerable scope for different people wanting different things. One tension is the possible misalignment of the student's needs and the test.

To give an example, a postgraduate student needs to reach a target of 6.5 IELTS in order to start their masters programme. This student knows that their writing needs improvement, and is highly motivated to write academic texts. Their EAP teacher supports this, but the student's sponsor is keen for their student to 'pass' the test, i.e. gain 6.5 on IELTS, and start their academic programme without further investment in EAP. The test, meanwhile, requires students to do two short writing tasks, one a data description of 150 words, the other a short essay (without citations) of 250 words. Finally, feedback from the university department centres on the importance for students entering the department to be skilled at writing longer (for example 2,000+ word) research papers, which constitute the main tasks and assessments on the academic programme.

In this example, the student's EAP teacher feels committed to doing all they can to help the student thrive in their future academic study. The EAP teacher fully understands the crucial role of academic writing in postgraduate assessment. If students enter their discipline unable to write a research essay, the MA programme, once it is under way, may be too highly pressured to allow much catch-up work in key areas such as using sources in a literature review, and as a result the student may fail the course. Clearly there is a need in the EAP preparation stage, such as a pre-sessional programme, to focus on writing longer academic texts, together with the academic skills these entail. While the international English tests assess short, relatively undeveloped student writing, the student's target need of writing research papers requires additional skills, language, and competences, notably researching and using sources in texts, writing in an appropriate academic style, and demonstrating criticality. In short, there is a tension between short-term goals (the need to pass the test) and longer-term needs (to cope with the intended academic course of study).

EAP teachers can play a pivotal role in cases like this and need to lead as well as follow. In this particular scenario, the EAP teacher may be able to open up vital discussions with the stakeholders and negotiate content. Without losing focus on the test in which the student needs reach their target, the EAP teacher can connect the student, and possibly their sponsor, with their department, for example by arranging a meeting between the student and departmental representative and by asking other students from the department to talk to potential new students, emphasizing and communicating the importance of being able to write research papers prior to entry. On the EAP programme itself, the teacher needs to manage the balance of time spent on potentially competing skills, in this case exam practice involving writing repeated short essays (which the student will not be writing in their discipline), and the more time-consuming but ultimately more fruitful work on writing research papers (which they will be writing).

Rationales and criticisms of international tests

For the purposes of admission, sometimes described as 'gate-keeping', many academic institutions around the world use commercial, internationally available proficiency tests.

Reasons for using international tests

From the perspective of the academic institution, international tests may used be for a number of reasons, including those given in Table 11.4.

Criteria	Explanation
Access	The major international tests are readily accessible in many countries and centres and/or via the internet, so the potential pool of international candidates (i.e. test-takers) can easily access the test
Convenience	The tests are available very frequently (e.g. weekly) or on-demand
Efficiency and controllable cost	For a fixed fee per candidate, any number of candidates can take the test, thereby eliminating the need to produce in-house tests which can be time consuming and difficult to write
Preparation	The widespread uptake of such tests has resulted in a wide choice of published materials—such as coursebooks—to support students in their test preparation; these can be used on preparation programmes
Recognition and status	The major international tests are widely accepted and recognized, unlike most locally produced tests; students can use their international test result to approach institutions worldwide
Security	Given the high stakes for applicants, test security is at a premium; high security is offered by the major international tests of English

Table 11.4   Reasons for using international tests

These reasons can be very compelling, and are supported by the evidence of the number of test-takers of the major international tests, which together are numbered in millions of candidates per year.

Reasons against using international tests

However, a number of criticisms may be levelled against international tests. Major criticisms of international tests are given in Table 11.5.

Criteria	Explanation
Authenticity	The widespread practice of taking a familiar test can lead to the emergence of new 'genres', e.g. the 'IELTS essay', which bears little resemblance to what lecturers in the disciplines might consider to be an academic essay
Effectiveness	The international tests are inevitably quite general in nature, and so may not meet specific needs effectively
Limitation in scope	The major international tests of academic English are unable to incorporate core academic practices such as citation and referencing
Inflexibility	The major international tests are well established and clearly defined, so it can be difficult and undesirable for the test providers to make fundamental or frequent changes to their format in response to changing needs and emerging technologies

Criteria	Explanation
Resources	Material to help students in the tests is widely available online and in print, including sample answers; this can result in predictability, homogeneity, and unoriginality of student responses in the tests
Washback	The tests can dominate the curriculum and teaching to the detriment of other work (i.e. skills not covered in the test), such as writing research papers

Table 11.5   Reasons against using international tests

A further point, which may not strictly result from the tests themselves, is that the student's target scores on the test may not be sufficient to equip them to cope academically and linguistically in the disciplines.

To some extent, these criticisms can be addressed by the EAP teacher and their institution, but some test providers arguably also need to play a role in defending their tests against such criticism. Indeed, this is starting to happen, as can be seen in the case of IELTS, which now provides guidance on how to apply entrance criteria.

The impact of international academic English tests

The three major international English tests have individually and collectively had a considerable impact on EAP and the wider context of acceptance into global English-medium of instruction (EMI) tertiary level programmes. The tests have contributed to a major industry involving not only the producers of the test but also test researchers and designers, publishers, and teaching operations such as university language centres and private language schools. For many teachers of EAP, exam preparation courses (for example IELTS) was their route into the field.

One of the most significant areas of impact is the washback of the tests. 'Teaching to the test' is neither a recent phenomenon, nor is it confined to EAP. If a high-stakes test contains a short essay of perhaps 250 words (as all three international academic tests do), one possible effect on teaching and learning is that many students and teachers will want to focus on this type of writing task. In this way, other writing tasks face being squeezed out of the available learning time. An example of such a writing task is research-based writing which involves among other things synthesizing material from reading texts into an original written text. Likewise, given the widespread use of multiple-choice items in both the more direct and indirect tests, students may want to focus on reading or exam practice materials with similar test items, at the expense of more open, unkeyable tasks, such as summaries.

Cramming for the test is another issue. Any or all of the parties involved in EAP provision may push for an intensive test-oriented programme. These parties include the students, their sponsors, EAP teachers, and the providing institution (for example language school). The result is likely to be an imbalanced programme of study which does not effectively meet the future study needs of the students.

Profiles of international tests of academic English

It is useful at this point to discuss the three international tests of academic English in greater detail. To give a little historical perspective, in the early years of EAP, higher-level general English examinations such as Cambridge English: Advanced (CAE) and Proficiency (CPE) were used for entry into many academic institutions. Students are normally required to achieve a specific grade, for example grade A on CAE or grade C or above on CPE. Although these general English examinations continue to be widely accepted, in the 1980s it came to be recognized that success in these examinations did not necessarily mean that students had the right skills, language, and academic literacy, to study successfully. Alternative general English tests from the USA became widely accepted, notably the Test of English as a Foreign Language (TOEFL) and, to a lesser extent, the Test of English for International Communication (TOEIC), which is targeted primarily at professional rather than academic candidates. The TOEFL exam has developed from purely multiple-choice answers into the productive skills.

Other examinations were launched, notably the International English Language Testing Service (IELTS) in 1989. IELTS is a comprehensively reworked version of the earlier English Language Testing Service (ELTS), which was itself based on an earlier test going back to the 1960s. To give an indication of its phenomenal growth, the number of candidates taking the test rose a hundredfold in little over 20 years. The ELTS test had 10,000 candidates in 1985, which rose to 43,000 for IELTS in 1995, to half a million by 2003, from which it doubled to a million in 2007 and to 1.5 million in 2010 (source: www.ielts.org). While these totals are not actual numbers of different students, as many students take the test more than once, they do illustrate the growth of students wishing to study in English.

IELTS and TOEFL together dominate the world market in gate-keeper EAP testing. IELTS is co-owned by the British Council, Cambridge English Language Assessment (formerly Cambridge ESOL), and IDP: IELTS Australia. It has become so widely accepted that for many students, teachers, and institutions it has the default status of industry standard. An indication of this is that a student is just as likely to be described as 'an IELTS 5' student than 'a high B1' student.

IELTS

IELTS has always been based on a direct testing approach, using proto- or pseudo-academic tasks such as short essay writing, reading comprehension, understanding lectures, and interviews. Initially, IELTS test developers sought to increase construct validity by developing discipline-specific versions of some papers, and by providing a thematic link across sets of papers. However, following research by Clapham (1996, cited in Brindley and Ross 2001: 152) and others, the IELTS test format is now non-subject specific. In her research, Clapham discovered the difficulties of sourcing texts to match disciplines as well as the reality that skills cross different disciplines (ibid.). In the current non-subject specific format, the reading, writing, listening and speaking components are still taken at a single sitting, but are no longer thematically linked.

There are two versions of the test: IELTS Academic and IELTS General Training, with the latter being aimed primarily at professional and vocational use. The four skills each constitute one paper. The speaking paper is a face-to-face interview. IELTS regularly publishes sets of past papers, and the official website (www.ielts.org) provides updated information on format, task types and duration to test takers, institutional users, and tutors seeking to prepare students for the test.

TOEFL

Developed in the 1960s and administered by the Educational Testing Service (ETS), the TOEFL (Test of English as a Foreign Language) test is now widely taken via the internet, and is known as the TOEFL iBT test.

TOEFL has historically taken an indirect and psychometric approach to test construction. In other words, rather than setting 'real-life' tasks, the test draws on large banks of discrete (i.e. freestanding and decontextualized) multiple-choice items, and has sought to assess both receptive and productive competence through underlying language features such as grammar, vocabulary, and pronunciation. Some direct test components for speaking and writing were later introduced, though still with an item banking approach. TOEFL moved to computer-based testing in 1998. The new iBT (internet-based TOEFL) was introduced in 2005 to replace the paper and computer versions, although the paper-based test is still available in locations without internet access.

The official website (www.ets.org/toefl) provides updated information on format, task types and duration to test takers, institutional users, and tutors seeking to prepare students for the test.

PTE

A more recent arrival in the global EAP test market is the Pearson Test of English (PTE). This test has a general and an academic version. Its unique and striking feature is that all four skills are assessed entirely by computer. This fact has generated some controversy, as users of the test—including EAP teachers— have needed some convincing in the ability of computer-based assessment software to accurately evaluate a student's use of English, as well as the quality and coherence of their arguments.

The official website (www.pearsonpte.com) provides updated information on format, task types and duration to test takers, institutional users, and tutors seeking to prepare students for the test.

Academic skills and criticality in international tests

The IELTS test has the least integration of the four language skills: each skill is taken in a separate section of the test. This is one factor in some candidates taking IELTS being given '**jagged profiles**', where the score band in one skill (for example speaking) is very different from that in another (for example writing). In contrast, both PTE and TOEFL integrate skills to a significant extent.

The academic version of IELTS does not enjoy a universal reputation among EAP teachers for being academically rigorous. As IELTS operates mainly at the level of understanding information presented in texts, it is grounded in the lower half of Bloom's taxonomy, which is discussed in Chapter 5. There is no requirement, for example, to synthesize information presented in different texts, as happens in TOEFL and PTE. For instance, a PTE task which requires students to orally describe information presented in more than one visually-presented source clearly moves quite far up the levels of Bloom's taxonomy. Given the use of multiple sources, students need to demonstrate skills in synthesis. The PTE therefore explicitly tests EAP rather than general English or discrete points of language. In this respect and because of the integrated nature of the tasks, the PTE test appears to resemble authentic academic tasks, thereby enhancing its validity.

However, institutions accepting these tests understand that language skill alone, even if it is arguably 'academic', is distinct from academic ability. The latter is validated through a candidate's academic qualifications.

On a practical note, students taking the PTE and the TOEFL iBT would benefit from having good typing skills. Since these tests are done entirely via a computer keyboard and headphones/microphone, and under strict timed conditions, a candidate with poor keyboard and typing skills would be disadvantaged. Arguably, this technical skill is a valid academic one, as in most academic institutions, coursework and projects have to be submitted electronically.

Test formats, scoring systems, and descriptors

With three major competing tests in the international market, users and stakeholders, including EAP teachers, need to develop a basic understanding of the test formats, scoring systems, and descriptors of specific scores or bands. Each test has a somewhat different approach to the assessment of English language skills, and there are further differences in the history and development of the tests which can inform users' understanding of them.

A comparison of test scores and descriptors

In accordance with their purpose, to assess students' preparedness for a range of study contexts, the three tests offer support and information through their official publications and websites. These provide detailed information on scoring, including sub-test scores, as well as information on how the scores should be interpreted by user-institutions.

IELTS bands

As a criterion-related test, IELTS uses a descriptor scale; this has nine points with whole- and half-band scores for each paper. The overall score is an average of these four scores, mathematically rounded up where necessary, for example a student scoring 5 in three skills and 4 in the fourth skill would gain an overall score of 5 (see Table 11.6 below).

Band 9: Expert user	Has fully operational command of the language: appropriate, accurate and fluent with complete understanding.
Band 8: Very good user	Has fully operational command of the language with only occasional unsystematic inaccuracies and inappropriacies. Misunderstandings may occur in unfamiliar situations. Handles complex detailed argumentation well.
Band 7: Good user	Has operational command of the language, though with occasional inaccuracies, inappropriacies and misunderstandings in some situations. Generally handles complex language well and understands detailed reasoning.
Band 6: Competent user:	Has generally effective command of the language despite some inaccuracies, inappropriacies and misunderstandings. Can use and understand fairly complex language, particularly in familiar situations.
Band 5: Modest user	Has partial command of the language, coping with overall meaning in most situations, though is likely to make many mistakes. Should be able to handle basic communication in own field.
Band 4: Limited user	Basic competence is limited to familiar situations. Has frequent problems in understanding and expression. Is not able to use complex language.
Band 3: Extremely limited user	Conveys and understands only general meaning in very familiar situations. Frequent breakdowns in communication occur.
Band 2: Intermittent user	No real communication is possible except for the most basic information using isolated words or short formulae in familiar situations and to meet immediate needs. Has great difficulty understanding spoken and written English.
Band 1: Non-user	Essentially has no ability to use the language beyond possibly a few isolated words.
Band 0: Did not attempt the test	No assessable information provided.

Table 11.6   IELTS score descriptors (www.ielts.org)

TOEFL scores

TOEFL describes performance in terms of marks out of 120. Compared with IELTS, much lower prominence is given to overall skills criterion. Table 11.7 gives basic descriptive information on TOEFL scores.

Skill	Score Range	Level
Reading	0–30	High (22–30) Intermediate (15–21) Low (0–14)
Listening	0–30	High (22–30) Intermediate (15–21) Low (0–14)
Speaking	0–30 score scale	Good (26–30) Fair (18–25) Limited (10–17) Weak (0–9)
Writing	0–30 score scale	Good (24–30) Fair (17–23) Limited (1–16)
Total Score	0–120	

Table 11.7   TOEFL score descriptors (www.ets.org/toefl)

Detailed TOEFL task marking-descriptors are available for the sub-section speaking and writing scores. Interestingly, these bands are broader than IELTS: a four-band scale for each speaking sub-skill; a five-band scale for writing sub-skills tasks.

PTE Academic Scores and use of CEFR scales

PTE provides detailed descriptions of the format and content of each section of the test in terms of what is being tested. There has been no attempt to date, however, to provide PTE-specific score descriptors. Instead, PTE aligns its numerical scores with the six-level performance descriptors developed by CEFR and ALTE. Table 11.8 gives the published CEFR equivalents for the PTE test.

		PTE Academic scores predicting the likelihood of successful performance on CEF level tasks		
CEFR descriptor	CEFR Level	Easiest	Average	Most Difficult
Proficient user	C2	80	85	n/a
	C1	67	76	84
Independent user	B2	51	59	75
	B1	36	43	58
Basic user	A2	24	30	42
	A1	n/a	n/a	n/a

Table 11.8   Pearson Test of English score equivalents (www.pearsonpte.com)

Interpreting test scores

Interpreting test scores for different tests has resulted in some controversies, particularly with regard to equivalences. For example, test providers do not always agree on their competitors' published equivalences relating to particular tests, scores, and the CEFR.

Issues and controversies on establishing equivalence

There is considerable pressure on the international EAP test providers to devise and publish equivalency tables. Users and stakeholders, such as university admissions staff, want clear information stating how each test relates to the CEFR, and indeed how the different tests compare. Such information has not always been sufficiently comprehensive, and equivalences between tests and the CEFR are periodically revised in the light of new research evidence.

In practical terms, the three tests have the same purpose, i.e. indicating a candidate's ability to perform at a given level of English with a view to studying through the medium of English. However, there remains some resistance to explicitly stating equivalence and correlation. One explanation lies in the variation in approaches to test design, and in particular the nature of direct and **indirect testing**.

PTE Academic authors argue that test providers need to clearly state the meaning of their claims of equivalence between test scores and CEFR bands. For example, the following statement appears on its web information pages:

> PTE Academic alignment with the CEF can only be fully understood if it is supported with information showing what it really means to be 'at a level'. In other words, are you likely to be successful with tasks at the lower boundary of a [CEF] level; do you stand a fair chance of doing well on any task, or will you be able to do almost all the tasks, even the most difficult ones, at a particular level?

(<http://pearsonpte.com/PTEAcademic/scores/Documents/Interpreting_the%20 PTE_Academic_Score_Report.pdf> accessed 26 August 2013)

IELTS and TOEFL, like PTE, also publish tables stating how their scores equate to the CEFR and ALTE frameworks. In addition, PTE and TOEFL both currently provide score converter tools on their websites which relate IELTS bands to scores in other tests. There is a similar tool on the TOEFL website to equate TOEFL scores to equivalent IELTS bands.

Issues and controversies on setting entry requirements

A further complex question concerns how institutions determine minimum score requirements for their programmes (foundation, undergraduate, and postgraduate/ research degrees) and different disciplines (for example mathematics and law). The perceived language demands of different disciplines affects score requirements. For example, the requirement for students applying to study law is typically higher than for mathematics. Further variations exist between institutions, with more prestigious institutions (i.e. typically higher-ranking in national and international league tables) demanding the highest test scores. Since it is by no means demonstrable or certain that studying, for example, law at Oxford University is more *linguistically* demanding than studying law at a less high-ranking university which asks for a lower English language test score, there would also appear to be market influences in the institutions' decision-making.

To assist their potential users, IELTS, TOEFL, and PTE provide guidance on setting score requirements. For example, Table 11.9 offers guidelines published by IELTS.

Band	Linguistically demanding academic courses e.g. medicine, law, linguistics, journalism, library studies	Linguistically less demanding academic courses e.g. agriculture, pure mathematics, technology. computer -based work, telecommunications	Linguistically demanding training courses e.g. air traffic control, engineering, pure/ applied sciences, industrial safety	Linguistically less demanding training courses e.g. animal husbandry, catering, fire services
9.0–7.5	Acceptable	Acceptable	Acceptable	Acceptable
7.0	Probably acceptable	Acceptable	Acceptable	Acceptable
6.5	English study needed	Probably acceptable	Acceptable	Acceptable
6.0	English study needed	English study needed	Probably acceptable	Acceptable
5.5	English study needed	English study needed	English study needed	Probably acceptable

Table 11.9   IELTS band score acceptability (<http://www.ielts.org/institutions/global_recognition/setting_ielts_requirements.aspx> accessed 26 August 2013)

This table might suggest that linguistically demanding courses, such as those at masters level which are likely to require more reading of academic journals, would set an IELTS entry level of 7.0 or 7.5. In reality, amid a competitive global market for international students, many university courses currently set lower requirements of 6.5 or even 6.0. Craven's (2011) study of the progress of university students through their academic programme uses IELTS scores as measures of progress, commenting that:

> If Australian universities are not inclined to raise English language proficiency requirements for entry to university courses […] then it is vital that they adopt a wide range of measures to ensure strategies to address issues of English language development are in place.

(Craven 2011: 43)

Many institutions also find themselves under market pressure to accept students with lower level IELTS scores onto shorter and shorter pre-degree preparation courses (some as short as four weeks). Yet studies such as Elder and O'Loughlin (2003) suggest that a realistic average gain for a ten- to twelve-week course may be no more than half a band overall.

Conclusion

This chapter has discussed the role of EAP assessments as tools to determine a student's academic progression (as summative assessments), and their role in evaluating the curriculum and teaching (as formative ones). Assessments have many types and purposes, but they are not neutral, add-on components of an EAP programme. Rather, they are integral to it and often highly influential through their effect on the curriculum and teaching. With a working knowledge of the major issues in test construction, the EAP teacher can contribute greatly to curriculum-based assessments including appropriate assessment criteria, through which they can positively influence their local EAP curriculum and teaching. This contribution will typically be through low-stakes assessments including classroom-based assessments. The influence of EAP teachers is likely to be more limited with regard to the wider context of the high-stakes assessments, notably IELTS, TOEFL, and PTE, although EAP teachers have an important role to play in balancing the effects of such tests in the programme and classroom. By focusing on assessments in a balanced way, EAP teachers are well-positioned to positively influence their students' outcomes both in terms of whether they proceed to the next stage of their academic study, and how successfully they cope with it.

Further reading

Blue, G., J. Milton and **J. Saville.** (eds.). 2000. *Assessing English For Academic Purposes*. Bern: Peter Lang Publications.

Carr, N. 2011. *Designing and Analyzing Language Tests*. Oxford: Oxford University Press.

Douglas, D. 2009. *Understanding Language Testing*. Abingdon: Hodder Education.

Hughes, A. 2002. *Testing for Language Teachers 2e*. Cambridge: Cambridge University Press.

McNamara, T. 2000. *Language Testing*. Oxford: Oxford University Press.

12

TECHNOLOGIES
Aisha Walker

Technologies as resources for communication and learning

Increasingly, digital technologies are becoming part of the way that people communicate and part of the context in which language is used. This is particularly the case in higher education (HE) as this sector was an early adopter in embracing technology for everyday teaching and learning and, for most students, digital tools will be an integral part of the way that they study. In addition, digital tools offer ways to support the teaching and learning of 'traditional' language and skills, including those needed for academic study.

In most teaching and learning contexts, the number of technologies potentially available is probably far greater than those that are actually used. In other words, teachers do not make full use of the technologies available. There may be good reasons for this, an important reason being that technologies, of themselves, are not necessarily useful unless they can be demonstrated to be so. For instance, equipping every classroom with an **interactive whiteboard** or issuing every student with a tablet may or may not result in better teaching and learning. Certainly there is the potential for better teaching and learning, but other factors are involved such as the effectiveness of the software; technical support; teaching and learning cultures; training and methodologies. Provision of the technologies is thus a starting point and not an end in itself, and their use needs developing and monitoring.

To enhance learning, technologies are best seen as resources rather than objects. In an EAP context, technologies can be used as highly productive resources to facilitate more effective teaching, learning, and communication. EAP teachers face two questions regarding the use of the increasing available technologies. The first is how they can prepare students for studying in such a technology-rich environment. The second is how teachers can use technology to enhance their teaching of EAP. Technologies have also contributed greatly to the resources that students and teachers use. An example of such a development is corpora, which Chapter 1 introduced as an important influence on EAP. Corpora have resulted in more accurate language reference resources, such as dictionaries and grammar books, and can be used in the classroom in their own right. This chapter focuses particularly on how EAP teachers and students can use technologies in the classroom, and how EAP teachers can maximize their use of technologies as resources for communication and learning.

21st-century learning contexts

In most teaching contexts, the majority of students are based in institutions and attend face-to-face classes. However, a substantial, and increasing, number of students are distance learners. For this latter group, it is very likely that course materials will be delivered online and that that any interaction with tutors or fellow students will also take place online. However, the boundaries between 'full-time', 'part-time' and 'distance' are blurring. Even students on full-time courses will find that at least some of the teaching materials and interactions will be online. Unless the course is designed for distance study, electronic resources will be intended to supplement rather than replace more traditional formats such as face-to-face lectures, seminars and tutorials.

Blended learning and the 'flipped classroom'

This combination of digital and traditional modes is known as **'blended learning'**, i.e. a mixture of face-to-face and virtual teaching and learning. For example, a face-to-face class may be followed by a virtual learning event such as an online discussion or by using a **wiki**. A wiki is simply a type of website that can be edited quickly by a number of authors; the word 'wiki' is said to come from the Hawaiian phrase *wiki-wiki* meaning 'quick' (Wikipedia is the best-known example of a wiki). Students can use wikis to write texts such as a collaborative report. In some cases, blended learning is used to facilitate a 'flipped classroom' approach. A more traditional teaching and learning approach is characterized by the presentation of new information in the classroom by the teacher, followed by student independent study to learn more about the topic through reading and listening outside the classroom. In a flipped classroom approach, the students have the responsibility for initially learning about the topic, which they can do by searching for and accessing relevant sources, including both traditional sources, such as books from the library and newer technologies, such as online lectures. Following this initial learning stage, the classroom time is used for face-to-face discussion, clarification, and other enquiry-based tasks. In either case, whether face-to-face teaching precedes online activities or the classroom is flipped, students are expected to take responsibility for completing the digitally mediated aspects of the course.

Using digital resources

Although most direct teaching remains face to face through lectures, seminars and tutorials, teaching and learning is increasingly supported, supplemented, and complemented through the use of technologies. A starting point is likely to be teachers putting their presentation slides and lecture handouts into a virtual learning environment (VLE) such as Moodle, so that students can access these materials before or after the lecture. Some tutors also record lectures, using audio or video, and upload them to the VLE. One effect of the increasing availability of materials online is that students may feel that it is no longer necessary to attend face-to-face classes, arguing that the course is all online. However, in a blended learning approach, the digital and traditional aspects of a course will be designed to work in tandem, and students who miss face-to-face sessions are likely to miss important aspects of a course. As Chapter 8 illustrates, a live lecture can involve more than the lecturer's 'script' alone, and other face-to-face events, such as discussions, offer invaluable opportunities to participate, which may not arise if the event takes place entirely online. Some teachers also make use of services such as Twitter to communicate with students, for example, by tweeting relevant readings or reminders about tutorial times. A useful resource for developing digital literacies is: <http://www.elanguages.ac.uk/digital_literacies.php>.

Library and digital resources

Digital publication has been the norm for academic journals since the 1990s. Students should expect that a large proportion of course readings will be in electronic form, as journal papers, e-books, or digitized materials, and they will therefore need to make use of electronic databases and to browse current journals on screen. However, it is important to note that, while a vast amount of resources are available online, many are not. A great number of books are not available online, nor as e-books, and only a fraction of the world's archives have been digitized. Libraries, therefore, remain a vital resource, especially in subjects that work with historical texts. For some students, the shift to digitized resources requires a change in expectation and attitudes; when books are unavailable in the library, they may be available online. EAP teachers can encourage their students to become familiar with online searches, particularly through training opportunities offered by university libraries. Libraries, now frequently known as 'information services' in recognition of their role in providing information to students and researchers generally, usually offer training in accessing and using digital resources. Navigating electronic databases and using search terms involve specific skills and techniques, and students need to learn these to be able to search for resources effectively.

Understanding and managing resources

Digital reading resources, like digital lecture notes, may appear easy to access and always available. However, availability is not the same as actually reading and understanding the materials. It may be straightforward to find and download large numbers of papers but, as shown in Chapter 6, students need the skills to read, interpret, make notes, summarize, and synthesize arguments from different sources. Summary and synthesis are particularly important with digital readings because it is so easy for students to copy and paste material. Moreover, because resources are always accessible some students may mistakenly think that they do not need to record bibliographic information when conducting a search. In doing so, students risk forgetting which journal/volume/issue contains the article they want to cite, especially when under pressure from an assignment deadline.

Electronic resources require careful management. One method of achieving this is through the use of reference management tools such as EndNote, Mendeley, and CiteULike. These resources have separate fields in which users can input each item of bibliographic information such as author names, journal names, page numbers, and other information and can enable the user to send the bibliographic information directly from a journal to the reference manager. However, it remains important to teach students to write their own summaries, and critical responses, rather than using only the abstract printed in the journal. It is through such teaching and learning that the student can learn to read, understand and respond to the paper. By contrast, building up a library of unread electronic resources is easily achieved, but until the student reads them, such resources have no use. The notes students create in the reference manager help them to remember what the paper was about, how it is relevant to their own studies and what they thought of it. Eventually, the notes may be incorporated into an assignment or thesis; something that cannot be done with the journal abstract.

Digital books

Many books are becoming available in digital as well as paper formats. Electronic books are extremely useful to university libraries and students as they enable multiple access to the same book by large numbers of students. Most library copies of digital books cannot be downloaded onto a student's personal **e-reader** but must be read using library facilities, which may be accessed remotely, for example via the library website. The availability of tools such as iBook Author and Kindle Bookmaker means that tutors can start to create interactive digital course texts instead of or in addition to conventional materials. Although academic iBooks are available through iTunesU, their use is limited due to the current lack of a universally agreed format for books. For example, Apple's iBooks can only be read on an iPad or iPhone. However, as the technology matures this may change and multimodal books, incorporating animations, video and interactive activities may become commonplace in academic settings.

Grey literature

Digital resources also include '**grey literature**' which means any digital or print publication 'not controlled by commercial publishing, i.e. where publishing is not the primary activity of the producing body' (<http://www.greynet.org>). Grey literature, which includes many important types of documents such as government reports, has always been available and in the pre-digital era was a problem for researchers and librarians because it was often difficult to access and to trace. However, the problem has now been reversed. There are many grey literature genres and resources are easy to find. The obvious advantage is that documents such as government or charity reports are now likely to be available online, but the drawback is that unofficial and informal texts such as blogs and tweets are also available online and accessible via web searches. The results of a search for almost any term will almost certainly start with a Wikipedia entry.

Wikipedia

EAP teachers frequently advise against using Wikipedia as a source to be cited in an academic text on the grounds that it is an intrinsically unreliable source, although it has been argued that this is not necessarily the case (West and Williamson 2009). Wikipedia can be a useful initial source of information during the early stages of learning about a topic; however its articles certainly do not meet the required academic standard of formal peer review. In academic peer reviews, peers are experts in the field working in academic institutions. The peer review process involves sending the text to the reviewers, usually 'blind' (i.e. without the names of the authors), who assess and evaluate aspects of the text relating to its quality and relevance. Wikipedia articles undergo a kind of review in that they can be edited by any user with internet access, in contrast with academic texts. Each Wikipedia article has a 'history' page which shows when, how and by whom the article has been edited and a 'talk' page in which contributors explain their edits and discuss how the topic should be presented and referenced in the main article. For those using Wikipedia for academic purposes, the talk page of an article can be a valuable resource when it comes to evaluating the reliability of an article. For example, below is an excerpt from the talk page for the Wikipedia article about 'dark matter'.

What is mass-energy?

"Dark matter is estimated to constitute 84% of the matter in the universe and 23% of the mass-energy."

I checked the source which this phrase links to and there is nothing about the differentiation between matter and mass-energy. Dark matter is said to constitute 23% of matter. So I think this phrase is inaccurate and needs to be fixed or else one should choose a different scientific source for it. Louigi Verona (talk) 12:17, 17 December 2012 (UTC)

I'll change it to energy density. As for the source, it's fine. Waleswatcher (talk) 21:02, 17 December 2012 (UTC)

'Mass-energy' simply refers to using mass–energy equivalence to compare the two. Energy density is technically fine as a term as well although it may obscure the point a bit more for the casual reader. 'Total energy' (of the universe) is probably a better choice, because that's what these percentages represent. There's nothing wrong with the conversion and comparison, by the way. It's commonly done in this context, e.g. in Ostriker & Steinhardt's review in Science, which is as reliable as it gets in this field. 188.26.163.111 (talk) 23:26, 31 January 2013 (UTC)

(<http://en.wikipedia.org/wiki/Talk:Dark_matter> accessed 10th April 2013)

Wikipedia has a review process by which articles can be nominated as 'good' or 'featured' articles. These criteria are similar to those by which academic work is judged, such as neutrality, comprehensiveness, and accuracy and use of citations. At the time of writing, the dark matter article does not meet the criteria for a 'good' article. However, as the excerpt above shows, contributors are taking some care to ensure that the article is correctly referenced and that the sources are reliable. This shows that a Wikipedia article does not necessarily represent only the opinion of one individual but can be produced by a team of contributors, who may not know each other in person, working together to ensure that information and sources are reliable. Looking at a Wikipedia article alongside its talk page can be a useful activity in an EAP classroom, especially as the discourse conventions of the two text types are different. It is helpful for students to learn to decipher the talk pages and to click on contributor names, which lead to a profile and/or an activity list, in order to gauge a contributor's level of expertise on the topic.

One concern with Wikipedia is that articles may be written by people with vested interests. For example, a commercial institution may write an article that, in effect, promotes its products or services, while neglecting to point out facts which might put the business in a negative light. Similarly, articles written about political events or figures may not be neutral. Neutrality cannot be assured, but this is true of any text and a key reading skill involves identifying bias in a text. Two factors which can mitigate bias in Wikipedia are the editing community, which tends to be vigilant and is likely to edit any text which is overly biased, and the Wikipedia rule of 'locking' articles which are particularly susceptible to biased or malicious editing. For example, whereas the Oxford University Press page is relatively uncontentious and can be edited by anyone (including rival publishers), the page for former US president George W. Bush is locked. The page content is limited to verifiable facts and does not include opinions about the rights or wrongs of his presidency.

Blogs

Blogs are another type of grey literature that can be problematic for students. The challenge here is to determine whether or not a blog (originally short for 'web log') is a reliable source due to the fact that anyone publish a blog (regardless of expertise), it is not subject to peer review, and the research may not be robust. As with Wikipedia articles, it could be argued that blog comments constitute a form of peer review. In academic journal peer reviews, the process is anonymous in that authors do not know who is reviewing their work, although the editors know the exact identity of each reviewer. When comments are made on blog posts, however, the commenters may be entirely anonymous, so there is no way to evaluate their expertise. Having said this, there are many reputable academics who write blogs, and it can be worthwhile for students to follow these blogs.

Academic blogs fall into two categories: those used by individuals to discuss important or emerging topics in their fields and those used by groups or teams to provide updates on the progress of research projects. One example of the first is kept by respected neuroscientist, Dorothy Bishop, who often uses her blog to critique science journalism and discuss wider questions relating to neuroscience or to child language development. Professor Bishop also argues that academic blogs are useful for 'post publication peer-review' (Bishop, 2013). This is an important point because a shortcoming of traditional journal publishing is that the process of disputing published work can take a long time. In this process, a new paper needs to be written, reviewed, and published in a journal, which can take up to two years. Bishop's argument came about because in her blog she critiqued a study published in a high-impact journal. She argued that the sample size was too small to justify the conclusions drawn by the authors. The study authors responded in the comments, saying that the proper route for critique was in the journal itself, preferably by conducting a second study to establish whether the findings could be replicated. However, this represents a major undertaking requiring both funding and time. Bishop's point is that the blog allows fast publication of a response and for discussion of the paper. The fact that the study authors responded to Bishop's post supports the validity of her argument. For academics this type of debate is challenging and exciting. Some, for example Moriarty (2013), argue that the commenting process should be taken further: that comment tools should be made available within online journals and the comments should be citable. For students, especially those at or below undergraduate level, online academic debate whether through blogs or Twitter, can introduce potentially confusing new levels. Many tutors state that only peer-reviewed academic journals should be trusted, yet in this example academic staff are publically questioning the process of peer review in practice. In addition, this questioning and subsequent discussion takes place via a medium (a blog) which students may have been told to distrust.

Student work

A considerable amount of assessed student work involves the use of technology. Coursework may take the form of essays or reports which normally need to be word-processed and may be submitted electronically, increasingly via text matching software such as Turnitin.

Plagiarism and Turnitin

Plagiarism and other forms of malpractice are matters of immense concern in higher education institutions, which is why the use of software such as Turnitin is now so widespread. Turnitin is an example of similarity-checking software in which documents are submitted and checked against a database which includes all previously submitted texts, and against a range of online texts including websites and academic journals. The submitted document is given a 'similarity score' which indicates how much of the text is similar to other sources. A high similarity index does not necessarily constitute evidence of plagiarism; if students have been asked to write on the same topic or using the same source material then there will be a natural level of similarity between assignments with key words or phrases occurring in several pieces of work. A suspicious Turnitin report needs to be interpreted by an academic staff member because 'suspicious' in this context would be difficult to define. Turnitin colour codes similarity reports, using blue (0%), progressing through green (<25%), yellow (25–49%) and orange (50–74%) to red (>74%). A red score looks clearly suspicious, but could simply indicate that a student has resubmitted a piece of work that had previously failed and has now been revised. Even a low score, coded green, may contain plagiarism if, on examination, the matching text is in one block that has been copied without attribution. Those working in institutions where Turnitin is used will be accustomed to students asking which score triggers an investigation. There is no simple answer; Turnitin does not, in itself, identify plagiarism, but simply makes it easier to track down the source(s) of plagiarized text.

Turnitin in institutions

There is varying practice with regard to student use of Turnitin. In some institutions it is viewed as a training tool with students encouraged to check their work before final submission whilst in others students are not allow to see Turnitin reports. Students may express concern about plagiarism, and electronic source material, such as online journals combined with modern writing tools, such as word processing, increase the likelihood of accidental plagiarism, i.e. inadvertently including copied text without intention to cheat. EAP teachers need to raise students' awareness of 'academic hygiene' at an early stage in the teaching programme. Good academic hygiene means recording bibliographic information alongside notes made when reading and making sure that copied text is clearly identified using a method such as changing the font colour. Summary is generally preferable to quotation, except in certain cases, such as comparing definitions or introducing concepts associated with an individual. With digital source texts students may naturally copy chunks of text into their notes as this is the fastest way to record important points. If copied text is a different colour then there is less risk that it will accidentally be copied again into the assignment, thereby leading to accidental plagiarism.

Collusion and purchasing assignments

There are types of plagiarism that are not picked up by text-matching software. These include collusion, and the purchasing of assignments. Collusion refers to the practice of receiving excessive help in writing an assignment, perhaps from another student, family member, or friend. This kind of help would leave no electronic trace, so would not be flagged up on Turnitin. Another problem is where students purchase assignments, typically from professional agencies or perhaps other students. Clearly, this is a form of academic dishonesty and, like collusion, would not be spotted by text-matching software.

Presentation tools

Student presentations are likely to involve the use of digital presentation tools such as PowerPoint or Prezi. Presentation visuals may be dependent on oral delivery or may need to stand alone, particularly if students are asked to create or upload online presentations for assessment. This is an important point for EAP tutors as it means that students need to learn how to structure and create stand-alone presentations. In these cases, some of the rules for oral presentations are reversed.

For example, a standard guideline for spoken presentations is that there should be a minimum amount of text on a slide because the audience cannot easily process spoken and written at the same time. If a presentation is to stand alone, the text needs to explain the argument in full, resulting in more content and structure than in a set of slides to support a live presentation. A list of bullet points is insufficient as these lack supporting contextual information. The text in this case may be only be written; as discussed in Chapter 8, a presentation or lecture may be multimodal and include audio, video and images. Unlike conventional academic texts, presentations need not be linear. With Prezi (www.prezi.com), for example, the user puts the elements into a path. Elements can be nested and also may appear more than once in the path. If the creator wants to take the viewer back to an earlier point, then the path can be designed to return to that section before moving to the next point. In addition, the nesting of elements allows each point to be presented in overview before the path zooms to the detail. There is a risk, though, that excessive movement between visual texts can cause viewers to feel physically uncomfortable, sometimes even inducing nausea. This can inhibit the viewer's ease of understanding. The important point, from a tutor's perspective, is that digital tools such as Prezi have added a new type of academic writing which is multimodal and fluid, and students need to be prepared for this.

Digital content in students' work

In many fields students may be asked to build a portfolio of evidence and, in most cases, this will consist of digital materials such as video, audio clips, photographs and text. Even where formal assessment does not include portfolios, students may be encouraged to create one so that there is a collection of evidence to show to a prospective employer. For example, Leeds University, in the UK, has a system called 'Leeds for Life' (<https://leedsforlife.leeds.ac.uk>). This is not part of the formal assessment procedures but is used to keep records of personal tutorial meetings and students are encouraged to add other material, for example, by recording voluntary work or student leadership roles. The idea is that, during the time that the student is at the university, the portfolio will become a resource that students can use when creating their CV and that tutors can use when writing references.

Wikis

Students may be asked to work online, for example using wikis, blogs, or **discussion boards**. Wikis contain 'articles', each with its own page, and a blog is another type of website which is edited by users. Generally speaking, blogs have 'posts' rather than 'articles' and the posts do not have individual pages but appear in a linear form with the most recent post at the top of the page, although most blog software archives posts by month which creates separate pages. Unlike wikis which are intrinsically collaborative, blogs may be authored individually, though there may be a group of authors. Where there are multiple authors, individual posts are usually written by one author, whereas a wiki page is usually written and edited by several authors. Both blogs and wikis are widely used in academic settings. Wikis may be used for any activity which requires collaborative writing, whilst blogs are particularly useful for situations where students might keep a diary or journal. Wiki articles always have associated 'talk' pages and blog posts have a facility for readers to add comments which means that both blogs and wikis can be used, to some extent, for discussion.

Discussion boards

Discussion boards, also known as 'forums' and 'conferences', are one of most long-established forms of online student work, having been in use since the 1990s. They can be found in most VLEs and are used for asynchronous discussions, i.e. where participants contribute at any time regardless of whether the other participants are online. **Text chat** and **virtual classrooms**, meanwhile, require all participants to be online together. Discussion boards may be used formally, with students expected and even required to make regular postings. Alternatively they may be used for less formal aspects of a course such as social interaction or student support. Where the boards are used formally then contributions may be assessed and count towards a student's final grade.

Social networking and digital footprints

Universities are tending to make greater use—both formally and informally—of social networking tools, such as Twitter and Facebook. Uses include for academic purposes, such as student discussions and group work, and for extra-curricular functions, such as organizing student society meetings. An unintended consequence is that students create a '**digital footprint**' The term 'digital footprint' refers to the online presence of an individual or institution, not only in their official website but also the trail that a person has created through interactions on social networking sites, online forums, newspaper comments and other online activities. In addition, the digital footprint will include things that other people have said about the individual. The easiest way to view a digital footprint is by entering someone's name into a popular search engines like Google. Although a digital footprint is not specifically related to academic study moving to study abroad, especially at tertiary level, is likely to lead to an increase in online interactions and therefore to creating or extending a digital footprint (Connaway et al 2013). Some universities are now starting to teach students how to manage a digital footprint to ensure that it gives a positive impression to prospective employers. EAP teachers can contribute to this management process by encouraging their students to avoid putting up controversial posts, such as comments on governments and corporations, or excessively personal posts, such as recollections of partying. By avoiding posts of this type, students can avoid creating a negative digital footprint, which may put off potential employers.

MOOCs

Massive open online courses (MOOCs) are a relatively recent development in higher education. MOOCs tend to be free or relatively low cost and are generally open to any student without pre-requisite qualifications or a formal application procedure. Typically, MOOCs do not offer certification or accreditation. Some people, for example Boxall (2012) claim that MOOCs constitute a disruptive force that can change the nature of higher education by removing current barriers to traditional university-level study, such as cost and qualifications. Certainly, early MOOCs have been extremely popular, especially when provided by world-famous institutions such as Stanford or Massachusetts Institute of Technology (MIT). An argument against MOOCs is that the provision of free university education to anyone who is interested will decrease the role and importance traditional fee-charging universities. However, it is these traditional universities who mainly provide the content for MOOCs, and ultimately the academic and support staff required to run the courses need to be paid. The MOOC model of education is based on providing resources for students to organize their own study. There are no formal assessments to be marked by tutors, no individual feedback from tutors and very little, if any, contact with academic staff. This type of learning can suit students who are highly motivated and driven by a desire to learn rather than to gain a qualification. These students, though, are probably in a tiny minority. Furthermore, whilst distance study suits some learning styles, many students prefer the environment and personal contact of a campus-based course. Current research (Jordan 2013; Parr 2013) shows that MOOC completion rates are extremely low (the best is 19%) which suggests that universities are not yet at risk from MOOCs. At the moment, it is not clear how widespread MOOCs will become and what their impact will be on HE, but it remains a development to watch.

Mobile learning (m-learning)

At the leading edge of technology and study is the use of mobile and portable devices, i.e. smartphones and tablet computers. Some institutions and even countries go as far as to equip all students with a particular model of phone or tablet which allows the institution to make far greater use of mobile learning and/ or assessment. Institutional forms of **m-learning** include apps related to general aspects of study, such as access to a VLE via a smartphone or tablet, such as Blackboard Mobile Learn. There may also be apps related to a particular subject area, possibly even tailored to a particular course (see for example Coulby et al. 2010). Some types of interactive digital books fall into this category, especially if they have been written for an individual programme of study. Students who own smartphones or tablets are likely to use them for listening to audio files or for watching video, and tutors may make use of this by supplying course material as m-friendly audio '**podcasts**' or video '**vodcasts**'. Smartphones are also used as a person's primary means of accessing social networking sites. Some tutors make use of this, for example, by asking students to post or to tweet comments and responses during a lecture. However, m-learning is currently a developing field and practices differ widely, even within a single institution, which makes engaging with m-learning less straightforward than using more established digital tools such as VLEs. It is very likely, for example, that an EAP student's final study destination will have a VLE and an online library (and so EAP teachers can prepare students for this), whereas it is difficult to accurately predict how much or what type of m-learning may be in use. There may be an overlap between desk-based technology use and m-learning, and this is likely to continue with a shift towards dominance of mobile devices in the future.

Technologies as resources for teaching EAP skills

Technologies provide resources that can be used not only for teaching 'new' study skills but also for teaching traditional EAP skills. This section explores some of the resources that are available to teachers and some of the ways in which they might be used.

Learning management systems

As it is likely that students will encounter Learning Management Systems (LMSs) or VLEs in their further studies it may be useful to introduce this way of working into the EAP classroom. In addition, an LMS can be a convenient way of tying together digital resources and tasks. Some EAP tutors may be based in institutions that already have a VLE or LMS such as Blackboard or Moodle. For those who do not, there are free alternatives such as Edmodo (<http://www.edmodo.com>) or Coursesites (<https://www.coursesites.com>).

Text handling and citation management

The internet, in itself, provides a vast range of written material which can be used for developing reading skills at any level. Citation management tools are valuable for academic work at any level but can also be used in the teaching of academic reading skills. Socially-oriented tools such as CiteULike (<http://www.citeulike.org>) and Bibsonomy (<http://www.bibsonomy.org>) allow people to create shared bibliographies. In a social bibliography users 'tag' entries, which means that they identify key words that express the overall topics of a text. Tags can be used to group entries and also as a way of searching for texts on specific topics. Key words are also widely used in journal abstracts, and students can learn to search for relevant material using such words.

When using a citation manager, there is a page or record for each individual text. This contains fields for bibliographic information such as author names, publication date, title of journal and other information, including the abstract, notes, and tags. Citations can be added manually or may be exported from the journal to the citation manager. For example, many online journals include a facility to export a reference to management tools like CiteULike, so the bibliographic information and abstract may be added to the record automatically.

A useful task is for students to create records manually in order to gain practice at finding bibliographic information.

Another activity would be to make use of the tags. For example, students could be given a set of abstracts and a set of tags and be asked to match the texts to the tags. Alternatively, students can read an abstract, or even a full paper, and suggest tags which can then be compared to tags that other readers have given to the same paper. In this task, different tags are not necessarily wrong; it may be that another reader has a different interpretation of the paper or has read it with a different focus.

Word clouds

A word cloud creator such as Wordle (www.wordle.net) produces an image made from the words in a text. The more frequently a word occurs in a text, the larger it appears in the word cloud image. These services are simple to use; all that it is necessary is to copy and paste text into the service and the word cloud will be created. Figure 12.1 shows a word cloud of an early draft of this chapter. In EAP contexts, a word cloud can have two main uses. The first is for the teaching of reading. The word cloud provides an overview of a text. The cloud could be used either as a pre-reading activity or students could be asked to quickly read a text and then create a word cloud to see if it matches their understanding of the salient points. The second use of a word cloud is in the teaching of academic writing. By pasting their text into the cloud creator, students can see at a glance what words occur frequently in their work. The word cloud might show that something that the student thinks is a vital point has been barely mentioned whilst something that is of little importance occurs several times. A word cloud can also help students to see when they are overusing idiosyncratic words which extend the length of a text without necessarily adding meaning.

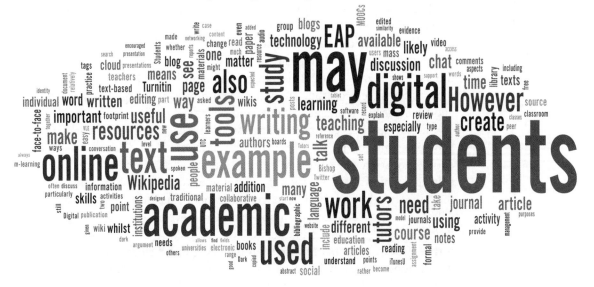

Figure 12.1   Chapter 12 word cloud

Figure 12.1, for example, shows the two hundred words that occurred most frequently in the draft of this chapter, excluding extremely common words such as 'the', 'and' or 'is'. Given the chapter topic of technology, a pre-reading activity might predict that the most common words might include 'computer', 'internet', 'smartphone' and 'tablet'. In reality, the word cloud shows that 'students' is by far the most frequent word, with well over 100 instances of 'student' and 'students'. This is an understandable and perhaps satisfying finding as it indicates that the emphasis of the chapter appears to be on students rather than technology i.e. how *people* can use the tools to support learning rather than what the *devices* can do. The word cloud also shows a reasonable amount of hedging in the chapter; words such as 'may' and 'likely' occur frequently. In this chapter, uncertainty is appropriate because technology is in a constant state of change and what suits one context may not fit another. There is also an enthusiasm for the adverbs 'however' and 'also', which perform useful discourse management functions and do not simply function as 'filler' words.

Wikis and real-time collaborative writing

Wiki tools are available with some VLEs and there are a number of websites providing wikis for educators, for example Wikispaces (<http://www.wikispaces.com>). Some education blog sites, for example Edublogs (edublogs.org) also allow users to create wikis. In education settings, wikis may be used for group projects or for other collaborative activities, such as creating a group or class resource bank. The history function of a wiki makes the tool particularly useful for assessed projects as it enables a tutor to see exactly which portions of a text have been contributed by each group member. This should lead to all members of the group contributing, as a 'silent' member can easily be identified.

The fact that wikis are becoming relatively common in Higher Education is, in itself, a strong argument for using them in the EAP classroom. They are also useful in their own right as tools for collaborative writing. All users of the wiki can create and edit text and use the 'talk' feature to explain and justify their choices. Many students do not like editing each other's work, or having their work edited by others. This means that collaborative writing tasks need to be set up with care so that students feel that they are part of a community engaged in a shared enterprise and that it is both safe, acceptable, and beneficial to change text written by each other. EAP teachers can point out to students that editing the work of other people is common practice in wikis, as Wikipedia itself demonstrates. Tutors can also demonstrate use of the talk/discussion pages to describe, explain, and justify editing decisions so that other group members can understand the reasons behind the edits. In addition, EAP teachers can explain that editing someone's work in a wiki is not a personal criticism but that ideas develop through shared thinking and discussion and also that students may be expected to do this kind of work in their further studies. Tutors can discuss and agree ground rules with students, which itself can be a useful wiki-based preparatory task, so that they understand how to engage in shared editing critically but respectfully.

Real-time writing tools

Generally speaking, wikis can only be used asynchronously, so their main use is for contexts where students are not expected to be online simultaneously. However, there are writing tools designed for real-time collaboration. Examples of these include Google Docs, Etherpad-based tools such as TitanPad <http://titanpad.com>), and PrimaryPad (<http://primarypad.com>). With Google Docs each user has an individual account. A user creates a document and then shares it with other people; sharing can be read-only or with editing privileges. Any author can work on the document alone, in which case the document works in a similar way to a wiki, but if more than one user is working at the same time then all authors can contribute and a chat window can be opened for synchronous discussion whilst editing the text.

Google Docs is an excellent choice for professional collaborative word-processing, but for educational purposes, especially classroom-based activities, it may be better to choose one of the Etherpad alternatives. With TitanPad, for example, there is no need to create a document and share it. Instead one author or the tutor creates an online 'pad', i.e. a writing space, and sends a link to other authors. There is no need for anyone, except perhaps the tutor, to create an account. Each author's text is highlighted in a different colour so that it is easy to identify each person's contributions and to see changes as they happen. There is also a chat window so that authors can discuss the text as they work on it. Walker and White (2013: 65) suggest that Etherpad tools can be used for one-to-one writing tutorials. Tutors can model editing by, for example, revising a paragraph so that it has a clear structure, explaining what they are doing and then asking students to revise a different paragraph in the same way. Students can use Etherpad to work collaboratively on writing tasks in real time, using the chat window to discuss the task as they write. By doing this, they can gain the benefits of collaboration in the writing and editing of their work, while the discussion itself involves articulating thoughts in writing. The tutor can use the text of the conversation to see what alternative ideas students have discussed, for example, with regard to structuring the text or choice of language, which may provide useful evidence for future teaching points, including text-based chat, which is discussed later in this chapter.

iTunesU and YouTubeEDU

iTunesU is provided by Apple.com as a platform for educational material including video, audio, digital books, and assignments. Content is free and the range of providers includes some illustrious universities such as Oxford, Stanford, and MIT and other institutions including libraries. There are various reasons why institutions make content available in this way: for some it is to provide samples of their courses, whilst for others, it is part of a commitment to open educational resources. For some institutions, iTunesU and/or YouTube EDU are easy ways to make content available to their own students. Whatever the reasons, iTunesU and YouTubeEDU both provide a rich resource of free material covering a wide range of subjects. Oxford iTunes (<http://itunes.ox.ac.uk>), for example, has more than 3,000 contributors, including many world-famous academics, who have provided video and audio material on subjects as diverse as 'The chemistry of the Botanic Garden' and 'Approaching Shakespeare'. Oxford iTunes also offers electronic books including Shakespeare's *First Folio*. Material obtained through iTunesU or YouTube EDU is presented by tutors from all over the world, thereby giving students exposure to many different accents and presentational techniques. This provides an invaluable set of resources that EAP tutors can use to help students develop academic reading and listening skills.

Academic discussions: Wikipedia and academic blogs

The Wikipedia article on 'dark matter' is also a useful resource for teaching EAP speaking skills. Whilst it may be relatively easy for students to practise general speaking in the classroom, it is harder to understand and practise the ways in which people speak in academic conversations. Many online academic conversations exist, and the talk page of 'dark matter' is an excellent example. For instance, the conversation below comes after some selections have been quoted from various websites.

> Quoted from the same article, one is the university source, the other is a notable science website. There are dozens more available through a quick search.

> Basically, they've proven that there is absolutely no predictable relationship between luminosity and mass, and they contend "dark matter" is most likely just "matter" that we can't see from Earth. — Preceding unsigned comment added by 71.60.33.136 (talk) 12:07, 19 September 2012 (UTC)

> You say "they've proven that there is absolutely no predictable relationship between luminosity and mass". I don't see where that comes from – the study seems to conclude that the relationship is more complex than was previously assumed, not that there is no relationship at all. I also can't see anything in these references that supports your assertion that the study concludes that dark matter is mostly baryonic. Gandalf61 (talk) 12:52, 19 September 2012 (UTC)

> I'll second Gandalf61's comment. They've adjusted the old model for estimating galaxy mass– a straight luminosity-to-mass ratio – and made a more complex model where different classes of galaxy have different luminosity-to-mass ratio. That has nothing to do with dark matter – and the vast majority of mass in all of these galaxies is still dark matter (dark matter is about 90% of galactic mass, and the updated estimates change by at most a factor of 3).

> The noteworthy elements from this work were a) an improved understanding of how luminosity relates to galaxy type (obvious in hindsight; galaxies with more star formation for a given mass will have more bright but short-lived stars), and b) improved techniques for measuring the mass and mass distribution within galaxies (by measuring the velocity distributions of stars at different locations within the galaxies, if I understand correctly).

Per Gandalf61, these releases say nothing at all about the nature of dark matter and very little about its distribution, so it's puzzling that you'd cite them as support for your position. --Christopher Thomas (talk) 20:36, 19 September 2012 (UTC)

(<http://en.wikipedia.org/wiki/Talk:Dark_matter> accessed 10 April 2013)

In many respects this conversation could have been recorded from a live discussion at a conference or in an academic seminar rather than typed online. Subject-specific language is used in conjunction with everyday expressions and general academic language in a similar way to face-to-face academic conversations, for example: 'I don't see where that comes from—the study seems to conclude that the relationship is more complex than was previously assumed'. The comments following the blogpost by Dorothy Bishop on 'Blogging as post-publication peer review' show similar characteristics, for example:

Pete Etchells 22 March 2013 09:54

The authors cite various (excellent) papers by Bavelier and colleagues regarding transfer of perceptual learning from game playing to other areas. However, as EJ Wagenmakers notes in this paper

(http://www.ejwagenmakers.com/submitted/DonGaming.pdf), this is actually a highly surprising effect – normally we only see context-specific perceptual learning effects. As such, the jury's out at the moment as to whether playing action video games does indeed confer benefits in other domains. We need much more solid evidence before assuming that they do

(<http://deevybee.blogspot.co.uk/2013/03/blogging-as-post-publication-peer.html?showComment=1363946093941#c8708682655819854858> accessed 23 May 2013)

Apart from the link to the paper by Wagenmakers, this is clearly part of a conversation which could have been either spoken or written. Online academic debates such as these show authentic uses of informal academic language; the samples have not been created for the use of language learners and thus provide useful resources for EAP tutors who want to demonstrate use of informal interactive academic language in context.

Text chat and virtual classrooms

Students can have an opportunity to practise academic discussion using synchronous text-based chat, in a simple chat room or in a virtual classroom such as Adobe Connect, (<http://www.adobe.com/uk/products/adobeconnect.html>) or WizIQ, (<http://www.wiziq.com>). These take place in a form that is slower than face-to-face conversation, and so provides time for consideration before sending. Text-based chat is particularly useful for less confident students as it allows them to express their opinions without worrying about pronunciation. Pronunciation remains important, but it is normal in international academic contexts for speakers to have a wide range of accents and effective communication is more important than sounding like a native speaker. However, some students may be inhibited by fear of sounding incorrect; text-based chat can relieve some of this pressure. Certainly, the evidence shows that quieter and less confident students are more likely to contribute to a text-based online discussion than to a normal spoken discussion (Warschauer, 1996).

Text-based chat requires participants to express their points in *writing* which means that such resources may serve as a useful bridge between spoken and written academic communication. It is important to establish ground rules for text-based chats, for example, that participants should be respectful and constructive when challenging each other, such as when asking for justification by providing supporting examples or evidence. In many disciplines these are important academic skills in both speech and writing, so it is very useful to be able to practise them in the safe and controlled environment of online text-based discussions. Furthermore, text-based chat tools automatically create a written record of the conversation which can be used as a reference or as material for further teaching. For example, one activity with a chat transcript might be for students to look for all the ways that disagreement was expressed or all the expressions used to introduce supporting evidence and then think of alternative options.

Another benefit of online text-based chat is for students who come from writing cultures whose academic style is different from English-language academic writing. For example, as Koutsantoni (2005) points out, Greek academic writing values a high level of formality and Greek writers 'command the respect of their colleagues by displaying the ability to use elaborate forms of expression' (Kousantoni 2005: 122). Many academic staff prefer their students' academic writing to be clear and direct, which can pose difficulties for students who have learned that academic writing should be intricate rather than simple.

A further point is that such written discussions can aid fluency. Although it is likely to be slower than speech, text-based chat can speed up writing in that students have to write quickly in order to get their points in before the discussion moves on. This process favours simpler writing, as there is little time for longer, more elaborate language. The same is true for using **microblogging** services such as Twitter: if an idea has to be expressed in 140 characters then it must be succinct.

Mind-mapping

Mind-mapping is a useful technique for both reading and writing. Mind-mapping involves putting down ideas in visual form, such as a spidergram or any personalized form. It can be used when reading to make and organize notes and then for planning and organizing ideas when writing. There are a number of digital tools for mind-mapping, some of which are designed to run on a personal computer, for example Freemind (< http://freemind.sourceforge.net>) or a tablet, for example MindMaple (<http://www.mindmaple.com>), whilst others are intended for online use, such as Bubbl.us (< https://bubbl.us/) or Popplet (<http://popplet.com>). Some have alternative modes such as online use or as a tablet app.

Online mind-mapping software can often be used collaboratively so that students can work together to create mind maps. Many mind-mapping tools allow fairly substantial amounts of text to be added to map branches as notes. The map can then be exported as a text file, which means that a map which started as notes for planning an assignment can become the nucleus of an essay. Figure 12.2 shows a mind map of the plan for this chapter (made with Bubbl.us).

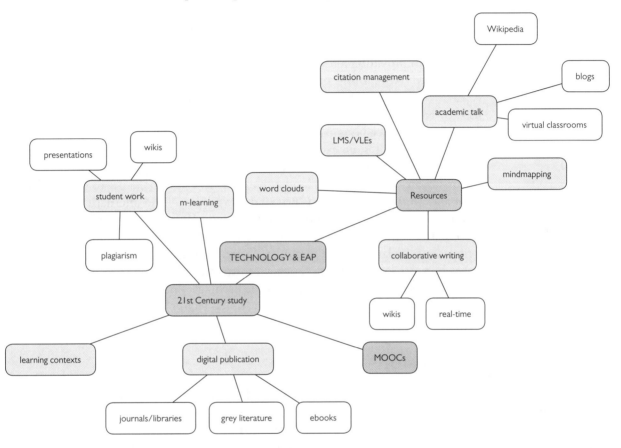

Figure 12.2   Mind map of the plan for this chapter

Quiz-making

Quiz-making software enables tutors to develop banks of questions to use in different tasks including reading/listening comprehension and grammar/vocabulary practice. For example, Quizlet (<http://quizlet.com>) allows users to create digital 'flashcards' that can be read, for example for revision, or used in 'test' mode as multiple-choice questions. These are perfect for activities such as vocabulary development. However, Quizlet is not only for teachers. Students can create their own flashcard sets either for personal use or to challenge each other in a class activity. This can be a real help to EAP tutors in multi-discipline classes where students are studying a wide range of subjects. For example, engineering students can create flashcards for their own specialized vocabulary whilst their classmates who are studying sociology can make resources appropriate to their own discipline. Alternative quizmakers include Quizstar (<http://quizstar.4teachers. org>) and Yacapaca (<http://yacapaca.com>).

Keeping up to date

Digital technology is in a continual state of development and change. Useful tools regularly appear, and may disappear equally quickly, or providers may decide to change from providing a resource for free to charging a fee. An example of this is Ning (<http://www.ning.com>): a platform for creating a social network. Until April 2010, Ning was free for educational purposes and had become very widely used by educators. When the site owners suddenly decided to move to a full subscription service Ning users either had to pay or to find an alternative platform. Ning was, and still is, an excellent site for teachers to create an easy and secure network for their classes—the tools include video/audio upload, online chat and discussion areas—but it is no longer free. Teachers who make use of technology want and need to know what is new and also where to find alternatives if their favourite resources are closed down or become unaffordable. The best way to keep up to date with technology is to follow some of the many education bloggers who write about the latest digital resources. Current good examples are José Picardo (www.boxoftricks.net) or Nik Peachey (<http://www.scoop.it/u/technogogy>). Twitter is another useful resource and the hashtags '#edtech' and '#langtech' are used to identify posts related to educational technology and language technology respectively.

Conclusion

Technology has made major changes to the way that course materials are presented and the way that students, in turn, are expected to prepare and submit their work. Without doubt, digital tools have changed the ways that tutors and students work and have made study more accessible and more fluid. There are fewer boundaries between 'study time' and 'non-study time' as tutors may create online activities for students to work on outside formal class times or may tweet additional resources for students. However, the basic skills and language needed for study in English remain relatively unchanged. An argument needs to be well-structured and coherently expressed, whether it is delivered in an essay or a multimodal presentation. Students still need to be able to listen to, understand, and remember academic information; they still need to read and interpret academic texts, and they still need to be able to express themselves in appropriate spoken and written language.

Further reading

Gillett, A. *Using English for Academic Purposes* (an online guide) (<http://www.uefap.com>)

Richardson, W.H. 2010. *Blogs, wikis, Podcasts and other Powerful Web Tools or Classrooms. Thousand Oaks, California: Corwin and London: Sage.*

Stanley, G. *2013. Language Learning with Technology: Ideas for Integrating Technology in the Classroom. Cambridge: Cambridge University Press.*

Walker A. and White G. *2013. Technology Enhanced Language Learning: Connecting Theory and Practice Oxford: Oxford University Press.*

CONCLUSION

This book has aimed to set out the field of EAP, starting from its early beginnings and ongoing influences, moving through teaching and learning in EAP in broad terms into in-depth exploration of its principle elements—language and critical thinking, skills, materials, assessment, and technologies. The discussions in these areas have been grounded in current theories and research, so that these can be applied to current EAP approaches and practice in a principled way. The material has illustrated the diversity and complexity of the field, and offered opportunities for reflection, application, and personalization.

These discussions have also shown that EAP is very much a work in progress: in its relatively short history the field of EAP has undergone significant changes, and is continuing its rapid development in response to local needs informed by diverse influences and new technologies. To varying degrees, such influences have informed and impacted on EAP in a very wide range of global contexts through people, publications, and practices, which have paved the way for the issues discussed in EAP today to emerge, such as the general-specific debate and approaches to the teaching and learning of skills, critical thinking, and language. By bringing together theory and practice through EAP influences, issues, and approaches, this book provides the opportunity for EAP teachers to reflect on their current practices and consider their current and future approaches in an informed way. Additionally, the discussions have brought out many commonalities between EAP students and teachers: in many instances there are similarities in what EAP students and teachers need to be able to do. The student focus in the skills chapters has underlined these commonalities.

I hope and trust that, in the light of the discussions in this book, EAP teachers can be stimulated to extend their knowledge and expertise in the field, innovate further in their practice, and build stronger links to other practitioners in academic life. As Chapter 1 notes, opportunities in the field of EAP are rapidly emerging around the world, and with their expertise EAP teachers can capitalize on these opportunities and positively influence individual students, institutions, and the wider educational and professional world.

APPENDIX

Text 1: Chapter 3

The number 700,000 is often cited in articles and editorials about science politics and economic development as an estimate of the number of scientists, technicians and engineers that the European Union will need by 2010 to keep up its current rate of growth. There might be some questions about how the figure is reached, but the message is clear: the European economies face a huge deficit of the trained people needed to sustain modern knowledge-based economies.

The problem of the availability of skilled personnel worries policy-makers worldwide, who solve it in different ways. Scientific research in the USA depends massively on young scientists from abroad who are attracted by the excellent reputation of US university education and research, and by the chance of finding a well-paid job. China and India are training a large number of scientists and engineers, and expect that there will be enough jobs for them once they graduate. There are similar plans in South American countries—notably Brazil and Mexico—that, in time, will also be able to retain their researchers. Smaller countries, such as Singapore, are also investing in high-tech industries and are becoming increasingly successful at attracting talented researchers from other countries. **Clearly the demand for trained scientists and engineers is increasing worldwide.**

This is good news for all students in science and engineering, and yet these subjects are not the first choice for most students now working towards their high-school graduation. **It is therefore worthwhile to reflect on this lack of interest in science, because the projected deficit in manpower will ultimately strangle economic development and delay the process of discovery and invention.**

Some of the problem might originate from the fact that science is often presented in an unattractive way, akin to focusing on grammar when learning a foreign language. It is therefore necessary to develop a more attractive mix of 'edutainment' and solid science to engage school children …

Another fact that discourages students from science is the widespread perception that the salaries of scientists are very low compared with those of medical doctors, lawyers or bankers, for example. Although this is true at the PhD and postdoctoral level, in advanced economies, scientists at the top professional level are well paid. Once students have finished their PhD training—which admittedly takes longer than the training for some other professions—they find a welcoming international marketplace that offers competitive salaries; but nobody seems to know that.

Worse still, the salaries of experienced researchers who reach the level of group leader or professor are rarely reported. The potential student is therefore left with the image of an impoverished career in science driven solely by the quest for knowledge …

(Extracts from **Gannon, F. 2008. 'The pipeline.'** *EMBO reports* 9/1.1. doi:10.1038/sj.embor.7401156. London: Nature Publishing.)

Text 2: Chapter 4

Intelligence: heredity versus environment

Various attempts have been made to explain where intelligence comes from. In the nineteenth and twentieth centuries the essential argument of heredity versus environment emerged. These terms are often known as 'nature' and 'nurture' respectively. Essentially the arguments are concerned with the extent to which intelligence is inherited through the genes a person is born with (heredity, or nature), or formed through a person's life and their surroundings (environment, or nurture).

These theories led to the concept of how to measure intelligence. Early attempts at measuring intelligence (e.g. Galton 1869) associated it with social inequalities. According to this point of view, the role of environmental factors had to be recognized alongside the part played by heredity. This work led to the construction of IQ (intelligence quotient) tests to measure intelligence. The measurement of IQ originated in the work of the statistician Spearman (1904), who introduced the concept of 'g' (general intelligence) to describe the general cognitive ability that he thought lay behind specific abilities and forms of intelligence (linguistic, mathematical, spatial, musical, etc.). The development of these tests seemed to promise the possibility that the relationship between material inequalities and social inequalities could be studied with mathematical precision.

Arguments that link inherited intelligence to social disadvantage rest on several assumptions, including:

- General intelligence (g) is a cognitive ability that underlies all other specific forms of intelligence and can be accurately measured by IQ tests.

- Measures of social advantage and disadvantage correlate highly with measures of general intelligence. Because the distribution of advantages and disadvantages reflects the distribution of intelligence, it can be seen as determined by differences in general intelligence.

- Intelligence is genetically determined. It is, therefore, fixed from birth: education and other environmental factors have little or no effect on the level of intelligence.

Each of these assumptions can be questioned. The concept of general intelligence has been heavily criticized, and there is no agreement that there is any such common factor behind particular abilities. Mathematical and verbal intelligence, for example, are not perfectly associated with one another. It may be more useful to regard intelligence as a set of intellectual capacities rather than a single one. Even if it is allowed that general intelligence exists, however, there is the problem of how it is to be measured.

Many have questioned the value of the IQ score as a measure of intelligence. Tests have been shown to be culturally biased towards Western (American and European) culture and, within this, towards white, middle-class men. The cultural differences that shape the ability to perform in the tests do not necessarily reflect any differences in intelligence. More fundamentally, perhaps, there are doubts about whether performance in pencil-and-paper tests can be a proper measure of a person's ability to perform in 'real' situations. Indeed, there are wider doubts about whether performance in A-level, degree, or other examinations is an adequate measure of a person's understanding of a subject or ability to apply it in real-life situations.

Intelligence is a complex process that brings together numerous aspects of brain function, and doubts have been raised about its genetic basis. It is inherited not as a fixed quantity but as a capacity to learn the kinds of skills and understandings that make up a particular ability. The realization of this capacity depends on the stimulation that is received in the first few years of life and, to a much lesser extent, in later life. It has been found that pre-school, primary socialization is critical in raising or lowering measured intelligence. Formal education can have a continuing, if smaller, effect, and educational action programmes can significantly raise the IQ of children who enter them with relatively low IQ. Cross-cultural studies have shown that the relatively high IQ of East Asians, as compared with North Americans, is due to the length and type of schooling, the extent of parental support, and the cultural support for disciplined work.

(**Fulcher, J.** and **J. Scott.** *Sociology 4e.* Oxford: Oxford University Press: 731–2.)

GLOSSARY

Only those items which have a special or technical meaning in ELT and EAP have been included here. Terms which have an accessible dictionary definition are not included. The definitions provided reflect their usage within this book; some terms may be used in other ways by other authors.

abstract: The text at the beginning of an academic article which summarizes the whole article, typically 100–200 words; abstracts are also available and searchable separately

academic staff: Teachers, lecturers, professors, and researchers in the disciplines

the academy: Tertiary academic contexts, usually taken to be universities, and the academic staff working in them

anaphoric: Referring back in a text to an item previously mentioned

analysis: Detailed examination of information or statistics, especially the results of research, in order to understand and classify it

antonym: A word with an opposite meaning to another word

apposition/appositive: Part of a complete noun phrase in which a noun phrase is added directly after the head noun, separated by a comma. The appositive, i.e. the second noun phrase, refers to the same entity as the head noun and adds identifying information to it. All parts are analysed as a complete noun phrase.

argument: A written or spoken discussion based on reason, logic, and evidence; an argument can be the main argument or a supporting argument

article: A type of text which presents facts and argument

association: A connection between two things where one is affected or influenced by the other in some way, especially one shown by research

audience: All the people who are likely to read a particular book or article, or attend a lecture or presentation

authenticity: In relation to a text: a text that has not been changed, adapted, reworded, or simplified; it can however be cut, i.e. extracts from the text can be used and these remain authentic. In relation to a task, a task that reflects real-life practice, which in EAP means academic practice, such as making notes while reading.

biased: Showing a tendency to favour a particular perspective or point of view; not presenting all sides of something fairly

blended learning: A mixture of face-to-face and virtual teaching and learning

blog: A type of website that is easy to edit and which contains posts (items) in chronological order; particularly useful for diaries and journals. A blend of 'web' + 'log'

case: A set of arguments and evidence intended to persuade others

case study: A detailed study of a particular situation, person, or group, especially over a period of time

cataphoric: Referring forward in a text to an item that will be mentioned

citation: A *summary*, *paraphrase*, or *quotation* which is from a source text

claim: The main point which the writer or speaker is trying to convince their audience of

clause: A grammatical unit which normally contains a subject, verb, and other parts of a sentence; a sentence may contain one clause, or two or more joined together using a coordinator or subordinator

coherence: How a text is connected in terms of meaning and ideas

cohesion: How a text is connected in terms of meaning and language

cohesive noun phrase: Carefully chosen noun phrases used to coherently link text, by encoding (summarising, labelling, evaluating) a previous stretch of discourse, and moving the text forward

cohort: The group of students who make up an intake, academic year group, or other group; often divided into smaller groups such as classes

collocation: Two words which frequently occur together

commentary: A written description or explanation to go with, for example, a graph or diagram

conference proceedings: A written report of the presentations given at a conference, published later, which can be read by a wider audience

construct validity: The measure of a test's fitness to measure the traits under investigation

content word: (see *lexical word*)

criterion-referenced (testing): An approach to presenting test scores which state a student's performance in relation to prepared statements or standards describing achievement on the test, or criteria

criticality: Relating to *critical thinking* practices

critical questions: Questions asked about the information given in a text or presentation in order to test how reliable or accurate it is

critical response: A written or spoken *evaluation* of a text, giving a subjective, evidence-based assessment of the ideas in the text; a critical response can include positive comments and/or criticisms (also known as a critique or *review*)

critical thinking: The state of mind and practice of challenging assumptions and making connections across entities and propositions through such processes as analysis, synthesis, evaluation, and creativity

curriculum: The educational programme which sets out what students are expected to learn. It typically states the aims, content, and assessments, and is realized in practice through the *syllabus* and *schemes of work*.

deductive: A language teaching approach which presents rules and patterns before students put them into practice; also, an approach to research and finding new information which uses an idea or *hypothesis* as a starting point which is then tested (see also *inductive*)

delivery: The way a speaker gives a lecture or presentation, including the speed, volume and clarity of their speech

digital footprint: The type of information that a websearch will produce about an individual or institution. May include webpages, tweets, Facebook mentions and any other information that is available online.

direct (testing): Assessment tasks that replicate 'real-life' performance as closely as possible, e.g. to assess a student's ability to understand a lecture a direct test would require students to listen to and take notes from a live lecture

discipline / in the disciplines: Relating to the academic departments in which students follow their programme of study. EAP programmes aim to enable students to study effectively in English in the disciplines.

discussion board: An online page, sometimes within a VLE, that allows asynchronous discussion, i.e. discussion at different times. Posts are usually 'threaded', i.e. replies are shown below the original topic. Normally, users need to be logged in to post but do not need to be online at the same time as each other.

e-reader: A device for reading electronic books. Tablets and smartphones may have e-reader software.

essential element: The major components of texts which are informed by the purpose of the text, e.g. cause, *citation*, *evaluation*.

ethnographic: Relating to qualitative research of people and their culture

evaluation: The writer's or speaker's subjective, evidence-based response to an idea in the text

evidence: Facts, information, statistics, arguments, or other material which show that a particular statement or argument is true or valid

exophoric: Referring to an item outside a text

expository: Explaining, describing, or defining something

fact: A piece of information which is widely accepted to be true because it can be proven

flipped classroom: An approach to learning in which students have the responsibility for initially learning about the topic outside the classroom, followed by classroom time which is used for face-to-face discussion, clarification, and other enquiry-based tasks

function word: A word, e.g. preposition, which expresses grammatical meaning, rather than meaning related to content (compare with *lexical word*)

generic language: Language which can express a wide range of meanings such as introducing definitions and describing characteristics, and which can be used in any discipline, e.g. '*X may be defined as …*'

genre: A particular type of written or spoken text with its own features, related to the audience and purpose of the text

genre analysis: The study of and research into genres, for example to identify typical organizational patterns and language which tend to occur across multiple samples of a particular genre; these descriptions can then be used in learning materials aimed at students who need to understand and/or produce the genre

grey literature: Literature which is published outside the academic system of books and peer-reviewed journals. Includes government documents, charity reports, newspapers, websites, blogs, Twitter, and Wikipedia

head noun: The main noun in a noun phrase around which other information can be added

hedge/hedging: The language and academic practice of 'softening' statements

hyponym: A type or example of something else, e.g. 'elephant' and 'mouse' are hyponyms of 'mammal', which is the *superordinate*

hypothesis: An idea which is based on existing evidence but which needs further evidence and research to be *validated*

indirect (testing): Tests which do not aim to replicate the real-life task directly, but in relation to traits, e.g. an indirect test of a student's ability to cope with lectures might be based on short recordings with multiple-choice listening comprehension items to test word stress, sentence stress, intonation, vocabulary, accent, lexis, and grammar

inductive: A language teaching approach which presents examples of language in use, e.g. through texts, which students use to look for rules and patterns; also, an approach to research and finding new information which involves gathering data without any preconceived question or idea as to what the data may show (see also *deductive*)

interactive whiteboard: (IWB) electronic version of the whiteboard which may be used both as a screen for projection and also be written on using special electronic pens

interpretation: Explanation of the possible meaning of something, such as the results of research

in-sessional programmes: EAP programmes designed for students already studying on their academic programmes in English, which aim to support and extend their skills, language, and competences in academic study

in-text reference: Information in a text showing the source of any citations; in-text references consist of the authors' name and the date of the source, or a number, which are linked to the full reference details in the *bibliography* or references section

jagged profile (testing): A test score on a skills-based test such as IELTS which shows different proficiency levels in different skills for a given candidate

journal: An academic publication which presents new research in *research articles*, reviews of existing research in *review articles*, and other material such as *reviews* and recent developments in the field

journal article: A written text, typically following a set structure, which is published in an academic *journal*

lexical word: A word (i.e. noun, verb, adjective, adverb) which expresses meaning related to content, rather than grammatical meaning (compare with *function word*)

limitation: The points that were not covered in a piece of writing or a research project, due to restrictions on time, space, etc., which affect how full and complete the conclusions can be

literature: What has been written, in academic books, *journal articles*, etc., about a particular topic

literature review: A written text, typically part of a longer piece of writing, which provides an overview of what has already been written about a particular topic or what research has already been done in the area; a literature review typically appears near the beginning of a text, after the introduction, or can be integrated throughout the text

LMS: Learning Management System, similar to a VLE. Includes a range of tools for digital delivery of learning materials, student activities, and managing students such as checking whether they have accessed materials

meronym: Words which are related in a 'whole to part' way, e.g. 'seed' and 'juice' are meronyms of 'apple'

metalanguage: The language used to talk about language, or more broadly learning and education

metaphor: Non-literal use of a word to express a key characteristic of another word

microblogging: A service which allows very short posts, for example, Twitter posts are limited to 140 characters

m-learning: Mobile learning, i.e. learning which uses technologies such as smart phones and which takes place to some extent independently

modality: The expression of meanings related to notions (e.g. time), logic (e.g. likelihood), and personal meanings (e.g. advice); modality is typically expressed through *modal verbs*

modal verb: Auxiliary verbs which express various meanings related to *modality*. Based on Biber et al. (1999, p.486) the order of frequency in which modal verbs are used in English academic texts is: *will, would, can, could, may, should, must, might, shall.*

modifier: A word which adds to or limits the meaning of another word

MOOC: Massive Open Online Course: a course at Higher Education level which is offered to thousands of students free and without entry requirements

morpheme: The smallest part of a word which expresses meaning. Morphemes can be lexical, i.e. expressing meaning related to content, or grammatical, i.e. performing a grammatical function such as indicating the word class of a word.

multimodality: The practice of communicating through multiple channels such as written texts, audio input, images and other visual material, and video

nominalization: The process in which a noun is formed from a different word class such as a verb, or a noun phrase from a clause

norm: Behaviour or a way of doing something which is typical or accepted within a particular context

norm-referenced (testing): An approach to presenting test scores which state a student's performance in relation to the other candidates who have taken the test, i.e. the whole population of test-takers

notion: Meanings used to communicate phenomena such as time, location, and causality

noun phrase: A phrase built round a head noun, which can be a noun or a pronoun. A noun phrase can include premodification and/or postmodification, and the whole phrase can be made up of one or more words

objective: Based only on facts and evidence, not influenced by personal judgments (see also *subjective*)

objective (testing): 'Objective tests' are tests where each item has one correct answer, or a limited set of correct answers, e.g. tests with multiple-choice items. Objective tests are widely used in writing and speaking (see also *subjective (testing)*)

opinion: A personal, subjective viewpoint which may be held and expressed without reference to supporting evidence

paraphrase: A piece of text which expresses similar ideas to another text of similar length but using different language

peer-reviewed: A process of determining whether a text is suitable for a particular purpose, e.g. determining whether an article submitted for inclusion in a particular journal is appropriate for publication in terms of relevance and quality. The peer review process involves sending the text to the reviewers, usually 'blind' (i.e. without the names of the authors), who assess and evaluate aspects of the text relating to its quality and relevance.

percentile: A score used in *norm-referenced* assessment criteria which ranks candidates in relation to those below them in the cohort, e.g. a percentile score of 80% indicates that the candidate has scored more highly than 80% of the other candidates taking the test

perspective: An essentially objective way of viewing something, e.g. from a medical perspective

phrase: A structure built round a noun, verb, adjective, adverb, or preposition

plagiarism: The use of someone else's work in your own writing without acknowledgment; plagiarism can involve using the exact words or the ideas of someone else without a correct reference or submitting work for assessment that has been submitted before (self-plagiarism)

podcast: Downloadable audio file

popular academic text: A book on an academic subject that has been written for general, non-academic readers e.g. a popular science book or a popular psychology book

position: A way of viewing something which is mainly subjective but based on evidence; someone can take a position on an issue and argue in support of or against it (see also *stance*)

postmodifier: The material in a phrase, e.g. a noun phrase, which comes after the head and adds information to it. Frequent noun phrase postmodifiers include prepositional phrases and relative clauses

prediction: A statement about what a person thinks may happen in the future, based on evidence

prefix: The first part of some words, which express a particular meaning or grammatical property (see also *suffix*)

premodifier: The material in a phrase, e.g. a noun phrase, which comes before the head, such as adjective(s) which come before the noun they modify

prepositional verb: A verb which contains a base verb + a preposition, e.g. *look into*. Prepositional verbs can refer to both physical and cognitive activities and are frequent in academic texts.

pre-sessional: EAP programmes designed to prepare students for their future academic study in English

primary research: Research that involves collecting new data, from experiments, measurement, observation, interviews, etc. (see also *secondary research*)

primary source: Texts in which new research is first published, such as research articles and case studies; or original contemporary documents and objects

proposition: An idea which is put forward for discussion and possible *validation*

purpose: What a piece of writing aims to achieve, for example, to describe or explain something, to discuss an issue, to evaluate something, etc.

quotation: A *citation* which uses the exact words of the original source

rationale: The reasons for doing something in a particular way, for example, the reasons for choosing a topic or taking a particular approach

references section: A list of sources (books, articles, etc.) used in writing a text; a references section typically appears at the end of the text and shows the full details of the author(s), date, title and publication. (Also known as a *bibliography* or a reference list.)

relative clause: A structure in a longer noun phrase which follows the head noun and adds extra information

reliability: In testing, the degree to which a test is able to provide consistent results; a reliable test should give a similar result when a student repeats the test or sits different versions of the test

research article: An article in an academic publication which presents new research

review article: An article in an academic publication which reviews existing research

research findings: The results of academic research

resolution: A situation in which agreement has been reached about the answer to a question, the solution to a problem, or how to deal with something

response: A reaction to new information (written or spoken) by asking questions, making comments, etc.

review: A written or spoken *evaluation* of a text, giving a subjective, evidence-based assessment of the ideas in the text; a review can include positive comments and/or criticisms (also known as a *critical response* or critique)

scheme of work: A document describing the realization of the *syllabus* in detail including the learning outcomes for each item of the syllabus, suggested materials and ways of teaching the items, specific dates and times, balance of time, resources, and assessments

scope: The range of ideas that a text, a presentation or a piece of research deals with

secondary research: Research that is based on reading about what others have already researched and written about, rather than conducting original new *primary research*

secondary source: Publications which are one step removed from the original research or event, e.g. textbooks and critical works

seminar: A class at a university where a small group of students and a teacher discuss a topic, having prepared for it by reading

smartphone: Mobile telephone which also offers internet access, email, games, camera/video and other applications (apps)

source: The original text from which a *citation* or reference is taken

stance: A way of viewing something which is essentially subjective but based on evidence, and connected to an *argument*

subjective: Based on personal judgments; in an academic context these judgments are typically informed by evidence and reading rather than personal opinion (see also *objective*)

subjective (testing): 'Subjective tests' involve answers which are not 'right' or 'wrong' but more open-ended. Unlike objective tests these answers need specialist markers, and are suited to the skills of listening and reading (see also *objective (testing)*)

suffix: The last part in some words, which expresses a particular meaning or grammatical property (see also *prefix*)

summary: A short text which expresses the main points and argument(s) of a longer text

superordinate: A word with a higher relational meaning to other words, e.g. 'vehicle' is a superordinate of 'car' and 'bus', which are *hyponyms*

syllabus: The description relating to the *curriculum* which states the order in which the content is to be covered; both curriculum and syllabus can state the methodological approaches to be followed

synthesis: A text or piece of work which contains material drawn from multiple sources; the process of selecting and putting together such material

tablet: A handheld computer which consists only of a touchscreen. Tablets run dedicated apps and when a keyboard is required it appears on the screen display.

text chat: Synchronous online conversations which use text rather than audio. Participants typically need to be online at the same time.

theory: A formal explanation of why or how something happens or exists, based on extended evidence and research

thesis: The main point which is argued for and supported with evidence in a piece of writing, typically expressed in a *thesis statement* in the introduction; the thesis reflects the writer's *stance*

thesis statement: The part of a text which briefly expresses some or all of the following: purpose, argument, aims, rationale, limitations, conclusion of the text (deductive style), and text organization

topic sentence: A sentence in a paragraph, often one of the first sentences, which expresses the topic of that paragraph

trait: In testing, a sub-component of a test which relates to knowledge and skills that are seen to underlie or contribute to target performance

valid: In testing, based on what is logical or true

validate/validation: The process of establishing the extent to which something is reliable or true

validity: In testing, the degree to which a test is able to measure the trait(s) under investigation

virtual classroom: An online tool that allows presentations and discussions. Virtual classrooms often include other tools such as filesharing or voting. All participants must be online at the same time although sessions can usually be recorded for later viewing.

vodcast: A downloadable video file

wiki: A type of website that can be edited quickly and which usually has multiple authors. Useful for collaborative writing.

word class: Also known as 'part of speech'; the way a word is used grammatically in a particular sentence

BIBLIOGRAPHY

Aarts, B., D. Denison, E. Keizer and **G. Popova.** (eds.) 2004. *Fuzzy Grammar*. Oxford: Oxford University Press.

Alexander, O. *(ed.)* 2007. *New Approaches to Materials Development for Language Learning: Proceedings of the 2005 joint BALEAP/SATEFL conference*. Bern: Peter Lang.

Alexander, O., S. Argent and **J. Spencer.** 2008. *EAP Essentials: A teacher's guide to principles and practice*. Reading, UK: Garnet Education.

Alexander, O. 2010. 'The leap into TEAP: EAP in university settings.' *Joint BALEAP/IATEFL international conference, Bilkent University*.

Andrews, R. 2010. *Argumentation in Higher Education: Improving Practice Through Theory and Research*. New York and Abingdon: Routledge.

Bacon, C. 2005. 'Confronting the Coffee Crisis: Can Fair Trade, Organic, and Specialty Coffees Reduce Small-Scale Farmer Vulnerability in Northern Nicaragua?' *World Development* 33/3: 497–511.

BALEAP. 2008. *BALEAP Competency Framework for Teachers of English for Academic Purposes*. BALEAP. Available at: <www.baleap.org.uk>.

BALEAP. 2013. *BALEAP Can Do Framework for EAP syllabus design and assessment*. BALEAP. Available at: <www.baleap.org.uk>

Basturkmen, H. 2010. *Developing courses in English for Specific Purposes*. Basingstoke: Palgrave Macmillan.

Bavelas, Janet B. 1978. 'The social psychology of citations.' *Canadian Psychological Review* 19: 158–63.

Beard, R. 1990. *Developing Reading 3–13 2e*. London: Methuen.

Beaven, B. (ed.). 2005. *IATEFL Cardiff Conference Selections 2005*. Canterbury: IATEFL.

Beaven, B. (ed.). 2007. *IATEFL Harrogate Conference Selections 2006*. Canterbury: IATEFL.

Beaven, B. (ed.). 2008. *IATEFL Aberdeen Conference Selections 2007*. Canterbury: IATEFL.

Beaven, B. (ed.). 2009. *IATEFL Exeter Conference Selections 2008*. Canterbury: IATEFL.

Beaven, B. (ed.). 2010. *IATEFL Cardiff Conference Selections 2009.* Canterbury: IATEFL.

Benesch, S. 2001. *Critical English for Academic Purposes: Theory, Politics and Practice.* Mahwah NJ: Lawrence Erlbaum Associates.

Benesch, S. 2009. 'Theorizing and practicing critical English for academic purposes.' *Journal of English for Academic Purposes* 8/2: 81–85.

Biber, D., S. Johansson, G. Leech, S. Conrad and **E. Finegan.** 1999. *Longman Grammar of Spoken and Written English.* Harlow: Longman.

Biber, D., S. Conrad and **G. Leech.** 2002. *Longman Student Grammar of Spoken and Written English.* Harlow: Longman.

Biber, D. 2006a. *University language: a corpus-based study of spoken and written registers.* Amsterdam: John Benjamins.

Biber, D. 2006b. 'Stance in spoken and written university registers'. *Journal of English for Academic Purposes* 5/2: 97–116.

Biber, D. 2008. *Variations across speech and writing.* Cambridge: Cambridge University Press.

Biber, D. and **B. Gray.** 2010. 'Challenging stereotypes about academic writing: Complexity, elaboration, explicitness.' *Journal of English for Academic Purposes* 9/1: 2–20.

Bishop, D. 2013. 'Blogging as post-publication peer review: reasonable or unfair?' <http://deevybee.blogspot.co.uk/2013/03/blogging-as-post-publication-peer.html> posted 21st March 2013. accessed 23 May 2013.

Bloom, B.S., M.D. Engelhart, E.J. Furst, W.H. Hill and **D.R. Krathwohl.** 1956. *Taxonomy of educational objectives: The classification of educational goals. Handbook 1: Cognitive domain.* New York: David McKay.

Blue, G. (ed.). 2010. *Developing Academic Literacy.* Bern: Peter Lang.

Blue, G., J. Milton, and **J. Saville.** (eds.). 2000. *Assessing English For Academic Purposes.* Bern: Peter Lang.

Bonnett, A. 2001. *How to Argue: A students' guide.* Harlow: Pearson.

Booth, W. C., G.G. Colomb and **J.M. Williams.** 2008. *The Craft of Research 3e.* Chicago: University of Chicago Press.

Boxall, M. 2012. 'MOOCs: a massive opportunity for higher education, or digital hype?'. *The Guardian* 8 August 2012. <http://www.guardian.co.uk/higher-education-network/blog/2012/aug/08/ mooc-coursera-higher-education-investment> accessed 23 May 2013.

Brindley, G. and **S. Ross.** 2001. 'EAP Assessment: Issues, models, and outcomes.' in **Flowerdew, J.** and **M. Peacock.** 2001. *Research Perspectives on English for Academic Purposes.* Cambridge: Cambridge University Press.

Brown, P., H. Lauder, and **D. Ashton.** 2011. *The Global Auction: the broken promises of education, jobs, and incomes.* New York: Oxford University Press.

Bruce, I. 2005. 'Syllabus design for general EAP writing courses: A cognitive approach.' *Journal of English for Academic Purposes* 4: 239–256.

Bruce, I. 2008. *Academic Writing and Genre: A Systemic Analysis.* London and New York: Continuum.

Bruce, I. 2011. *Theory and Concepts of English for Academic Purposes.* Basingstoke: Palgrave Macmillan.

Bruce, I. 2013. 'The centrality of genre in EAP instruction.' in **Wrigglesworth, J.** 2013. *Proceedings of the 2011 BALEAP Conference. EAP Within the Higher Education Garden: Cross-Pollination Between Disciplines, Departments and Research.* Reading, UK: Garnet Education.

Brumfit, C. 1991. 'Language Awareness in teacher education.' in **James, C.** and **P. Garrett.** (eds.). *Language Awareness in the Classroom.* Harlow: Longman.

Bryman, A., and **E. Bell.** 2011. *Business Research Methods 3e.* Oxford: Oxford University Press.

Cambridge Advanced Learner's Dictionary 3e. 2008. Cambridge: Cambridge University Press.

Candlin, C., J.M. Kirkwood and **H.M. Moore.** 1975. 'Developing study skills in English.' in *E.T.I.C., English for Academic Study: Problems and Perspectives.* London: The British Council.

Candlin, C. N. and **Hyland, K.** (eds.). 1999. *Writing: Texts, Processes and Practices.* Harlow: Addison Wesley Longman Limited.

Cargill, C. and **S. Burgess.** 2008. 'Introduction to the Special Issue: English for Research Publication Purposes.' *Journal of English for Academic Purposes* 7/2.

Carr, N. 2011. *Designing and Analyzing Language Tests.* Oxford: Oxford University Press.

Carter, R., and **M. McCarthy.** 2006. *Cambridge Grammar of English.* Cambridge: Cambridge University Press.

Chamberlain, D. and **R.J. Baumgardner.** 1988. *ESP in the Classroom: Practice and Evaluation.* Modern English Publications in association with the British Council.

Charles, M., D.D. Pecorari, and **S. Hunston.** (eds.). 2011. *Academic writing: at the interface of corpus and discourse.* London: Continuum.

Charlesworth, B. and **D. Charlesworth.** 2003. *Evolution: A Very Short Introduction.* Oxford: Oxford University Press.

Christie, F. and **K. Maton.** (eds.). 2011. *Disciplinarity: Functional linguistic and sociological perspectives.* London: Continuum.

Clanchy, J. and **B. Ballard.** 1981. *How to Write Essays.* Melbourne: Longman Cheshire.

Clapham, C. 1996. *The Development of IELTS: A Study of the Effect of Background Knowledge on Reading Comprehension* in **Flowerdew, J.** and **M. Peacock.** 2001. *Research Perspectives on English for Academic Purposes.* Cambridge: Cambridge University Press.

Coffin, C., M.J. Curry, S. Goodman, A. Hewings, T.M. Lillis, and **J. Swann.** 2003. *Teaching Academic Writing: A Toolkit for Higher Education.* London and New York: Routledge.

Coffin, C. and **J.P. Donohue.** (eds.). 2012. 'English for Academic Purposes: Contributions from systemic functional linguistics and Academic Literacies'. *Journal of English for Academic Purposes, Special Issue,* 11/1: 1–78.

Coffin, C. and **J. P. Donohue.** 2012. *'Academic Literacies and systemic functional linguistics:* How do they relate?' in **Coffin, C.** and **J. P. Donohue,** (eds.). 2012. 'English for Academic Purposes: Contributions from systemic functional linguistics and Academic Literacies' *Journal of English for Academic Purposes, Special Issue,* 11/1: 1–78.

Collins COBUILD *Advanced Dictionary.* 2009. Glasgow: HarperCollins.

Connaway, L.S., D. White, D. Lanclos, and **A. Le Cornu.** 2013. 'Visitors and Residents: What Motivates Engagement with the Digital Information Environment?'. *Information Research.* 18/1 (paper 556). <http://InformationR.net/ir/18-1/paper556.html > accessed 26 August 2013.

Conrad, S. and **D. Biber.** 2000. 'Adverbial Marking of Stance in Speech and Writing.' in **Hunston, S., G Thompson.** (eds.). *Evaluation in Text: authorial stance and the construction of discourse.* Oxford: Oxford University Press.

Cotton, F. 2004. 'Evaluative language use in academic writing: a cross-cultural study.' Talk at the Institute of Education. London. 24 November 2004.

Cotton, F. 2009. 'Different not deficit: towards a more critical EAP pedagogy.' in **Whong, M.** (ed.) 2009. *Proceedings of the 2007 BALEAP Conference, EAP in a Globalizing World: English as an Academic Lingua Franca.* Reading, UK: Garnet Education.

Cotton, F. 2010. 'Critical Thinking and Evaluative Language Use in Academic Writing: A Comparative Cross-Cultural Study.' in **Blue, G.** (ed.). *Developing Academic Literacy.* Bern: Peter Lang.

Cottrell, S. 2005. *Critical Thinking Skills: Developing Effective Analysis and Argument.* Basingstoke: Palgrave Macmillan.

Coulby, C., J.C. Laxton, S. Boomer, N. Davies and **K. Murphy**. 2010. 'Mobile Technology and Assessment – A case study from the ALPS programme.' *in* **Pachler, N., C. Pimmer and J. Seipold** (eds.). *Work-based mobile learning: concepts and cases. A handbook for academics and practitioners.* Peter Lang: Oxford.

Coulthard, M. 1986. 'Talking about Text: Studies Presented to David Brazil on his Retirement.' *Discourse Monographs* 13. University of Birmingham: English Language Research.

Coulthard, M. (ed.). 1994. *Advances in written text analysis.* London: Routledge.

Coxhead, A. 2000. 'A new academic word list.' *TESOL Quarterly 34/2:* 213–238.

Coxhead, A. and **P. Nation.** 2001. 'The specialized vocabulary of English for academic purposes.' in **Flowerdew J.** and **M. Peacock**. *Research Perspectives on English for Academic Purposes.* Cambridge: Cambridge University Press.

Craven, E. 2011. 'The quest for IELTS Band 7.0: Investigating English language proficiency development of international students at an Australian university.' *IELTS Research Reports Volume 13.*

Creme, P. and **M. R. Lea.** 2008. *Writing at University: A guide for students 3e.* Maidenhead: Open University Press, McGraw-Hill Education.

Crystal, D. 2003. *A Dictionary of Linguistics and Phonetics 5e.* Oxford: Blackwell Publishing.

Deane, M. and **O'Neill, P.** (eds.). 2011. *Writing in the Disciplines.* Basingstoke: Palgrave Macmillan.

de Chazal, E. 2005. 'Symposium on Academic Writing report.' in **Beaven, B.** *(ed.). IATEFL Cardiff Conference Selections 2005.* Canterbury: IATEFL.

de Chazal, E. 2006. 'Mind the GAP'. In **Fletcher de Tellez, I**. *Talking Point. London:* Trinity College London.

de Chazal, E. 2007. 'Symposium on Academic Writing report: The Adverbial Cycle.' in **Beaven, B.** (ed.). *IATEFL Harrogate Conference Selections 2006.* Canterbury: IATEFL.

de Chazal, E. 2008a. 'How Deep is Your Word? Excavating etymological evidence.' in **Beaven, B.** (ed.). *IATEFL Aberdeen Conference Selections 2007.* Canterbury: IATEFL.

de Chazal, E. 2008b. 'Ten Steps to Better Academic Writing.' in **Krzanowski, M.** 2008. *Current Developments in English for Academic, Specific and Occupational Purposes.* Reading, UK: Garnet Education.

de Chazal, E. 2009a. '"So what?" Evaluation in academic writing: what, where, why, how?' in **Beaven, B.** (ed.). *IATEFL Exeter Conference Selections 2008.* Canterbury: IATEFL.

de Chazal, E. 2009b. 'The future's bright. The future's periphrastic.' *English Teaching Professional.* 63.

de Chazal, E. 2010a. '7 Wonders of advanced English grammar: phenomena, patterns, pedagogy.' in **Beaven, B.** (ed.). *IATEFL Cardiff Conference Selections 2009.* Canterbury: IATEFL.

de Chazal, E. 2010b. 'Two "howevers" and "moreovers" do not a cohesive text make.' Talk given at *44th IATEFL annual international conference.*

de Chazal, E. 2010c. 'Academic English: building competences, transferring knowledge'. *EAP in university settings,* joint BALEAP/IATEFL international conference. Bilkent University 18 June 2010.

de Chazal, E. 2011a. 'Two "howevers" and "moreovers" do not a cohesive text make.' in **Pattison, T.** (ed.). *IATEFL Harrogate Conference Selections 2010.* Canterbury: IATEFL.

de Chazal, E. 2011b. 'Integrating skills, language and critical thinking in EAP materials.' Talk given at *3rd Annual Staff Conference on 'Integration – the key to success'.* INTO Exeter University, UK.

de Chazal, E. 2012a. 'Critical thinking: what the heck?' in **Pattison, T.** (ed.). *IATEFL Brighton Conference Selections 2011.* Canterbury: IATEFL.

de Chazal, E. 2012b. 'Putting EAP into practice'. Talk at British Council, Manchester. <http://englishagenda.britishcouncil.org/seminars/putting-eap-practice> accessed 26 August 2013.

de Chazal, E. 2013a. 'EAP in practice: integrating skills, language, tasks, and critical thinking.' in **Pattison, T.** (ed.). *IATEFL Glasgow Conference Selections 2012.* Canterbury: IATEFL.

de Chazal, E. 2013b. 'The general – specific debate in EAP: which case is the most convincing for most contexts?' *Journal of Second Language Teaching and Research.* 2/1. <http://pops.uclan.ac.uk/index.php/jsltr/index> accessed 26 August 2013.

de Chazal, E. and **Y. Aldous.** 2006. 'From Japanese to Anglo-Saxon academic writing culture: a practical framework and a personal journey.' *The East Asian Learner Journal* 2/2. Oxford: Oxford Brookes University. <http://cs3.brookes.ac.uk/schools/education/eal/eal-2-2/vol2-no2-contents.html> accessed 26 August 2013.

de Chazal, E. and **S. McCarter.** 2012. *Oxford EAP Upper Intermediate/B2+ Student's Book.* Oxford: Oxford University Press.

de Chazal, E. and **L. Rogers, L.** 2013. *Oxford EAP Intermediate/B1+ Student's Book.* Oxford: Oxford University Press.

de Chazal, E. and **J. Moore.** 2013. *Oxford EAP Advanced/C1+ Student's Book.* Oxford: Oxford University Press.

Dudley-Evans, T. and **M.J. St John.** 1998. *Developments in English for Specific Purposes: A multi-disciplinary approach.* Cambridge: Cambridge University Press.

Ehrenberg, V. 1973. *From Solon to Socrates: Greek history and civilization during the 6th and 5th centuries BC.* London: Methuen.

Elder and **O'Loughlin.** 2003. 'The Relationship between Intensive English Language Study and Band Score Gains on IELTS.' *IELTS Research Reports:* 207–254.

Etherington, S. (ed.). 2011. *Proceedings of the 2009 BALEAP Conference: English for Specific Academic Purposes*. Reading, UK: Garnet Education.

Ewer, J. R. and **G. Hughes-Davies.** 1971. 'Further notes on developing an English programme for students of science and technology (1).' *English Language Teaching:* 26/1.

Fairbairn, G. and **C. Winch.** 2011. *Reading, writing and reasoning: a guide for students 3e*. Maidenhead: McGraw-Hill Education.

Feak, C. 2011. 'Culture shock? Genre shock?' in **Etherington, S**. (ed.). *Proceedings of the 2009 BALEAP Conference: English for Specific Academic Purposes*. Reading, UK: Garnet Education.

Feak, C. and **J. Swales.** 2009. *Telling a Research Story: Writing a Literature Review*. Ann Arbor: University of Michigan Press.

Feak, C. and **J. Swales.** 2011. *Creating Contexts: Writing Introductions across Genres*. Ann Arbor: University of Michigan Press.

Field, J. 2005. 'Second language writing: a language problem or a writing problem?' Talk at *IATEFL Special Interest Group Conference*. Cambridge. 26 February 2005.

Field, J. 2008. *Listening in the Language Classroom*. Cambridge: Cambridge University Press.

Field, J. (ed.). 2011. 'Into the mind of the academic listener.' *Journal of English for Academic Purposes Special Issue: Listening in EAP* 10/2: 102–112.

Field, J. 2013. 'Listening tests and tasks versus listening in the real world.' Talk given at *47th IATEFL annual international conference*. Liverpool. 10 April 2013.

Fletcher de Tellez, I. 2006. *Talking Point*. London: Trinity College London.

Flowerdew, J. (ed.). 1994. *Academic Listening: Research perspectives*. Cambridge: Cambridge University Press.

Flowerdew, J. and **M. Peacock, M.** 2001. *Research Perspectives on English for Academic Purposes*. Cambridge: Cambridge University Press.

Flowerdew, J. 2005. *Second Language Listening*. Cambridge: Cambridge University Press.

Foucault, M. 1980. 'Power and strategies.' In **Gordon. C.** (ed.) *Power/Knowledge: Selected Interviews and Other Writings, 1972–1977*. New York: Pantheon Books.

Francis G. 1986. 'Labelling discourse: an aspect of nominal-group lexical cohesion', in **Coulthard, M.** 1986. *Talking about Text: Studies Presented to David Brazil on his Retirement. Discourse Monographs* 13. University of Birmingham: English Language Research.

Friere, P. 1994. *Pedagogy of Hope: Reliving Pedagogy of the Oppressed* (Trans. A. M. A Freire and P. Freire). New York: Continuum.

Fulcher, J. and **J. Scott.** 2011. *Sociology 4e.* Oxford: Oxford University Press.

Gannon, F. 2008. 'The pipeline'. *EMBO reports 9/1/1. doi:*10.1038/sj.embor.7401156. London: Nature Publishing.

Gee, J.P. 2011. *How to do Discourse Analysis: A Toolkit.* Abingdon: Routledge.

Gibbons, A. 2012. *Multimodality, Cognition, and Experimental Literature.* New York/Abingdon: Routledge.

Gibbons, P. 2009. *English Learners, Academic Literacy, and Thinking: learning in the challenge zone.* Portsmouth, NH: Heinemann.

Gilbert, G. N. 1977. 'Referencing as persuasion.' *Social Studies of Science 7:* 113–22.

Gillett, A. Using English for Academic Purposes. <http://www.uefap.com/> accessed 26 August 2013

Godfrey, J. 2009. *How to Use Your Reading in Your Essays.* Basingstoke: Palgrave Macmillan.

Godfrey, J. 2011. *Writing for University.* Basingstoke: Palgrave Macmillan.

Godfrey, J. 2013. *The Academic Phrase Book: Vocabulary for Writing at University.* Basingstoke: Palgrave Macmillan.

Goodman, K. S. 1967. 'Reading: A psycholinguistic guessing game.' *Journal of the Reading Specialist* 4: 126–35.

Gordon. C. (ed.). 1980. *Power/Knowledge: Selected Interviews and Other Writings, 1972–1977.* New York: Pantheon Books.

Gough, P. B. 1972. 'One second of reading.' *Visible Language 6/4:* 291–20.

Grabe, W. and **F. Stoller.** 2002. *Teaching and Researching Reading.* Harlow: Longman.

Grabe, W. 2009. *Reading in a Second Language: Moving from Theory to Practice.* Cambridge: Cambridge University Press.

Grainger, S. and **M. Paquot.** 2009. 'Lexical Verbs in Academic Discourse: A Corpus-driven Study of Learner Use.' in **Charles M., D. Pecorari,** and **S. Hunston.** (eds.). 2009. *Academic writing: at the interface of corpus and discourse.* London: Continuum.

Gray, B. and **D. Biber.** 2012. 'Current Conceptions of Stance.' In **Hyland, K.** and **C. Sancho Guinda.** (eds.). 2012. *Stance and Voice in Written Academic Genres.* Basingstoke: Palgrave Macmillan.

Grellet, F. 1981. *Developing Reading Skills.* Cambridge: Cambridge University Press.

Guse, J. 2011. *Communicative Activities for EAP.* Cambridge: Cambridge University Press.

Halliday, M. A. K. 1989. *Spoken and written language.* Oxford: Oxford University Press.

Halliday, M. A. K. 1994. *An Introduction to Systemic Functional Grammar*. London: Edward Arnold.

Halliday, M. A. K. and **R. Hassan.** 1976. *Cohesion in English*. Harlow: Longman.

Hamp-Lyons, L. and **Heasley, B.** 2006. *Study Writing 2e*. Cambridge: Cambridge University Press.

Hannam, S. 2012. 'ELT under the microscope: critical ELT.' In **Schwetlick, A.** (ed.) *IATEFL Voices* (Issue 226). Canterbury: IATEFL.

Harper, D. (ed.). 1986. *ESP for the University*. Oxford: Pergamon Press.

Hinds, J. 1987. 'Reader versus writer responsibility: A new typology.' in **Connor, U.** and **R. B. Kaplan.** (eds.). *Writing across languages: analysis of L2 text*. Reading, MA: Addison-Wesley.

Hobson, P. 2001. 'Aristotle.' in **Palmer, J.** (ed.). *Fifty Major Thinkers on Education: from Confucius to Dewey*. Abingdon: Routledge.

Hoey, M. 1983. *On the surface of discourse*. London: George Allen and Unwin.

Hoey, M. 2005. *Lexical Priming: a new theory of words and language*. Abingdon: Routledge.

Hudson, T. 2007. *Teaching Second Language Reading*. Oxford: Oxford University Press.

Hughes, A. 2002. *Testing for language teachers* 2e. Cambridge: Cambridge University Press.

Hunston, S. and **G. Thompson.** (eds.). 2000. *Evaluation in Text: authorial stance and the construction of discourse*. Oxford: Oxford University Press.

Hutchinson, T. and **A. Waters.** 1987. *English for Specific Purposes: a learning-centred approach*. Cambridge: Cambridge University Press.

Hyland, K. 1999. 'Disciplinary discourses: writer stance in research articles.' in **Candlin, C. N.** and **K. Hyland.** (eds.). 1999. *Writing: Texts, Processes and Practices*. Harlow: Addison Wesley Longman.

Hyland, K. 2002. 'Authority and invisibility: authorial identity in academic writing.' *Journal of Pragmatics 34*.

Hyland, K. 2003. *Second Language Writing*. Cambridge: Cambridge University Press.

Hyland, K. 2004. *Genre and Second Language Writing*. Ann Arbor: University of Michigan Press.

Hyland, K. 2006. *English for Academic Purposes: an advanced resource book*. Abingdon: Routledge.

Hyland, K. 2011. 'Discipline and divergence: evidence of specificity in EAP.' in **Etherington, S.** (ed.). *Proceedings of the 2009 BALEAP Conference: English for Specific Academic Purposes*. Reading, UK: Garnet Education.

Hyland, K. 2012. 'Welcome to the machine: thoughts on writing for scholarly publication.' *Journal of Second Language Teaching and Research.* 1/1.

Hyland, K., and **F. Hyland.** (eds.). 2006. *Feedback in Second Language Writing: Contexts and Issues.* Cambridge: Cambridge University Press.

Hyland, K. and **J. Milton.** 1997. 'Qualification and certainty in L1 and L2 students' writing.' *Journal of Second Language Writing* 6/2: 183–206.

Hyland, K. and **P. Tse.** 2007. 'Is there an "Academic Vocabulary"?' *TESOL Quarterly* 42/2: 235–253.

Hyland, K. and **C. Sancho Guinda.** (eds.). 2012. *Stance and Voice in Written Academic Genres.* Basingstoke: Palgrave Macmillan.

IELTS. *Common European Framework [Website].* <http://www.ielts.org/researchers/common_european_framework.aspx> accessed 16 November 2011.

Institute of Science Index (ISI). <http://www.isi-thonsomreuters.org/au.php> accessed May 1st 2013.

James, C. and P. Garrett. (eds.). 1991. *Language Awareness in the Classroom.* Harlow: Longman.

Jenkins, J. 2007. *English as a Lingua Franca: Attitude and Identity.* Oxford: Oxford University Press.

Jenkins, J. 2009. *World Englishes: A Resource Book for Students 2e.* Abingdon: Routledge.

Jesperson, O. 1924. *The Philosophy of Grammar.* London: George Allen & Unwin. Chapter 4: 'Parts of Speech' reprinted in **Aarts, B., D. Denison, E. Keizer** and **G. Popova.** (eds.). 2004. *Fuzzy Grammar.* Oxford: Oxford University Press.

Johns, A. 1997. *Text, Role, and Context: Developing Academic Literacies.* Cambridge: Cambridge University Press.

Johns, A. and **M. A. Snow.** 2006. 'Introduction to special issue: Academic English in secondary schools (Editorial).' *Journal of English for Academic Purposes* 5/4: 251-336.

Jones, C., J. Turner and **B. Street.** 1999. *Students writing in the university: Cultural and epistemological issues.* Amsterdam/Philadelphia: John Benjamins.

Jordan, K. 'MOOC Completion Rates: The Data' <http://www.katyjordan.com/MOOCproject.html> accessed 23 April 2013.

Jordan, R. R. 1997. *English for Academic Purposes: a guide and resource book for teachers.* Cambridge: Cambridge University Press.

Jordan, R. R. 1999. *Academic Writing Course* 3e. London: Longman.

Judge, B., P. Jones, P. and **E. McCreery.** 2009. *Critical Thinking Skills for Education Students.* Exeter: Learning Matters.

Kafes, H. 2008. 'A corpus-based study on the use of nouns to construct stance by native and non-native academic writers of English.' Paper presented at the *2008 Conference on Writing Research Across Borders, Santa Barbara, CA.* 24 February 2008.

Khoch, E. 2013. 'Exploring the intercultural dimension of academic writing: Hedging in Russian (L1) and English (L1/2) research articles.' Talk at the 2013 BALEAP Conference *The Janus Moment in EAP: Revisiting the Past and Building the Future.* 21 April 2013.

Koutsantoni, D. 2005. 'Greek Cultural Characteristics and Academic Writing.' *Journal of Modern Greek Studies* 23/1: 97-138.

Krathwohl, D. R. 2002. 'A Revision of Bloom's Taxonomy: An Overview'. *Theory into Practice* 41/ 4. Ohio: The Ohio State University.

Kress, G. 2010. *Multimodality: A Social Semiotic Approach to Contemporary Communication.* London/New York: Routledge.

Krzanowski, M. 2008. *Current Developments in English for Academic, Specific and Occupational Purposes.* Reading, UK: Garnet Education.

Kubota, R. 1999. 'Japanese Culture Constructed by Discourses: Implications for Applied Linguistics Research and ELT.' *TESOL Quarterly* 33/1: 9–35.

Lakoff, G. 1972. 'Hedges: a study in meaning criteria and the logic of fuzzy concepts.' in *Papers from the Eighth Regional Meeting, Chicago Linguistic Society:* 183–228 in **Swales, J.** 1990. *Genre Analysis: English in academic and research settings.* Cambridge: Cambridge University Press.

Lea, M. and **B. Street.** 1998. 'Student writing in higher education: An academic literacies approach.' *Studies in Higher Education* 23/2: 157–72.

Lea, M. and **B. Street.** 1999. 'Writing as academic literacies: Understanding textual practices in higher education.' in **Candlin, C. N.** and **K. Hyland.** (eds.). 2000. *Writing: Texts, Processes and Practices.* London: Longman.

Lea, M. and **B. Street.** 2000. 'Student writing and staff feedback in higher education: An academic literacies approach.' in **Lea, M.** and **B. Stierer.** (eds.). *Student writing in higher education: New contexts.* Buckingham: The Society for Research into Higher Education and Open University Press.

Lea, M. and **B. Stierer.** (eds.). 2000. *Student writing in higher education: New contexts.* Buckingham: The Society for Research into Higher Education and Open University Press.

Lee, J. J. 2009. 'Size matters: an exploratory comparison of small and large class size university lecture introductions.' *English for Specific Purposes* 28: 42–57. in **Lynch, T.** 'Academic listening in the 21st century: Reviewing a decade of research' *Journal of English for Academic Purposes* 10/2: 79–88.

Leech, G. 2001. 'The Role of Frequency in ELT: New Corpus Evidence Brings a Re-appraisal.' *Foreign Language Teaching and Research 33/5.*

Leech, G. and **J. Svartvik.** 1975. *A Communicative Grammar of English.* Harlow: Longman.

Leech, G.,P. Rayson and **A. Wilson.** 2001. *Word Frequencies in Written and Spoken English, based on the British National Corpus.* London: Longman.

Leki, I. 1991. 'The preferences of ESL students for error correction in college-level writing classes.' *Foreign Language Annals* 24: 203–218.

Liu, J., Y. Chang, F. Yang, and **Y. Sun.** 2011. 'Is what I need what I want? Reconceptualising college students' needs in English courses for general and specific/academic purposes.' *Journal of English for Academic Purposes* 10: 271–280.

Longman Dictionary of Contemporary English 4e. 2009. Harlow: Pearson.

Lynch, T. 2009. *Teaching Second Language Listening.* Oxford: Oxford University Press.

Lynch, T. 2011. 'Academic listening in the 21st century: Reviewing a decade of research' *Journal of English for Academic Purposes* 10/2: 79–88.

Mabe, M. 2003. 'The growth and number of journals.' *Serials 16/2.*

Macmillan English Dictionary for Advanced Learners 2e. 2007. Oxford: Macmillan Education.

Marsh, B. 2007. *Plagiarism: Alchemy and Remedy in Higher Education.* New York: State University of New York Press.

Martin, J. R. 1992. *English text: System and structure.* Amsterdam: John Benjamins.

Martin, J. R. 2011. 'Bridging troubled waters: interdisciplinarity and what makes it stick.' in **Christie, F.** and **K. Maton.** (eds.). *Disciplinarity: Functional linguistic and sociological perspectives.* London: Continuum.

McCarter, S. and **P. Jakes.** 2009. *Uncovering EAP: How to Teach Academic Writing and Reading.* Oxford: Macmillan.

McCarthy, M. 1991. *Discourse Analysis for Language Teachers.* Cambridge: Cambridge University Press.

McCarthy, M. and **F. O'Dell.** 2008. *Academic Vocabulary in Use: Vocabulary reference and practice.* Cambridge: Cambridge University Press.

Mitchell, S. and **R. Andrews.** (eds.). 2000. *Learning to argue in higher education.* Portsmouth, NH: Heinemann/Boynton-Cook.

Moon, J. 2008. *Critical Thinking: An exploration of theory and practice.* Abingdon and New York: Routledge.

Moriarty, P. 2013. 'Spwhile and Spriouser.' *Times Higher Education* <http://www.timeshighereducation.co.uk > accessed 26 August 2013.

Munby, J. 1978. *Communicative Syllabus Design.* Cambridge: Cambridge University Press.

Myers, G. 1994. 'The narratives of science and nature in popularizing molecular genetics.' in **Coulthard, M.** (ed.). *Advances in written text analysis.* London: Routledge.

Nation, I. S. P. 2006. 'How Large a Vocabulary is Needed For Reading and Listening?' *Canadian Modern Language Review/La revue canadienne des langues vivantes* 63/1: 59-82.

Nesi, H. and **S. Gardner.** 2012. *Genres across the Disciplines: Student writing in higher education.* Cambridge: Cambridge University Press.

Nuttall, C. 2005. *Teaching Reading Skills in a Foreign Language 3e.* Oxford: Macmillan.

Oshima, A. and **A. Hogue.** 2005. *Writing Academic English 4e.* New York: Pearson Education.

Oxford Advanced Learner's Dictionary of Current English. 2010. 8e. Oxford: Oxford University Press.

Palmer, J. (ed.). 2001. *Fifty Major Thinkers on Education: from Confucius to Dewey.* Abingdon: Routledge.

Paltridge, B. 2001. 'Linguistic research and EAP pedagogy.' in **Flowerdew, J.** and **M. Peacock.** *Research Perspectives on English for Academic Purposes.* Cambridge: Cambridge University Press.

Paltridge, B. 2012. *Discourse Analysis: An Introduction. 2e.* London: Bloomsbury.

Paquot, M. 2010. *Academic Vocabulary in Learner Writing.* London: Continuum.

Parr, C. 2013. How many stay the course? A mere 7%. *Times Higher Education* No. 2.100/9. 15 May 2013.

Paterson, K. with **R. Wedge.** 2013. *Oxford Grammar for EAP: English grammar and practice for Academic Purposes.* Oxford: Oxford University Press.

Pattison, T. (ed.). 2011. *IATEFL Harrogate Conference Selections 2010.* Canterbury: IATEFL.

Pattison, T. (ed.). 2012. *IATEFL Brighton Conference Selections 2011.* Canterbury: IATEFL.

Pattison, T. (ed.). *IATEFL Glasgow Conference Selections 2012.* Canterbury: IATEFL.

Quirk, R., S. Greenbaum, G. Leech. and **J. Svartvik.** 1985. *A Comprehensive Grammar of the English Language.* Harlow: Longman.

Ravetz, J. R. 1971. *Scientific knowledge and social problems.* Oxford: Oxford University Press.

Reinhart, S. M. 2002. *Giving Academic Presentations.* Ann Arbor: University of Michigan Press.

Richards, J. C. and **T. S. Rodgers.** 2001. *Approaches and Methods in English Language Teaching 2e.* Cambridge: Cambridge University Press.

Riddle, M. 2000. 'Improving argument by parts.' in **Mitchell, S.** and **R. Andrews.** (eds.). *Learning to argue in higher education.* Portsmouth, NH: Heinemann/ Boynton-Cook.

Rumelhart, D. E. 1977. 'Towards an interactive model of reading.' In **Dornic,** S. (ed.). *Attention and Performance VI: Proceedings of the Sixth International Symposium on Attention and Performance, Stockholm, Sweden, July 28–August 1 1975.* Hillsdale, NJ: Lawrence Erlbaum Associates.

Ryan, J. 2012. 'A whole of institutional approach to teaching and supporting international students.' Talk at the *UK Higher Education Academy.* Retrieved from <http://www.heacademy.ac.uk/assets/documents/disciplines/biosciences/2012/ BathInternationalisation/Ryan.pdf> accessed 26 August 2013

Rundell, M. 2011. 'Dictionaries, language technology, and EAP: the state-of-the-art in corpus-based reference resources.' Talk at *EAP@SouthBank Seminar Series.* 6 May 2011.

Saito, H. 1994. 'Teachers' practices and students' preferences for feedback on second language writing: A case study of adult ESL learners.' *TESL Canada Journal* 11/2: 46–70.

Santos, B. 1992. 'Ideology in composition: L1 and ESL.' *Journal of Second Language Writing* 1/1: 1–15.

Schwetlick, A. (ed.). 2012. *IATEFL Voices (Issue 226).* Canterbury: IATEFL.

Scholfield, P. 1990. *MA courses in Linguistics 1990–91: Guide to MA courses in linguistics.* Bangor: University College of North Wales Department of Linguistics.

Scott, M. 1999. In **Jones, C., J. Turner** and **B. Street.** 1999. *Students writing in the university: Cultural and epistemological issues.* Amsterdam/ Philadelphia: John Benjamins.

Shen, J. 2001. 'Confucius.' In **Palmer, J.** (ed.) *Fifty Major Thinkers on Education: from Confucius to Dewey.* Abingdon: Routledge.

Smith, R. 2013. 'History of EAP.' Talk at *BALEAP Conference.* Nottingham. 20 April 2013.

Stainthorp, R. 2005. 'Writing: the ultimate juggling act.' Talk at *IATEFL Special Interest Group Conference.* Cambridge. 26 February 2005.

Strevens, P. 1988. 'ESP after twenty years: A re-appraisal' in **Flowerdew, J.** and **M. Peacock.** 2001. *Research Perspectives on English for Academic Purposes.* Cambridge: Cambridge University Press.

Sutherland-Smith, W. 2008. *Plagiarism, the Internet, and Student Learning.* New York and Abingdon: Routledge.

Swales, J. 1971. *Writing Scientific English.* Sunbury-on-Thames, UK: Nelson.

Swales, J. 1985. *Episodes in ESP.* Oxford: Pergamon Press.

Swales, J. 1990. *Genre Analysis: English in academic and research settings.* Cambridge: Cambridge University Press.

Swales, J. 2004a. 'Then and now: A reconsideration of the first corpus of scientific English.' *Iberica* 8: 5–21.

Swales, J. 2004b. *Research genres: Explorations and Applications.* New York: Cambridge University Press.

Swales, J., U. K. Ahmad, Y-Y. Chang, D. Chavez, D. F. Dressen and **R. Seymour. 1998.** 'Consider This: The Role of Imperatives in Scholarly Writing." *Applied Linguistics* 19/1: 97–121.

Swales, J. and **C. Feak.** 2000. *English in Today's Research World: a writing guide.* Ann Arbor: University of Michigan Press.

Swales, J. and **C. Feak.** 2012. *Academic Writing for Graduate Students: essential skills and tasks 3e.* Ann Arbor: University of Michigan Press.

Swan, M., and **C. Walter.** 1984. *The Cambridge English Course 1 Teacher's Book.* Cambridge: Cambridge University Press.

Thompson, G. and **Y. Ye.** 1991. 'Evaluation in the reporting verbs used in academic papers.' *Applied Linguistics* 12: 365–382.

Tomlinson, B. (ed.). 2011. *Materials Development in Language Teaching 2e.* Cambridge: Cambridge University Press.

Toulmin, S. E. 1958/2003. *The Uses of Argument.* Cambridge: Cambridge University Press.

Tribble, C. and **U. Wingate.** 2011. 'Academic Literacies versus EAP: Contrasting origins, common ground, new directions.' Talk at *EAP@SouthBank Seminar Series.* 6 May 2011.

Tribble, C. 2005. 'Who sets the standards for academic writing?' Talk at *Writing Revisited: New approaches to second language literacy conference.* Cambridge, 25–27 February 2005.

UNESCO. 'Global flow of tertiary-level students.' <http://www.uis.unesco.org/Education/Pages/international-student-flow-viz.aspx> accessed 27th May 2013.

Vandergrift, L. 2006. 'Second language listening: listening ability or language proficiency?' *Modern Language Journal.* 90: 6–18 in **Lynch, T.** 2011. 'Academic listening in the 21st century: Reviewing a decade of research.' *Journal of English for Academic Purposes* 10/2: 79–8.

Wacks, R. 2008. *Law: A Very Short Introduction.* Oxford: Oxford University Press.

Wallace, M. and **A. Wray.** 2011. *Critical reading and writing for postgraduates 2e.* London: Sage Publications.

Warschauer, M. 1996. 'Comparing Face-to-Face and Electronic Discussion in the Second Language Classroom.' *CALICO Journal.* 13/2: 7–26

Weissberg, R. and **S. Buker.** 1990. *Writing Up Research.* Englewood Cliffs, N.J.: Prentice Hall Regents.

West, K. and **J. Williamson.** 2009. 'Wikipedia: Friend or foe?' *Reference Services Review* 37/3: 260–271.

West, M. 1953. *A General Service List of English Words.* London: Longman.

White, R. and **D. McGovern.** 1994. *Writing.* Hemel Hempstead: Phoenix ELT/ Prentice Hall.

Whitley, B. E., and **P. Keith-Spiegel.** 2002. *Academic Dishonesty: An Educator's Guide.* Mahwah and London: Lawrence Erlbaum Associates.

Whong, M. (ed.). 2009. *Proceedings of the 2007 BALEAP Conference, EAP in a Globalizing World: English as an Academic Lingua Franca.* Reading, UK: Garnet Education.

Widdowson, H. 1983. *Learning Purpose and Language Use.* Oxford: Oxford University Press.

Wilkins, D. 1976. *Notional Syllabuses.* Oxford: Oxford University Press.

Willis, D. and **J. Willis.** 2007. *Doing Task-based Teaching.* Oxford: Oxford University Press.

Wray, A. 2002. *Formulaic language and the lexicon.* Cambridge: Cambridge University Press.

Wrigglesworth, J. 2013. *Proceedings of the 2011 BALEAP Conference. EAP Within the Higher Education Garden: Cross-Pollination Between Disciplines, Departments and Research.* Reading, UK: Garnet Education.

Yule, G. 1998. *Explaining English Grammar. Oxford:* Oxford University Press.

Zhang, S. 1995. 'Re-examining the affective advantages of peer feedback in the ESL writing class.' *Journal of Second Language Writing* 4/3: 209–222.

INDEX

Page numbers annotated with 'g' refer to glossary entries. Those annotated with 't' or 'f' refer to information in tables or figures respectively.

empathy 65t, 130t

empathy writing 188, 189t

English as a *lingua franca* 41

entities 137

EOP (English for occupational purposes) 5

epistemology 123

ERPP (English for research publication purposes) 47

ESAP (English for specific academic purposes) 3–4, 18t, 35–6
  see also EGAP/ESAP debate

ESL/ESOL (English as a second language) 4

ESP (English for Specific Purposes) 4–5, 6, 18t

essays 189t, 191 3, 192 3t
  see also research essays

essential elements 62–6, 349g
  and context 165–6
  and critical thinking 126, 128–30, 128–30t
  in language reference books 130–1
  stages in production of 127–8, 127f
  taxonomy 64–5t, 128–30t
  and text management functions 126–7, 126f, 131
  in writing 189

EST (English for science and technology) 4, 5

ethnographic 349g

evaluation 64t, 124, 184t, 349g
  and cohesion 80
  criteria 174–5, 174t, 184–5
  and critical thinking 129t, 135, 136–7, 138, 174–5, 174t

evaluative language 139, 139t, 140t, 171–2

evidence 10–11, 349g

Ewer, J.R. 20

examinations *see* assessment; international tests of academic English

exemplification 64t, 129t

exercises 189t

exophoric reference 73–4, 349g

explanation 65t, 129t, 189t

exposition 65t, 129t

expository books 60, 350g

facts 11, 184t, 185, 186, 350g

Fairbairn, G. 142

falsification 122–3

Feak, C. 37, 69–70, 111, 139, 140t, 166, 201, 204, 279, 280

Field, J. 208, 217, 224

'flipped classrooms' 176t, 320, 350g

Flowerdew, J. 217, 220

fluency 210t

focus 134

focusers 76–7, 343–4

form, function, and meaning 92–3

Foucault, M. 204

Francis, G. 69

Freire, P. 204

Fulcher, J. 164, 172, 201, 345–6

function words 89–90, 90t, 350g

functions 63, 65t, 129t

Gannon, F. 74, 343–4

Gardner, S. 180, 188, 189t, 191

gender, in academic style 114

General Service List of English Words 20, 102, 107, 108, 115

generalizability 134t

general–specific debate *see* EGAP/ESAP debate

generic language 14, 173, 350g

genre 14, 58–9, 187
  audience and purpose 59–60, 162–3, 189, 206
  definition 22, 59, 350g
  in the disciplines 188–9, 189t
  listening 220–4
  non-academic genres 61–2
  primary sources 60
  secondary sources 60–1
  student genres 62
  tertiary sources 61
  writing approaches 204

genre analysis 22, 276t, 350g

Gibbons, A. 219

Gibbons, P. 143

Gilbert, G.N. 195

'given–new' pattern 70, 87t

globalization 15, 28–9, 41–2, 47, 213, 277t

glossaries 164t

Godfrey, J. 131, 201

Goodman, K.S. 149

Gough, P.B. 149

Grainger, S. 108

grammar 13, 84
  academic language 108–11
  evaluative language 140t
  frequency 115–16
  lexical and function words 89–90, 90t
  selection criteria 115–17
  see also clauses; nominalization; noun phrases; nouns

grammatical words *see* function words

Gray, B. 78, 87, 88t, 140t, 154, 187

Grellet, F. 280

grey literature 322, 350g
  blogs 324–5, 327–8, 334–5, 338, 348g
  Wikipedia 61, 323–4, 334–5

group projects
  characteristics 222t, 245t
  speaking competencies 247t, 248t

Halliday, M.A.K. 20, 22, 35–6, 67, 86

Hamp-Lyons, L. 203

Hannam, S. 24–5

Harvard referencing system 199

Hasan, R. 67

head nouns 96, 350g

Heasley, B. 203

hedging 141, 350g
  in Russian 141–2

Hinds, J. 213

Hippocrates 122

Hobson, P. 122

Hoey, M. 22, 63, 66, 102

Hogue, A. 203

Hughes-Davis, G. 20

Hunston, S. 136–7, 138

Hutchinson, T. 279, 286

Hyland, F. 179

Hyland, K. 21, 22, 25–6, 35–6, 37, 45, 103, 113, 139, 140t, 179, 187, 213, 240, 280, 301

hyponyms 69, 350g

hypotheses 65t, 129t, 184t, 185, 350g

IATEFL (International Association of Teachers of English as a Foreign Language) 24

ideas 146–7, 147t, 184, 184t

idioms 117, 140t

IELTS (International English Language Testing Service) 15, 311–12
  and EAP 9
  and entrance criteria 310, 317–18, 317t
  score descriptors 314, 314t
  score equivalence 316–17
  skills and criticality 313

imperatives 74

in-class observation 293t

in-sessional programmes 26, 34, 351g

in-text reference 10, 199, 351g

independence 80, 175–6, 176t, 209, 210t

indexes 164t

indirect testing 298–9, 351g

inductive method/inductivism 122, 350g

inference 65t, 129t

influences on EAP 19, 27
  academic literacies 6, 25–6